Becoming Disabled

Health and Aging in the Margins

Series Editor: Alexandra "Xan" C.H. Nowakowski,
Florida State University

Health and Aging in the Margins expands the horizons of mainstream and academic understandings of living and aging at the intersection of diverse health experiences and marginalized biographies. Interest in life course perspectives on health and aging has expanded dramatically in recent decades. However, most attention to this topic in extant academic books has focused on more dominant social and cultural groups. This series will build on groundwork laid by these traditions to focus explicitly on the health and aging experiences of marginalized people and groups. These specific topic areas may include, but are not limited to

Racism and People of Color	Kink Practitioners
Stigmatized Conditions	High Risk Occupations
First Generation Students	Community and Police Violence
Adoption and Donor Conception	Ethnic Discrimination
Religious and Spiritual Minorities	Asexualities
Working Class Lives	Invisible Disabilities
Unemployment	Sexism and Feminism
Intimate Partner Violence	Hate Crimes and Survivorship
Homelessness and Housing Insecurity	Food Insecurity
Rare Diseases	Sizeism and Fatphobia
Contested Disorders	Dementia and Cognitive Impairment
Social and Intellectual Differences	Communication Differences
Progressive Diseases	Childfreedom
Trans and Nonbinary Experiences	Infertility and Sterilization
Immigrant and Migrant Families	Gay / Lesbian / Bi / Pan Sexualities
Intersex Lives	Consensual Nonmonogamies
Transgender Studies	Early Mortality

The series centers ethnographic and narrative approaches to explore and understand the health and aging experiences of marginalized populations. Recruitment of authors will focus strongly on amplifying the voices of scholars who themselves have experienced intersectional marginalization, and who engage those elements of their personal biography in scholarly activity. Recent titles in the series include:

Becoming Disabled: Forging a Disability View of the World, by Jan Doolittle Wilson

Becoming Disabled

Forging a Disability View of the World

Jan Doolittle Wilson

LEXINGTON BOOKS

Lanham • Boulder • New York • London

Published by Lexington Books
An imprint of The Rowman & Littlefield Publishing Group, Inc.
4501 Forbes Boulevard, Suite 200, Lanham, Maryland 20706
www.rowman.com

6 Tinworth Street, London SE11 5AL, United Kingdom

British Library Cataloguing in Publication Information Available

Library of Congress Cataloging-in-Publication Data

Names: Wilson, Jan Doolittle, 1972- author.
Title: Becoming disabled : forging a disability view of the world / Jan Doolittle Wilson.
Description: Lanham : Lexington Books, [2021] | Series: Health and aging in the margins | Includes bibliographical references and index.
Identifiers: LCCN 2021018624 (print) | LCCN 2021018625 (ebook) | ISBN 9781793643698 (cloth) | ISBN 9781793643704 (epub)
Subjects: LCSH: People with disabilities—Social conditions. | Sociology of disability. | Disabilities—Social aspects.
Classification: LCC HV1568 .D66 2021 (print) | LCC HV1568 (ebook) | DDC 305.9/08—dc23
LC record available at https://lccn.loc.gov/2021018624
LC ebook record available at https://lccn.loc.gov/2021018625

For Zoey

Contents

Acknowledgments

The cover art for this book is the painting "The Beautiful Colors of Kids Like Me" by San Diego-based intuitive artist Jeremy Sicile-Kira. Diagnosed with autism at an early age, Jeremy began painting the images that he saw in his dreams and uses his gift of synesthesia to capture the emotions and spirituality of each of his subjects. I am so grateful to Jeremy for giving me permission to use his painting, which reflects the beauty and diversity of the autism spectrum.

Throughout this book, I call on each of us to recognize, make visible, and appreciate our dependency on a complex web of relationships that support and sustain us as we move through life. During the eight years that it took me to write this book, I was deeply aware of and grateful for my dependency on my own indispensable web of support. Two sabbatical leaves from the University of Tulsa bookended this project—I started researching and writing during my first sabbatical in Fall 2013 and completed the final revisions during my next sabbatical in Spring 2021. Subsequent research and travel grants from the University of Tulsa, particularly from the Center for Global Education, provided me with the invaluable opportunity to observe attitudes and approaches to social welfare in other parts of the world. I am especially grateful to Helle Rytkønen, Brynhildur Heiðar-og Ómarsdóttir, Freyja Haraldsdóttir, Yuri Ohlrichs, and the members of Tabú for welcoming me into their spaces and sharing their stories. The COVID-19 pandemic, which devastated the world during 2020 (and continues to devastate as of February 2021 when I write these acknowledgements), has deepened my gratitude for healthcare professionals, first responders, teachers, food service and agricultural workers, grocery store employees, and so many other essential workers who are vital to a functioning and thriving society but who so often remain invisible and undervalued. The pandemic has also magnified my respect for countries such as Iceland and Denmark that provide such a strong social safety net for their citizens, and it has refueled my anger over the injustices and inequalities created by the dearth of state responsibility for social welfare in my own country.

My book has benefitted tremendously from the expertise of the editorial staff at Lexington Books. I am especially grateful to Becca Rohde Beurer for her early interest in my work and to my editor, Courtney Lachapelle Morales, for so wisely shepherding this book through the production process and for trusting my vision every step of the way. It has been a joy to work with you. From my relationships with friends, colleagues, and students, I have received rich sources of information, wisdom, and support. Thank you to Paulo Tan, Christine Ruane, Janet Cairns, Madison Connell, Kristen Oertel, Jennifer Airey, Tamara Piety, Sheila Sonzzini Ferreira, Holly Laird, Lara Foley, Susan Chase, Kelsey Hancock, Carly Putnam, Clare Ryan, Nicole Bauer, Alex Wade, Jazzmin Wilson, Zachary Harvat, Leanna Duncan, Diane Britton, Jessica LaPlant, Tori Burris, Cassandra Meador, Whitney Cipolla, Daniela Rosales, and Emily Folsom. Several of these individuals read drafts of chapters or provided critical feedback on many of the ideas in this book. Their insights have made me a better scholar, teacher, and advocate. My understanding of disability has been shaped by the tremendous scholarship and activism of Susan Wendell, Ari Ne'eman, Lydia X. Z. Brown, Lennard Davis, Mia Mingus, Melanie Yergeau, Alison Kafer, Tobin Siebers, Simi Linton, Alice Wong, and so many others. I am especially grateful to Rosemarie Garland-Thomson, whose phenomenal book *Staring: How We Look* sparked my fascination with critical disability studies and started me down a new academic path. My respect and admiration for her incredible body of scholarship has no bounds.

Over the years, my web of support has evolved and expanded to encompass a group of professionals without whose wisdom, dedication, and compassion my family could not have survived. Thank you to Wendy Huckeba, Pam Moore, Uyen Le, Cheryl LaFortune, Katie Brander, Lynnah Huxall, Lindsay Smith, Dixie Highberger, Laura Zenthoefer, Hannah Brandt, Sherilyn Walton, and Michelle Hubner. You have all contributed an important verse to our powerful play. Thank you most of all to Janet Borden for your calm, steady reassurance, for emphasizing above all Zoey's personal empowerment, and for nurturing and delighting in every stage of Zoey's becoming. We are forever changed because of you.

From my family, I receive a deep reservoir of support, encouragement, and love that never runs dry. Thank you to Raymond Wilson, Sharon Wilson, Julie Shahan, Jill Austin, and Tara Rhoades. To my parents, Jerry and Leanne Doolittle, I am especially grateful. My father's gentle spirit, intellectualism, and unflagging championship of the ambitions and hopes of his three daughters have sustained and enriched my life and have provided a model of manhood from which the rest of the world could surely benefit. My mother is my rock, the first person with whom I want to share good news and the one to whom I turn when things look bleak. From her, I have received such wisdom and strength and unwavering faith and love. And from her, I have learned the meaning and beauty of what it is to give loving, generous, and respectful care to another person. My grandmother, Rose Cunning, was a tremendous shaping influence on my life and on the pages of this book. She was the best person I have ever known. I am so sad that my children never got to know her as I did, that her life was ending just as their lives were beginning. But in sharing her stories, in showing that her disability experience matters, I am ensuring that she will never be forgotten. She is with me, always.

In my husband, Nathan Wilson, I have a true partner and friend. Nathan, our shared journey and your own standards of scholarly excellence have made your critical responses to my work all the more valuable. For all of the times when you have done more than your share, taken care of the kids and the dogs so that I could write, and propped me up when my strength and courage faltered, I am truly grateful. My son, Connor, is a great, shining source of my joy and happiness. With your sweet spirit, cleverness, humor, and wisdom, you fill my world with such delight and purpose. The next book is for you, buddy.

And, finally, there is you, Zoey, the point from which all things in this book flow. This book is because of you and for you. Thank you for contributing your stories, poems, and songs from your own journal. Thank you for reading this manuscript and for providing feedback. Thank you for letting me share our journey. I desperately hope that I have done so respectfully and in ways that honor your dignity and personhood. Thank you for how you have contributed to the production of knowledge about autism and disability within these pages. Thank you for the joy and meaning you bring to my life every single day. Thank you for being you. I love you.

Introduction

Becoming Disabled

I became disabled in 2009 at the age of thirty-seven. People's reaction when I tell them this is fairly predictable. They ask me what happened, assuming of course that my disability came about through some sort of accident or sudden illness. And they tend to react sympathetically, as if my disablement was a tragedy or a stroke of misfortune. Their reaction is illustrative of a widespread cultural assumption that understands "able-bodiedness" as a normal, desirable state of being and therefore sees disability as abnormal, lesser than, an impairment of one's body or mind—a state of being that is unquestionably undesirable.[1]

When I say that I became disabled at the age of thirty-seven, I do not mean that I was not disabled before then. I was born hard of hearing, began to experience obsessive-compulsive disorder at the age of seven, and was diagnosed with an autoimmune disorder in young adulthood. But I did not recognize nor understand myself as disabled; rather, I believed that I had individual "problems" that I would need to manage on my own through hard work and a bit of ingenuity. I learned to adapt to unaccommodating or inhospitable environments through various strategies that I developed over time. Within my school environment, for example, it proved to be a distinct advantage that teachers endlessly arranged their classroom seating charts according to the alphabet. Because my last name began with a "D," I was always assigned to the front row in my classrooms, a position from which I could better hear the teachers' lessons. From elementary school all the way through graduate school, I compensated for my struggles with auditory learning through intensive reading of course materials, which allowed me to perform well on exams and written work. If I found myself in a setting in which I could not escape exposure to triggering content (church was a

1

leading candidate in this regard), I learned the technique of dissociation, creating elaborate stories in my mind to block out words or images that were emotionally traumatizing. Over time, I began to perform mental and physical rituals and compulsions (counting, performing tasks in a certain order, mentally reciting certain words or phrases, among others) to ward off harm. The idea that I could ask for help, that I could receive accommodations to make my movement through life less challenging, or that there might be others who shared my experiences never occurred to me. Without alternative ways of thinking about or understanding disability, I lived in and accepted as normal a world in which I had to succeed by trying to fit into existing structures or fail through my inability to do so.

I had lived my entire life with disability, but I did not become disabled until my daughter, Zoey, was diagnosed with various neurodiversities, including autism, starting at the age of four. My position by Zoey's side as we navigated hostile environments and spaces gave me a particular vantage point from which I began to see and evaluate my world in dramatically new ways.[2] As I watched Zoey struggle to fit into a world that was not made for her, I began to recognize how society pathologizes, misrepresents, excludes, and even criminalizes disability. In our interactions with doctors, therapists, and educators, I discovered a depth of discrimination against disabled people that I never could have imagined previously. In the books that I read and the movies and television shows that I watched, I began to notice how often disability was ignored, marginalized, or stereotyped. I began to recognize how the words used to describe disability in news stories, social media, and everyday conversations stigmatized and patronized lived disability experiences. The parenting memoirs, "expert" advice books, and so-called autism advocacy organizations that I had previously found so helpful now seemed to contribute to the pathologizing and medicalization of disability. In nearly every physical space that I inhabited, I began to notice multiple access barriers preventing the full and equal inclusion of disabled people. Discouraged by the near absence of disability in the courses taught at my university, including my own, I began an exhaustive exploration of disability history and culture and the rich body of knowledge produced by disability scholars and activists, many of whom I would eventually call my friends. Through this exploration, I discovered the tremendous gap between disability representation and lived disability experiences, between disability rights in legislation and the lack of disability rights in practice. I began to question everything I had thought to be true about disability and to critique existing discourses, practices, and institutions. I drew from my lived disability experiences and connections to the wider disability community to think differently about concepts such as neurodiversity, interdependency, access, and care and to reimagine my approaches to parenting, teaching, research, and social interactions. Ultimately, this journey led me to reevaluate my own history and to recognize and proudly claim my own disability identity.

When I say that I became disabled, then, I mean that I gained a new consciousness and a radically new way of viewing and understanding the world.[3] Becoming disabled is to think about disability in ways that depart from and challenge dominant discourses and systems that shape and reproduce disability stigma and discrimination. It is to create alternative understandings that validate and even celebrate the multiple ways of being in the world. It is to connect with other disabled people to promote disability rights and justice and to create systems and environments that are fully inclusive and accepting of all forms of human diversity. Using my own "disability becoming" as a jumping off point, this book offers a view of the world through the powerful prism of disability.

A DISABILITY VIEW OF THE WORLD

"Disability is everywhere in history," writes historian Douglas Baynton, and disabled people have always existed.[4] Today, people with disabilities number approximately one billion worldwide and constitute about 26 percent of the United States' population. Disability cuts across every demographic and touches the life of every person on the planet—whether intimately, consistently, intermittently, and/or relationally. Some experience disability from birth while others acquire disability suddenly and without warning. Some experience temporary disabilities throughout their lives, and some slide gradually toward disability as they age. Nearly everyone experiences disability on some level via their relationships with disabled family members, friends, and coworkers. Disability, then, is the common human experience.[5] It is a dynamic form of embodiment and an identity used both to justify discrimination and marginalization of disabled people and one claimed by disabled people themselves as a form of positive self-actualization, a source of community, and the basis for collective movements for disability justice.[6]

Disability is everywhere and not just in the lived experiences of those with disabilities. It is part of a pervasive, meaning-constituting system—what Rosemarie Garland-Thomson calls the "ability-disability system"—that classifies certain bodies and minds as broken, diseased, ugly, deviant, or unnatural and in the process marks other bodies as whole, healthy, beautiful, normal, and natural.[7] It decides which ways of knowing, communicating, and existing in the world are legitimate and marks alternative ways of knowing, communicating, and existing for intervention, cure, or erasure. And then it models the ideological, social, and physical environments on a mythical human norm.

Even today, thirty years after the passage of the Americans with Disabilities Act (ADA), those whose bodies and minds fit most comfortably within this norm slide fairly easily throughout the world. Most never have to give a single thought to the height of grocery store shelves, the out-of-service elevator at the subway station, the time constraints of the final exam, the booming sounds of the movie theater, the narrow bathroom stall, the fragrances wafting from the department store perfume counters—the environment is tailored to their specifications. Disability is what happens, then, when the environment does not take into consideration that minds and bodies are extremely varied; when it does not value the many ways of thinking about and moving through the world; and when it fails to accommodate and embrace all forms of human diversity.

Despite being "everywhere," disability is "curiously absent" or woefully misrepresented in the histories that we write and in the popular culture that we produce.[8] When disabled people do appear in scholarly or popular texts, they are usually marginal to the central narrative, serve as a plot device to advance or foil the journey of the story's protagonist, or function to inspire the audience through their courage, kindness, and plucky attitude. A tremendous disparity exists, then, between the reality of disability and the depiction of disability in our culture. Perhaps this is due to the common assumption that disability is relevant only to a small group of people with visible, physical impairments, which ignores the tremendous variability of disability and leaves invisible and unrecognized the many ways in which seemingly nondisabled people benefit from unearned privileges of the ability/disability system. The assumption that disability applies only to disabled people is similar to the assumption that race affects only people of color, that gender shapes only the lives of women, or that sexuality is relevant only to the experiences of LGBTQ+ people. Perhaps the disparity stems from a general discomfort with or fear of disability—its reminder that that we are mortal, that we will all eventually experience alterations of our bodies and minds, that our bodies are vulnerable and dependent on a multitude of supports for sustenance and survival. The notion that only people with disabilities are dependent on others, while nondisabled people are completely autonomous and self-sufficient is a tremendous fallacy that contributes to the dread of disability and so much of the discrimination, control, and abuse of disabled people. Perhaps the disparity is a product of the ongoing exclusion of disabled people from full participation in the creation, production, and performance of the stories that we tell about disability. The vast majority of these stories are not written by or for people with disabilities but by nondisabled people for an imagined nondisabled audience, whose nervousness about disability needs to be assuaged. We can therefore watch a feature-length movie about a quadriplegic woman assured in the knowledge that her "pitiful" life will end mercilessly with a friend-assisted suicide and that the actor who plays her will be able to stride up the aisle at the Academy Awards ceremony a few months later to collect her Oscar. Instead of news reports that detail the impediments to justice and equality for disabled people—such as high poverty and unemployment rates, the prevalence of sexual abuse and assault, lack of access to voting rights, education, housing, adequate transportation, and medical care—we are inundated with segments about disabled people who "overcome" their disability through heroic achievements. On the Internet, we are bombarded by depictions of nondisabled people's acts of kindness toward disabled people through heartwarming images captured on cell phone cameras and circulated on social media platforms usually without the consent of those filmed. And we are regularly exposed to public service announcements that use the threat of disability to discourage us from risky or dangerous behaviors. Given that most members of the public form their understanding of disability from media representations, it is little wonder, then, that our collective view of disability is so skewed and rooted in fear, misperception, and pity.

Throughout this book, I make two key arguments. First, by demonstrating that the ways in which we currently define, represent, legislate, educate, and parent disability are deeply problematic, I argue that disability is a natural, legitimate, valuable human variation that demands and deserves fully accommodating and accepting environments. This requires nothing less than a radical reconceptualization of disability and the restructuring of social, economic, and ideological institutions. Second, I argue for interdependence as a "natural" and desirable human condition crucial to success and happiness. Our stubborn insistence on independence as the hallmark of a worthy life undermines the value of disabled lives, denies the reality of our need for one another, and dismisses the public responsibility for social welfare. In truth, no one is autonomous or self-sufficient. We are all dependent on human relationships, institutional support systems, and environmental factors in order to survive and flourish. Far from something that deprives us of our humanity, this sort of dependency is the essence of what it is to be human; it is what connects us to one another. Instead of moving toward the unattainable and undesirable goal of independence, this book argues that we should be further enmeshing ourselves in the complex web of relationships and social systems that, if fully recognized, cultivated, and offered generously and equally, can sustain us, give us the support we need to care for one another, and make us feel truly valued and loved.[9] These two arguments comprise this book's central claim: Analyzing the world through the powerful prism of disability creates a revolutionary and irreversibly transformative understanding of the human experience, one that magnifies our appreciation for human differences, deepens our commitment to social justice, and leads us to embrace our need for one another.

This book uses an autoethnographic approach, defined as one in which an author draws on personal experiences to analyze and create meaning about larger social, cultural, and political phenomena.[10] "The intent of autoethnography," writes sociologist Sarah Wall, "is to acknowledge the inextricable link between the personal and the cultural and to make room for nontraditional forms of inquiry and expression."[11] In each chapter, I draw on my own distinct experiences—particularly how parenting Zoey led to my "disability becoming"—and my social location to make original knowledge claims about the social and political meanings attached to disability and the histories and lives of disabled people. In addition to my experiences, I use scholarship from disability, feminist, and queer history and studies to analyze language, history, media, public policy, cultural practices, and educational, economic, and familial systems in order to understand how meanings of disability are formed in specific contexts among specific communities of people; how these meanings change over time; how some meanings emerge as normative; how normative meanings affect the material reality of disabled people's lives; and what all of these processes reveal about the role of power, history, and culture in producing knowledge about minds and bodies. Embracing the mantra "Nothing About Us Without Us," my book assumes that people with disabilities are authorities over their own lives and experiences and must be full participants in the knowledge produced about them. Hence, I also draw on previously untapped or underutilized sources written and created by people with disabilities—including blogs, articles, websites, documentaries, YouTube videos, and memoirs—to explore how disabled people have challenged and offered alternatives to dominant meanings of disability in order to transform institutions and attitudes and to achieve social justice. Inclusion of these sources allows me to center the intersectional perspectives and lived experiences of a range of people with disabilities, many of whom have been marginalized within or excluded from traditional forms of knowledge production.

In my use of "nontraditional forms of inquiry and expression," I am attempting to push against the boundaries that privilege traditional forms of knowledge building, boundaries that, according to sociologist Sharlene Nagy Hesse-Biber, "mark who can be a knower and what can be known."[12] As feminist, critical race, postmodern, and postcolonial theorists have long demonstrated, there are multiple, legitimate methods for the creation and sharing of knowledge.[13] Throughout the book, I use experiential and subjugated knowledges as key sources for providing critical insights about disability, recognizing that rich new meanings are created when we place the experiences of marginalized groups at the center of social inquiry. While autoethnography characterizes the book as a whole, some chapters are written in a formal academic style while others read more like creative nonfiction. Using techniques drawn from journaling, memoir, and hauntology, a few chapters are deeply intimate and even conversational. Other chapters adopt a more distanced, pedagogical tone. My autoethnographic, multimodal, and shifting narrative approach is another way for me to push against the boundaries of traditional methodologies, but it is also an illustration that knowledge is communicated most effectively not through one method but through multiple means that address the diverse, unpredictable ways in which audiences perceive, comprehend, and engage information. While some readers may find my shifts in style and tone jarring, I agree with disability scholars Cynthia Lewiecki-Wilson and Jen Cellio that the "fault lines" of plural methods "can engender productive dissonance, opening up opportunities for reconsiderations for . . . how we believe we know."[14]

My unconventional narrative style is perhaps, most importantly, an attempt to demonstrate that this book is not a product but a process, a journey of sorts that is far from complete. Knowledge production is never linear, neutral, or conclusive, but halting, transitory, and even messy, and I wanted my narrative to reflect this. I do not claim to have "true" knowledge of or final authority on the issues that I discuss. Rather my intent is to open a liminal, dialogic space that invites consideration, debate, and even contestation of the arguments that I present in these pages toward the larger goal of creating meaning for social change.[15] My understanding of and perspectives on disability flow from the identities and experiences of my social locations that are various, shifting, and intersectional. I identify here as a disability studies scholar, a person who has come to identify as disabled, and as the mother of an autistic daughter named Zoey. These identities—like all identity categories—are not uniform, static, or unrelated but rather fluid, dynamic, and deeply interconnected. The ways in which I experience these identities are particular and partial—what is true for me is not necessarily true for others—and are shaped by the interaction of my various other social locations, including my gender, race, age, sexuality, culture, and nationality. When my identities shift—due to the accumulation of new experiences and forms of knowledge, the passage of time, and changes in my location—so too do my perspectives on disability. I wrote this book over the span of eight years, and each chapter captures a snapshot of a particular stage in my journey. Naturally, then, each chapter varies in tone, style, and emphasis.

My identification as disabled is not without complications and risk. I lived with congenital and acquired disabilities but had no language or community through which to articulate disability as a positive identity or category of analysis until I began my journey with Zoey. On this journey, where I discovered disability history, culture, and politics and connected to disability communities, I "became" disabled. Yet, the fact that my disabilities are mostly invisible has indelibly shaped my particular disability identity. On most days, there is nothing immediately noticeable about my body or how my mind interacts with my world that signals to others that I am disabled. While this invisibility sometimes puts me in the tiresome position of having to explain my disabilities and even justify the need for accommodations, it also gives me a degree of privilege not afforded those whose alterity is clearly visible and who are marked and treated as disabled whether or not they identify as such. While claiming disability makes me vulnerable to forms of discrimination and stigma, I recognize that my many privileges (or sets of unearned benefits that I receive because I belong to groups/categories that my society erroneously deems superior to others) as a white, educated, straight, middle-class, cisgender person mitigate some of this vulnerability in ways not possible for those who do not share my privileges. Claiming disability also runs the risk of solidifying identity categories that in some ways are best challenged and deconstructed. For example, disability exists in a mutually constituting and dependent relationship to its perceived opposite—ability—a binary that reifies the presumption that these categories are homogenous, discrete, and static instead of heterogeneous, fluid, and unstable. Most of us, after all, do not live in the boxes of either "disabled" or "nondisabled" but occupy shifting, slippery positions in the spaces in between. Furthermore, when I say that I am disabled, what information am I communicating about myself? In announcing this identity, I am making important claims about my own experience and attempting to disrupt normative discourses about disability, but I cannot reasonably predict nor control the public interpretation and outcome of my claims.[16]

Despite the risks, I believe that defining one's relationship to disability does important work. Borrowing from feminist and queer studies' identity-based critical perspectives, disability scholars like Corbett Joan O'Toole and Rosemarie Garland-Thomson argue that disability coming-out stories serve "to expose what was previously hidden, privatized, and medicalized in order to enter into a political community" and to provide positive "counternarratives" about what it means to have a disability.[17] Claiming disability, in other words, challenges the misperception that being identified as disabled is shameful or undesirable. Particularly when someone who appears to be non-disabled identifies as disabled, claiming disability has the potential to disrupt normative expectations for how disabled bodies and minds are supposed to look and behave. It provides an epistemological vantage point from which to share knowledge and to interrogate ableist economic and social structures and ideologies. And it creates rewarding connections to other disabled people who have formed a heterogeneous community of invaluable support, resources, and strategies.[18]

My identity as the mother of a child with autism also has risks and complications. I am well aware of the concern expressed by many autistic people about the tendency of some parents to speak for their autistic children or to conflate their experiences as parents with their child's actual lived experiences.[19] As autistic activist Aaron Herman has noted:

> Parents of autistic people tend to assert that because they know their children so well, they should be able to speak on their children's behalf with just as much authority. The public subscribes to both of these beliefs, but they are misguided. A parent can love, understand and listen to their child, but they are not their child. No matter how much they "get it," they will never be more qualified to talk about autism than an autistic person, and they should recognize that in their thoughts and actions.[20]

Several autistic writers and activists, like Amy Sequenzia, caution parents about the unwitting damage they are inflicting on their children and to public perceptions of disability in general by sharing on social media platforms private information about their kids or posting videos of their children experiencing meltdowns or other challenging behaviors. These "martyr parents," writes Sequenzia, claim that they are helping other families and fighting the "good fight" against autism. In actuality, she argues, they are fighting their children by demonizing an essential part of who they are and disrespecting their child's humanity in the process.[21]

From my reading of numerous writings by and conversations with autistic adults, I have gained valuable insights about how to frame my identity as the parent of an autistic child and how to share Zoey's experiences in ways that respect her dignity and humanity. Though I started writing this book several years ago, I have consciously delayed publishing it until Zoey was old enough to read and understand it and to give it her stamp of approval. Certainly, my life and experiences are shaped in intimate connection to Zoey's. When she moves, I move. With her by my side, I have navigated through the health care, educational, and social systems and have been exposed to a depth of ableism, discrimination, judgment, and hostility I could not have previously imagined. But the way in which I have experienced these things differ fundamentally and crucially from the way that Zoey has experienced them. Our experiences are not equivalent. And so, this book is written from my perspective; my job is to help Zoey to recognize the power of her own voice so that perhaps one day, she will tell her own story.

I have also consciously tried to avoid the trappings of the "typical" memoir written by parents of children with disabilities, many of which have the tendency to reify rather than challenge oppressive cultural models of disability. As described by the late feminist scholar Alison Piepmeier, many parental memoirs emphasize grief over a child's diagnosis, frame their child's disability at least in part through a medicalized model, and "represent the child not as a person but as a problem with which the parents have to grapple."[22] Regardless of the parents' intentions, then, these memoirs often bolster some of the worst cultural stereotypes of disability. I hope that, by contrast, my book provides a space of resistance to, not reinforcement of, these stereotypes. While not ignoring or romanticizing Zoey's many challenges and struggles, I emphasize that she is disabled primarily from unaccommodating and unaccepting structures, attitudes, and environments. When I do describe aspects of her life, I am not attempting to "speak" for her or to claim authority over her lived experiences with disability but instead offering a portrait of a fantastic human being from an intimate, loving vantage point that most others do not get to see.[23] In so doing, I hope to challenge the many public misperceptions of what it is like to parent a child with a disability, to shift the way in which people with disabilities are often framed, and to complicate and reconceptualize the ways in which we define, think about, articulate, and represent disability in our homes, schools, media, and everyday conversations.

This book is structured in four parts, each of which analyzes and challenges a particular understanding of disability and proposes alternate policies and attitudes that can magnify appreciation for human differences and promote social justice. Part I, "Identifying Disability" (chapters 1 and 2) examines how meanings of disability are constructed through language, history, and culture and how various groups have attempted to reassign meaning through scholarship and activism. Chapter 1 explores the difficulties of defining disability, given the tremendous variability of disabled bodies and minds, and offers a brief history of the medicalization of disability, the emergence of the disability rights movement, and ongoing struggles for disability justice and self-advocacy. By examining how disability experiences are shaped by intersecting social locations determined by race, gender, sexuality, and class, chapter 2 considers some of the possibilities and limitations of disability identity politics and the potential of crip theory to broaden and strengthen coalitions for disability justice. Part II, "(Re)imagining Disability" (chapters 3 and 4) considers how social institutions are powerful producers of knowledge about disability. Through the ways in which they arrange, represent, categorize, and treat different bodies and minds, social institutions send powerful and deeply influential messages about which lives and experiences matter and which do not. The chapters in this section explore two of the most powerful meaning-producing institutions—media and education—and how they have been sources of the perpetuation of disability stigma and discrimination, as well as spaces in which new, more positive reimaginings of disability have developed. In chapter 3, I explore displays of disability created and recycled in popular media and evaluate the extent to which they can be useful mechanisms for analyzing and critiquing popular understandings of disability and the treatment of disabled people in specific historical and cultural locations.

The chapter also examines the power of alternative narratives created by disabled people, who have been finding a larger visibility, community, and voice since the passage of the ADA, the proliferation of social media platforms, and wider opportunities for self-expression in the past few decades. In chapter 4, I analyze the many inadequacies of so-called "inclusive education" approaches as currently practiced in American public schools and call for a radical reimagining of the learning environment through the implementation of Universal Design for Learning (UDL). A social justice approach to education that accommodates and takes into consideration the diverse learning needs of all students, UDL, I argue, has the potential to radically transform the meaning of inclusive education and the very concept of disability.

Part III, "Locating Disability" (chapters 5 and 6) analyzes how disability is a powerful social location from which to form new, positive identities, to connect to others in networks of community and support, and to create approaches to care that are guided by the principles of inclusion, respect, and self-determination. In chapter 5, I discuss how my grandmother's disability experiences taught me the importance of "access intimacy," described by disability writer and educator Mia Mingus as those relationships in which disabled bodies and minds can feel safe and comfortable; where help and support are not a form of charity or an obligation but woven into the very fabric of what it means to love and care for another person; and where help and support are understood as just another form of the interdependency that characterizes all human relationships.[24] I also argue for an expanded disability theory that creates space for experiences of pain, discomfort, trauma, and sorrow and that embraces the messiness, the dangers even, of actual lived disability experiences that do not fit neatly into existing disability studies' discourses. In chapter 6, I discuss how my care of Zoey has been informed by the principles of access intimacy, as well as the work of autistic self-advocates, who recognize neurodiversity as a valid and important human variation that deserves acceptance and accommodation. From them, I have learned to reject care approaches that attempt to "normalize" Zoey and to seek out instead whatever supports, services, therapies, educational tools, and assistive technologies are necessary for Zoey to participate fully in society. Part IV, "Mothering Disability" (chapters 7 and 8) analyzes how socially constructed ideas of the "good mother" serve as a mechanism by which all mothers are regulated, disciplined, and punished and how they perpetuate the harmful but still widespread notion that successful childrearing depends on an individual woman's perseverance and self-sacrifice. Throughout chapters 7 and 8, I use my own parenting experiences as a window into the many problems with the "heroic mothering" paradigm, as well as a global framework (drawing comparisons between the United States and countries with strong social welfare systems such as Denmark) to demonstrate that disrupting the "good mother" and "heroic mothering" paradigms requires that we keep offering up alternative models of motherhood. Such models do not depend on wealth, whiteness, ability, and heteronormativity but encourage mothers to help their children develop eventually into self-advocates equipped to fight the obstacles of disabling environments, structures, and attitudes. They recognize that good mothering depends largely on community support, state resources, and public responsibility for social welfare. And they acknowledge that a mother's self-care is not an act of indulgence but is in fact crucial both to her ability to care for others and to her own happiness and well-being.

NOTES

1. Rosemarie Garland-Thomson, "Becoming Disabled," *The New York Times*, August 19, 2016, https://www.nytimes.com/2016/08/21/opinion/sunday/becoming-disabled.html.

2. Corbett O'Toole writes that a family member of a disabled person gains valuable insights and new perspectives about disability and disability discrimination when they travel through the world by the side of their loved one. "We need language that respects the lessons learned by nondisabled family members who live with disabled people," she argues, even as we need to be careful not to conflate relational and lived disability experiences nor to ignore how nondisabled family members benefit from ableist privilege. I agree with her. See Corbett Joan O'Toole, "Disclosing Our Relationships to Disabilities: An Invitation for Disability Studies Scholars," *Disability Studies Quarterly* 33:2 (2013), http://dsq-sds.org/article/view/3708/3226.

3. Several scholars with disabilities have written about how they "became disabled" by gaining a new consciousness of themselves and their society, and I want to acknowledge their influence on my thinking in this Introduction and throughout this book. See, for example, Rosemarie Garland-Thomson, "The Story of My Work: How I Became Disabled," *Disability Studies Quarterly* 34:2 (2014), https://dsq-sds.org/article/view/4254; Georgina Kleege, *Sight Unseen* (New Haven and London: Yale University Press, 1999); and Simi Linton, *Claiming Disability* (New York: New York University Press, 1998).

4. Douglas Baynton, "Disability and the Justification of Inequality in American History," in *The New Disability History: American Perspectives*, eds. Paul K. Longmore and Lauri Umanski (New York: New York University Press, 2001), 52.

5. See, for example, Tom Shakespeare, *Disability: The Basics* (New York: Routledge, 2018), 1 and Rosemarie Garland-Thomson, "Integrating Disability, Transforming Feminist Theory," *NWSA Journal* 14:3 (Autumn 2002): 5, http://www.jstor.org/stable/4316922.

6. Tobin Siebers, *Disability Theory* (Ann Arbor: University of Michigan Press, 2008), 11.

7. Garland-Thomson, "Integrating Disability," 21.

8. Baynton, "Disability and the Justification of Inequality in American History," 52.

9. Kim Q. Hall, "Toward a Queer Crip Feminist Politics of Food," *philoSO-PHIA* 4:2 (Summer 2014): 178, https://muse.jhu.edu/article/565882.; Chris Cuomo, *Feminism and Ecological Communities: An Ethic of Flourishing* (New York: Routledge, 1998), 74.

10. Tessa Muncey, "Doing Autoethnography," *International Journal of Qualitative Methods* 4:3 (2005): 69–86, https://doi.org/10.1177/160940690500400105; William Neuman, *Social Research Methods: Qualitative and Quantitative Approaches* (Needham Heights, MA: Allyn and Bacon, 1994).

11. Sarah Wall, "An Autoethnography on Learning About Autoethnography," *International Journal of Qualitative Methods* 5:2 (2006): 146, https://doi.org /10.1177/160940690600500205. See also Carolyn Ellis, *The Ethnographic I: A Methodological Novel about Autoethnography* (Walnut Creek, CA: AltaMira, 2004); Camilla Stivers, "Reflections on the Role of Personal Narrative in Social Science," *Signs: Journal of Women in Culture and Society* 18:2 (1993): 408–425, https://doi.org /10.1086/494800; and Norman Denzin and Yvonna Lincoln, *The Sage Handbook of Qualitative Research* (Thousand Oaks: Sage Publications, 2005), x.

12. Sharlene Nagy Hesse-Biber, ed., *Handbook of Feminist Research: Theory and Praxis*, 2nd ed. (Thousand Oaks, CA: Sage Publications, 2012), 3.

13. See, for example, Terry Eagleton, *The Illusions of Postmodernism* (Oxford: Blackwell, 1996); Sandra Harding, *The Science Question in Feminism* (Ithaca: Cornell University Press, 1986); Michèle Barrett and Anne Phillips, *Destabilizing Theory: Contemporary Feminist Debates* (Stanford: Stanford University Press, 1992); Patricia Hill Collins, *Black Feminist Thought: Knowledge, Consciousness, and the Politics of Empowerment* (New York: Routledge, 1990); Gayatri Chakravoty Spivak, "Can the Subaltern Speak?" in *Colonial Discourse and Post- Colonial Theory: A Reader*, eds. Patrick Williams and Laura Chrismen (New York: Columbia University Press, 1994), 66–111; Trinh T. Minh-ha, *Framer Framed* (New York: Routledge, 1991); and Nancy Tuana, ed., *Feminism and Science* (Bloomington: Indiana University Press, 1989).

14. Cynthia Lewiecki-Wilson and Jen Cellio, "Introduction: On Liminality and Cultural Embodiment," in *Disability and Mothering: Liminal Spaces of Embodied Knowledge*, eds. Cynthia Lewiecki-Wilson and Jen Cellio (Syracuse: Syracuse University Press, 2011), 11.

15. Andrew Miller, "Personalising Ethnography: On Memory, Evidence, and Subjectivity: The Writing and Learning Journey," *New Writing* 5:2 (September 2008): 89–113, https://doi.org/10.1080/14790720802209971.

16. Here I borrow from Judith Butler, who originally asked these questions about identity in her seminal work "Imitation and Gender Insubordination," in *Inside/ Out: Lesbian Theories, Gay Theories,* ed. Diana Fuss (New York: Routledge, 1991), 13–31.

17. O'Toole, "Disclosing Our Relationships to Disabilities"; Garland-Thomson, "Integrating Disability," 21–22.

18. O'Toole, "Disclosing Our Relationships to Disabilities."

19. O'Toole, "Disclosing Our Relationships to Disabilities."

20. Aaron Herman, "Ableism at Tufts and the 'Life, Animated' Screening," *The Tufts Daily*, March 13, 2017, https://tuftsdaily.com/opinion/2017/03/13/op-ed-ableism-at-tufts-and-the-life-animated-screening/.

21. Amy Sequenzia, "Privacy and Parental Behavior," *Ollibean*, accessed July 19, 2018, https://ollibean.com/privacy-and-parental-behavior/. See also Mary Langan, "Parental Voices and Controversies in Autism," *Disability & Society* 26:2 (2011): 193–205, https://doi.org/10.1080/09687599.2011.544059; and Sara Ryan and Katherine Runswick-Cole, "Repositioning Mothers: Mothers, Disabled Children, and Disability Studies," *Disability & Society* 23:3 (2008): 199–210, https://doi.org/10.1080/ 09687590801953937.

22. Alison Piepmeier, "Saints, Sages, and Villains: Endorsement of and Resistance to Cultural Stereotypes in Memoirs by Parents of Children with Disabilities," *Disability Studies Quarterly* 32:1 (2012), http://doi.org/10.18061/dsq.v32i1.3031.

23. Piepmeier, "Saints, Sages, and Villains."

24. Mia Mingus, "Access Intimacy: The Missing Link," *Leaving Evidence*, May 5, 2011, https://leavingevidence.wordpress.com/2011/05/05/access-intimacy-the-missing-link/.

Part I

IDENTIFYING DISABILITY

Chapter 1

Meanings of Disability

My Zoey is a bright, precocious, funny, quirky girl who loves Ariana Grande, mint chocolate chip ice cream, French bull dogs, and the television show *Stranger Things*. Zoey is also autistic, a neurodiversity[1] that shapes the creative, unique, insightful, and sometimes challenging ways that she interacts with her world—a world, she learned early on, that often treats difference as something to be mitigated or stamped out. One day during a session with one of Zoey's therapists, I referred to Zoey as an "autistic child." At this, the therapist drew in a quick breath and quickly corrected me: "We never say 'autistic child,'" she admonished. "Always say instead, 'a child with autism.'" Seeing my puzzled look, she went on to explain that it is important to "put the person first" in order to emphasize the person's humanity and value and to avoid identifying the person with his or her "disorder." As I mulled over this, I grew increasingly uneasy. Why would calling Zoey an autistic child diminish her humanity or her value? When the therapist called for the need to disassociate Zoey from her autism in order to demonstrate her humanity and value, was she suggesting that autism has nothing to do with Zoey's humanity and value or that Zoey cannot be seen as having humanity and value if she is associated with autism? None of these things could be true, I concluded. Separating Zoey from her autism does not give her humanity and value—she has humanity and value at the same time that autism is an inherent part of her identity. In fact, as autistic writer and activist Lydia X. Z. Brown argues, "It is impossible to affirm the value and worth of an Autistic person without recognizing his or her identity as an Autistic person. Referring to me as 'a person with autism,' or 'an individual with ASD' demeans who I am because it denies who I am."[2] Without autism, Zoey would not be the same Zoey, and there was nothing about Zoey's personhood that I wanted to change.

Ultimately, the therapist's attempt to separate Zoey from her autism was a tacit acknowledgment that autism is wrong or undesirable. Likewise, to separate the person from the disability is to perpetuate the terribly damaging idea that disability itself is a misfortune. This idea is already well grounded in the public understanding, along with widespread and sometimes contradictory assumptions that disabled people are pathetic and helpless; that disability is an abnormality to be corrected or cured; that life with a disability is an unending burden both for disabled people and their caregivers; that people with mental "illnesses" are violent, dangerous, and/or sexually predatory; that people with cognitive or developmental disabilities have extraordinary gifts and abilities; and that people with disabilities, through their courage and grace, have a special purpose to inspire nondisabled people to be benevolent, generous, and more grateful for their "able-bodiedness." Shaped and reified by historical and contemporaneous ideas in medicine, science, religion, social theory, and media, writes historian Laurie Block, these popular perceptions of disability have proven stubbornly resilient, transcending time and geographical boundaries. "They still have power today to alter and affect the lives of individuals with disabilities," Block observes, "as well as the lives of their family members and care providers."[3]

In part I of this book, I examine how meanings of disability are constructed through language, history, and culture and how various groups have attempted to reassign meaning through scholarship and activism. In this chapter, I attempt to trace the factors that have led to current understandings of disability rooted in tragedy and pathology and the impact that these understandings have had on the lives and experiences of people with disabilities. I also discuss how people with disabilities have pushed back against stereotypical definitions of disability by advancing their own meanings and how they have challenged discriminatory and exclusionary laws, policies, and attitudes by forming rights-based and self-advocacy groups to fight for full inclusion, equality, and justice. In chapter 2, I consider the possibilities and limitations of both identity-based politics and forms of activism that call for the reworking or dismantling of identity categories in order to build more inclusive coalitions for change.

DEFINING DISABILITY

On a whim one afternoon, I typed the word "disability" into the Google search box, and the following definition popped up on my screen: "Disability: a physical or mental condition that limits a person's movements, senses, or activities; synonyms: handicap, disablement, incapacity, impairment, infirmity, defect, abnormality; a disadvantage or handicap, especially one imposed or recognized by the law."[4] This is a definition that equals individual affliction, a limitation on a person's movements, senses, and activities. It means loss, undesirability, incapacity, abnormality, and even tragedy. So entrenched are these negative associations with disability, notes Mia Mingus, that "just the idea that we can understand disability as 'not wrong'" requires "a huge shift in thinking."[5] Therefore, a key project of disability scholars and activists, writes disability scholar Simi Linton, is to challenge current understandings of disability and to formulate new meanings "consistent with a sociopolitical analysis."[6]

But in rejecting a definition of disability rooted in tragedy and pathology, what alternative definitions can we offer? This question is not easily answered. Like all identity categories, disability is an incredibly incoherent category that defies easy definition. According to the U.S. Census Bureau, sixty-one million Americans live with a disability, and people with disabilities comprise approximately 26 percent of the U.S. population.[7] The disability population is not only enormous but incredibly diverse; disability assumes a multitude of different forms, including physical, cognitive, sensory, neurological, and intellectual disabilities, as well as a wide array of chronic diseases. There is no singular disability experience, and no one person will experience disability in exactly the same way as others similarly disabled. Nor will one's individual experience of disability remain static over time. How a person experiences disability is due to a huge number of factors, including not only the type of disability one has but also whether the disability is congenital or acquired; how the disability is perceived by others; the level of stigma attached to the disability; whether one's disability is visible to others; how one's disability experience intersects with one's experiences of gender, race, class, sexuality, age, geographic location, and religion (among other factors); and one's access to adequate health care, education, employment, family and community support, and social services.

The categories of disabled and nondisabled are not static, universal, discrete, or self-evident but rather have shifted over time and across cultures. In fact, culturally constructed and historically shifting ideas of disability shape medical and popular understandings of "impairment" itself. Who is defined as "impaired" and, therefore, who gets counted among the disabled population are largely political and cultural decisions. Each society has constructed its own version of the human ideal with its own set of cultural norms and expectations for health, functioning, and levels of performance, and individuals within those societies hold various positions in relationship to those norms and expectations. Yet, built environments, policies, and attitudes make little room for this sort of human variation. Instead, they are modeled on, and thus privilege, bodies and minds perceived as fit, competent, and intelligent and thus devalue, stigmatize, and subjugate bodies and minds viewed as ugly, deformed, and incompetent.[8] When individuals "fail" to think, move, act, and look in ways that fit expected norms, they are rendered "disabled." But, as disability scholar Susan Wendell asks, how much does one have to vary from expected norms to be classified as disabled? How closely does one have to adhere to expected norms to be classified as able-bodied? How have these classifications shifted across time and place? And who has the power to make these classifications?[9] The answer to these questions varies widely depending on the activities a given society values, whether social resources are widely available and equitably distributed, and the extent to which lawmakers, medical authorities, and insurance companies have the power to determine what constitutes a disability.

We might also ask how these classifications affect the identities and experiences of individuals included in these classifications and those excluded from them. Often, individuals categorized or perceived as having a disability do not identify as disabled either because they do not experience limitations in activities or opportunities or because, for a variety of reasons, they do not wish to be associated with a stigmatized group. By contrast, there are many other individuals who experience various impairments but are not recognized as disabled by public or medical and legal authorities; consequently, they are not able to access needed medical or social services. In addition, changes in political leadership and shifting medical decisions often create new populations of disabled people and remove others previously classified as disabled from disability categories. With a change in blood pressure guidelines from the American College of Cardiology and the American Heart Association in November 2017, for example, eight million people were suddenly characterized as having hypertension and advised to start blood pressure medication.[10] In 1998, twenty-nine million Americans were newly classified as overweight when the federal government lowered the optimal weight threshold based on the controversial body mass index.[11] Millions of people who were classified as having a mental disorder due to their sexual orientation were suddenly depathologized in 1973 when the American Psychiatric Association removed the diagnosis of "homosexuality" from the second edition of the Diagnostic and Statistical Manual of Mental Disorders (DSM).[12] Forty years later, the American Psychiatric Association replaced the previously separate diagnostic labels of Autistic Disorder, Asperger's Disorder, and PDD-NOS with the umbrella term "Autism Spectrum Disorder" and adopted more restrictive diagnostic criteria.[13] A report from the Child Study Center at the Yale School of Medicine estimated that under the new criteria, approximately 75 percent of individuals previously diagnosed with Asperger's and 85 percent of those diagnosed with PDD-NOS would no longer meet the criteria for a diagnosis of Autism Spectrum Disorder and would potentially be unable to access needed services.[14]

Disability categories, definitions, and diagnostic criteria are also the product of dominant assumptions about race, class, and gender, as the historical and current medical understandings of autism so clearly demonstrate. In some of the first clinical descriptions of autism, psychologist Leo Kanner wrote that many of the children he treated were white boys from financially secure families.[15] Kanner and other early autism researchers did not consider that these were the types of children whose families were most likely to seek expensive autism "treatment" and thus helped to perpetuate the assumption—which lingers to this day—that autism is a white, male, middle-class "disorder."[16] Studies by the Centers for Disease Control and Prevention (CDC) show that rates of autism are essentially identical across racial and ethnic groups.[17] Recent studies also suggest that autism is much more common in girls than previously believed.[18] Yet, white children are 30 percent more likely to receive an autism diagnosis than Black children and 50 percent more likely than Latinx children; boys are four times more likely than girls to be diagnosed with autism.[19] Girls and children of color are also diagnosed significantly later than white boys.[20] This racial and gender disparity is explained in part by the fact that the diagnostic criteria for autism has been based largely on the behavioral characteristics and etiology of boys and men,[21] which is consistent with the well-documented historical gender and racial biases within the field of medical research as a whole.[22]

Definitions of disability, then, are not simply the result of some sort of universal, objective process, but the product of relations of power that are historically and socially contingent. The assignation of medical meanings to disability has had several repercussions for disabled people, both beneficial and harmful. Medical discoveries and treatments have prevented or treated illness and disease, saved lives, and increased the well-being of countless individuals. Without a medical diagnosis, many people cannot receive medications or access educational accommodations and other needed services. But, as I will demonstrate throughout this chapter, the medicalization of disability has also marked human variations as deviant, pathological, and tragic.[23] Those with the power to diagnose and treat disability shape the discourses that produce knowledge about disabilities, which, in turn, influence the experiences and material realities of disabled people. News stories, for example, frequently report that people with spinal cord injuries are "confined" to their wheelchairs, or that children "suffer from" autism. Words such as "crazy," "insane," "psycho," "retarded," "dumb," "moron," and "lame" are used frequently in everyday conversations to insult someone, to invalidate a person's point of view, or simply to characterize something as "bad." When we describe someone's neglectfulness as "blindness," when we portray ambivalent feelings as "schizophrenic" or "bipolar," when we claim that people are having "OCD," "ADD," or "senior moments," or when we comment on the "crippling" effects of a winter storm, we are contributing to, as disability advocate Rachel Cohen-Rottenberg puts it, "a narrative that says that disabled people are wrong, broken, dangerous, pitiful, and tragic."[24] Such narratives mostly go unchallenged, and when challenges are raised, they usually focus on those being disparaged by a disability comparison instead of how the comparison itself is disparaging to people with disabilities. For example, when Joy Behar, a cohost on the ABC talk show *The View*, joked that Vice-President Mike Pence's conversations with Jesus were symptomatic of a mental illness, many conservatives, including Pence himself, were outraged by Behar's insult to those of the Christian faith but left unrecognized Behar's insult to people with neurological disabilities in her use of mental illness as a device to ridicule.[25]

The language that we use to describe disability has a tremendous impact on public attitudes and ideas about disabled people and thus influences the experiences and material realities of disabled people. As Cohen-Rottenberg writes, "If a culture's language is full of pejorative metaphors about a group of people, that culture is not going to see those people as fully entitled to the same housing, employment, medical care, education, access, and inclusion as people in a more favored group."[26] So, words are never just words. They are powerful shapers of meaning that create real-world economic, social, and political consequences for the millions of people who live with a disability. "What people say matters," argues disability scholar and activist Emily Rapp Black. "It is another form of accessibility, another way of being inside, or outside, the narrative of our culture. Every time we hear the words 'lame' or 'cripple' or 'freak' it is clear we are still living outside the perimeters of that culture."[27]

THE MEDICAL MODEL OF DISABILITY

Concerns over avoiding language that perpetuates disability oppression have led to long-standing and often heated debates among disability advocates, caregivers, and professionals over "person-first language," as my experience with Zoey's therapist illustrates. Fundamentally, the debate over person-first language is reflective of a larger schism in the understanding and interpretation of disability. Person-first language seems consistent with the medical model of disability, which locates disability in a person's body and/or mind and seeks to eradicate this disability through medical interventions and cures. Separating the person from the disability makes sense in this model, as the disability is understood as disease, disfunction, or misfortune. But as Rosemarie Garland-Thomson notes, "[t]his impulse to rescue people with disabilities from a discredited identity" works to delegitimate disability as a positive form of self-identification as important to many people as racial or gender identities.[28] Disability identity is more nebulous, however, than other identities based on race, gender, and sexuality because there is no defini- tive, collective notion of what it means to be disabled. As Garland-Thomson acknowledges, nondisabled people may assign disability to someone in a wheelchair, a person with a guide dog, or a child with Down syndrome, but most do not understand that these disparate individuals share a social iden- tity and political status. Rather, "they merely seem to be people to whom something unfortunate has happened, for whom something has gone terribly wrong. The one thing most people do know about being disabled is that they don't want to be that."[29]

Such attitudes are reflective of what disability scholar Tobin Siebers calls the "ideology of ability" that pervades cultural perceptions of disability and is deeply embedded in economic, social, legislative, and educational institutions. According to this ideology, ability is the norm of humanity and disability is therefore a deviation from this norm. Ability and dis- ability are two self-evident, discrete, and opposing categories; people are either able-bodied or disabled. The ideology of ability assumes that being able-bodied is not only the natural, normal state but also the desirable one; being disabled is an unnatural, undesirable state that represents a loss of ability. According to this logic, then, all disabled people would choose to be able-bodied if they could. Finally, the ideology of ability understands dis- ability as an individual problem located in the body, one that should be treated medically or overcome through hard work, determination, and a positive attitude.[30]

This ideology of ability is at the heart of the medical model of disability that depoliticizes disability by framing it as an individual problem or disease that is best approached through curing, treating, normalizing, or eliminat- ing the "afflicted" individual. The medical model gained ascendency in the United States through a long and complex series of events that started in the nineteenth century. Amid the tremendous upheavals created by rapid and massive industrialization, urbanization, and immigration, the end of slav- ery, and women's growing demands for political equality by the later half of the century, there was an urgent need to impose order and control over the nation's institutions and populations so that the inevitable march toward human progress guided by Darwin's theory of evolution could continue unimpeded.[31] As historian Douglas Baynton explains, this need spurred the growth of the social sciences and the use of statistics to produce new under- standings of what constituted "average" human bodies and minds. Those who fell within and particularly above the average range were considered ideal and "normal," worthy participants in humanity's pull away from barbarism and upward movement toward perfection.[32] Those who fell below the average range were considered "abnormal" and defective, a drain on evolutionary progress who must be improved, fixed, or even eliminated.

Ideas of evolutionary progress and the human ideal provided new "scientific" justifications for the continued discrimination and unequal treatment of people with disabilities. But as Baynton points out, the concept of disability was also applied to other marginalized groups in order to justify discrimination against the members of these groups and to prevent them from obtaining political and social equality. For example, opponents of women's suffrage stressed that women were inferior to the male norm due to their physical weaknesses, emotionality, and irrationality.[33] Arguments that pointed to the innate mental and physical inferiority of people of African descent were used to justify slavery and, later, the continued denial of rights under the Jim Crow system.[34] Disability was also used to defend increasingly restrictive U.S. immigration policies that denied entry to "lunatics," "idiots," and people with a wide range of mental and physical disabilities, as well as immigrants from Asia and Southern and Eastern Europe who might "disable" the "native" population through racial pollution.[35] The new human ideal, then, emerged from the "imperative of the norm," as disability scholar Lennard Davis writes. It was bolstered "by the notion of progress, human perfectibility, and the elimination of deviance," and culminated as "a dominating, hegemonic vision of what the human body should be."[36]

Throughout history, the consequences of the medical model of disability have been tragic; disabled people have been subjected to dangerous medical interventions, institutionalization, murder, immigration restriction, and segregation. Disabled women have been particularly vulnerable to forced sterilization. By the early twentieth century in the United States, approximately thirty states legally sanctioned the forced or coerced sterilization of individuals with disabilities as part of their efforts to improve society's genetics and to avoid the burden of supporting the offspring of individuals with disabilities. Under these state laws, more than 60,000 individuals with disabilities were involuntarily sterilized.[37] In 1927, the U.S. Supreme Court upheld the constitutionality of state sterilization laws in the notorious *Buck v. Bell* decision. At issue was whether the state of Virginia was constitutionally permitted to sterilize Carrie Buck, a young woman then institutionalized in the Virginia State Colony for Epileptics and the Feebleminded, though she was neither epileptic nor mentally disabled. Rather, she was the offspring of a woman who had previously been confined to the Virginia Colony and the destitute mother of a child born out of wedlock. Officials at the Virginia Colony asserted that Carrie and her mother shared the hereditary traits of feeblemindedness and sexual promiscuity and that Carrie had likely passed these traits on to her own illegitimate daughter. Writing the majority opinion, Justice Oliver Wendell Holmes declared: "It is better for all the world, if instead of waiting to execute degenerate offspring for crime, or to let them starve for their imbecility, society can prevent those who are manifestly unfit from continuing their kind . . . Three generations of imbeciles are enough."[38]

Involuntary eugenic sterilization that targeted women with disabilities, particularly Black, Latinx, and Native American women, continued in the United States until the 1970s.[39] Fannie Lou Hamer, for example, was a prominent civil rights activist who helped to organize Student Nonviolent Coordinating Committee (SNCC) voter registration drives and cofounded the Mississippi Freedom Democratic Party. Hamer was a polio survivor and lived with physical disabilities resulting from injuries sustained when she was savagely beaten by police in a Mississippi jailhouse for her participation in a lunch counter sit-in.[40] During an operation to remove a small uterine tumor in 1961, Hamer was sterilized without her knowledge or consent when the surgeon performed an unnecessary hysterectomy,[41] a practice so commonly forced on poor Black and/or disabled women as a form of racialized population control that it was known as a "Mississippi Appendectomy."[42] In 1973, the case of two young Black girls in Alabama helped to publicize the issue of sterilization abuse. Sisters Minnie Lee and Mary Alice Relf, ages fourteen and twelve, were declared mentally incompetent and sterilized by a Montgomery doctor after their mother, who was illiterate, consented to what she was told was merely the administration of long-term birth control. The Relfs joined a class action lawsuit in federal court, which uncovered hundreds of thousands of similar cases in the region. The overwhelming majority of the women sterilized were Black and were either declared mentally incompetent or threatened with the loss of government benefits for failure to comply.[43]

These practices are not relics of a less enlightened age but continue in various forms to this day. In 2004, for example, a seven-year-old girl named Ashley, described as having "static encephalopathy of unknown etiology," was subjected to a growth attenuation treatment involving a hysterectomy, a bilateral mastectomy, and the administration of estrogen. Designed to keep Ashley permanently small and childlike, the treatment would enable Ashley's parents to continue to lift and to move her easily—thus permitting her continued participation in family and recreational activities—and would allow them to care for her at home instead of being forced to commit her to an institution after she transformed into adulthood.[44] When Ashley's story—ultimately known as the "Ashley X case"—became public in 2006, many people with disabilities and advocates in the disability rights movement expressed shock and outrage at what they described as a gross violation of human rights through the performance of a nonconsensual, unalterable, and medically unnecessary sterilization of a developmentally disabled individual.[45] As philosopher Eva Feder Kittay has written, the Ashley X case is part of the "long, cruel, and gruesome history" of the medical abuse of people with severe cognitive disabilities, which is usually justified on the mistaken assumption "that these people don't know the difference" or do not understand that they are being mistreated.[46] And, as Kittay suggests, the Ashley X case fits squarely within a depoliticized, medical model of disability that attempts to alter the disabled person rather than the sociopolitical landscape.[47] That Ashley's parents felt that they had no choice but to resort to such a drastic medical "solution" to Ashley's disability is a deeply disturbing commentary on the inability of many disabled people and their caregivers to access resources and services—such as social security payments, in-home aides, and respite care—that would mitigate many of the consequences of a disabling environment and allow family members to care for disabled loved ones in their own homes.

The medical model of disability has led not only to the performance of drastic and irreversible surgical procedures on the bodies and minds of disabled individuals but also to the implementation of therapies intended to "normalize" those with cognitive, developmental, and intellectual disabilities. In the name of "curing" autism, for example, some parents seek out "alternative" therapies on the Internet, where they find dozens of websites and Facebook groups hawking breakthrough products and miracle cures and unproven, anecdotal claims about treatments that improve or even eliminate autism. Usually expensive, frequently hazardous, and sometimes deadly, these treatments often link mercury exposure to the development of autism— even though there is no scientific evidence for such a link[48]—and thus try to remove mercury and other toxins from the body using a variety of dangerous and unsupported methods. Chelation therapy, which involves giving children chelating agents such as dimercaptosuccinic acid (DMSA) to remove mercury and other heavy metals from the body, can cause kidney damage and heart failure.[49] The painful, daily injection of multiple high doses of Lupron, a drug sometimes used to chemically castrate sex offenders, to shut down the production of testosterone—erroneously believed to make the removal of mercury from the body more difficult—interferes with natural puberty and potentially weakens children's hearts and bones.[50] In addition to detoxification treatments, some parents resort to other risky, fringe therapies whose peddlers claim can improve cognitive and social functioning. Hyperbaric oxygen therapy, which involves breathing oxygen in a pressurized chamber, can damage the eardrum and sinuses, trigger seizures, and cause oxygen toxicity.[51] The administration of "miracle mineral solution," a mixture containing hydrochloric acid and chlorine bleach, causes nausea, vomiting, and sometimes kidney failure.[52] Other popular but unproven therapies include vitamin supplements, topical ointments, antifungal agent therapy, secretin injections, clay baths, restrictive diets, brain scans, transcranial magnetic stimulation, and stem-cell therapy.[53]

While these sorts of unscientific and unproven approaches to treating autism exist outside of mainstream medicine, other approaches that treat autism as a disorder requiring therapeutic interventions have developed from within it. Aversion therapy—a form of behavior therapy in which an aversive (causing a strong feeling of dislike or disgust) stimulus is paired with an undesirable behavior in order to reduce or eliminate that behavior—was developed as a treatment for autism and neurological disabilities by psychologists like Matthew Israel. In 1971, Israel established the Behavior Research Institute, later renamed the Judge Rotenberg Center (JRC), as a school for autistic people and individuals with intellectual disabilities.[54] Influenced by the behaviorist ideas of B.F. Skinner, Israel devised an aversive "treatment" approach for the school's residents that included spraying them in the face with water; pinching or spanking them; and forcing them to smell ammonia, eat hot peppers, or wear static-emitting white noise helmets.[55] To reduce physical struggles between staff and students and to make the administration of aversives more consistent, Israel began to use electrical shocks—administered remotely through a graduated electronic decelerator (GED)—as the preferred aversive technique at the JRC by the late 1980s. Students who exhibited particularly challenging or self-injurious behaviors might receive thousands of shocks per day.[56] Writing of her horrific experiences during her time at the JRC, one autistic survivor (who wrote anonymously in a 2013 letter to then-president of TASH, Nancy Weiss) explained that she was physically injured and emotionally scarred through multiple applications of the GED. Most of the time, she was shocked for tics or other involuntary movements or for coping behaviors like covering her ears when noises became unbearable.[57] Falling into a deep depression after several weeks in the program, she contemplated suicide nearly every night as she lay in bed with her body strapped to two metal electrodes across her chest—even during sleep, residents were not spared the potential for GED shocks. Nor were they spared from witnessing the trauma of their fellow residents:

> We were always having to watch others getting shocked in the room. Hearing others scream, cry, beg to not be shocked. Students would scream "I'm sorry, No, Please!!" all day. I, like other students, would cringe and feel sick and helpless while watching others getting shocked. I was so anxious about getting shocked that I would many times bang my head just to get it over with. The GED often was the cause of my behavior problems. The students that get shocked the most at JRC are non-verbal. So they cannot speak up.[58]

In addition to being physically and emotionally scarring, JRC aversive techniques were sometimes deadly. In 1985, Vincent Milletich, an autistic young man in his early twenties, suffered a seizure and died after he was put in

restraints and forced to wear a white-noise helmet. Five years later, staff punished nineteen-year-old Linda Cornelison for her refusal to eat by spanking
her with a spatula, pinching and squeezing her fingers and muscles, and forcing her to inhale ammonia. It turned out that Linda had a perforated stomach,
and she died a few hours later during emergency surgery.[59]

In 2011, the human rights organization Disability Rights International
(DRI) filed a report with the United Nations that argued that the JRC's inflic-
tion of pain on its residents through electric shock, restraints, and social
isolation constituted a form of torture specifically prohibited by the UN
Convention. "The fact that these individuals have disabilities," the report
read, "that they are placed in institutions by parents who have consented to
treatment on their behalf, and that they are in a position of complete power-
lessness at the hands of state authorities are all factors that bring this form
of mistreatment to the level of torture."[60] But despite the wealth of evidence
presented in the DRI Report, the eventual condemnation of JRC practices by
the UN Special Rapporteurs on Torture, and the dozens of abuse allegations
from survivors filed with the Massachusetts Disabled Persons Protection
Commission, the Judge Rotenberg Center remains open to this day.[61]

In the decade before the founding of the JRC, Ole Ivar Lovaas, a psychology professor at UCLA, had pioneered the use of slaps and electric jolts to
modify the behavior of autistic kids. Lovaas eventually abandoned these
methods as ineffective, noting in a 1993 interview, "These people are so
used to pain that they can adapt to almost any kind of aversive you give
them."[62] Instead, he turned to applied behavior analysis (ABA), a therapy he
developed based on B.F. Skinner's principles of behavior and Lovaas's own
work with "gender-deviant" boys considered at risk for homosexuality in his
federally funded Feminine Boy Project. Lovaas used a range of rewards and
punishments to produce desired behaviors in the boys. When they displayed
effeminate traits, such as showing an interest in dolls, they were subjected
to physical punishment and emotional abuse; when they displayed behaviors
considered appropriately masculine, they were given toys or rewarded with
attention and affection from their mothers.[63] In a now infamous 1974 study,
Lovaas, along with his former student George Rekers, hailed the success
of the Feminine Boy Project by writing about a four-year-old boy named
"Kraig," a gentle child with effeminate mannerisms and speech patterns
who liked to wear girls' clothing and play with dolls. When Kraig displayed
undesirable feminine behaviors, his father spanked him and his mother
ignored him—even when he sobbed and grew hysterical by her inattention.
When Kraig displayed appropriately masculine behaviors, he was rewarded
with toys, praise, and affection. Following the ten-month treatment program,
Lovaas declared that Kraig had been "cured."[64] In 2003 at the age of thirty-
eight, "Kraig," whose real name was Kirk Murphy, committed suicide, a

tragedy that his older brother Mark attributes to the long-lasting trauma that Kirk experienced as a result of Lovaas and Rekers's treatment plan.[65]

Thus, out of a therapy created to "train out the queer" in young children—the forerunner of today's destructive reparative therapy—Lovaas developed ABA, the goal of which was to make children with autism as neurotypical as possible.[66] This was accomplished by forcing them to participate in intensive behavioral training programs—usually up to forty hours a week—based on positive reinforcements and a range of aversive techniques (including with-holding meals, slapping, and use of a shock stick) to reduce undesirable behaviors, such as stimming, rocking, and lack of eye contact.[67] In a 1969 article published in the *Journal of American Psychotherapy*, Lovaas and his team described their use of ABA with autistic children in the Young Autism Project at UCLA as an overwhelming success.[68] Lovaas claimed that his methods resulted in dramatic improvements in the functioning and social skills of autistic children and that ABA therapy, especially if implemented early and exhaustively, would allow autistic individuals to refrain from self-harm, participate in their communities, and avoid institutionalization. As its popularity spread, ABA became the leading "treatment" for autism and other developmental disabilities and widely demanded by parents, who believed that ABA would keep their children out of an institution and give them the best hope for a "normal" life.[69]

Today, ABA remains the most widely used and recognized behavioral therapy for autistic children and adults, but not without considerable contro-versy.[70] Some behavior analysts, such as Andrea Ridgway, argue that current ABA therapists reject Lovaas's harsh methods and instead use reinforcement-based interventions rather than aversive procedures to increase socially appropriate replacement behaviors. "Over the years, ABA has become more of a touchstone—an approach . . . that is applied more flexibly," Ridgway writes. "It's a broad umbrella that covers many different styles of therapy."[71] Some experts, however, question the long-term effectiveness of ABA; children might display desired behaviors when offered food or other treats but might not be able to exhibit these behaviors outside of a clinical setting in real-world situations.[72] And many parents and autistic people charge that while ABA may no longer include Lovaas's harshest methods, the repetitive drills and the forty-hours a week regimen still constitute a form of cruel and abusive treatment.[73] Maxfield Sparrow, a transmasculine autistic author who blogs under the name "Unstrange Mind," describes the ten years of ABA therapy they endured as painful and damaging: "I can tell you that being pushed repeatedly to the point of tears with zero sense of personal power and knowing that the only way to get the repeated torment to end was to comply with everything that was asked of me, no matter how painful . . . was trau-matizing to such a degree that I still carry emotional scars decades later."[74]

Especially condemnatory for many is the attempt of ABA to curb behaviors that seem socially inappropriate but serve an important emotional or sensory function for autistic individuals, whose bodies and minds often move, think, and communicate in ways that differ from neurotypical individuals.[75] For many autistic people, stimming and other repetitive behaviors—such as flapping, walking on tip-toes, using echolalia, or rocking—are a natural expression of certain feelings or a way of adapting to and regulating overwhelming sensory input (lights, sounds, smells, among others) in the environment. Hence, preventing an autistic person from engaging in self-regulatory behaviors potentially causes emotional damage and even physical pain.[76] Ari Ne'eman, cofounder and former president of the Autistic Self Advocacy Network (ASAN), argues that "the emphasis on things like eye contact or sitting still or not stimming is oriented around trying to create the trappings of the typical child without acknowledging the reality that different children have different needs. It can be actively harmful when we teach people from a very early age that the way they act, the way they move is fundamentally wrong."[77]

Ne'eman's observation strikes at the heart of why some autistic people object to ABA therapy. Unchanged since Lovaas's day, the primary goal of ABA, they argue, is to make autistic people less autistic and "indistinguishable from their peers." Sparrow, for example, argues that the most damaging aspect of ABA therapy is that it teaches children that who they are is "fundamentally wrong and unacceptable," which leads to self-hatred and potentially destructive behaviors. They learn that love, praise, and even basic needs are not unconditional but earned by stifling their own desires and impulses and concealing "any trace of autism from others."[78] While Sparrow understands that parents who pursue ABA therapy desire only the best for their children and want to see them fully included in their social and educational environments, they caution that the "exhaustion and trauma" of ABA is not the route through which to pursue these aims. John Elder Robison, who was diagnosed with Asperger syndrome at the age of forty, agrees. ABA could be a useful therapy, he notes, as long as it does not attempt to eradicate the autism but focuses instead on teaching a child important self-care, communication, and social skills, such as making friends. "'That is life-changing in a good way,' he says."[79] ABA, then, is "effective" in the sense that it makes autistic people look and act less autistic. But, as a former ABA therapist has noted, "if we're measuring whether ABA helps Autistic people feel safe, accommodated, and accepted in a largely neurotypical world, then it's very ineffective, according to the overwhelming evidence from the Autistic community."[80]

ABA's goal to modify or to "normalize" autistic people in order to make them fit within society's expectations for human behavior is consistent with the goal of the largest and best-known autism "advocacy" group in the United

States, Autism Speaks. With its ubiquitous publicity campaigns and glittery array of celebrity backers, Autism Speaks spends the vast majority of its $60 million annual budget on researching causation and prevention of autism and less than 4 percent on family service grants aimed at improving the quality of life of autistic people.[81] Autism Speaks draws the base of its support from families of young children with autism but has earned the criticism of autistic adults, many of whom claim that Autism Speaks "does not speak for them" because the organization does not include autistic people in its governance and because its priorities do not accord (and sometimes directly conflict) with the interests of the very population it claims to represent.[82]

For example, Autism Speaks has perpetuated the widespread but mistaken presumption that people with autism are broken and defective, that their lives are miserable and unhappy, and that autism is a disease that needs to be cured. In 2007, Autism Speaks produced a film that premiered at the Sundance Film Festival. Titled *Autism Every Day*, the film consists of a series of clips of mothers discussing in front of their autistic children the pitifulness of their children's lives and the misery and heartbreak of their caregiving roles. In one of the film's more infamous moments, then executive vice-president of Autism Speaks, Alison Singer, admits that she had contemplated killing her autistic daughter and herself by driving off of the George Washington Bridge but ultimately decided against it because of her other, neurotypical daughter. Horrifically, she makes this admission within earshot of her autistic daughter, who is seen playing in the background.[83] In 2009, Autism Speaks created a video written by Grammy-nominated songwriter Billy Mann and directed by Academy Award-winning director Alfonso Cuarón. Titled *I Am Autism*, the video depicts a series of images of autistic children accompanied by an ominous voice-over that compares autism to debilitating and deadly diseases, such as AIDS, cancer, and diabetes, and that warns of autism's destructive impact: "I am Autism . . . I will fight to take away your hope. I will plot to rob you of your children and your dreams. I will make sure that every day you wake up you will cry, wondering who will take care of my child after I die?"[84] The films *Autism Every Day* and *I Am Autism* earned swift condemnation from disability advocacy groups, including the Autistic Self Advocacy Network, American Disabled for Attendant Programs Today (ADAPT), and the American Association of People with Disabilities, who charged that they propagated fear, stigma, and misinformation about autistic people.[85] Ari Ne'eman, for example, argued that "'portraying autistic people as less than human'" has serious material consequences. "'This [portrayal] is really damaging if you're trying to get your child included in school or if you're an autistic person trying to find a job or get included in society more broadly.'"[86] John Elder Robison served for a time as a member of Autism Speaks' Science and Treatment boards but ultimately resigned his position because he could not seem to convince organization leaders that their methods and rhetoric were emotionally and materially damaging to autistic people. "We do not like hearing that we are defective or diseased," he wrote in an open letter explaining his resignation. "We are not problems for our parents or society, or genes to be eliminated. We are people."[87]

THE SOCIAL MODEL OF DISABILITY

Most disabled activists and scholars reject the medical model of disability in favor of a social model. In the social model, disability is not an individual problem but a human variation that needs to be accommodated through improvements in social, ideological, and economic structures and through the elimination of attitudinal and institutional barriers that interfere with the opportunity of all individuals to participate fully in society.[88] Adherents to the social model argue that impairments are located not entirely or even primarily in any condition of their bodies or minds but in built environments, attitudes, and policies that exclude and stigmatize them and that fail to include the vast array of human particularities.[89] As Susan Wendell points out, "much of the world is . . . structured as though everyone is physically strong, as though all bodies are 'ideally shaped,' as though everyone can walk, hear and see well, as though everyone can work and play at a pace that is not compatible with any kind of illness or pain, as though no one is ever dizzy or incontinent or simply needs to sit or lie down."[90] Disability occurs, then, when a body enters a space that was not meant for it, a space constructed on a very narrow perception of how a body should function within it. Disability occurs when people whose bodies and minds do not fit expected norms are forced to uncomfortably inhabit such spaces or be excluded from full participation in public life by remaining outside of them. And disability occurs when we assume that navigation of such spaces is an individual instead of a public responsibility. Exasperated with the pervasive public assumption that disability is a limitation to be overcome simply through a sunny disposition, the late activist and comedian Stella Young remarked:

> And that quote, *The only disability in life is a bad attitude*, . . . it's just not true . . . . You know, no amount of smiling at a flight of stairs has ever made it turn into a ramp. Never. Smiling at a television screen isn't going to make closed captions appear for people who are deaf. No amount of standing in the middle of a bookshop and radiating a positive attitude is going to turn all those books into Braille. It's just not going to happen.[91]

According to the social model, then, the "problem" of disability is best solved not through medical intervention, normalization, or individual effort but through social and political changes.[92]

Because the medical model of disability, with its emphasis on disability as tragic and burdensome, has been so stigmatizing and oppressive, many disability activists and scholars who adhere to the social model are understandably wary of cure narratives and other medical approaches to disability. Certainly, there is nothing wrong with wanting to end pain, fix injuries, or eliminate deadly and debilitating diseases such as smallpox, polio, and tuberculosis, notes disability scholar Michael Bérubé. But when people start promoting the eradication of all disabilities "as a general, unqualified species good," he writes, "some of us get kinda antsy."[93] Adherents to the social model of disability do not deny that disabilities sometimes create difficulties and challenges; rather, they understand that disability "is as much a social as a medical phenomenon," as Ne'eman puts it, "and that the 'cure' approach is not the best way forward for securing people's quality of life."[94]

Still, the social model's deemphasis on the disabling effects of the body has sometimes produced a marginalizing effect for those who experience chronic fatigue, illness, and pain, for example, and who recognize that changes in social and physical structures will do little to target their particular disabilities. It has also led in some cases to criticism of disabled people who have sought medical treatment or cure for their disabilities. Perhaps no other disabled person has divided the disability community like Christopher Reeve, an actor who was paralyzed when he was thrown from his horse during an equestrian competition in 1995. From the time he was injured until he died nine years later, Reeve fought tirelessly to publicize and raise funds for research, treatments, and a cure for spinal cord injuries.[95] While he was widely admired by members of the public and many members of the disability community, some disabled activists criticized his emphasis on finding a cure instead of eliminating disabling environmental barriers.[96] Reeve should have used his high public profile and substantial financial resources, some claimed, to advocate for measures that would improve the lives of disabled people instead of raising false hopes in his campaign for an elusive cure, a campaign that they charged perpetuated damaging stereotypes about life with a disability.[97] Aware of these criticisms, Reeve responded on one occasion: "I feel I have the right to put my energies where I want them, as does any other individual with a disability. In my condition I would prefer to walk rather than not walk. That's where I am coming from and if there are other people to whom that is not as important than that's their choice and so be it."[98] Some members of the disability community sympathized with Reeve's position. In a piece written shortly after Reeve's death, disability scholar Tom Shakespeare defended Reeve's approach to disability by noting that "a total rejection of the concept of cure seems self-defeating" and that it is possible to support medical research that has the potential to ease pain and enhance function while also advocating for civil rights and removal of barriers. Working to prevent or minimize impairments that are painful or limiting, he pointed out, is not the equivalent of attacking disability identity or undermining the value and contribution of disabled people. For those who live with such impairments, he argued, the finding of a cure is often as important as the achievement of civil rights.[99] Disability scholar Alison Kafer agrees that it is possible both to seek a cure for one's disability and to champion disability rights, and that the social model of disability needs to "make room" for those who mourn and/or seek medical intervention for a change in form or function. She cautions, however, that such interventions always need to be understood within the larger context of hegemonic cultural practices and ideologies that value some bodies and minds and devalue others.[100]

While the social model continues to serve as a core principle of disability studies and activism, leading disability theorists have developed more sophisticated approaches that complicate the relationship between the body and environment. Tobin Siebers, for example, offers an interesting approach to the dilemma posed by the need to both reject a medical model that rests entirely on embodiment and a social model that sometimes ignores or minimizes corporeality. According to his theory of "complex embodiment," disability is the result of disabling environments but can also be the result of bodily conditions, such as chronic pain, disease, and aging. Embodied forms of disability and socially produced disabilities are mutually inexclusive and reinforcing, he notes, and exist within the broad spectrum of human variability. Likewise, Kafer recognizes disability as both a condition of the body and an effect of inaccessible environments. Yet, in her political-relational model of disability, she argues that making a sharp distinction between embodiment and environment prevents us from recognizing that both are culturally produced, that neither can exist without the social context that gives them meaning. "What we understand as impairing conditions—socially, physically, mentally, or otherwise—shifts across time and place," she notes, "and presenting impairment as purely physical obscures the effects of such shifts."[101]

DISABILITY IDENTITY POLITICS

Disability is more than the product of a complex relationship between the body and its environment. It is a social location, a situated knowledge, from which hegemonic and oppressive claims about disability can be questioned, critiqued, and overturned. This sort of epistemological privilege derived from the social location of disability has led disabled people to understand themselves as part of a minority group; to recognize that their mistreatment is political, systemic, and collective; to articulate a vision of disability that is fundamentally different from that of the dominant group; and to pursue meaningful change through group protest and cooperative action.[102] This collective understanding is the crucial precondition for disability identity politics.

Disability identity politics emerge when oppressed social locations create identities, perspectives, histories, and experiences among disabled people that are different from, challenge, expose, and offer valuable knowledge about ideas of disability perpetuated by dominant groups. Disabled people's common experiences with ableism have been especially crucial to shaping disability identity politics. Ableism is defined as the institutional, symbolic, legal, and attitudinal discrimination, marginalization, and oppression of people with disabilities and the unquestioned and often unconscious presumption that "able-bodiedness" is superior and infinitely preferable to being disabled. Similar to maleness, whiteness, and heterosexuality, able-bodiedness is an invisible and unquestioned norm that becomes remarkable only when juxtaposed with its presumed opposite—disability. To be able-bodied is to enjoy certain privileges, almost all of which are invisible and unacknowledged, but nonetheless very real in conferring a higher social status. Abled privilege means that you can move about the world reasonably confident that your body and mind can and will be accommodated in public places; that your physical or mental state will not be a factor in your ability to obtain an education or adequate employment; that you can inhabit public spaces fairly anonymously without being subject to stares or looks of pity; that you can perform routine daily tasks without being told how inspirational or courageous you are; that you are able to watch a television show, see a movie, or read a book and find numerous diverse people of your ability represented.

Disability identity, then, originates from oppression, from the denial of privileges automatically conferred on nondisabled people, and is thus formed from and in reaction to able-bodied identity. Hence, for some, disability identity is undesirable because it seems to reify and even to celebrate the very identity created and perpetuated by dominant groups to maintain power over marginalized groups.[103] But for that very reason, writes Susan Wendell, disability identity "is also a politically useful and socially meaningful category to those who are in it."[104] A disability lens, she argues, renders visible unacknowledged ableist privileges, exposes as fallacies "cultural mythologies" about the body, and creates new, revolutionary knowledge about the meaning and value of bodies and minds.[105] "Disabled people share forms of social oppression," she writes, "and the most important measures to relieve that oppression have been initiated by disabled people themselves."[106]

But disability identity is formed not just from experiences with oppression and discrimination. It is an identity formed from a recognition that disability is a core part of one's self, a marker of pride, and a form of positive group identification. As Rosemarie Garland-Thomson notes, identifying as disabled "means moving from isolation to community, from ignorance to knowledge about who we are, from exclusion to access, and from shame to pride."[107] Disability identity is understanding disability as part of a happy, fulfilling life and as a natural and "normal" part of the human experience. Laura Hershey, who participated in annual protests organized by disability activists outside of the Muscular Dystrophy Association Telethon until her death in 2010, wrote: "I've encountered people who, never having tried it, think that living life with a disability is an endless hardship. For many of us, it's actually quite interesting, though not without its problems."[108] Similarly, Ari Ne'eman stresses that most people on the autism spectrum "do not wake up in the morning and wish that we had never been born. Insofar as we desire normalcy, it tends to be as a mechanism for achieving the things we cannot access in our lives due to lack of support, inaccessible environments—social and otherwise—and education and medical systems that are not responsive to our needs."[109]

This recognition of disability as just another type of human variation and a positive form of self-identification is at the core of the concept of neurodiversity. Promoted by self-advocacy groups like ASAN and other autism and disability rights organizations, neurodiversity is the idea that all neurological variations—including autism, learning disabilities, intellectual disabilities, and mental health disabilities—should be accommodated, valued, and even celebrated. As John Elder Robison asserts: "I celebrate the gifts autism brings us . . . Consequently, I support the idea of changing society to make it more accommodating for people who are different."[110] For many autists (autistic people), autism forms an essential part of their identity; to eliminate the autism, then, is to eliminate a fundamental and valued feature of who they are. "My autism is part of who I am," remarks musician Anya Ustaszewski, and "is not something 'extra' that can be taken away from me to suit the agenda of an intolerant society. My abilities, challenges and perception of the world all go hand in hand. If I were to be 'cured' of my autism, the person that I am would cease to exist."[111]

In addition to creating a new, positive self-consciousness, identity politics, writes Tobin Siebers, have been "the most practical course of action by which to address social injustices against minority peoples and to apply the new ideas, narratives, and experiences discovered by them to the future of progressive, democratic society."[112] Identity politics have formed the basis of disability rights movements that have challenged the dominant understandings of disability; led to the creation of laws that prohibit discrimination against disabled people; and expanded opportunities for disabled people to lead lives of self-determination. For example, the League of the Physically Handicapped, organized by disabled men and women during the

Great Depression, fought disability-based discrimination from work-relief agencies during the 1930s and "contested the ideology of disability that dominated early twentieth-century public policies, professional practices, and societal arrangements."[113] In 1948, psychiatric patients at Rockland State Hospital in New York founded the organization We Are Not Alone to help newly released patients transition from institutional life to integrated community living. Nine years later, actor Billy Barty founded Little People of America, an advocacy group that offers peer and parent support, medical resources and referrals, scholarships, and social programs that benefit the dwarfism community.[114] Ed Roberts and John Hessler formed the "Rolling Quads" group to protest the lack of housing options for disabled students like themselves at the University of California, Berkeley during the 1960s. Their efforts led to the Disabled Students Program at UCLA, which arranged living accommodations for students with disabilities, influenced university architecture and planning, and inspired the independent living movement.[115]

In 1975, a group of activists in Denver organized a demonstration modeled on the civil disobedience tactics of the Black Civil Rights Movement to protest the lack of wheelchair accessibility on the city's public buses. Calling themselves the "Gang of 19," they held up transportation by lying down in front of buses and chanting "We Will Ride!" until local transportation officials agreed to listen to their demands. Similar demonstrations broke out in other places across the country and led eventually to the formation of ADAPT, originally American Disabled for Accessible Public Transit (changed later to American Disabled for Attendant Programs Today).[116] For twenty-five days in the spring of 1977, disability activists occupied the Department of Health, Education, and Welfare (HEW) San Francisco office to advocate for enforcement of Section 504 of the Rehabilitation Act, which prohibited recipients of federal aid from discriminating against those with disabilities. Disability scholar Susan Schweitz notes that the sit-in's longevity and ultimately successful outcome sprang from the skills, dedication, and experiences of its participants—many of whom had learned the tactics of successful movement building through their work in the Black, Chicano, and queer civil rights movements and the women's movement—and the crucial matrix of support from community groups. Members of the Butterfly Brigade (who patrolled city streets to protect gay people from violence), Glide Church, labor unions, drug rehab programs, Mission Rebels (a Chicano youth-development group), and the Black Panther Party delivered food and offered political support and other crucial resources to the protesters. Schweitz argues that the support from the Black Panthers best demonstrates "the fluid and intricate dynamics of alliance" that comprised the core of the sit-in's power. The Black Panthers extended their support, she points out, because of Bradley Lomax, a disabled Panther and longtime disability rights/independent living movement leader, who was participating in the sit-in with his care attendant and fellow Panther, Chuck Jackson.[117] "Without the presence of Brad Lomax and Chuck Jackson," observed sit-in participant Corbett O'Toole, "the Black Panthers would not have fed the 504 participants occupying the HEW building. Without that food, the sit-in would have collapsed."[118] In 1988, students at Gallaudet University led the "Deaf President Now" protest that resulted in the appointment of the university's first Deaf president, I. King Jordan, since its founding in 1864.[119] Starting in the 1990s, individuals with muscular dystrophy began protesting the Jerry Lewis Labor Day Muscular Dystrophy Association Telethon and its promulgation of the pity model of disability,[120] while disability activists led by Diane Coleman founded the organization Not Dead Yet to fight against the legalization of physician- assisted suicide and the cultural misperception that disabled lives are "not worth living."[121]

In the first decade of the twenty-first century, a strong autism self-advocacy movement emerged to advance equality, access, and opportunities for autistic people and to change public perceptions of autism. Led by and for autistic people, groups such as Autism Network International and the Autistic Women & Nonbinary Network were created to empower autistic people to take control of their own lives and to become agents in the conversations and policies that affect their lives. In 2004, Gareth and Amy Nelson founded Aspies for Freedom (AfF) to promote autism pride and to challenge harmful and pathologizing practices and attitudes about autism promoted by popular media. Aspies for Freedom has been an important source of networking, support, and community for autistic people through its chatrooms, meet-ups, and events, such as the annual Autistic Pride Day (created by AfF in 2005) celebrated on June 18 each year by autistic groups and individuals around the world. Ari Ne'eman founded the Autistic Self Advocacy Network in 2006 when he was still in college and served as the organization's president for the next ten years. ASAN gained national attention when it initiated a grassroots campaign to protest a 2007 autism awareness campaign from the New York University Child Study Center that featured a series of "ransom notes" on billboards and kiosks and in widely circulated magazines. Addressed to parents of autistic children, the ransom notes contained messages like, "We have your son. We will make sure he will not be able to care for himself or interact socially as long as he lives," and "We have your son. We are destroying his ability for social interaction and driving him into a life of complete isolation. It's up to you now."[122] Outraged by the campaign's stigmatization and false characterization of people with autism as miserable outcasts incapable of living functioning, fulfilling lives, self-advocates from ASAN and the autism and disability rights communities launched a coordinated, grassroots effort that resulted in a shutdown of the campaign. With their slogan "Nothing

About Us Without Us," they "served notice to autism professionals," as Joseph Kras writes, "that autistics need to be consulted when there are issues that concern them."[123]

In what became the legislative pinnacle of the disability rights movement, disability activists finally secured passage of the Americans with Disabilities Act (ADA), a federal civil rights law that prohibits discrimination against individuals with disabilities in all areas of public life, including jobs, schools, transportation, and all public and private places that are open to the general public. When the ADA stalled in Congress due to opposition from public transit companies over strict regulations for accessibility, members of ADAPT and other disabled activists mounted a protest at the Capitol.[124] To highlight the enormous challenges of physical barriers faced by disabled people on a daily basis, the activists put aside their wheelchairs, walkers, and crutches, got down on their hands and knees, and slowly pulled themselves up the eighty-three steps of the Capitol's west entrance. The "Capitol Crawl," as this iconic moment in the disability rights movement has become known, captured national attention and prodded members of Congress to pass the ADA, the most comprehensive civil rights law in U.S. history.[125] Signing the ADA into law on July 26, 1990, President George H.W. Bush remarked, "Let the shameful wall of exclusion finally come tumbling down."[126]

The Americans with Disabilities Act has served as a crucial legal tool to fight pervasive discrimination against people with disabilities. In 1995 with the help of the Atlanta Legal Aid Society, two women with mental and developmental disabilities, Lois Curtis and Elaine Wilson, for example, brought suit against the state of Georgia in federal district court for a violation of the ADA. Following completion of Curtis and Wilson's medical treatment at the psychiatric unit of Georgia Regional Hospital, mental health professionals at the hospital admitted that the women no longer met the state's requirement for institutional confinement, but they refused to release them to live within community-based programs.[127] Attorneys representing Curtis and Wilson argued that individuals with a mental or physical disability could not be forced to remain in an institutional environment if they could be served in a more integrated, community-based setting. On June 22, 1999, the U.S. Supreme Court held in *Olmstead v. L.C.* that unjustified segregation of persons with disabilities constitutes discrimination in violation of Title II of the ADA.[128] A landmark decision, *Olmstead* created a legal precedent for people with disabilities and their families to demand a full range of community services as alternatives to services provided in institutional settings.[129] Today, Lois Curtis, an African American woman who spent most of her youth in mental health institutions, lives with a host family and serves as an advocate for people with developmental disabilities. In a 2014 interview, Curtis reflected on her role in the community integration movement, her hopes for developmentally disabled individuals, the pleasure of meeting President Barrack Obama—who recognized her for her role in the *Olmstead* decision at a White House reception—and the joys of daily living. When asked what her life is like today, Curtis answered:

> Well, I make grits, eggs, and sausage in the morning and sweep the floor. I go out to eat sometimes. I take art classes. I draw pretty pictures and make money. I go out of town and sell me artwork. I go to church and pray to the Lord. I raise my voice high! In the summer I go to the pool and put my feet in the water. Maybe I'll learn to swim someday. I been fishing. I seen a pig and a horse on a farm. I buy clothes and shoes. I have birthday parties. They a lot of fun. I'm not afraid of big dogs no more. I feel good about myself. My life a better life.[130]

Enforcement of the *Olmstead* decision has been uneven, however. According to Ira Burnim, Director for the Judge Bazelon Center for Mental Health Law in Washington, D.C., some cities have an excellent record on integration of people with disabilities into the community, but such efforts have not been consistent across the nation as a whole. "There are also people in terrible situations—at home with no support, or stuck in awful institutions for no other reason than governmental ineptitude or public meanness," he acknowledges. "What makes the difference is whether the leadership of the public systems are progressive and effective, and whether they really believe in community integration."[131]

Despite President Bush's ringing optimism, then, the ADA did not immediately nor completely result in a "tumbling" of the wall of exclusion. Thirty years after its passage, people with disabilities still face tremendous discrimination in education and employment and experience disproportionate rates of homelessness and poverty.[132] They also face discrimination within the criminal justice system. People with disabilities—especially those with cognitive, developmental, and mental health disabilities—are dramatically overrepresented in the nation's state and federal prisons.[133] And disabled people, particularly disabled people of color, comprise an astonishing one-third to one-half of all individuals killed by law enforcement.[134]

Due to significant loopholes in the Americans with Disabilities Act and lack of compliance and enforcement, people with disabilities still struggle to access community services and public spaces. Title III of the ADA requires that "the goods, services, privileges, or activities provided by places of public accommodation be equally accessible to people with disabilities" but provides few guidelines for compliance. Hence, the meaning of "equal access" has been subject to the interpretation of the courts and to the Department of Justice, especially when it comes to newer technologies that did not exist when the ADA was written. For example, while the Department of Justice in 2018 confirmed that Title III applies to the websites of public accommodations, it failed to issue website accessibility regulations and thus permitted businesses and organizations a great deal of flexibility in how to comply. Furthermore, the language of Title III makes significant exceptions for existing businesses (those constructed prior to the ADA's passage) for whom modifications to remove barriers to accessibility would be too difficult or costly. When building accommodations required by the ADA have been made, they often have been tacked on hastily and haphazardly, leading to spaces that are difficult or even impossible to navigate. Luticha Doucette, a wheelchair user, notes that "segregation and limiting the movement of disabled persons in public spaces is commonplace and accepted," even in the nation's capital:

> As a black woman I am keenly aware of the irony of being ushered through back ways, sketchy hallways, side entrances and kitchens to enter restaurants, bars and other establishments. My favorite bar up the street has its accessible entrance down an alley, with a steep ramp that leads to a door in the bowels of the building. There's no signage, no security cameras, and I once saw a bloody towel covering the fire alarm. At another local restaurant, I have to enter from a side door, through the kitchen and then to the dining room. It is a running joke with my friends that if the accessible entrance is not up front, you're going to end up needing a map to find your way through.[135]

Even with newer buildings and spaces, inclusive design that accommodates and considers all bodies and minds is rare. The new $41.5 million Hunters Point Library, which is part of the Queens, New York, public library system, was hailed as a design marvel when it opened in September 2019 but quickly met with widespread criticism for its many architectural barriers.[136] Designed to provide breathtaking views of the Manhattan skyline, the library's stacks ascend over five stories of landings and terraces, most of which are accessible only to people who can climb to them. When some people complained that many books in these sections (including the entire adult fiction collection) were out of reach to those unable to use stairs, library officials responded that library staff could simply retrieve items in these sections for disabled patrons. "'To me, that is the response of somebody who never had the experience of going somewhere and not being able to fully participate,' said Christine Yearwood, founder of the disability rights group, Up-Stand. 'Part of what universal design is about is allowing everyone to independently enjoy spaces. Having to ask someone else to help you is, at worst, demeaning, and at best, a limiting experience.'"[137]

Three decades after passage of the ADA, an estimated 30 percent of disabled people experience difficulties accessing transportation.[138] Because the ADA addresses only public transportation, few options exist for people with disabilities where no public transportation is available, and private companies such as Uber and Lyft have consistently denied that they are subject to ADA requirements.[139] Even public transit agencies often fail to comply with ADA regulations, such as the requirement to announce bus stops. Problems persist with the maintenance of accessibility equipment, such as elevators in subway stations, lifts on buses, and proper securing of mobility equipment like wheelchairs and scooters. Too often, drivers do not stop for people with disabilities.[140] Writing about her frustration with public transportation, Emily Rapp Black noted that the bus she rode for two years from Roxbury to Cambridge, Massachusetts experienced habitual problems with broken or malfunctioning wheelchair lifts, which took drivers and support staff thirty minutes or more to resolve while angry passengers glared out of their windows at the person in the wheelchair "shivering on the icy sidewalk" waiting to board. "So many times I heard people say, and not under their breath, 'damn cripples' or some variation."[141] When people with disabilities are kept out of public spaces due to lack of transportation, there is a substantial individual and community loss, notes the American Association of People with Disabilities. When people with disabilities cannot leave their homes, they cannot work, vote, shop, or participate in community life and are thus prevented "from making valuable contributions to our society as individuals, as workers, as consumers, and as taxpayers."[142]

The promise of the ADA has been hampered not only by loopholes, non-compliance, and uneven enforcement but also by a reporting system that places an unfair burden on people with disabilities. The ADA Education and Reform Act of 2017 stipulates that before civil actions can be brought against a public accommodation for failure to remove an architectural barrier, the "aggrieved person" must submit a written notice to the business identifying the barrier and specifying the conditions under which the accommodation was denied.[143] The business owner then has sixty days to respond with either a plan to remove the barrier or an acknowledgment that the removal will require "additional time as a result of circumstances beyond the control of the owner or operator."[144] Annie Segarra, who lives with Ehlers–Danlos syndrome, argues that disabled people should not bear the responsibility for reporting and following up on ADA violations. "'I'll ask repeatedly, for years, for accessibility to be implemented,' she notes, '[only] for these requests to go completely ignored. The onus should not be on disabled people and their allies [to enforce the ADA], it should be enforced through inspection.'"[145] With its reliance on individual enforcement, then, the ADA unfortunately treats violations as personal problems requiring individual solutions rather than systemic problems best solved through public responsibility.

While the ADA has had a significant impact on attitudes and understandings of disability, it has not managed to produce a revolution in the public consciousness. Many people today oppose disability-based discrimination and speak out against the mistreatment of disabled people, evidenced, for example, by the public outrage over Donald Trump's mocking of Serge Kovaleski, a reporter with arthrogryposis, during the 2016 presidential campaign. But the idea that disability is, at best, a misfortune and, at worst, a tragedy maintains a stubborn hold on the public perception. Stuck in a medical model of disability, few people outside of the disability community are able to conceive of disability as simply another human variation, let alone a positive good or an identity to be celebrated and embraced. Public reactions to the neurodiversity movement comprise an illuminating case in point. Following a 2008 *Good Morning America* segment on the autism rights movement, anchor Diane Sawyer "seemed utterly perplexed" by the concept of neurodiversity and suggested that it was "just a beautiful way of justifying heartbreak."[146] Emily and Ralph Savarese point out that some people are not just skeptical but infuriated by the very idea of neurodiversity, as evidenced by online websites and blogs dedicated to "exposing the lies of a collection of scoundrels who oppose curing autism."[147] Contributors to these sites—many of them parents of autistic children—make a distinction between "high-functioning" and "low-functioning" autism and contend that "neurodiversity is a luxury only those with milder forms of autism or Asperger syndrome can afford." They also tend to charge that proponents of neurodiversity refuse "to recognize autism as a disability," ignore "its sometimes debilitating challenges," and dismiss the difficulties and disruptions autism creates in the lives, relationships, and families of parents and caregivers.[148] These criticisms are deeply problematic for several reasons. First, neurodiversity proponents do not deny that autism is a disability that often brings significant challenges. Lydia X. Z. Brown, for example, defines autism as a developmental disability marked by forms of communication and sensory and information processing that differ "from a typical neurological profile." For some autists, these differences are experienced positively while for others, they can be fairly challenging, Brown notes.[149] Nor do neurodiversity proponents reject safe and respectful therapies and interventions that teach useful skills, work to ameliorate challenges, or help to alleviate troubling symptoms.[150] They recognize that for many autistic children and adults, physical therapy, speech therapy, occupational therapy, and augmentative and assistive communication technologies are helpful and should be widely available and affordable to anyone who needs them. But they oppose programs or treatments that attempt to eliminate, cure, or "normalize" autistic people.[151] Second, the high-functioning/low-functioning binary is an artificial, medical construction that assigns a rigidity and discreteness to categories that are in fact fraught with instability and uncertainty. How one functions is highly individualized, dependent on a myriad of environmental factors, and determined through comparisons to expected norms. What traits or abilities does one have to possess to be classified as high-functioning? What traits or abilities does one have to lack to be considered low-functioning? How are these traits and abilities a reflection of what we as a society privilege and what we undervalue? And who gets to make these judgments? As Melanie Yergeau notes: "We don't have a stable definition of what functioning is because of this normalized (not to mention unregulated) constructedness."[152] Fundamentally, as Yergeau observes, an autistic person's assignment to a "functioning level" is determined by the extent to which their abilities and behavior match those of neurotypicals and the social environment that is built for neurotypical needs and expectations.[153]

While the ADA has failed to create equal opportunity for disabled people, then, it remains a landmark piece of legislation in disability history. It created a framework for the personhood of disabled people. And by solidifying into law the principle that people with disabilities deserve the right to participate fully in every aspect of society, it has made disabled people more cognizant and demanding of this right. Disability activist John Smith notes that the ADA has made inaccessibility and disability discrimination more visible. The lack of wheelchair ramps in public places or inappropriate questions about disability during job interviews, for example, now "stick out like a sore thumb." The ADA gives a person the right "to say something or to step back again and say, 'You know what? I'm out of here.'"[154] And, as Smith indicates, the successful campaign for passage of the ADA demonstrated the effectiveness of identity politics and the power of a coalition of diversely disabled people coming together to fight for their rights.[155] Particularly for disabled people who were born after passage of the ADA—what Joseph Shapiro calls the "ADA generation"[156]—the Americans with Disabilities Act not only heightened expectations about equality and fair treatment in public life but contributed to a growing willingness to claim and to celebrate disability as a positive form of identity.

NOTES

1. As John Elder Robison describes, neurodiversity is "the idea that neurological differences like autism and ADHD are the result of normal, natural variation in the human genome. This represents a new and fundamentally different way of looking at conditions that were traditionally pathologized." See John Elder Robison, "What is Neurodiversity?" *Psychology Today*, October 7, 2013, https://www.psychologytoday.com/blog/my-life-aspergers/201310/what-is-neurodiversity.

2. Lydia X. Z. Brown, "The Significance of Semantics," *Autistic Hoya*, August 4, 2011, http://www.autistichoya.com/2011/08/significance-of-semantics-person-first.html?m=1.

3. Laurie Block, "Stereotypes about People with Disabilities," *Disability History Museum*, accessed July 31, 2019, https://www.disabilitymuseum.org/dhm/edu/essay.html?id=24.

4. "Definition of Disability," *Google*, accessed January 15, 2017, https://ww w.google.com/search?source=hp&ei=ORFCXc_GO6GzggeAu6G4BQ&q=definition +of+disability.

5. Mia Mingus, "Changing the Framework: Disability Justice," *Leaving Evidence*, February 12, 2011, https://leavingevidence.wordpress.com/2011/02/12/c hanging-the-framework-disability-justice/.

6. Simi Linton, *Claiming Disability: Knowledge and Identity* (New York: New York University Press, 1998), 10.

7. Centers for Disease Control and Prevention, "Disability Impacts All of Us," accessed July 31, 2019, https://www.cdc.gov/ncbddd/disabilityandhealth/infographic -disability-impacts-all.html.

8. Rosemarie Garland-Thomson, "Integrating Disability, Transforming Feminist Theory," *NWSA Journal* 14:3 (Autumn 2002): 5, http://www.jstor.org/stable/4316922.

9. Susan Wendell, "Toward a Feminist Theory of Disability," *Hypatia* 4:2 (Summer 1989): 107, https://doi.org/10.1111/j.1527-2001.1989.tb00576.x.

10. Paul K. Whelton, et al., "Guideline for the Prevention, Detection, Evaluation, and Management of High Blood Pressure in Adults," A Report of the American College of Cardiology/American Heart Association Task Force on Clinical Practice Guidelines, *Hypertension* 71:6 (November 13, 2017): 13–115, https://doi.org/10.1161 /HYP.0000000000000065.

11. Office of the Surgeon General (U.S.), Office of Disease Prevention and Health Promotion (U.S.), Centers for Disease Control and Prevention (U.S.), National Institutes of Health (U.S.), "The Surgeon General's Call To Action To Prevent and Decrease Overweight and Obesity," Office of the Surgeon General, 2001, accessed July 31, 2019, https://www.ncbi.nlm.nih.gov/books/NBK44210/.

12. Jack Drescher, "Out of DSM: Depathologizing Homosexuality," *Behavioral Sciences* 5:4 (December 2015): 565–575, https://doi.org/10.3390/bs5040565.

13. American Psychiatric Association, "DSM-5 Development, Neurodevelopmental Disorders, 2012," accessed June 3, 2017, http://www.dsm5.org/ meetus/pages/neurodevelopmental%20disorders.aspx.

14. James C. McPartland, et al, "Sensitivity and Specificity of Proposed DSM-5 Diagnostic Criteria for Autism Spectrum Disorder," *Journal of the American Academy of Child & Adolescent Psychiatry* 51:4 (April 2012): 382, https://doi.org /10.1016/j.jaac.2012.01.007. See also Bethan Chambers, et al., "'Sometimes Labels Need to Exist': Exploring How Young Adults with Asperger's Syndrome Perceive its Removal from the *Diagnostic and Statistical Manual of Mental Disorders* Fifth Edition," *Disability & Society* 35:4 (2020): 589–608, https://doi.org/10.1080/096875 99.2019.1649121.

15. Leo Kanner, "Autistic Disturbances of Affective Contact," *Nervous Child: Journal of Psychopathology, Psychotherapy, Mental Hygiene, and Guidance of the Child* 2 (1943): 217–250.

16. Steve Silberman, "The Invisibility of Black Autism," *UNDARK*, May 17, 2016, https://undark.org/article/invisibility-black-autism/.

17. Jon Baio, et al., "Prevalence of Autism Spectrum Disorder Among Children Aged 8 Years—Autism and Developmental Disabilities Monitoring Network, 11

Sites, United States, 2014," *MMWR Surveillance Summaries* 67 (April 27, 2018): 1–23, http://doi.org/10.15585/mmwr.ss6706a1.

18. Judith Gould and Jacqui Ashton-Smith, "Missed Diagnosis or Misdiagnosis: Girls and Women on the Autism Spectrum," *Good Autism Practice* 12:1 (2011): 34–41, https://doi.org/10.1177/1362361317706174; Tyler McFayden, et al., "Brief Report: Sex Differences in ASD Diagnosis—A Brief Report on Restricted Interests and Repetitive Behaviors," *Journal of Autism and Developmental Disorders* 49:4 (April 2019): 1693–1699, https://doi.org/10.1007/s10803-018-3838-9; Allison Ratto, et al., "What About the Girls? Sex-Based Differences in Autistic Traits and Adaptive Skills" *Journal of Autism and Developmental Disorders* 48:5 (2018): 1698–1711, https://doi.org/10.1007/s10803-017-3413-9.

19. Jason Travers, et al., "A Multiyear National Profile of Racial Disparity in Autism Identification," *Journal of Special Education* 47:1 (2013): 41–49, https://doi.org/10.1177/0022466911416247; David Mandell, et al., "Racial/Ethnic Disparities in the Identification of Children with Autism Spectrum Disorders," *American Journal of Public Health* 99:3 (2009): 493–498, https://doi.org/10.2105/AJPH.2007.131243; John Constantino and Tony Charman, "Gender Bias, Female Resilience, and the Sex Ratio in Autism," *Journal of the American Academy of Child and Adolescent Psychiatry* 51:8 (August 2012): 756–758, https://doi.org/10.1016/j.jaac.2012.05.017; Centers for Disease Control and Prevention, "Racial and Ethnic Differences in Children Identified with Autism Spectrum Disorder," *Community Report on Autism*, 2018, https://www.cdc.gov/ncbddd/autism/addm-community-report/documents/differences-in-children-addm-community-report-2018-h.pdf.

20. David Mandell, et al., "Race Differences in the Age at Diagnosis among Medicaid-Eligible Children with Autism," *Journal of the American Academy of Child and Adolescent Psychiatry* 41:12 (December 2002): 1447–1453, https://doi.org/10.1097/00004583-200212000-00016; Ruby M. Gourdine, et al., "Autism and the African American Community," *Social Work in Public Health* 26:4 (2011): 454–470, https://doi.org/10.1080/19371918.2011.579499.

21. Svenny Kopp and Christopher Gillberg, "The Autism Spectrum Screening Questionnaire (ASSQ)-Revised Extended Version (ASSQ-REV): An Instrument for Better Capturing the Autism Phenotype in Girls?" *Research in Developmental Disabilities* 32:6 (November-December, 2011): 2875–2888, https://doi.org/10.1016/j.ridd.2011.05.017; Simon Baron-Cohen, "The Extreme Male Brain Theory of Autism," *Trends in Cognitive Sciences* 6:6 (2002): 248–254, https://doi.org/10.1016/S1364-6613(02)01904-6.

22. See, for example, Maya Dusenbery, *Doing Harm: The Truth about How Bad Medicine and Lazy Science Leave Women Dismissed, Misdiagnosed, and Sick* (New York: HarperOne, 2018); and Harriet Washington, *Medical Apartheid: The Dark History of Medical Experimentation on Black Americans from Colonial Times to the Present* (New York: Harlem Moon, 2006).

23. Linton, *Claiming Disability*, 11.

24. Rachel Cohen-Rottenberg, "On Normalcy and Identity Politics," *Disability and Representation*, March 24, 2014, http://www.disabilityandrepresentation.com/?s=language.

25. Maria Eltagouri, "'The View's' Joy Behar calls Mike Pence to Apologize for Calling his Christian Faith a 'Mental Illness,'" *The Washington Post*, March 8, 2018, https://www.washingtonpost.com/news/acts-of-faith/wp/2018/03/08/joy-behar -called-mike-pences-faith-a-mental-illness-then-she-called-to-apologize/.

26. Rachel Cohen-Rottenberg, "Doing Social Justice: Thoughts on Ableist Language and Why It Matters," *Disability and Representation*, September 14, 2013, http://www.disabilityandrepresentation.com/2013/09/14/ableist-language/.

27. Emily Rapp Black, "Why is Our Existence as Humans Still Being Denied?" *The New York Times*, July 26, 2017, https://www.nytimes.com/2017/07/26/opinion/ why-is-our-existence-as-humans-still-being-denied.html.

28. Rosemarie Garland-Thomson, "Becoming Disabled," *The New York Times*, August 19, 2016, https://www.nytimes.com/2016/08/21/opinion/sunday/becoming-d isabled.html.

29. Garland-Thomson, "Becoming Disabled."

30. Tobin Siebers, *Disability Theory* (Ann Arbor: University of Michigan Press, 2008), 7–8.

31. Douglas Baynton, "Disability and the Justification of Inequality in American History," in *The New Disability History: American Perspectives*, eds. Paul K. Longmore and Lauri Umansky (New York: New York University Press, 2001), 33; 35–36.

32. Baynton, "Disability and the Justification of Inequality in American History," 36.

33. Sharon Lamp, "'It is For the Mother': Feminists' Rhetorics of Disability during the American Eugenics Period," *Disability Studies Quarterly* 26:4 (2006), https:// dsq-sds.org/article/view/807.

34. Scott Plous and Tyrone Williams, "Racial Stereotypes from the Days of American Slavery: A Continuing Legacy," *Journal of Applied Social Psychology* 25:9 (1995): 795–817, https://doi.org/10.1111/j.1559-1816.1995.tb01776.x.

35. Baynton, "Disability and the Justification of Inequality in American History," 45–46.

36. Lennard Davis, *Enforcing Normalcy: Disability, Deafness, and the Body* (London: Verso, 1995), 17.

37. Roberta Cepko, "Involuntary Sterilization of Mentally Disabled Women," *Berkeley Journal of Gender, Law, and Justice* 8:1 (September 1993): 121–165, https://doi.org/10.15779/Z38729X; Rebecca Kluchin, *Fit to be Tied: Sterilization and Reproductive Rights in America, 1950–1980* (New Brunswick, NJ: Rutgers University Press, 2009), 17.

38. *Buck v. Bell*, 274 U.S. 200 (1927).

39. See, for example, Alexandra Minna Stern, *Eugenic Nation: Faults and Frontiers of Better Breeding in Modern America* (Oakland: University of California Press, 2015).

40. Fannie Lou Hamer, "Testimony Before the Credentials Committee at the Democratic National Convention, Atlantic City, New Jersey, August 22, 1964," in *The Speeches of Fannie Lou Hamer: To Tell It Like It Is*, eds. Maegan Parker Brooks and Davis W. Houck (Jackson: University Press of Mississippi, 2011), 42–45.

41. Chana Kai Lee, *For Freedom's Sake: The Life of Fannie Lou Hamer* (Urbana: University of Illinois Press, 1999), 9, 11.

42. Dorothy Roberts, *Killing the Black Body: Race, Reproduction, and the Meaning of Liberty* (New York: Pantheon Books, 1999), 90.

43. Molly Ladd-Taylor, "Contraception or Eugenics? Sterilization and 'Mental Retardation' in the 1970s and 1980s," *CBMH/BCHM* 31:1 (2014): 192–193, https://doi.org/10.3138/cbmh.31.1.189. See also Molly Ladd-Taylor, *Fixing the Poor: Eugenic Sterilization and Child Welfare in the Twentieth Century* (Baltimore: Johns Hopkins University Press, 2017), 211–213.

44. Eva Feder Kittay, "Forever Small: The Strange Case of Ashley X," *Hypatia* 26:3 (Summer 2011): 610–612, https://doi.org/10.1111/j.1527-2001.2011.01205.x.

45. Dave Reynolds, "'Ashley Treatment Was Illegal,' Watchdog Group Says," *Inclusion Daily Express*, May 8, 2007, http://www.inclusiondaily.com/archives/07/05/09/050807waashleyx.htm; Sam Howe Verhovek, "Parents Defend Decision to Keep Disabled Girl Small," *Los Angeles Times*, January 3, 2007, https://www.latimes.com/archives/la-xpm-2007-jan-03-na-stunt3-story.html.

46. Kittay, "Forever Small," 623–625.

47. Kittay, "Forever Small," 626.

48. Luke E. Taylor, et al., "Vaccines Are Not Associated with Autism: An Evidence-Based Meta-Analysis of Case-Control and Cohort Studies," *Vaccine* 32:29 (June 17, 2014): 3623–3629, https://doi.org/10.1016/j.vaccine.2014.04.085; Anjali Jain, et al., "Autism Occurrence by MMR Vaccine Status among U.S. Children With Older Siblings With and Without Autism," *JAMA* 313:15 (2015): 1534–1540, https://doi.org/10.1001/jama.2015.3077.

49. Alisa Opar, "The Seekers: Why Parents Try Fringe Therapies for Autism," *Spectrum*, September 21, 2016, https://www.spectrumnews.org/features/deep-dive/the-seekers-parents-who-find-fringe-therapies-for-autism/; Autism Science Foundation, "Beware of Non-Evidence-Based Treatments," accessed May 4, 2019, https://autismsciencefoundation.org/what-is-autism/beware-of-non-evidence-based-treatments/.

50. Trine Souderos, "Miracle Drug Called Junk Science," *Chicago Tribune*, May 21, 2009, http://www.chicagotribune.com/lifestyles/health/chi-autism-lupron-may21-story.html.

51. Opar, "The Seekers."

52. Autism Science Foundation, "Beware of Non-Evidence-Based Treatments."

53. Autism Science Foundation, "Beware of Non-Evidence-Based Treatments."

54. Quentin Davies, "'Prisoners of the Apparatus': The Judge Rotenberg Center," *Autistic Self Advocacy Network*, August 9, 2014, https://autisticadvocacy.org/2014/08/prisoners-of-the-apparatus/.

55. Davies, "'Prisoners of the Apparatus.'"

56. Jennifer Gonnerman, "The School of Shock," *Mother Jones*, August 20, 2007, https://www.motherjones.com/politics/2007/08/school-shock/.

57. xxx, "Judge Rotenberg Center Survivor's Letter," *Autistic Hoya*, January 15, 2013, http://www.autistichoya.com/2013/01/judge-rotenberg-center-survivors-letter.html.

58. xxx, "Judge Rotenberg Center Survivor's Letter."

59. Davies, "'Prisoners of the Apparatus.'"

60. Laurie Ahern, "Torture Not Treatment: Electric Shock and Long-Term Restraint in the United States on Children and Adults with Disabilities at the Judge Rotenberg Center," *Disability Rights International*, 2010, 28, https://www.driadvoc acy.org/wp-content/uploads/USReport-accessible.doc.

61. American Disabled for Attendant Programs Today (ADAPT), "Judge Rotenberg Center: A History of Torture," accessed July 31, 2019, https://adapt.org /jrc/.

62. Gonnerman, "The School of Shock."

63. George Rekers and O. Ivar Lovaas, "Behavioral Treatment of Deviant Sex-Role Behaviors in a Male Child," *Journal of Applied Behavior Analysis* 7:2 (1974): 173–190, https://doi.org/10.1901/jaba.1974.7-173.

64. Rekers and Lovaas, "Behavioral Treatment," 187.

65. Scott Bronstein and Jessi Joseph, "Therapy to Change 'Feminine' Boy Created a Troubled Man, Family Says," *CNN*, June 10, 2011, http://www.cnn.com/2 011/US/06/07/sissy.boy.experiment/index.html.

66. Melanie Yergeau, *Authoring Autism: On Rhetoric and Neurological Queerness* (Durham: Duke University Press, 2018), 29.

67. O. Ivar Lovaas, et al., "Building Social Behavior in Autistic Children By Use of Electric Shock," *Journal of Experimental Research in Personality* 1 (1965): 99–109.

68. James Q. Simmons III and O. Ivar Lovaas, "Use of Pain and Punishment as Treatment Techniques with Childhood Schizophrenics," *American Journal of Psychotherapy* 23:1 (April 2018): 23–36, https://doi.org/10.1176/appi.psychotherapy .1969.23.1.23.

69. Elizabeth Devita-Raeburn, "The Controversy over Autism's Most Common Therapy," *Spectrum*, August 10, 2016, https://www.spectrumnews.org/features/deep -dive/controversy-autisms-common-therapy/.

70. Devita-Raeburn, "The Controversy over Autism's Most Common Therapy."

71. Andrea Ridgway, "A Response to 'The Controversy over Autism's Most Common Therapy,'" *Autism Spectrum Therapies*, August 29, 2016, http://autismth erapies.com/blog/a-response-to-the-controversy-over-autisms-most-common-the rapy/.

72. "Why I Left ABA," *Socially Anxious Advocate*, May 22, 2015, https://sociall yanxiousadvocate.wordpress.com.

73. A collection of writings about ABA from the perspective of autistic people can be found at Socially Anxious Advocate's post "Why I Left ABA."

74. Devita-Raeburn, "The Controversy over Autism's Most Common Therapy."

75. "Why I Left ABA."

76. "Why I Left ABA."

77. Devita-Raeburn, "The Controversy over Autism's Most Common Therapy."

78. Maxfield Sparrow, "ABA," *Unstrange Mind*, October 20, 2016, http:// unstrangemind.com/aba/.

79. Devita-Raeburn, "The Controversy over Autism's Most Common Therapy."

80. "Why I Left ABA."

81. Autistic Self Advocacy Network, "Before You Donate to Autism Speaks, Consider the Facts," accessed November 22, 2018, https://autisticadvocacy.org/wp-content/uploads/2017/04/AutismSpeaksFlyer_color_2017.pdf.

82. Eli Ramos, "Autism Speaks Doesn't Speak for Me," *Odyssey*, September 18, 2017, https://www.theodysseyonline.com/autism-speaks-doesnt-speak; Elsa Henry, "Autism Speaks Does Not Speak For Me," *Feminist Sonar*, November 13, 2013, http://feministsonar.com/2013/11/autism-speaks-does-not-speak-for-me/; Little Moon Whimsy, "Autism Speaks Doesn't Speak for Autistics," *Saplings of Hope*, November 12, 2013, http://saplingstories.blogspot.com/2013/11/autism-speaks-doesn-speak-for-autistics.html?m=0; Kirsten Schultz, "A Roundup of Posts Against Autism Speaks," *Medium*, March 29, 2017, https://medium.com/@KirstenSchultz/a-roundup-of-posts-against-autism-speaks-5dbf7f8cfcc6; Autistic Self Advocacy Network, "Statement on Autism Speaks Board Appointments," December 7, 2015, https://autisticadvocacy.org/2015/12/statement-on-autism-speaks-board-appointments/.

83. Autism Speaks, *Autism Every Day*, Milestone Video, 2006, https://www.youtube.com/watch?v=O0vCz2KWMM0.

84. Autistic Self Advocacy Network, "Horrific Autism Speaks 'I am Autism' Ad Transcript," September 23, 2009, https://autisticadvocacy.org/2009/09/horrific-autism-speaks-i-am-autism-ad-transcript/.

85. Michelle Diament, "Groups Outraged over Video Released By Autism Speaks," *Disability Scoop*, September 25, 2009, https://www.disabilityscoop.com/2009/09/25/autism-speaks-video/5541/.

86. Diament, "Groups Outraged over Video."

87. John Elder Robison, "I Resign My Roles at Autism Speaks," *Look Me in the Eye*, November 13, 2013, http://jerobison.blogspot.com/2013/11/i-resign-my-roles-at-autism-speaks.html.

88. Michael Oliver, *The Politics of Disablement: A Sociological Approach* (New York: St. Martin's, 1990).

89. Tom Shakespeare and Nicholas Watson, "Defending the Social Model," *Disability & Society* 12:2 (1997): 293–300, https://doi.org/10.1080/09687599727380; Laura Hershey, "From Poster Child to Protestor," *Independent Living Institute*, accessed August 1, 2019, https://www.independentliving.org/docs4/hershey93.html.

90. Wendell, "Toward a Feminist Theory of Disability," 111.

91. Stella Young, "I'm Not Your Inspiration, Thank You Very Much," filmed April 2014 at TEDxSydney, Sydney, Australia, video, 9:04, https://www.ted.com/talks/stella_young_i_m_not_your_inspiration_thank_you_very_much?language=en.

92. Ben Mattlin, "Cure Me? No, Thanks," *The New York Times*, March 22, 2017, https://www.nytimes.com/2017/03/22/opinion/cure-me-no-thanks.html; Alison Kafer, *Feminist, Queer, Crip* (Bloomington: Indiana University Press, 2013), 6.

93. Michael Bérubé, Blog, accessed June 13, 2019, http://www.michaelberube.com/index.php/weblog/comments/877/.

94. Ari Ne'eman, "The Future (and the Past) of Autism Advocacy, Or Why the ASA's Magazine, *The Advocate*, Wouldn't Publish This Piece," *Disability Studies Quarterly* 30:1 (2010), http://dsq-sds.org/article/view/1059/1244.

95. Jerome Groopman, "The Reeve Effect," *The New Yorker*, November 2, 2003, https://www.newyorker.com/magazine/2003/11/10/the-reeve-effect.

96. Elizabeth Scherman, "The Speech that Didn't Fly: Polysemic Readings of Christopher Reeve's Speech to the 1996 Democratic National Convention," *Disability Studies Quarterly* 29:2 (2009), http://dsq-sds.org/article/view/918/1093.

97. See, for example, multiple posts by William Peace at *Bad Cripple*, accessed August 1, 2019, http://badcripple.blogspot.com/search?q=christopher+reeve; Charles Krauthammer, "Restoration, Reality and Christopher Reeve," *Time*, February 14, 2000, http://content.time.com/time/magazine/article/0,9171,996064,00.html; S. E. Brown, "Super Duper? The (Unfortunate) Ascendancy of Christopher Reeve," *Independent Living Institute*, October 1996, http://independentliving.org/docs3/brown96c.html.

98. Chet Cooper, "The Road I Have Taken: Christopher Reeve and the Cure; An Interview with Christopher Reeve and Fred Fay," *ABILITY Magazine*, accessed August 1, 2019, https://www.abilitymagazine.com/reeve_interview.html.

99. Tom Shakespeare, "Christopher Reeve, "You'll Believe a Man Can Walk," *Ouch!*, October 29, 2004, http://www.bbc.co.uk/ouch/features/christopher-reeve-you -ll-believe-a-man-can-walk.shtml.

100. Kafer, *Feminist, Queer, Crip*, 6.

101. Kafer, *Feminist, Queer, Crip*, 7.

102. Siebers, *Disability Theory*, 70–95.

103. Anna Mollow, "Identity Politics and Disability Studies: A Critique of Recent Theory," *Michigan Quarterly Review* 43:2 (Spring 2004), http://hdl.handle.net/2027/spo.act2080.0043.218.

104. Wendell, "Toward a Feminist Theory of Disability," 108.

105. Wendell, "Toward a Feminist Theory of Disability," 119–120.

106. Wendell, "Toward a Feminist Theory of Disability," 108.

107. Garland-Thomson, "Becoming Disabled."

108. Hershey, "From Poster Child to Protestor."

109. Ne'eman, "The Future (and the Past) of Autism Advocacy."

110. Robison, "I Resign My Roles at Autism Speaks."

111. Anya Ustaszewski, "I Don't want to be 'Cured' of Autism, Thanks," *The Guardian*, January 14, 2009, https://www.theguardian.com/commentisfree/2009/jan /14/autism-health.

112. Siebers, *Disability Theory*, 70–95.

113. Paul K. Longmore and David Goldberger, "The League of the Physically Handicapped and the Great Depression: A Case Study in the New Disability History," *The Journal of American History* 87:3 (December 2000): 888, https://doi.org/10.2307 /2675276.

114. Little People of America, "What is LPA?" accessed August 1, 2019, https:// www.lpaonline.org/about-lpa_.

115. Joseph Shapiro, *No Pity: People with Disabilities Forging a New Civil Rights Movement* (New York: Three Rivers Press, 1993), 41–74.

116. Susan Schweik, "Lomax's Matrix: Disability, Solidarity, and the Black Power of 504," *Disability Studies Quarterly* 31:1 (2011), http://dsq-sds.org/article/view/1371/1539; see also ADAPT's organizational website at https://adapt.org.

117. Schweik, "Lomax's Matrix."

118. Schweik, "Lomax's Matrix."

119. Shapiro, *No Pity*, 74–104.

120. "Jerry's Orphans Protest the MDA Telethon," *The Kids are All Right*, accessed September 20, 2017, http://www.thekidsareallright.org/story.html.

121. Not Dead Yet, "Who We Are," accessed August 1, 2019, http://notdeadyet.org/about.

122. Joseph Kras, "The Ransom Notes Affair: When the Neurodiversity Movement Came of Age," *Disability Studies Quarterly* 30:1 (2010), http://dsq-sds.org/article/view/1065.

123. Kras, "The Ransom Notes Affair."

124. Shapiro, *No Pity*, 132–141.

125. Shapiro, *No Pity*, 133–141.

126. Shapiro, *No Pity*, 140.

127. Disability Justice, "Olmstead v. L.C.," accessed December 11, 2016, http://disabilityjustice.org/olmstead-v-lc/.

128. *Olmstead v. L.C.* 527 U.S. 581 (1999).

129. Disability Justice, "Olmstead v. L.C."

130. Lee Sanders, "Lois Curtis on Life after *Olmstead*," *Impact*, accessed June 1, 2018, https://ici.umn.edu/products/impact/281/13.html.

131. Robyn Rayne, "Unlocked: The Lois Curtis Story," November 27, 2010, https://assignmentatlanta.wordpress.com/2010/11/27/unlocked-the-lois-curtis-story/. See also Paul Milner and Berni Kelly, "Community Participation and Inclusion: People with Disabilities Defining Their Place," *Disability & Society* 24:1 (2009): 47–62, https://doi.org/10.1080/09687590802535410; and Glen White, et al., "Moving from Independence to Interdependence: A Conceptual Model for Better Understanding Community Participation of Centers for Independent Living Consumers," *Journal of Disability Policy Studies* 20:4 (2010): 233–240, https://doi.org/10.1177/1044207309350561.

132. Julia Rivera Drew, "Disability, Poverty, and Material Hardship Since the Passage of the ADA," *Disability Studies Quarterly* 35:3 (2015), https://dsq-sds.org/article/view/4947/4026.

133. Jennifer Bronson, et al., *Disabilities among Prison and Jail Inmates, 2011–2012* (Washington: Bureau of Justice Statistics, 2015), http://www.bjs.gov/content/pub/pdf/dpji1112.pdf.

134. David M. Perry and Lawrence Carter-Long, *The Ruderman White Paper on Media Coverage of Law Enforcement Use of Force and Disability: A Media Study (2013–2015) and Overview* (Newton, MA: Ruderman Family Foundation, 2016), http://www.rudermanfoundation.org/news-and-events/ruderman-white-paper.

135. Luticha Doucette, "If You're in a Wheelchair, Segregation Lives," *The New York Times*, May 17, 2017, https://www.nytimes.com/2017/05/17/opinion/if-youre-in-a-wheelchair-segregation-lives.html.

136. Sharon Otterman, "New Library Is a $41.5 Million Masterpiece. But About Those Stairs," *The New York Times*, November 5, 2019, https://www.nytimes.com/2 019/11/05/nyregion/long-island-city-library.html.

137. Otterman, "New Library Is a $41.5 Million Masterpiece."

138. The American Association of People with Disabilities and The Leadership Conference Education Fund, "Equity in Transportation for People with Disabilities," *The Leadership Conference on Civil and Human Rights*, accessed July 20, 2018, http://www.civilrightsdocs.info/pdf/transportation/final-transportation-equity-disabi lity.pdf.

139. Bryan Casey, "Uber's Dilemma: How the ADA May End the On Demand Economy," *UMass Law Review* 12:1 (2017), https://scholarship.law.umassd.edu/ umlr/vol12/iss1/3.

140. The American Association of People with Disabilities and The Leadership Conference Education Fund, "Equity in Transportation for People with Disabilities."

141. Black, "Why is Our Existence as Humans Still Being Denied?"

142. The American Association of People with Disabilities and The Leadership Conference Education Fund, "Equity in Transportation for People with Disabilities."

143. "H.R.620 — 115th Congress (2017–2018)," *Congress.gov*, accessed July 27, 2020, https://www.congress.gov/bill/115th-congress/house-bill/620/text.

144. "H.R.620 — 115th Congress."

145. Anna Hamilton, "30 Years after the ADA, It's Time to Imagine a More Accessible Future," *Bitch Media*, July 20, 2020, https://www.bitchmedia.org/article/ reimagining-americans-with-disabilities-act-anniversary.

146. Emily Thornton Savarese and Ralph Savarese, "The Superior Half of Speaking," *Disability Studies Quarterly* 30:1 (2010), http://dsq-sds.org/article/view /1062/1230.

147. See, for example, "Hating Autism" at http://hatingautism.blogspot.com/ and "Finding Cooper's Voice" at https://www.findingcoopersvoice.com/2017/02/11/con fessions-of-a-special-needs-parent/.

148. Savarese and Savarese, "The Superior Half of Speaking."

149. Lydia X. Z. Brown, "Disability is a Social Construct: A Sociological Perspective on Autism and Disability," *Autistic Hoya*, November 1, 2011, http://www .autistichoya.com/2011/11/disability-is-social-construct.html.

150. Robison, "I Resign My Roles at Autism Speaks."

151. Savarese and Savarese, "The Superior Half of Speaking."

152. Melanie Yergeau, "Circle Wars: Reshaping the Typical Autism Essay," *Disability Studies Quarterly* 30:1 (2010), http://dsq-sds.org/article/view/1063/1222.

153. Yergeau, "Circle Wars."

154. John Smith, "Why the Americans with Disabilities Act is Important to Me," *Impact*, accessed August 13, 2018, https://ici.umn.edu/products/impact/281/4.html.

155. Smith, "Why the Americans with Disabilities Act is Important to Me."

156. Joseph Shapiro, "Disability Pride: The High Expectations of a New Generation," *The New York Times*, July 17, 2020, https://www.nytimes.com/2020/07 /17/style/americans-with-disabilities-act.html.

Chapter 2

Cripping Disability Identities

PROBLEMATIZING DISABILITY IDENTITY POLITICS

Disability identity has been the foundation of broad alliances among disabled people that have fought for and won important legislative victories resulting in better access, inclusion, and protections from discrimination. Yet, disability identity is not without its problems and limitations. Like all identity categories, disability as a category is inherently unstable and incoherent. As queer theorists like Michel Foucault and Judith Butler have pointed out, identity is a cultural fiction due to the irresolvable diversity between and within the subjects it claims to represent.[1] Referring to lesbian identity, for example, Butler argues that the specificity of any identity category can be articulated only through exclusions that, in so naming, disrupt the identity category's "claim to coherence."[2] Similarly, disability is not a self-evident or discrete category. As I discussed in chapter 1, who or what gets included in the disability category, who or what gets excluded, and who gets to make these decisions are political processes, products of power, that shift and are contested over time and place. Furthermore, because marginalized identities are products of oppression, claiming them can extend and perpetuate dominant discourses and thus work as "instruments of regulatory regimes."[3] Still, it is possible both to acknowledge the inherent problems with identity categories and to recognize them as politically useful "sites of necessary trouble." In fact, for Butler, the deconstruction of identity categories—the calling into question of their coherence and potential to extend regulatory and oppressive systems—does not prohibit the claiming and political deployment of identity, but rather constructively leads to a greater consideration of the purposes and costs of identity politics and "establishes as political the very terms through which identity is articulated."[4]

Disability identity politics, then, can help us to think more deeply about the power mechanisms behind how disability is defined, who is permitted to do the defining, who is included and who is left out of such definitions, and the benefits and drawbacks of identity categories themselves. For example, despite the tremendous heterogeneity in disabled populations and experiences, disability studies as an academic discipline has not been fully inclusive of people with nonphysical and/or invisible disabilities or adequately attentive to how disability intersects with racial, sexual, gender, and other identities.[5] Even in many disability movements, diversity and difference are often minimized or erased in the name of building political alliances.[6] Probing into these issues and doing the hard work of addressing them can make disability scholarship and activism more inclusive and effective as vehicles for social justice.[7]

Scholars like Anna Mollow correctly note that many of the foundational theories of disability studies were modeled on the experiences of those with physical disabilities.[8] While those with neurological disabilities have gained more academic recognition over the past few years, they remain marginalized within the field.[9] The greatest outliers, perhaps, are those diagnosed with mental "illness," a controversial term challenged by psychiatric survivors and mad pride proponents who reject the category of mental illness as nothing more than a cultural fiction invented by modern psychiatry. What psychiatrists call mental illnesses, they claim, are in reality neurodivergences, or minds that process information and emotions in ways that differ from but are not inferior to neurotypical minds.[10] Their willingness to share their personal experiences of forced institutionalization, nonconsensual drug therapies, sexual abuse, and harmful treatments has been important to raising awareness of how those diagnosed with mental health disabilities have been deprived of their autonomy, privacy, dignity, and basic human rights.[11] This has been particularly true for African Americans, who, because of racial stereotypes, are disproportionately diagnosed with "severe mental illnesses" like schizophrenia, prescribed high dosages of antipsychotic medications, and involuntarily institutionalized.[12] Still, while many disability theorists and activists support movements to increase the self-determination of those with mental disabilities and to end the stigma surrounding psychiatric disorders, they remain deeply ambivalent about whether to "normalize" sometimes debilitating mental "illnesses" such as schizophrenia, bipolar disorder, depression, and anxiety.[13] Writers such as Meri Nana-Ama Danqua and Susan Wendell, for example, depart in some ways from the psychiatric survivor movement and the social model of disability by pointing out that some people with disabilities are indeed ill and actively seek out treatment or cure to end their pain and suffering.[14] According to Mollow, Danqua's experiences also serve as an important reminder that many people with mental health disabilities suffer not only from the involuntary imposition of psychiatric treatment but also from a lack of treatment access. As a poor Black woman, Danqua sought but was unable to access treatment for her depression due to the prohibitive cost of therapy and prescriptions and because her doctors relied on racial and gender stereotypes of the "crazy" or "malingering" Black woman to dismiss her depressive symptoms. Unlike many within the psychiatric survivors movement, then, Danqua "sees adequate medical treatment for her depression as a necessity, to which poverty, racism, and gender bias have created almost insurmountable barriers."[15] Still, even for those whose mental health conditions sometimes cause pain and suffering, there is a shared belief in the importance of agency and control over medical treatment and a rejection of the silence and shame surrounding mental disabilities. The late disability scholar, Alison Piepmeier, for example, acknowledged that while her own neurological disabilities often produced significant challenges, she could not deny that they formed an important part of her identity and how she experienced her world. "Denying them, or seeing them as shameful," she concluded, "is harmful to me, to other people who experience mental illness or neurological disorders, and to my efforts at celebrating human diversity."[16]

The tendency of disability studies to frame disability "as a visual, objectively observable phenomenon"[17] means that those who live with invisible disabilities occupy a rather uneasy location within the disability community. Because they appear to be nondisabled, people with invisible disabilities often escape the public discrimination, scrutiny, condescension, pity, and invasion of personal space so frequently experienced by those whose disabilities are more noticeable.[18] The idea that people with nonvisible disabilities are able to "pass" more easily than those with more visible disabilities has been a divisive issue within the disability community. "Passing" in this context refers to the ability of some people with disabilities to pass as nondisabled either through a conscious attempt to conceal markers of one's disability (active passing) or through the imposition by others of a nondisabled identity on a person whose disabilities are not obvious or apparent (reactive passing).[19] Interestingly, while the act of passing has received a plethora of attention from scholars in race, sexuality, and gender studies, it has received less attention from scholars of disability studies, who sometimes assume that the ability to pass is a marker of privilege and who connect passing to the perpetuation and even internalization of disability stigma.[20]

While those with invisible disabilities no doubt derive certain benefits from anonymity, they have challenged the idea that the ability to pass as nondisabled is a marker of privilege or that the act of passing is always a form of internalized ableism. For example, nonvisibly disabled people are routinely subject to what Ellen Samuels calls an "invasive surveillance" that nearly always results from a perceived disconnect between their appearance and the identity that they seem to be claiming through particular actions. Hence, they frequently endure "a daily struggle for accommodation and benefits that reflects the dominant culture's insistence on visible signs to legitimate impairment."[21] In many ways, the ability to pass is "just another type of disadvantage"[22] that can involve considerable effort, cost, sacrifice, and isolation. The sophisticated tactics that disabled people often use to avoid invasive questions, discrimination, or violence, writes Tobin Siebers, can cause emotional and mental stress and even exacerbate existing conditions. Amputees, for example, may be able to avoid the prying eyes of strangers by wearing cosmetic prostheses but often do so at the loss of functionality provided by more mechanical, practical devices.[23] In an attempt to escape workplace discrimination, people with chronic fatigue syndrome may try to work the same hours and at the same pace as their colleagues but ultimately suffer a worsening of their condition and even long-term health consequences.[24] To avoid stigma and ostracism from their peers, students with learning disabilities may not seek classroom accommodations and thus experience even greater learning challenges.[25] To gain social acceptance, people with autism may suppress their need to flap, spin, or engage in other stimming behaviors, which can lead to emotional and physical exhaustion and severe mental strain.[26] Remaining "closeted" in one's disability also means an inability to connect with and find support from other disabled people, which can result in feelings of intense loneliness and isolation.[27]

The ability to pass as nondisabled, then, should not be understood simply as a mark of privilege but as a complicated experience that brings both benefits and particular forms of oppression. Importantly, disability passing tells us much about the power mechanisms that create social expectations for bodies and minds and that either reward or punish individuals based on the extent to which they can fulfill them. Even active passing, or the conscious attempt to conceal one's disability, is rarely an uncomplicated product of internalized ableism but rather a strategy that disabled people across different historical time periods and particular cultural locations have developed to avoid stigma, find acceptance within families and communities, and negotiate the general challenges and barriers of an ableist world.[28] Hence, for disability scholars Jeffrey Brune and Daniel Wilson, "it is more productive, and more just, to challenge the ableism that compels people to pass rather than blame the individuals who choose to do so."[29]

Like other academic disciplines and social justice movements, disability scholarship and activism have not always reflected the tremendous diversity of the disabled population nor the intersectional perspectives of lived disability experiences. For example, the histories, realties, and needs of women with disabilities, argues Rosemarie Garland-Thomson, "remain on the margins of the social justice movements that should represent them—the women's movement, the disability rights movement, and the civil rights movement—leaving disabled women and girls of all backgrounds essentially invisible."[30] This is particularly true for disabled women of color. Lydia X. Z. Brown—an "autistic, multiply otherwise neurodivergent and disabled, queer, asexual-spectrum, genderqueer/non-binary and sometimes read as feminine, and transracially and transnationally adopted east Asian person of color from China (into a white adoptive family)"—argues that the founders and leadership of autistic self-advocacy groups and the most popular books and blog posts from those in the autistic and neurodiverse communities are overwhelmingly white. At most autistic-specific events, Brown is often the only person of color in attendance. This "unacknowledged erasure of autistic people of color, and public discourse about autism as essentially a 'white people issue,'" they write, means that autists of color are far "too often left out of the spaces that are supposedly for us."[31] Vilissa Thompson, creator of the website *Ramp Your Voice!* and the hashtag #DisabilityTooWhite, agrees that the public "face" of disabled women within the media and within disability studies and activism is white, leading to the invisibility of Black disabled women and the erasure of their particular experiences. The excuse from those within the disability community that Black disabled people are difficult to locate, she writes, is spurious given the ubiquity of Black disabled writers on social media. Therefore, those who use this excuse simply "aren't looking hard enough TO find us." She calls on white disabled people to recognize their racial privileges, to seek out and listen to disabled people of color, and ultimately to recognize the different "realities of others that live and look differently from you as a disabled person."[32]

To illustrate the need for greater attention to intersectionality in the disability rights movement, Thompson, along with disability activist and writer Alice Wong, used the Twitter hashtag #GetWokeADA26 to solicit and document personal stories from "individuals representing various people of color communities, disability types, ages, and sexual identities and orientations." The stories, which they summarized and published on the *Ramp Your Voice!* website, demonstrate how disabled people of color traverse, occupy, but often feel invisible within the multiple communities to which they belong.[33] Reyma McCoy McDeid, an "African American Aspergian," acknowledges that "I often feel pressured to pick a movement. . . . I . . . am a person who experiences layers of diversity and, therefore, wish to represent that within the 'disability rights' movement." Finn, "a queer, black, autistic, disability advocate," notes that he often feels as if "I'm only allowed one marginalised identity, not several, so I might get treated as though I'm JUST black, rather than black and queer, or black and autistic, or all three of those things. It makes me feel pretty invisible at times." Jae Jin Pak, "Korean, Disabled, Male, Straight, American," remarks that it is rare for him to see other Asians

at disability related events. "Feeling like I am a minority has caused me to
feel tension and alone at times," he claims. Ellen Erenea, "a Filipina with
dwarfism, mother of two," acknowledges that "I feel as though I'm the only
one representing the API community, where I know there are more. I do feel
welcome in the disability community. However, it's the differences within
differences that eventually leave me feeling alone mostly."[34]

Queer and transgender disabled people have rarely been at the center of
disability studies or rights-based movements and have sometimes struggled
to find a comfortable and accepting home for their ideas and activism. Within
trans and queer spaces, their disability identity often goes unacknowledged,
and within disabled spaces, their trans and nonbinary gender identity often
feels erased.[35] Wanting to address this sort of marginalization and to foster
community among queer, disabled scholars and activists, disability scholar
Eli Clare helped to found the Queerness and Disability Conference, which
held its first meeting in 2002 at San Francisco State University. The conference brought together United States and international artists, activists, and
scholars to explore a wide range of issues, including the pathologization of
queer and disabled bodies, sex and relationships, personal attendant care, and
queer-disabled performance. "Those 48 hours," Clare wrote, "were fueled
by the explosion of energy that often happens when peoples who have lived
in incredible isolation first find each other. . . . Many of us felt relief not
having to explain homophobia to straight disabled people or ableism to nondisabled queer people. The sheer, stunning variety of bodily differences was
both ordinary and awesome."[36] And yet, it became very clear to conference
organizers at the closing plenary session that within this affirming, empowering community, many people continued to feel marginalized and erased. The
complete transcript of this session at the Queer Disability Conference website
demonstrates that the conference organizers were all white, that conference
participants were overwhelmingly white, and that conference presentations
largely ignored issues of race, neurological disabilities, gender, religion,
class, bisexuality, and other important issues. The transcript also illustrates
that Clare and other conference organizers acknowledged these problems,
arranged for members of the psychiatric disabilities and people of color cau-
cuses to address them, and opened the floor for audience members to discuss
them. Ultimately, these conversations—fraught with anger, frustration, and
grief—illustrated how unacknowledged privileges often influence the shape
of disability scholarship and activism and how painful but crucial it is for the
future of disability studies and disability rights movements to unpack, examine, and dismantle them.[37]

Discouraged by the disability rights movement's "invisibilization" of disabled people who simultaneously inhabit multiple identity categories and who
live at "intersecting junctures of oppression,"[38] disabled activists such as Patty

Berne, Mia Mingus, Stacey Milbern, Leroy Moore, Eli Clare, and Sebastian Margaret have called for a disability justice framework. Such a framework understands ableism in relation to white supremacy, heteropatriarchy, colonialism, and capitalism within intersecting systems of domination and exploitation and guides the work of community-based movements led by queer disabled people of color.[39] Working within and across organizations such as the National Black Disability Coalition, Sins Invalid, Helping Educate to Advance the Rights of Deaf communities (HEARD), Coalición Nacional para Latinxs con Discapacidades (National Coalition for Latinxs with Disabilities), and Asians and Pacific Islanders with Disabilities of California (APIDC), disability justice advocates address intersecting, systemic oppressions by centralizing and working on issues that have received scant attention in the disability rights movement, including income inequality, homelessness, unequal access to healthcare, reproductive justice, immigrant and refugee rights, militarization, incarceration, anti-colonialism, and sexual violence.[40]

For decades, many disability justice advocates have fought to highlight the particular vulnerability of disabled Black, Indigenous, people of color (BIPOC) to police violence, an issue that has received heightened scrutiny in the midst of renewed Black Lives Matter (BLM) protests over racial injustice sparked by the May 25, 2020, killing of George Floyd, a Black man who died from injuries sustained when a white police officer knelt on his neck for over eight minutes. Frustrated that disability is usually ignored or marginalized within BLM and other movements that protest state-sanctioned violence against BIPOC, activists like Talila Lewis have fought for recognition that an estimated one half of those killed by law enforcement have been disabled people, a disproportionate number of whom have been from BIPOC, trans, and/or low-income communities. Because individuals targeted by police violence are most often multiply marginalized, Lewis argues, "any conversation about their murder that does not recognize and honor their multiple identities dishonors them through and through. We actually deal a heavy blow to our own liberation struggles when we engage in this kind of violent erasure."[41]

The disparity in law enforcement's treatment of marginalized and privileged bodies has a long, egregious history but was illustrated most publicly, perhaps, on January 6, 2021, when a mob of Donald Trump-supporters violently invaded the Capitol Building in an attempt to overthrow the legitimate outcome of the November 2020 presidential election. Three years prior, police had responded to a peaceful disability rights protest at the Capitol over a Republican proposal to cut Medicaid funding by handcuffing and literally dragging disabled protesters—many of whom were Black women—out of the Capitol Building.[42] Throughout May 2020, police in Washington, D.C. used pepper spray, tear gas, and rubber bullets against Black Lives Matter activists. When faced by a mob of aggrieved, entitled, angry, mostly white, right-wing men, however, law enforcement members responded with an incredible amount of restraint. Many Capitol police officers largely stood by while throngs of shouting, cursing insurrectionists smashed their way into the Capitol, rampaged through hallways and private offices, destroyed property, threatened violence against the vice-president and members of Congress, terrorized the press corps, toted weapons, and carried Confederate flags and other symbols of white supremacy. In the hours and days that followed the insurrection at the Capitol, which ultimately resulted in the deaths of five people, many activists and leaders bitterly pointed out that if Black people had mounted this sort of domestic terrorism, the police response would have been immediate and far deadlier. Placed side by side, an examination of the widely divergent responses to disability and BLM protestors on the one hand and Trump-supporting insurrectionists on the other painfully demonstrates once again what disability justice activists have long argued—that certain bodies and lives are given a level of deference and value that other bodies and lives are not.[43]

THE POSSIBILITIES OF CRIP THEORY

Crip theory has been an important response to the homogenizing tendencies of disability studies, activism, and identity. Crip is a play on the word "cripple," a pejorative term that some disabled theorists and activists have reclaimed to assert a positive, unapologetic, and unpatronizing view of disability that "jolt[s] people out of their everyday understandings of bodies and minds, of normalcy and deviance."[44] Unlike so-called polite terms such as "handicapped" or "disabled" and in stark contrast to cutesy euphemisms like "differently abled" and "handicapable"—terms despised by many disabled people—the word *cripple* is "a sock in the eye with gnarled fist,"[45] as the acclaimed poet and performer Cheryl Marie Wade so delightfully put it. It is an "in your face" demand that disability be seen and recognized and an insistence that people confront their unease and even disgust with bodies and minds that do not meet their expectations. "People—crippled or not—wince at the word 'cripple,'" wrote essayist Nancy Mairs. "Perhaps I want them to wince."[46] Agreeing with this perspective, Caitlin Wood, editor of the excellent anthology *Criptiques*, writes:

> Crip is my favorite four-letter word. Succinct and blunt, profane to some, crip packs a punch. Crip is unapologetic. Audacious. Noncompliant. Crip takes pleasure in its boldness and utter disinterest in appearing "respectable" to the status quo. It's a powerful self-descriptor, a cultural signifier, and a challenge to anyone attempting to conceal disability off in the shadows. . . . Crip is outspoken with no patience for nonsense. Crip is my culture and it's where I want to be.[47]

Like queer, crip is used not only as a noun and an adjective but as a verb. As disability scholar Carrie Sandahl explains, to crip is to view dominant ideas about disability from a disability perspective in order to expose their ableist assumptions. To crip is to deconstruct the binaric distinctions between abled and disabled, to analyze how disability has been used throughout history to justify the oppression of women, people of color, and immigrants, and to highlight "the negative social ramifications of attempts to homogenize humanity."[48] Crip embraces disability justice, which Mia Mingus describes as "moving away from an equality-based model of sameness and 'we are just like you' to a model of disability that embraces difference, confronts privilege and challenges what is considered 'normal' on every front. We don't want to simply join the ranks of the privileged; we want to dismantle those ranks and the systems that maintain them."[49] Or, as Wood puts it, "[c]rip is my community filled with badass freaks and outcasts who are classified as abnormal by society and wear that designation as a badge of honor. Because we're not trying to assimilate into a culture that doesn't know what to do with us in the first place."[50]

Understandings of disability and impairment, crip theorists argue, are not rooted in any sort of biological facts about bodies and minds that are immutable or self-evident but are instead the products of particular historical moments, societal imperatives, and the political decisions that give them meaning. Crip theorists point out the incoherence of disability identity in order to build wider coalitions for disability justice and to expose the instability of nondisabled identity and the ableist assumptions that undergird it. Deliberately fluid and nebulous, crip locates disability identity not in embodiment or diagnosis but in a political "collective affinity." Crip has the potential, then, to strengthen disability activism by bringing together diverse individuals and groups committed to dismantling systems of oppression and pursuing justice for disabled people. Crip makes room for chronic illnesses, neurological disabilities, fatness, madness, invisible disabilities, for those who seek a cure and for those who do not. Crip extends beyond single-issue identity politics to recognize how identities of race, sexuality, gender, class, and nationality, for example, intersect with disability to create diverse experiences and perspectives. Crip includes those debilitated by environmental hazards, police violence, war, colonialism, and other weapons of bodily harm produced by biopolitical regimes of authoritarian power.[51] Crip accommodates those who self-diagnose, as well as people who claim or identify with crip as a desirable location due to their relationship with disabled parents, children, or partners.[52] And crip prompts us all to ask "what is my relationship to disability"[53] by reminding us that all bodies and minds occupy slippery locations on a wide spectrum that shift and slide with age and through engagement with our social and built environments. Crip holds forth the tantalizing possibility of *"what might arise"* from coalitional theory and politics by the "joining of our different bodies/minds/desires/behaviors," writes Sami Schalk. "We can only know what our differences might create if we are willing to risk such proximity to one another."[54]

By exposing the instability and fluidity of identity categories, crip calls into question the naturalness and superiority of nondisability and the ableist assumptions that sustain it. There is tremendous radical potential for changing dominant understandings of disability, for example, when a person read and understood as "perfectly able-bodied" turns out to be disabled. Despite the real risks of doing so, particularly for those who are already marginalized by other identities, those with invisible disabilities have the potential to create important counternarratives about disability when they "uncover" or expose their disabilities to others. By "naming myself a crazy girl, neuroatypical, mentally disabled, psychosocially disabled" while at the same time appearing "healthy as a horse," as disability scholar Margaret Price points out, "I am trying to reassign meaning."[55] Making the invisible visible, then, has the potential to educate, to challenge the epistemological certainty of the stare, and to create new knowledges about disability.[56] There is also a great deal of epistemological potential in recognizing that "ability" is something that can be appropriated. If "able-bodiedness" can be imitated and performed by those with disabilities, then the categories of nondisabled and disabled cannot be fixed, static, or the expression of some a priori identity. In fact, it is the performance itself—repeated, practiced, stylized—that constitutes the identity "even as it produces the very notion of the original as an *effect* and consequence of the imitation," writes Judith Butler, who has theorized how the practice of drag performance creates and reproduces gender and sexuality identities.[57] For Butler, then, there is no preexisting gender identity, no gendered subject that simply performs gender; rather, "identity is performatively constituted by the very 'expressions' that are said to be its results."[58] In much the same way, we can understand the act of performing ability not as the imitation of a "false" identity through the masking of the "true" one but as a performance that constructs all identities. The performance of "able-bodiedness" by those with disabilities, then, can unsettle ableist notions about the fixed nature of identities and what is "normal" and "natural" by revealing that nondisabled identities are as constructed and performative as the imitations of them.

Finally, by dismantling the ableist fallacy that equates nondisability with independence and disability with dependence, crip theory emphasizes the limitations of all bodies and minds and, hence, the dependency of all individuals on external supports to survive and flourish. In a 2010 appearance on *The Colbert Report*, Aimee Mullins, a Paralympian and disability activist, made this point explicitly in response to host Stephen Colbert's amazement that she had managed to walk competently onto the set on two prosthetic legs:

Colbert: "That completely changes my image of what it means to not have a leg. Cause I've got to tell you, that looks a lot like a leg to me and you just walked out here completely confident and completely poised. What has happened to prostheses in the last few years that I don't know about evidently?"

Mullins: "Well, you do know. You put on prosthetics every day. You have them on your face."

Colbert: "You mean the latex chin they put on me every— . . . You mean my glasses?"

Mullins: "It's glasses, yeah of course. Anything that functions as part of your body that you wear outside of your body is really a prosthetic, whether it's clothes, your cell phone, scissors, your glasses. So, the fact that so many new technologies right now are really allowing people to rebuild bodies and push past the limits that nature would impose on them, it's completely redefining what we think of as ability and disability."[59]

As Mullins noted, all bodies depend on an array of prosthetics and supports to increase functioning and to reduce pain and limitations. These supports are unconsciously built for the needs of nondisabled people but are either inaccessible to or obtained only through great struggle by those who are disabled. "The additional difficulty, expense, and challenge associated with securing necessary support for those of us who diverge from that majority," Ari Ne'eman argues, "stems from the reality that we live in a world that is geared only to a particular kind of person."[60] And we tend to think of such supports in terms of dependency and "special" forms of accommodation only when people with disabilities use them. Stephen Colbert needs glasses in order to see clearly. Aimee Mullins needs prosthetic legs to walk. Stephen Colbert is not a medal-winning athlete. Aimee Mullins has set world records in sprinting and long jump. Yet, curiously, he is not regarded as disabled and she is.

This curiosity is an example of what Alison Kafer calls the invisibility of nondisabled access and the hypervisibility of disabled access. Both steps and ramps, she notes, are forms of accommodation but only steps go "unmarked as access; indeed, it is only when atypical bodies are taken into account that the question of access becomes a problem."[61] Similarly, Tobin Siebers argues that the built environment is full of technologies and interventions that allow people considered "able-bodied" to survive, flourish, or to function more easily. Stairs, escalators, washing machines, leaf blowers, eggbeaters, chainsaws, and other tools help to relax physical standards for performing certain tasks. These tools are nevertheless viewed as natural extensions of the body, and no one questions their use. Nor does anyone question nondisabled people's reliance on computers, babysitters, protective laws, or warm clothing on a cold day. Yet, technologies and interventions designed to make disabled people's lives easier—wheelchairs, caregivers, assistance dogs, disability laws, and psychotropic drugs—are often viewed as expensive additions, unnecessary accommodations, special treatment, or a burden on society.[62] In reality, notes Lennard Davis, all bodies and minds are limited and incomplete and depend on external supports to improve form, function, and wellness.[63]

This crip recognition that disability is not one half of a binary but part of a wide spectrum that encompasses every person is not to indulge in the problematic and ableist claim that "we are all disabled,"[64] which erases the embodied, material experience of disability and ignores the particular experience of oppression that accompanies disability within various contexts. While pointing out the constructed messiness of identity categories, disability scholars continue to recognize the importance of disability identity to self-actualization, for accessing needed services, for calling attention to the discriminatory treatment of disabled people, and for collective action to address this treatment. Garland-Thomson argues, for example, that "while the borders of the category *disabled* need to be recognized as porous, contextual, and dynamic, to dismiss the political category of disabled as it functions in the material and social world in which we live at this moment in the service of some anti-normative critical move ignores the reality that most disabled people who identify as disabled or are identified as disabled are excluded from life-sustaining resources because the extant world cannot accommodate us."[65] Instead of "dematerializing" disability, Robert McRuer calls for a "contestatory relationship" with it that widens and complicates its dimensions.[66] And as Kafer notes, by questioning and complicating the binary between disabled and nondisabled, crip does not minimize the particularities of disabled experiences but in fact forces us to think more carefully about how all bodies and minds are differentially treated; so positioned, disability becomes "a set of practices and associations that can be critiqued, contested, and transformed."[67]

By emphasizing that the crip project is transformation, not solely critique and contestation, Kafer hints at how dismantling the binary between ability and disability is not just a deconstructive exercise but a potentially creative act that generates new, radical forms of identity. In this regard, invisible disability is once again particularly illustrative. While no one's experience of disability is completely static, those with nonvisible disabilities—such as chronic fatigue syndrome, rheumatoid arthritis, obsessive-compulsive disorder (OCD), or depression (to name just a few)—that flare and subside in different contexts and environments tend to occupy a space somewhere in between the worlds of disability and nondisability.[68] By inhabiting and traveling in and out of both of these worlds, they are able to reveal their permeability and instability and thus work to dismantle the identity borders that exclude and oppress people with disabilities.[69] Yet, this location of in-betweenness is one of tremendous generative potential. In her seminal book, *Borderlands/La Frontera*, writer Gloria Anzaldúa, for example, demonstrated the productive possibilities of her multiple and sometimes conflicting locations in various cultures, races, nationalities, and sexualities: "Soy un amasamiento, I am an act of kneading, of uniting and joining that not only has produced both a creature of darkness and a creature of light, but also a creature that questions the definitions of light and dark and gives them new meanings."[70] This "new mestiza consciousness" that Anzaldúa describes not only "tolerates" and sustains contradictions and ambiguities of identity but becomes a powerful tool by which to straddle cultures, break down paradigms, and create new histories, new narratives, and new possibilities.[71] Disability scholar Shayda Kafai offers an effective illustration of this sort of transgression and creation that occurs in the borderlands through the narratives she constructs from her "mad border body." By existing simultaneously in the border spaces of sanity and madness, she is able to challenge the dominant meanings of both sanity and madness and to transcend the false binary dividing these categories. "If dominant culture begins to acknowledge the mad border body, that individuals can exist simultaneously in states of sanity and madness," she argues, "then it must also question the belief that sanity is stable."[72] For her, the mad border body is a location of transgression and protest, a site from which to deconstruct binaries and to challenge oppressive regimes. But, like Anzaldúa's borderlands, it is also a site of the creation of new stories and new identities that fundamentally shift the meaning of what it is to be "mad."[73]

Crip, then, is not incompatible with the movement for disability rights and the identity politics that fuel it. When disability identity is based not on any set of essential, biological attributes, but rather on political affinities rooted in shared social locations, it becomes a powerful site for the creation of meaning and the implementation of real social change. Disability scholars Lennard Davis and Margrit Shildrick, for example, argue that disability is a powerful location from which to advance a "malleable view of the human body."[74] In other words, by demonstrating how all bodies and minds are limited, messy, vulnerable, and dependent on a wide variety of external supports, this recognition exposes the absurdity of claims about bodily autonomy, normalcy, and completeness.[75] "Impairment is the rule, and normalcy is the fantasy," Davis notes.[76] Jasbir Puar cautions that this view of the human body as inherently limited and vulnerable may serve the interests of neoliberal, capitalist regimes who profit from the selling of commodities promising to "fix" bodily deficiencies, and that privileged bodies are more easily able to access the promise of rehabilitation.[77] But as Shildrick points out, the understanding that no bodies "escape the tentacles of neo-liberalism" prompts us to think more carefully about the factors that create differences in how we each experience "immersion in debility and slow death."[78] "My desire not to lose the specificity of debility in the more general term survives the test," she writes, "and the ambivalence of where precisely distinctions matter and where they do not is productive rather than disturbing."[79] Indeed, Davis's theory of "dismodernism" argues for "a commonality of bodies within the notion of difference. It is too easy to say, 'We're all disabled.' But it is possible to say that we are all disabled by oppression of various kinds. We are all nonstandard, and it is under that standard that we should be able to found the dismodernist ethic."[80]

Despite the risks, this is a potentially powerful claim, because if all bodies and minds are limited and interdependent, then it makes sense to build our environment, to structure our institutions, and to craft our ideologies to make them fit the needs of all individuals. Imagine how different our world would be and how differently we would think about disability if our buildings, schools, economy, health care system, and government were truly responsive to, inclusive of, and accessible for all people regardless of age, race, size, gender, class, sexuality, religion, appearance, and disability. Imagine the possibilities of truly intersectional collective action that fought not simply to ensure the inclusion of a particular group into existing cultural, economic, and political institutions but to transform radically the body politic into a system of fair and equitable distribution of social resources. Imagine what would happen to our current understandings of disability, accessibility, "special needs," dependency, autonomy, beauty, health, knowledge, quality of life, and happiness if we universally designed our physical, structural, and ideological environments to accommodate all forms of human diversity. As Rosemarie Garland-Thomson eloquently expressed, "How would the public landscape change if the widest possible diversity of human forms, functions and behaviors were fully accommodated? . . . What would be the political significance of such inclusion?"[81]

NOTES

1. See Judith Butler, *Gender Trouble: Feminism and the Subversion of Identity* (New York: Routledge, 1990) and Michel Foucault, *The History of Sexuality, Volume 1* (New York: Pantheon Books, 1978).

2. Judith Butler, "Imitation and Gender Insubordination," in *Inside/Out: Lesbian Theories, Gay Theories* ed. Diana Fuss (New York: Routledge, 1991), 13–31.

3. Butler, "Imitation and Gender Insubordination," 13–31.

4. Butler, "Imitation and Gender Insubordination," 13–31.

5. See Christopher Bell, ed., *Blackness and Disability: Critical Examinations and Cultural Interventions* (Germany: LIT Verlag, 2011); Alice Wong, *Disability Visibility: First-Person Stories from the Twenty-First Century* (New York: Vintage,

2020); and Sami Schalk, "Coming to Claim Crip: Disidentification with/in Disability Studies," *Disability Studies Quarterly* 33:2 (2013), http://dsq-sds.org/article/view/3705.

6. Schalk, "Coming to Claim Crip."

7. See Bell, ed., *Blackness and Disability* and Schalk, "Coming to Claim Crip."

8. Anna Mollow, "Criphystemologies: What Disability Theory Needs to Know about Hysteria," *Journal of Literary & Cultural Disability Studies* 8:2 (2014): 185–201, muse.jhu.edu/article/548850.

9. Anna Mollow, "'When Black Women Start Going on Prozac': Race, Gender, and Mental Illness in Meri Nana-Ama Danquah's *Willow Weep for Me*," *MELUS* 31:3 (Fall, 2006): 70, https://doi.org/10.1093/melus/31.3.67.

10. Peter Beresford, "'Mad,' Mad Studies and Advancing Inclusive Resistance," *Disability & Society* 35:8 (2020): 1337–1342, https://doi.org/10.1080/09687599.2019.1692168; Cynthia Lewiecki-Wilson, "Rethinking Rhetoric through Mental Disabilities," *Rhetoric Review* 22:2 (2003): 156–167; Catherine Prendergast, "On the Rhetorics of Mental Disability," in *Towards a Rhetoric of Everyday Life*, eds. Martin Nystrand and John Duffy (Madison: The University of Wisconsin Press, 2003): 189–207; Heather Hillsburg, "Mental Illness and the Mad/woman: Anger, Normalcy, and Liminal Identities in Mary McGarry Morris's *A Dangerous Woman*," *Journal of Literary & Cultural Disability Studies* 11:1 (2017): 1–16, https://doi.org/10.3828/jlcds.2017.1.

11. Mollow, "When Black Women Start Going on Prozac," 71.

12. Mollow, "When Black Women Start Going on Prozac," 74.

13. Elizabeth Donaldson and Catherine Prendergast, "Introduction: Disability and Emotion: 'There's No Crying in Disability Studies!'" *Journal of Literary & Cultural Disability Studies* 5:2 (2011): 129–135, https://doi.org/10.3828/jlcds.

14. Mollow, "When Black Women Start Going on Prozac," 75–76; Susan Wendall, "Unhealthy Disabled: Treating Chronic Illnesses as Disabilities," *Hypatia* 16:4 (Autumn 2001): 17-33.

15. Mollow, "When Black Women Start Going on Prozac," 72.

16. Alison Piepmeier, et al., "Disability Is a Feminist Issue: Bringing Together Women's and Gender Studies and Disability Studies," *Disability Studies Quarterly* 34:2 (2014), http://dsq-sds.org/article/view/4252/3592.

17. Mollow, "When Black Women Start Going on Prozac," 68.

18. Aimee Burke Valeras, "We Don't Have a Box": Understanding Hidden Disability Identity Utilizing Narrative Research Methodology," *Disability Studies Quarterly* 30:3/4 (2010), https://dsq-sds.org/article/view/1267/1297.

19. Daniel G. Renfrow, "A Cartography of Passing in Everyday Life," *Symbolic Interaction* 27:4 (2004): 489, https://doi.org/10.1525/si.2004.27.4.485.

20. Jeffrey Brune and Daniel Wilson, "Introduction," in *Disability and Passing: Blurring the Lines of Identity*, eds. Jeffrey A. Brune and Daniel Wilson (Philadelphia: Temple University Press, 2013), 2, 4–5; Ellen Samuels, "My Body, My Closet: Invisible Disability and the Limits of Coming-Out Discourse," *GLQ: A Journal of Lesbian and Gay Studies* 9:1–2 (2003): 240, 244.

21. Samuels, "My Body, My Closet," 245.

22. Naomi Chainey, "Passing is Not a Privilege," *Ramp Up*, June 6, 2014, https://www.abc.net.au/rampup/articles/2014/06/06/4018773.htm.

23. Rosemarie Garland-Thomson, *Staring: How We Look* (Oxford: Oxford University Press, 2009), 129.

24. Tobin Siebers, *Disability Theory* (Ann Arbor, University of Michigan Press, 2008), 118.

25. Siebers, *Disability Theory*, 118.

26. "Passing for Neurotypical," *Learn from Autistics*, October 27, 2015, https://www.learnfromautistics.com/passing-for-neurotypical/.

27. Siebers, *Disability Theory*, 118; Simi Linton, *Claiming Disability* (New York: New York University, 1998), 21.

28. Brune and Wilson, "Introduction," 5; Linton, *Claiming Disability*, 19–21.

29. Brune and Wilson, "Introduction," 5.

30. Rosemarie Garland-Thomson, "Re-shaping, Re-thinking, Redefining: Feminist Disability Studies," *Center for Women Policy Studies*, 2001, https://www.womenenabled.org/pdfs/Garland-Thomson,Rosemarie,RedefiningFeministDisabilitiesStudiesCWPR2001.pdf.

31. Vanessa Leigh, "Critical Conversations: Lydia X. Z. Brown on Ableism and the New Anthology *All the Weight of Our Dreams*," *Adios Barbie*, July 18, 2016, http://www.adiosbarbie.com/2016/07/critical-conversations-lydia-x-z-brown-on-ableism-and-the-new-anthology-all-the-weigh-of-our-dreams/. See also Lydia X. Z. Brown, et al., eds., *All the Weight of Our Dreams: On Living Racialized Autism* (Lincoln: DragonBee Press, 2017); Malcolm Matthews, "Why Sheldon Cooper Can't Be Black: The Visual Rhetoric of Autism and Ethnicity," *Journal of Literary & Cultural Disability Studies* 13:1 (2019): 57–74, https://doi.org/10.3828/jlcds.2019.4; Paul Heilker, "Autism, Rhetoric, and Whiteness," *Disability Studies Quarterly* 32:4 (2012), https://dsq-sds.org/article/view/1756; and Carrie Arnold, "Autism's Race Problem," *Pacific Standard*, May 25, 2016, https://psmag.com/news/autisms-race-problem.

32. Monique Jones, "Exclusive Interview: #DisabilityTooWhite Creator Vilissa Thompson," *Just Add Color*, May 24, 2016, http://colorwebmag.com/2016/05/24/exclusive-interview-disabilitytoowhite-creator-vilissa-thompson/. See also Elizabeth Mulderink, "The Emergence, Importance of #DisabilityTooWhite Hashtag," *Disability Studies Quarterly* 40:2 (2020), https://dsq-sds.org/article/view/6484/5565.

33. See also Wong, *Disability Visibility*.

34. Vilissa Thompson and Alice Wong, "#GetWokeADA26: Disabled People of Color Speak Out, Part Two. Ramp Your Voice!" *Disability Visibility Project*, July 26, 2016, http://wp.me/p4H7t1-MLn.

35. Mahdia Lynn, "Here's What Transgender People With Disabilities Want You To Know," *BuzzFeed*, August 19, 2017, https://www.buzzfeed.com/mahdialynn/heres-what-disabled-transgender-people-want-you-to-know.

36. Eli Clare, "Sex, Celebration and Justice," Queerness and Disability Conference, 2002, accessed June 2, 2018, https://eliclare.com/what-eli-offers/lectures/queer-disability.

37. "Proceedings: Panel: Closing Plenary," *Disability History*, accessed June 2, 2018, http://www.disabilityhistory.org/dwa/queer/panel_closing.html.

38. Patty Berne, "Disability Justice—A Working Draft by Patty Berne," *Sins Invalid*, June 9, 2015, https://www.sinsinvalid.org/blog/disability-justice-a-working -draft-by-patty-berne.

39. Nomy Lamm, "This is Disability Justice," *The Body is Not an Apology*, September 2, 2015, https://thebodyisnotanapology.com/magazine/this-is-disability -justice/.

40. Berne, "Disability Justice."

41. Talila Lewis, "Emmett Till and the Pervasive Erasure of Disability in Conversations about White Supremacy and Police Violence," *Talila A. Lewis*, January 28, 2017, https://www.talilalewis.com/blog/emmett-till-disability-erasure.

42. Robyn Powell, "The Women with Disabilities Who Fought for Your Health Care This Year," *Vice*, December 20, 2017, https://broadly.vice.com/en_us/article/w jp5px/the-women-with-disabilities-who-fought-for-your-health-care-this-year.

43. Quoted in Steve Inskeep, "How Police Handled Pro-Trump Mob Compared With Protesters for Black Racial Justice," *NPR*, January 7, 2021, https://www.npr .org/sections/insurrection-at-the-capitol/2021/01/07/954410419/how-the-u-s-capitol -mob-was-treated-differently-than-earlier-black-protesters.

44. Alison Kafer, *Feminist, Queer, Crip* (Bloomington: Indiana University Press, 2013), 15.

45. Cheryl Marie Wade, "I Am Not One of The," *Sinister Wisdom* 35 (Summer/ Fall 1988): 24, http://www.sinisterwisdom.org/sites/default/files/Sinister%20Wisd om%2035.pdf.

46. Nancy Mairs, *Plaintext* (Tucson: University of Arizona Press, 1986), 9.

47. Caitlin Wood, "Introduction: Criptiques: A Daring Space," in *Criptiques*, ed. Caitlin Wood (Portland, OR: May Day, 2014), 1–2, https://criptiques.files.wordpress. com/2014/05/crip-final-2.pdf.

48. Carrie Sandahl, "Queering the Crip or Cripping the Queer?: Intersections of Queer and Crip Identities in Solo Autobiographical Performance," *GLQ: A Journal of Lesbian and Gay Studies* 9 (April 1, 2003): 37, https://doi.org/10.1215/10642684-9-1 -2-25.

49. Mia Mingus, "Changing the Framework: Disability Justice," *Leaving Evidence*, February 12, 2011, https://leavingevidence.wordpress.com/2011/02/12/changing-the -framework-disability-justice/.

50. Caitlin Wood, "Tales from the Crip: Ready, Willing, and Disabled," *Bitch Media*, September 25, 2012, https://www.bitchmedia.org/post/tales-from-the-crip-rea dy-willing-and-disabled.

51. Jasbir Puar, *The Right to Maim: Debility, Capacity, Disability* (Durham: Duke University Press, 2017), 15, 69. See also Robert McRuer, *Crip Times: Disability, Globalization, and Resistance* (New York: New York University Press, 2018).

52. Kafer, *Feminist, Queer, Crip*, 13.

53. Corbett Joan O'Toole, "Disclosing Our Relationships to Disabilities: An Invitation for Disability Studies Scholars," *Disability Studies Quarterly* 33:2 (2013), http://dsq-sds.org/article/view/3708/3226.

54. Sami Schalk, "Coming to Claim Crip."

55. Margaret Price, *Mad at School: Rhetorics of Mental Disability and Academic Life* (Ann Arbor: University of Michigan Press, 2011), 20.

56. Garland-Thomson, *Staring*, 15, 194.

57. Butler, "Imitation and Gender Insubordination," 21.

58. Butler, *Gender Trouble*, 34.

59. The *Colbert Report*, Comedy Central, April 15, 2010, https://www.cc.com/e pisodes/ktt9wb/the-colbert-report-april-15-2010-aimee-mullins-season-6-ep-52.

60. Ari Ne'eman, "The Future (and the Past) of Autism Advocacy, Or Why the ASA's Magazine, *The Advocate*, Wouldn't Publish This Piece," *Disability Studies Quarterly* 30:1 (2010), http://dsq-sds.org/article/view/1059/1244.

61. Kafer, *Feminist, Queer, Crip*, 138.

62. Siebers, *Disability Theory*, 31.

63. Lennard Davis, *Bending Over Backwards: Disability, Dismodernism, and Other Difficult Positions* (New York: New York University Press, 2002), 30.

64. Kafer, *Feminist, Queer, Crip*, 9.

65. Rosemarie Garland-Thomson, "The Story of My Work: How I Became Disabled," *Disability Studies Quarterly* 34:2 (2014), http://dsq-sds.org/article/view /4254/3594.

66. Robert McRuer, *Crip Theory: Cultural Signs of Queerness and Disability* (New York: New York University Press, 2006), 71.

67. Kafer, *Feminist, Queer, Crip*, 9.

68. Susan Wendell, *The Rejected Body: Feminist Philosophical Reflections on Disability* (New York: Routledge, 1996), 76.

69. Samuels, "My Body, My Closet," 243.

70. Gloria Anzaldúa, *Borderlands/La Frontera: The New Mestiza* (San Francisco: Aunt Lute Books, 1987), 81.

71. Anzaldúa, *Borderlands/La Frontera*, 79.

72. Shayda Kafai, "The Mad Border Body: A Political In-betweenness," *Disability Studies Quarterly* 33:1 (2013), http://dsq-sds.org/article/view/3438/3199.

73. Kafai, "The Mad Border Body."

74. Davis, *Bending Over Backwards*, 26.

75. Margrit Shildrick, *Embodying the Monster: Encounters with the Vulnerable Self* (London: Sage Publications, 2002), 4.

76. Davis, *Bending Over Backwards*, 31.

77. Puar, *The Right to Maim*, 153. See also David Mitchell and Sharon Snyder, *The Biopolitics of Disability: Neoliberalism, Ablenationalism, and Peripheral Embodiments* (Ann Arbor: University of Michigan Press, 2015).

78. Shildrick, *Embodying the Monster,* 22. The concept of "slow death" comes from Lauren Berlant, "Slow Death: Sovereignty, Obesity, Lateral Agency," *Critical Inquiry* 33 (2007): 754–780, https://doi.org/10.1086/524831.

79. Shildrik, *Embodying the Monster,* 22.

80. Davis, *Bending Over Backwards*, 31–32.

81. Rosemarie Garland-Thomson, "First Person: Rosemarie Garland-Thomson," *Emory Report* 56 (July 6, 2004), http://www.emory.edu/EMORY_REPORT/erarch ive/2004/July/er%20july%206/7_6_04firstperson.html.

Part II

(RE)IMAGINING DISABILITY

Chapter 3

Disability on Display

It is Monday night, which means an evening of *Dancing with the Stars* (DWTS).[1] Airing on network television since 2005, DWTS is a show in which professional dancers and their celebrity amateur partners compete over the course of several weeks for judges' points and audience votes until the last remaining couple is awarded the coveted mirror ball championship trophy. Zoey and I rush to clear up after dinner, feed the dogs, and assemble our snacks (usually big bowls of popcorn) before tucking ourselves into the oversized chair in our family room as we await the start of the telecast. While we watch, we cheer on our favorite couples, loudly signal our disapproval of objectionable comments from the judges, and sometimes get up from our chair and dance around the family room along with the contestants on the screen. Throughout its multiple seasons, DWTS has typically featured at least one celebrity with a disability in its cast of amateur dancers, including Heather Mills (amputee, leg), Marlee Matlin (deaf), J.R. Martinez (burn survivor), Amy Purdy (bilateral amputee, legs), Noah Galloway (double amputee, arm and leg), Nyle DiMarco (deaf), Danelle Umstead (blind), and Terra Jole (achondroplasia). In addition to the glitzy costumes, intense coaching sessions, and often spectacular performances, the regularity with which DWTS includes people with disabilities is one of the reasons that Zoey and I began watching the show. This medium, among others, provides a safer forum for Zoey to learn to appreciate and to ask questions about bodily differences. Yet, the show consistently positions disabled contestants within narratives that perpetuate damaging stereotypes about disability. Regardless of their skills on the dance floor, dancers with disabilities receive effusive praise from the judges, who routinely call them "inspirational," "brave," and a shining example for anyone facing adversity or hardship. Judge Carrie Ann Inaba is especially prone to gushing tearfully over the "heroism" of disabled contestants. She once called Amy Purdy a "shining beacon of light," told J.R. Martinez that it "broke her heart" to give him a low score for his mediocre performance because he was "so courageous and inspiring," and thanked Noah Galloway for "changing her perception of what dance looks like" (in a comment that suggested her ignorance of the way in which disabled dancers have been redefining dance for decades).

On this particular night, as I listen to Inaba crow yet again over how inspired she is by the performance of a contestant with a disability, I am reminded of Rosemarie Garland-Thomson's observation that throughout history, disabled people have been put on display for the benefit of nondisabled people "while being politically and socially erased."[2] From the monstrous wonders of the ancient world, to the sideshow attractions of nineteenth-century freak shows, to the pathologized subjects of medical inquiry, to the participants of modern reality television, disability has been continually on display.[3] Disability has featured prominently in folklore, literature, movies, and television. Yet, actual disabled people and lived disability experiences have been "conspicuously absent in the histories we write," as Douglas Baynton puts it, barely present in the media narratives that we produce, largely excluded from the public spaces we construct, and rejected as unworthy from full and equal participation in the political, economic, and social spheres that we maintain.[4] In *Dancing with the Stars*, disability is on display. The language, music, and visual representation by which disabled contestants are positioned make it very clear that the true value of these contestants lies not so much in their individual skills (which for some are considerable), but in their ability to provide inspiration to others and to teach us all that achievement is a consequence of determination and a good attitude.

During a commercial break, Zoey and I are exposed to a very different type of disability display. We listen to a preview of a news report about yet another measles outbreak caused by vaccine denialism. Many parents are refusing to have their children administered with the MMR (measles, mumps, rubella) vaccine, the newscaster explains, due to their belief that it causes autism spectrum "disorder."[5] A father whose interview would be included in the full news report airing later in the night appears in closeup at the end of the preview, tearfully explaining that following an MMR vaccination, his son "became autistic," and that he was telling his story as a cautionary tale for other parents. After the preview, Zoey suddenly grows very quiet. Then, she turns to me and asks, "Mama, what does that mean? Why don't those parents want their kids to be autistic? What's wrong with autism?" What she seems to be asking, of course, is, "What's wrong with me?"

For some parents, the fear that their children might develop autism—despite the fact that numerous scientific studies have found no association between autism and the MMR vaccine[6]—outweighs the risk of their children contracting a highly infectious, potentially deadly disease. Apparently for these parents, autism is a fate worse than death. "Someone who refuses to vaccinate their children because they're afraid of autism," writes Sarah Kurchak, "has made the decision that people like me are the worst possible thing that can happen to their family, and they're putting everyone at risk because of it."[7] As Kurchak indicates, the anti-vaccine campaign is loaded with implications and outright declarations of who does and who does not have the right to live in the world. Drawing on pseudo-scientific evidence and spurious claims, anti-vaxxers regularly use autism as a scare tactic to manipulate people into believing that vaccines are dangerous.[8] Such scare tactics have given the anti-vax campaign wide publicity for its false information and thus an outsized influence on parents' vaccine decisions. The repercussions for public health have been serious, with once-eradicated diseases like measles and whooping cough circulating among unvaccinated populations.[9] In fact, the World Health Organization included "vaccine hesitancy" alongside air pollution, climate change, influenza, and Ebola in its 2019 list of the top ten threats to global health.[10] And by using autism as a scare tactic to persuade others to their way of thinking, anti-vaccine activists perpetuate the idea that autism is a disease, a misfortune, and even a tragedy for the individuals and families who live with or in proximity to it.

Unfortunately, arguments for the safety of vaccines too often focus on debunking the link between vaccines and autism without challenging these basic assumptions about autism itself, thus indirectly contributing to the fear, stigma, and misunderstandings surrounding autism and disabilities more generally. Significantly, pro-vaccination arguments, similar to anti-vaccination arguments, seem to be most effective when they tap into public fears of disease and debility. According to a 2015 study in the *Proceedings of the National Academy of Sciences*, parents are much more likely to be persuaded to vaccinate their children when they are presented with graphic photos or read firsthand accounts of children with diseases such as mumps, measles, and rubella. Such "scare tactics," the report concluded, were much more effective than fact-based approaches that presented parents with scientific studies that debunked the connection between vaccines and autism.[11]

The exploitation of public fears about disability in media-driven public health campaigns is certainly not unique to the anti- and pro-vaccination movements. In 2012, the Centers for Disease Control and Prevention (CDC) launched a national tobacco education campaign called "Tips From Former Smokers" (TFFS) consisting primarily of a series of television advertisements that feature "real people who are living with serious long-term health effects from smoking and secondhand smoke exposure."[12] In one advertisement, a young man named Brandon explains that he contracted Buerger's disease from years of smoking, which resulted in the amputation of both of his legs and several fingertips. He describes in gruesome detail how his limbs grew infected and then gangrenous and how he nearly gagged on the smell of his putrid flesh. As Brandon tells his story, the camera lingers on close-up shots of his scarred stumps while he sits on the edge of his bed slipping on silicone liners over his residual limbs. He struggles to walk down a staircase on his prosthetic legs and is featured staring out of windows and sitting dejectedly, completely alone and isolated in a monochromatic room—the lighting is dim and his clothing drab. In his biography on the CDC website, Brandon mourns his disabled body as an impediment to daily functioning and his enjoyment of parenting. Putting on his prosthetic legs is too bothersome when he has to use the bathroom in the middle of the night, he notes, and so he often resorts to crawling on the floor. Too much time spent on his prosthetics causes painful sores, forcing him to use a wheelchair much of the time. For Brandon, the worst consequence of his smoking and subsequent disability is the impact on his relationship with his son. "I can sit on the floor with him now when he's a baby," he says, "but when he gets older, I won't be able go out and run and play football with him."[13]

Clearly the intended message in Brandon's story and others in the TFFS series is that disability equals isolation, misery, and an inability to lead a functional and fulfilling life. Disability is the warning, the cautionary tale, the horrible consequence of smoking. Do not smoke or this pitiful creature could be you, the TFFS ads seem to say, and this warning has proven to be extremely effective. According to the CDC, years of advertisements, warnings, and public service campaigns that linked smoking to early death were largely ineffective. Most smokers acknowledge that fear of death provides little motivation to stop smoking. But fear of lifelong disability? Well, that is a different matter, apparently. As the CDC reports, scientific studies have shown that "emotionally evocative tobacco education media campaigns featuring graphic images of the health effects of smoking" are effective in helping people to quit. Since the launch of the TFFS campaign, "more than 5 million smokers have attempted to quit because of the campaign; and an estimated 500,000 have quit for good . . . . In addition, in the first year of the campaign alone, an estimated 6 million nonsmokers talked with friends and family about the dangers of smoking."[14] While the effort to reduce the number of smoking-related diseases and deaths is important and laudable, the TFFS campaign unfortunately pursues this effort by manipulating the already pervasive public fear and disgust of disability, thus contributing to the stigmatization of disabled bodies.

The displays of disability in both *Dancing with the Stars* and in many public health campaigns share a feature typical in most media. Disabled bodies are understood and positioned only in terms of their relationship to nondisabled bodies. In other words, disabled bodies are worthy subjects of media attention only when they provide something beneficial for those without disabilities, either by inspiring them or discouraging them from engaging in dangerous behaviors. Whether framed as inspiration or as a scare tactic, disability on display tells us much about public perceptions of disability and the way in which media both reflect and help to shape them.

Media serve as a tool of self-actualization, influencing the way that we think about ourselves in relationship to the images and messages we see reflected back at us on the page or screen. Media are also "a lens through which we view the world" and a primary means by which we encounter individuals and groups whose identities and experiences differ from our own.[15] For those whose interactions with disabled people are infrequent, narrow, or perfunctory, media representations are particularly powerful in creating knowledge and shaping attitudes about disability. Media messages are not absorbed uncritically, of course. But they "are key to the setting of agendas and focusing public interest on particular subjects," write media scholars Catherine Happer and Greg Philo, "which operates to limit the range of arguments and perspectives that inform public debate."[16] When media displays of disability distort and misrepresent actual lived disability experiences, therefore, they help to produce and perpetuate public misperceptions of disability that, in turn, contribute to the stigma surrounding disability and systemic discrimination against disabled people.

In some cases, however, media have the potential to disrupt dominant understandings of disability and to serve as a catalyst for social change. Particularly when their depictions are nuanced and complex, media representations of disability give audiences the opportunity to engage with disabled individuals in ways not always possible in the real world and encourage them to question their society's negative misperceptions and fears surrounding disability. Depictions of disability have the greatest "subversive power," argues Mia Harrison, when they grant the most stigmatized and marginalized characters the agency to reject their society's perception of them; when they present disability as the product of disabling environments and attitudes; and when they depict disability not as a feature of a handful of freakish outsiders but as a common, natural part of the human experience.[17]

In this chapter, I explore some ubiquitous displays of disability created and recycled in popular media, including television shows, movies, news stories, literature, and social media platforms. The displays that I have chosen are useful vehicles for addressing questions of disability representation in media more generally. What makes a particular representation of disability "good" or "bad," for example? Are these categories discrete and self-evident? What constitutes "authentic" disability representation? Who gets to decide? Are disability tropes always wholly negative or can they be useful mechanisms for analyzing and critiquing popular understandings of disability and the treatment of disabled people in specific historical and cultural locations? Ultimately, I demonstrate that we cannot improve disability representation in media simply through the greater presence of disabled people or the addition of more disabled characters—even when these characters are richly developed—but through wider structural changes that allow people with disabilities to participate fully in the creation, production, and performance of the stories that we tell. And so, the chapter concludes with an examination of the power of alternative narratives created by disabled people, who have been finding a larger visibility, community, and voice since the passage of the ADA, the proliferation of social media platforms, and wider opportunities for self-expression in the past few decades.

THE MEDIA'S ABLEIST GAZE

Disabled people currently comprise 15 percent of the global population, by far the world's largest minority group.[18] In the United States, more than one in four people live with a disability.[19] Disability is "everywhere," as historian Douglas Baynton has observed, yet "curiously absent" or woefully misrepresented in the stories that we create.[20] On television, the number of regular characters with disabilities on original scripted series reached only 2.1 percent during the 2018–2019 television season.[21] In the 100 highest-grossing movies of 2018, only 1.6 percent of speaking characters were portrayed as having some form of disability. The vast majority of disabled characters in media are white, cisgender, heterosexual men. Over 70 percent of characters in the top 100 movies of 2018 were male, while less than a third of characters with disabilities were women. Nearly three-quarters of disabled characters were white, while only 36.9 percent were from underrepresented racial or ethnic groups. Just two characters with a disability were from the LGB community, and no characters were transgender.[22] When television shows and movies feature characters with disabilities, disabled actors are rarely hired to portray them; in fact, more than 95 percent of characters with disabilities on television are played by nondisabled actors.[23]

A tremendous disparity exists, then, between the preponderance of disability in the real world and the near absence of disability in the stories that we tell. This disparity has significant consequences for disabled viewers, whose lack of positive representation in media can lead to poor self-esteem resulting from unfavorable comparisons with the "nondisabled ideal they see" in television and movies.[24] This was the case for Javy Gwaltney, a person with dysgraphia, who did not see himself positively reflected in the video games he loved to play as a child. "If I had had numerous role models influencing not just me, but the rest of the culture I inhabit as well, telling us that disabled people were strong and intelligent and valuable," he questions, "would I be as anxious and ashamed of a condition I have absolutely no control over?"[25] For disabled people of color, positive media representation is almost nonexistent. Growing up, singer and disability activist Lachi Offoha was unable to imagine for herself a future in the performing arts because there was absolutely no one on television who looked like her. "I had no ability to kind of visualize myself on screen or to visualize myself in front of crowds and audiences because . . . there was nothing [in media] to see."[26] Underrepresented and often invisible in media, disabled people rarely see themselves and their experiences reflected in popular culture and thus are more likely to believe that their lives are less valuable and their dreams and hopes unattainable.[27]

When disabled people do appear in popular media, they are rarely central to the narrative but serve instead to advance, foil, or add comic relief to the journey of the story's protagonist. The underrepresentation of disabled people as creators and producers of mainstream media means that disability is presented overwhelmingly through an "ableist gaze," that is, from the perspective of those without disabilities in service to an imagined audience of nondisabled people, and represented through negative, unrealistic, and stereotypical characters and storylines. Typically, disabled characters fit within a narrow range of constantly recycled disability tropes. The most ubiquitous tropes connect disability to violence and criminality (the "evil cripple"); portray disability as a tragic or pitiable condition best met through miraculous cure or a merciful death (the "tragic cripple"); link disability to the possession of extraordinary or supernatural abilities (the "supercrip" or the "mystic cripple"); or use disability to inspire nondisabled audiences to lead more authentic lives and to measure their own experiences more favorably by comparison ("inspiration porn").[28]

Perhaps the most recognizable disability trope in media is that of the "pitiful cripple." Symbolized most infamously by the character Tiny Tim in Charles Dickens's *A Christmas Carol*, the pitiful cripple is a sweet but tragic child or childlike figure whose "broken" and impaired body or mind evokes the pity and sympathy of nondisabled people. Spanning historical epochs and cultural genres, the pitiful cripple includes Quasimodo from *The Hunchback of Notre Dame*, John Merrick from *The Elephant Man*, Beth March from *Little Women*, Lennie from *Of Mice and Men*, and Boo Radley from *To Kill a Mockingbird*. One particularly insidious version of the pitiful cripple trope has appeared in several popular and critically acclaimed films from the last couple of decades in which central characters choose death over a life with paralysis. A recent example is the 2016 movie *Me Before You*, based on the bestselling novel by JoJo Moyes. In the film, a young and quirky woman named Louisa becomes caretaker of a deeply depressed man named Will, who had been paralyzed in an accident and no longer finds joy or value in his life. A formerly athletic, highly successful individual, Will experiences only pain, misery, and isolation following his spinal cord injury and considers himself a burden on his family and caretakers. Though Louisa, whose voice and perspective drive the narrative of the book and the film, tries desperately to "save him" with her Manic Pixie Dream Girl[29] charm and devotion, Will ultimately decides that a life with disability is not worth living and commits assisted suicide at the Dignitas Institute in Switzerland.

The film version of *Me Before You* sparked protest from many in the disability community over its terribly inaccurate and damaging portrayals of life with paralysis. Like the highly acclaimed and even award-winning films *The Sea Inside* and *Million Dollar Baby* (both released in 2004) before it, *Me Before You* cemented the widespread public assumption that paralysis was an unimaginable tragedy that foreclosed the possibility of a happy and fulfilling life.[30] As filmmaker Dominick Evans writes: "You can find success, love, fulfillment even if you happen to use a wheelchair. It is not the end of the world, and these films need to stop scaring people into thinking it is. We cannot change the narrative about disability when these kinds of films continued [sic] to be made."[31] Nor can we change the narrative when films like *The Sea Inside*, *Million Dollar Baby*, and *Me Before You* continue to present suicide as a brave and selfless action—the only viable and even responsible "choice"—for disabled people whose lives have been stunted by "tragedy." Such portrayals ignore the fact that real choice is not defined by being presented with only two poor options—that is, to take one's life or to live with a disability in an unaccommodating world. As disability scholar Beth Haller notes, "Society provides the option of death through assisted suicide to disabled people, but not the option of living in a supportive culture that values them as human beings."[32] People with disabilities, then, sometimes come to the conclusion that life is not worth living not so much because of the disabilities themselves, writes disability activist Kevin Irvine, but because of their inability to afford personal assistance needed to live independently at home, their inability to find decent employment due to discrimination, and the pervasive message from media and the public that their lives are tragic and pitiable. Fearing the impact, particularly on newly disabled people, of constant media messages preaching the "death over disability" doctrine, Ben Mattlin, who has spinal muscular atrophy, writes: "[H]ow many of those who are struggling to maintain self-esteem, who feel unsure of their right to exist, possess the courage and sheer chutzpah to withstand the invidious message that they're better off dead? That the world might be better off without them taking up space?"[33] Far too often in media and debates over the enactment of physician-assisted suicide laws in the states, the "death over disability" mantra rests on a highly medicalized view of disability that assumes that life with paralysis or other "crippling conditions" is intolerable due to the brokenness or inadequacies of the body itself instead of considering whether the intolerability stems largely from an inaccessible environment. Instead of working to secure laws that make it easier for a person with a disability to die, Irvine writes, "I think we should fight to make his or her life better—with adequate health care, home and community services, jobs, public transit, benefits—and role models who've successfully dealt with the same disability."[34]

The pitiful cripple trope is at the center of the charity model of disability, which depicts disability as an unfortunate medical problem to be solved by voluntary contributions from benevolent strangers, rather than an unjust social condition to be remedied by political action.[35] Historically, the charity model has driven many fundraising efforts for disability issues and causes, none more infamously than the Muscular Dystrophy Association (MDA) annual telethon hosted by the comedian/actor Jerry Lewis. Every Labor Day weekend starting in 1966 for over twenty hours on live television, Jerry Lewis would perform "his telethon shtick," writes historian Jon Wiener, "parading little kids in wheelchairs across the Las Vegas stage, making maudlin appeals for cash, alternatively mugging and weeping, and generally claiming to be a friend to the doomed."[36] Lewis's most notorious moment, perhaps, was during the 1973 telethon, when he held up a child with muscular dystrophy and declared, "God goofed, and it's up to us to correct his mistakes."[37] Year after year, the MDA telethon largely ignored adults living with muscular dystrophy and the burgeoning disability rights movement and instead centralized the sorrowful tales of little children—whom Lewis called "His Kids"—to elicit pity and big donations from viewers. Solely in terms of fundraising, the MDA telethon was a huge success—in its nearly fifty-year history, it raised over 2.5 billion dollars. But for many disabled people, the telethon's horribly misguided methods, goals, and rhetoric ended up causing greater harm to the very people it intended to benefit. In a now famous 1981 op-ed in the *New York Times*, Evan Kemp—the disability rights champion, Equal Opportunity Employment Commissioner, and executive director of the Disability Rights Center who himself lived with muscular dystrophy—argued that the MDA's presentation of disabled people as "childlike, helpless, hopeless, nonfunctioning and noncontributing members of society" perpetuated disability stigma and harmed disabled people's self-respect and efforts to live independent lives. By focusing singularly on a cure, Kemp wrote, the MDA failed to highlight the barriers to employment, transportation, education, housing, and recreation that "can be more devastating and wasteful of our lives than the diseases from which we suffer."[38] Similarly, former MDA poster child and disability activist Laura Hershey memorably wrote in a 1993 essay that while pity was an effective means of raising money, it was a major factor in disabled people's inability to achieve equality and respect. If you feel sorry for a person, she wrote, it is nearly impossible for you to see that person as your equal or to imagine them living or working alongside you.[39] For these views, however, Jerry Lewis had nothing but contempt. When correspondent Martha Teichner asked Lewis about the disability community's criticism of his and the MDA's pity approach to fundraising during a 2001 interview with *CBS News Sunday Morning*, he angrily responded that he was "just . . . telling people about a child in trouble," and "[i]f it's pity, we'll get some money." "Pity?" he scoffed. "You don't want to be pitied because you're a cripple in a wheelchair? Stay in your house!"[40]

Growing outrage over Lewis's offensive comments and the MDA's stigmatizing methods ultimately sparked organized protests from disability activists, including many who were, like Laura Hershey, former MDA poster children. In 1990, for example, Mike Ervin founded "Jerry's Orphans," a group of former "Jerry's Kids" who began to stage protests at the local broadcast of the telethon in Chicago. Soon, Jerry's Orphans grew into a nationwide network of disability activists committed to protesting the telethon and its use of the pity model to raise funds directed almost exclusively toward finding a cure.[41] Due to years of protests from Kemp, Ervin, Hershey, and dozens of other activists, the MDA finally decided in 2011 to end Lewis's tenure as host of the annual telethon—a decision that heralded "a great day for people with disabilities"[42]—and ended its telethon tradition altogether in 2014.[43] Just six years later, however, the MDA announced that it planned to offer a "reimagined" telethon that promised to depict people with disabilities in a positive and empowering light, an announcement that sparked immediate backlash from the disability community.[44] Using the hashtag #EndTheTelethon, disability activists like Dominick Evans and Emily Wolinsky organized protests on Twitter and other social media platforms to remind people of the telethon's damaging legacy and impact on the lives, self-image, and opportunities of so many disabled people.[45] Broadcast live on YouTube on October 24, 2020, "The MDA Kevin Hart Kids Telethon" dispensed with some of the more egregious methods and messages of the MDA telethon of old but still "missed the mark," according to many disability activists, by continuing to rely on cure narratives and images of (mostly white) children and by failing to centralize the most significant access barriers facing the disability community.[46]

Despite decades of protests from disability activists, representations of disability as pitiful and tragic remain common and even celebrated in the media landscape. In 2017, Zoey and I started watching a new reality competition show called *World of Dance* featuring dancers from all over the world competing for judges' points and the championship prize of one million dollars. During the season one semifinals of the competition, a dancer who is one half of the dancing duo known as Les Twins badly injured his ankle and was told by his doctor that he would not be able to compete. Determined to carry on, he decided to perform his part of the routine in a wheelchair, much to the astonished delight of the judges and audience. As Zoey and I watched their performance, my unease in seeing the dancer appear in a wheelchair quickly turned to disgust. Unlike his dancing partner brother, who was costumed in a sharp looking suit and tie and holding a briefcase, he appeared in tattered and disheveled clothes holding a cardboard sign that read, "Help Me!!! Destiny Uncertain." He might as well have been holding a tin cup and chirping "God bless us, everyone!" as he looked in supplication to his partner, who danced magnanimously above him while he groaned and held his head in despair. At the end of the routine, the crowd predictably screamed its approval while the judges praised the dancers for their provocative, emotive performance and expressed amazement that a dancer could perform so spectacularly while "confined" to a wheelchair.

The performance by Les Twins, the audience reaction, and the judges' comments all seem to be a product of the internalization of the pity and charity models of disability, an unquestioned assumption that people with disabilities are pitiful and depend solely on the benevolence and assistance of others to rescue them. The phrase "confined to a wheelchair," which is extremely common in the media and everyday conversation, is another manifestation of this assumption. A blogger named Karin writes that the phrases "confined to a wheelchair" and "wheelchair bound" are problematic not only because they evoke pity and limitations but also because they inaccurately characterize disabled people's relationship to their wheelchairs. No one is truly "bound" to a wheelchair, she accurately notes. Many people who use wheelchairs can walk to some extent and are able to get out of their chairs when they need to reach something or get into a car or restaurant booth, for example. Even those who cannot walk leave their wheelchairs to bathe or sleep. Furthermore, she points out, a wheelchair is not confining but a mobility device that allows its users to go nearly anywhere they choose. "Without my wheelchair, I would be bound and confined," she writes. "With it, I am free."[47]

In contrast to but no less stigmatizing than the pity model of disability is the "evil cripple" trope, which connects disability to villainy, violence, and criminality. Long a staple of popular media, the evil cripple trope has found expression in characters like Captain Ahab from *Moby Dick,* Captain Hook from *Peter Pan*, Mr. Potter from *It's a Wonderful Life,* the Joker from the Batman comics, Scar from *The Lion King*, and, more recently, Twisty the Clown from *American Horror Story.* The trope is particularly noticeable in media that feature characters with mental and/or intellectual disabilities, neurodiversities, or mental illnesses. Generated by the tremendous commercial success of the 1960 film, *Psycho*, the "mad is bad" stereotype features prominently in Hollywood films such as *Halloween, The Silence of the Lambs, Single White Female, Misery, American Psycho, The Village,* and, perhaps most notoriously, the 2016 film *Split* in which a man with dissociative identity disorder kidnaps and tortures a group of young women. Such depictions of characters with mental disabilities or some sort of unnamed psychoses committing horrific, gruesome acts contribute to the public perception that individuals with mental disabilities are inherently violent, even though such individuals are no more likely to commit violent acts than other members of the population and are, in fact, much more likely to be the victims, rather than the perpetrators, of violent crime.[48] Nevertheless, the "mad is bad" trope maintains a prominent place in popular culture and contributes to the stigma surrounding mental health disabilities. This stigma, in turn, contributes to the precarity of mentally disabled people, who have tremendous difficulties securing adequate employment and housing; accessing education and health care; and locating community support and services. Consequently, people with mental health disabilities experience staggeringly high rates of arrest, police violence, and incarceration.[49] This is especially true for Black people with disabilities who are victimized by policing protocols that scrutinize and target communities of color.[50]

While the stigmatizing impact of the pitiful and evil cripple tropes seems abundantly clear, the harms perpetrated by seemingly benevolent stereotypes of disability in popular media are perhaps less obvious. Most ubiquitous among these so-called "benevolent stereotypes" is the "supercrip" trope, in which disabled people are depicted as exceptional simply for managing to perform regular, everyday tasks—such as shopping for groceries or driving a car—or because they accomplish extraordinary activities—such as climbing a mountain or running a marathon.[51] Both of these supercrip narratives contribute to the marginalization of people with disabilities. As Sami Schalk points out, while the "regular supercrip" narrative "shows a person with a disability doing something 'just like everyone else,' the creation of the representation is premised upon the ableist assumption that people with disabilities do not do these things and thus are not just like everyone else."[52] And by demonstrating that disabled people are capable of accomplishing extraordinary feats, the "glorified supercrip narrative," writes Amita Kama, sends the clear message that the majority of disabled people who cannot demonstrate similar achievements "seem to be lacking in willpower and self-discipline. In other words, supercrips eclipse their peers who are thus negatively judged."[53] Such accomplishments, moreover, are nearly always portrayed as the result of individual determination, hard work, and courage and very rarely take into account how race and class privileges and a number of structural factors contribute to making such accomplishments possible.

One highly prominent manifestation of the supercrip trope in popular media is what Schalk calls the "superpowered supercrip," or "a character who has abilities or 'powers' that operate in direct relationship with or contrast to their disability." These superpowers overcompensate for the character's perceived physical or mental disability through displays of stunning physical strength, extraordinary mental acuity, or feats of bravery.[54] Examples include the Marvel Comics hero Daredevil, whose blindness following an accident provides him with "mutagenetically heightened" senses of smell, touch, and hearing; the character Gazelle from the movie *Kingsman: The Secret Service,* a bilateral amputee whose bladed leg prostheses serve as powerful weapons for taking out her enemies; or the characters Adrian Monk and Carrie Mathison from the shows *Monk* and *Homeland*, respectively, whose mental disabilities (OCD and bipolar disorder) give them extraordinary insights and crime-solving abilities.

As illustrated by the Monk and Mathison characters, the supercrip narrative often equates certain neurodiversities, especially autism, with genius-like or supernatural abilities. The quintessential example of the autism=genius narrative is the 1988 film *Rain Man* starring the allistic (a nonautistic person) actor, Dustin Hoffman. In the film, Hoffman plays an autistic man whose "deficiencies" in social interaction, language, and sensory processing are far outweighed by his extraordinary gifts for math and memory. One of the earliest depictions of autism in a major Hollywood film, *Rain Man* led to a proliferation of the autistic savant stereotype in other films, television shows, and novels and remains a central cultural referent for autism in the public mind thirty years later.[55] Despite the fact that only a tiny percentage of people with autism have savant-like abilities, there are very few autistic characters without these abilities in popular films, television shows, and literature.[56] Perhaps the most prominent example to date is Dr. Shawn Murphy, a fictional character with autism at the center of the television drama *The Good Doctor*. A massive hit with audiences since its premiere on the ABC network in the fall of 2017, the show chronicles the experiences of "a young surgeon with autism and Savant syndrome" as he works in "the pediatric surgical unit of a prestigious hospital."[57] Like *Rain Man* and other popular media sources—including the bestselling novel *The Curious Incident of the Dog in the Nighttime*—*The Good Doctor* once again offers a narrow and stereotypical view of autism through the image of a white man whose extraordinary gifts make up for the inherent "deficits" of his "disorder." Despite the abundance in recent years of books, blogs, websites, and YouTube videos created by autistic people that reflect the wide range of lived autism experiences, these types of popular media remain the sources from which many allistic individuals obtain their perceptions of people with autism,[58] and these perceptions have far-reaching consequences for autistic people. The blogger "breathingglass," for example, explains that she is often reluctant to share her autistic identity with her friends, all of whom have been convinced by books, films, television shows, and news stories that autistic people are super-talented geniuses. These sorts of expectations, she notes, make her feel inadequate in her ordinariness and send the message that she and other autistics are required to "make up for" their social "deficits" by excelling in other areas.[59]

It is in perpetuating the definition of autism in terms of social deviancy that shows like *The Good Doctor* inflict the most damage on the autism community, perhaps. In early advertisements prior to *The Good Doctor's* premiere, for example, a tagline for the show asked: "[C]an a person who doesn't have the ability to relate to people actually save their lives?"[60] In claiming that Dr. Shawn Murphy "doesn't have the ability to relate to people," *The Good Doctor* contributes to the harmful stereotype that all autistic people fundamentally lack "theory of mind," or the capacity to have empathy for and understanding of the intentions, thoughts, and beliefs of others. Most closely associated with the work of British psychologist Simon Baron-Cohen, theory of mind has become accepted wisdom in the field of psychology and remains the key explanation for understanding "deficits" in autistic cognition and behaviors within academic, medical, and therapeutic literature.[61] Coining the term "mindblindness" to describe this cognitive deficiency, Baron-Cohen wrote that "theory of mind difficulties seem to be universal among" autistic people, who do not understand that other people have their own mental states, lives, and experiences.[62] Yet, as Rachel Cohen-Rottenberg points out, nonautistic people who make similar mistakes in reading the beliefs and motives of neurodivergent people are considered "normal." Such a contradiction, she observes, demonstrates that theory of mind uses a neurotypical model for determining what and how a "normal" mind should be able to intuit and therefore pathologizes minds that do not work in the same way.[63] Even more damaging, as Melanie Yergeau notes, theory of mind calls into question the very humanity of autistic people. According to Baron-Cohen, theory of mind is "one of the quintessential abilities that make us human."[64] If theory of mind is integral to one's humanity, what does this mean for the humanity of those who do not seem to possess it? For Yergeau, the message is clear. If "h]umans are human because they possess a theory of mind," then "autistics are inhuman because they do not."[65] If autistic people are seen as less than fully human, it is much easier to speak on their behalf, to refuse them equal opportunities, to deny their autonomy over their own bodies, and to medicate and institutionalize them against their will. By pathologizing neurodivergent minds and robbing autistic people of their agency and humanity, Yergeau argues, theory of mind and the discourses that perpetuate it contribute to the disfranchisement and violence continually inflicted on the bodies of autists and other neurodiverse individuals.[66]

Quite often, autism, mental disabilities, or other vague neurodiversities give characters in literature, television, and movies not only savant-like gifts but also supernatural, psychic, or paranormal abilities. The plot of Stephen King's 1979 novel *The Dead Zone*, for instance, centers on a man whose brain injury from a car accident results in a powerful form of psychometry, which he uses to help the local police force solve crimes. In the short-lived television series *Touch,* a boy with autism who is obsessed with numbers and cell phones is able to predict the future by detecting invisible threads of energy that bind the world together. And in the Marvel comics series *Legion,* the eponymous character's dissociative identity disorder gives him multiple superpowers, including telepathy, telekinesis, and pyrokinesis.

Neurodiverse characters with supernatural abilities used for selfless purposes fit within a larger tradition of the "Magical Other," usually defined by a character with some sort of vague, often unnamed neurodiversity or social disability that gives them supernatural or genius-like gifts used in service of the story's protagonist. Magical Others appear in media most notoriously through characters of color, whose sole narrative purpose is to teach white characters important values or life lessons. Indigenous people, in particular, have long been mispresented in media through the Magical Other trope. From Iron Eyes Cody (who was not, in fact, an Indigenous person but played one on TV) who cried over white men's carelessness with the Earth's natural resources in the infamous 1970s "Keep America Beautiful" public service announcement; to Jacob Black (played by non-Indigenous actor Taylor Lautner) who used his shape-shifting abilities less to defend his fellow Quileutes and more to protect the white heroine from murderous vampires in Stephanie Meyer's *Twilight* book series; to the Navajo skin walkers who serve as early examples of Animagi in J.K. Rowling's deeply problematic digital story collection, *History of Magic in North America,* Indigenous characters are important exclusively for their ability to inspire white characters through the examples of their own innate spirituality, mysticism, and connection to the earth.

Another racially offensive subset of the Magical Other trope is the "Magical Negro," a humble, pure, and folksy Black character with magical abilities sometimes related to a disability that he or she uses exclusively to redeem a troubled or broken white (usually male) main character.[67] For example, in the film *The Green Mile* (1999), a Black man with an unidentified intellectual or developmental disability has magical healing powers and spends the entire movie trying to cure various white characters, including his jailers, instead of using his gifts to free himself from his wrongful incarceration. In the film *The Legend of Bagger Vance* (2000), a vagrant and preternaturally wise Black man, played by Will Smith, mysteriously appears in the narrative solely to guide a traumatized World War I veteran and golfer, played by Matt Damon, back on the path of happiness and wholeness. Criticizing the Magical Negro trope during a talk at Yale University in 2001, director Spike Lee questioned why Black characters with magical powers in films like *Ghost, What Dreams May Come,* and *The Family Man* used their abilities to benefit white people instead of themselves. Referring to *Bagger Vance* specifically, he said:

"Blacks are getting lynched left and right [in 1930s America] and [Bagger Vance is] more concerned about improving Matt Damon's golf swing! . . . . They're still doing the same old thing ... recycling the noble savage and the happy slave."[68]

Many media that feature Magical Others receive critical praise and popular approval for their inclusion of diverse characters, "progressive" portrayals of cooperation between differently situated individuals, and empowerment of people from traditionally marginalized groups. But magical othering is simply a modern incarnation of the same damaging stereotyping of minorities disguised as progressive and emancipatory. Writing specifically about the Magical Negro trope in Hollywood films, historian Matthew Hughey responds to the celebration of the greater visibility of African Americans in ostensibly sympathetic roles by pointing out that "[v]isibility and acceptance is not a guarantee of legitimacy or decency, but it is a precondition of regimes of surveillance."[69] The relationship between the lowly but wise Black supporting character and the white protagonist, he continues, "reinforces a normative climate of white supremacy within the context of the American myth of redemption and salvation whereby whiteness is always worthy of being saved, and strong depictions of blackness are acceptable in so long as they serve white identities."[70] Fundamentally, the selfless, saintly, humble Magical Negro is an acceptable and even celebrated identity in mainstream Hollywood films, Hughey argues, because it offers white audiences powerful but anodyne Black characters and palatable narratives that affirm their overt or subconscious belief in the superiority of whiteness over blackness. Most importantly, perhaps, the Magical Negro trope represents the possibility of racial harmony predicated on individual acts of kindness instead of the messier, harder, and more painful work of real structural and institutional change.[71]

In many ways, Hughey's analysis is applicable to magical disabled characters. The greater visibility of disabled characters in films and on television might suggest on the surface the public's growing acceptance of and comfort with disability in the real world. Yet, the persistence and pervasiveness of the Magical Other demonstrates that this does not seem to be the case. Magical Others are rarely well-rounded or complex; instead, they tend to be one-dimensional characters who exist in the narrative solely because of their magical abilities. "They're rarely just a regular person dealing with their own crap alongside the rest of the cast," as Corinne Duyvis notes. "Instead, their disability and their ability—and the seeming contradiction thereof— are defining aspects of their characters."[72] In whatever form it appears, then, the Magical Other trope does not advance the representation of traditionally marginalized individuals but rather highlights their differences from, and thus inferiority to, hegemonic norms. Disabled characters can never just be "regular" characters whose disabilities do not constitute their only identity and purpose in the narrative. Much like savantism is imprinted on autistic characters who would otherwise be unworthy of visibility, magical powers are given to disabled characters to give these characters purpose and to make them more palatable to presumably nondisabled audiences who find disabilities repugnant or disturbing. Disabled characters, then, need to possess magical or extraordinary abilities and—this is key—always use these abilities to benefit nondisabled characters in order to transcend the "deficits" attached to their identities and to ease society's fear and loathing of disability.

As illustrated in the supercrip and Magical Other tropes, media stories about disability are rarely meant to be about people with disabilities; rather, their purpose is to teach the nondisabled protagonist some important life lesson or to inspire him or her to be a better person. The idea that disabled people exist in the story, or in real life for that matter, for the benefit of nondisabled people is known as "inspiration porn." Pervasive in all forms of mass media and widely circulated through social media platforms such as Facebook and Twitter, inspiration porn includes "heartwarming" images, videos, or stories about how nondisabled people are so inspired by the lives and actions of disabled people—even when these actions are quotidian and mundane—that they are motivated to improve their own lives or to perform some sort of selfless act. The late comedian, writer, and activist, Stella Young—who coined the term "inspiration porn"—spoke at length during her 2014 TEDxSydney talk about how her Osteogenesis imperfecta made her the frequent subject of inspiration porn narratives. There was the time when she was fifteen, for example, when a local community organization wanted to give her a community achievement award simply because she was disabled and not because she had "actually achieved anything." Years later while speaking to a group of high schoolers about defamation law, she was interrupted by a student who wanted to know when she was going to "start her speech." Puzzled, she asked him to what speech he was referring, to which he replied, "'You know, like, your motivational speaking. You know, when people in wheelchairs come to school, they usually say, like, inspirational stuff? It's usually in the big hall.'" This comment, she explained, led to her sudden realization that this student, like most other people, had only ever experienced disabled individuals as objects of inspiration:

> For lots of us, disabled people are not our teachers or our doctors or our manicurists. We're not real people. We are there to inspire. . . . I've lost count of the number of times that I've been approached by strangers wanting to tell me that they think I'm brave or inspirational, and this was long before my work had any kind of public profile. They were just kind of congratulating me for managing to get up in the morning and remember my own name.[73]

Inspiration porn includes the dozens of images of smiling children running on prosthetic legs with captions like, "What's Your Excuse?" or "Your Excuse is Invalid!" It includes the story of the homecoming queen who was celebrated for giving up her crown to a student with cerebral palsy.[74] It includes the tale of the high school wrestler who was called a hero for allowing himself to be beaten by an opponent with an intellectual disability.[75] And it includes the viral video of a Qdoba restaurant employee who was praised for helping a customer in a wheelchair eat her meal.[76] Regardless of how large or small the act, notes blogger Kim Sauder, social media users treat nondisabled people who interact in any positive way with disabled people as heroes whose generosity "restores our faith in humanity" and "teaches us the meaning of kindness."[77]

Far from innocuous, feel-good stories and images that celebrate the generosity of the human spirit or the achievements of disabled people, inspiration porn perpetuates damaging misperceptions about people with disabilities that contribute to their "othering" and marginalization. As Stella Young noted, the purpose of stories and images that portray people with disabilities accomplishing magnificent feats is not to convince their audience of the worth and equality of disabled people. Rather, their purpose "is to inspire you, to motivate you, so that we can look at them and think, 'Well, however bad my life is, it could be worse. I could be that person.' But what if you are that person?"[78] Similarly, stories that highlight nondisabled people's acts of kindness toward those with disabilities reinforce disabled people's otherness by framing them as appropriate and necessary recipients of pity and charity—as the story about the nondisabled student who allowed his disabled opponent to win the wrestling match effectively illustrates. While the nondisabled wrestler might have had the best of intentions, as journalist John Altmann notes, he reinforced "segregation by laying down for his opponent rather than giving him his best." "His sympathy became toxic."[79]

Perhaps most consequently, inspiration porn harms people with disabilities by perpetuating the neoliberal idea that disability is an individual problem best solved through individual effort or through the magnanimity of nondisabled saviors.[80] While there is certainly nothing wrong with applauding and admiring the individual achievements of disabled people, we perpetuate harm when we assume that such achievements are simply the result of individual determination or that such achievements are available to all people with disabilities with a bit of pluck and hard work. Within this individualist, neoliberal framework, people with disabilities who have not managed to climb Mount Everest, run a marathon, produce works of art, solve complex mathematical equations, or warm the hearts of others through their courageous, noble spirit are perceived as having failed somehow, of having not tried hard enough, and are thus less deserving of rights and public recognition. Such a framework also depoliticizes disability by shifting attention away from institutional and systemic barriers. One little recognized aspect of the Qdoba story, for example, was the inaccessibility of the restaurant's entrance, which forced the disabled customer to sit outside in her wheelchair until a store employee or patron opened the door for her. What could have become an important and influential story about the disabling impact of obstacles in the built environment became instead an inspirational tale in which one woman's disability was "overcome" through the generosity of a caring employee. "It seems to me that if everybody in the world would just use the little simple gift that they have to maybe benefit somebody else," one customer who observed the charitable act noted, "think what the world would be like."[81] As the media coverage of the Qdoba incident and so many other stories illustrate, inspiration porn perpetuates harm by refusing to recognize how disability is largely a product of unequal access to health care and education, discriminatory hiring practices, and institutional and attitudinal barriers.

Ultimately, inspiration porn is harmful because it robs disabled people of mastery over their own stories. Inspiration porn uses the images and experiences of disabled people—often without their knowledge or consent—for the benefit of nondisabled people, who are always the central subjects of the narrative. Circulated through media outlets and social media platforms, the Qdoba story was characterized again and again as a person's "simple act of kindness" toward someone less fortunate and an example of the generosity of the human spirt. And yet, as Sauders points out, the video was filmed by another customer and posted online without the consent of the woman with the disability, whose name and background were unidentified. Created by and for nondisabled people, inspiration porn, then, uses disability as a plot point to say something about the goodness and generosity of nondisabled heroes while erasing disabled people's identity and agency by appropriating their "stories for the consumption of others."[82] As Mat Fraser, an actor with phocomelia, succinctly puts it, "Inspiration porn's what happens when you leave a story around disability in a room with nondisabled people who don't know many disabled people."[83]

CREATING MORE "AUTHENTIC"
DISABILITY REPRESENTATIONS

Popular media have a long tradition of misrepresenting disability primarily because disabled people have been largely excluded from participation in crafting the stories about their own lives and experiences. Perhaps the most glaring example of this exclusion is the persistent casting of nondisabled actors to play characters with disabilities. Known as "disappropriation,"

or "cripping up," the widespread phenomenon of nondisabled actors playing disabled characters in films, theater, and television shows is sometimes
equated with the tradition of blackface in order to illustrate the offensiveness
of the practice. Yet, many disability activists rightly point out that uncomplicated comparisons between cripping up and blackface are a form of cultural
appropriation that ignores the way in which these practices are rooted in
very particular histories and cultural specificities and that such comparisons
contribute to the invisibility and erasure of Black disabled people.[84] As disability rights media activist MaeLee Johnson explains, "'comparing disabled
mimicry to blackface . . . ignores the fact [that] black disabled folks have to
deal with both racism and ableism'" and that they experience these forms of
oppression simultaneously.[85] Or as Anita Cameron, a disability rights activist
with ADAPT and Not Dead Yet, more succinctly puts it: "'When cripface is
compared to Blackface, it is insulting, inappropriate and flat out wrong. Just
don't do it.'"[86]

The practice of cripping up rarely receives criticism outside of the disability
community; in fact, there is a long list of nondisabled actors who have earned
critical praise and even Oscars for playing disabled characters in films.[87]
Hollywood loves disability performances but not disabled actors, apparently.
In its more than ninety-year history, the Academy of Motion Picture Arts
and Sciences has given acting awards to only two people with disabilities.
In 1947, Harold Russell won a supporting actor Oscar for the film *The Best
Years of Our Lives* in which he portrayed a wounded World War II veteran.
His performance reflected his own experience during the war, when he lost
both of his hands in an accidental explosion while performing a training demonstration. Forty years later, Deaf actress Marlee Matlin won the top acting
Oscar for her role in *Children of a Lesser God*, in which she played a custo-
dian at a school for deaf and hard of hearing students. Attempting to explain
why disabled actors are rarely cast to play disabled characters, Christopher
Shinn, a disabled playwright, argues that cripping up is fundamentally the
product of mainstream audience's unease with confronting the actual lived
experiences of disability. Performances of disability by nondisabled actors,
he writes, give the audience "the comforting assurance that we are not
witnessing the actual pain and struggle of real disabled human beings; it is
all make believe."[88] Fundamentally, then, audiences do not want to be confronted with actual disabilities, only the illusion of disability, and are much
more interested in disability as a metaphor—meant to symbolize "the triumph
of the human spirit, or the freakishness we all feel inside"—rather than disability as an actual experience.[89] Finally, the presence of a disabled body on
screen is a far too potent reminder of the impermanence and vulnerability
of our own bodies and the disability that we will all inevitably face, either
through illness, injury, or the process of aging. As Alyssa Armbar Andrews,

who identifies as disabled and queer, notes: "Disability is something that can happen to any person at any time—and that's a reality that's hard to face. It's hard to face when you are disabled, why wouldn't it be hard to face when you are able-bodied and aware that you could become disabled?"[90]

When disabled people are excluded from participation in the crafting and performance of stories about disability, the stories are much more likely to portray people with disabilities in stereotypic and less authentic ways. Pointing to the movie *Me Before You* as one example, Dominick Evans notes that disabled people were not included nor even consulted in the making of the film (and many disability advocates were quick to point out that the book on which the film was based was authored by a nondisabled woman who did not consult any individuals with quadriplegia when writing her narrative). "Even the main actor is an able-bodied actor," Evans writes, "which prevents him from knowing how accurate his acting, how harmful his portrayal, and how inauthentic the script really are." As Evans's comment suggests, the lived experiences of disability bring a genuineness to portrayals of disabled characters that the portrayals by nondisabled actors cannot. "We are better at playing ourselves than other people," Mat Fraser argues. "We just are."[91] For actor Rachel Handler, disability creates a particular identity and world-view, and having a disabled body shapes how one moves, inhabits spaces, and interacts with other people. "A non-disabled actor," she argues, "is not able to understand or portray these subtle, but crucial differences."[92] Such inauthentic and stigmatizing representations of disability in media have damaging consequences for disabled individuals in the real-world. "Hollywood continues to make life harder for us," Evans notes, "because this is all people see, and they assume it's true." But "if Hollywood showed more disabled actors . . . and the stories were more reflective of the disabled experience, then people would believe disabled lives were worth living."[93]

When people with disabilities are not intimately and actively involved in creating stories about their lives, these stories are not only inauthentic but also potentially harmful. One recent illustration is the controversial 2020 film, *Music*, directed and cowritten by Australian pop star Sia. The film follows the journey of a character named Zu, who takes over the guardianship of her nonverbal, autistic sister, Music. Played by nonautistic performer Maddie Ziegler, Music is a "magical little girl" whose savant-like abilities allow her to interpret her world through song and dance and whose sole purpose in the narrative is to inspire her sister and those around her to live fuller, richer lives. Early trailers for the film featuring a grinning, rocking, flapping, head-bobbing Ziegler sparked a flood of criticism from members of the autistic community, who criticized the casting of a neurotypical actor in the eponymous role and the film's narrow, stereotypical, and inauthentic representation of life on the autism spectrum.[94] Charlie Hancock, for example, wrote that such representations only magnify pervasive misconceptions about autism and have "serious implications for impacting how people perceive the condition and autistic people. It can even make it harder for autistic people, especially women, to get a diagnosis if they don't fit the mould of autism that Hollywood has perpetuated over the years."[95] But most egregious for autism rights advocates was a scene in the film where Music is physically restrained while she is experiencing a meltdown. In a joint statement from CommunicationFIRST, the Autistic Self Advocacy Network, and the Alliance Against Seclusion and Restraint, Zoe Gross—ASAN's Director of Advocacy—noted that "MUSIC doesn't just promote harmful stereotypes about autistic people—it shows restraints that have killed members of our community as necessary and loving acts. . . . This film should never have been made, and it shouldn't be shown."[96]

Angered by the backlash to her film, Sia responded to her critics in a series of furious social media posts that only confirmed her ignorance of the complexity of autism and the existence of a thriving community of autistic self-advocates, none of whom had been consulted in the creation of the film.[97] Despite her insistence that her screenplay was based on three years of autism research, her claim that people with autism are not disabled but have "special abilities"; her praise for the "purity" of the "special abilities people" who bring light and inspiration to a dark and violent world; her acknowledgment that the Music character was based on a boy with autism she once knew; her description of the film as "*Rain Man* the musical, but with girls"; her insistence that casting an autistic performer at Music's "level of functioning" would be untenable and even "cruel"; her claim that she had "no idea" that Autism Speaks (which was apparently involved in promoting the film) was a "polarizing" organization; and her unawareness of the dangers and illegality of physical restraints demonstrate the paucity and misguidedness of her so-called "research efforts."[98] Facing mounting criticisms, particularly after the film was nominated for two Golden Globe awards, Sia finally apologized to the autistic community through a February 3 tweet in which she acknowledged that her "research was clearly not thorough enough" and that she had "listened to the wrong people."[99] She also announced that a warning would be added to the film stating that "MUSIC in no way condones or recommends the use of restraint on autistic people" and that those scenes would be removed from "all future printings."[100]

As films like *Me Before You* and *Music* (and so many others) demonstrate, the continual failure to cast, include, or even consult disabled people in the creation of stories about disability leads to stereotypic and dangerous portrayals that have serious consequences for the disability community. Likewise, the widespread reluctance to hire disabled actors to play characters not specifically identified as disabled contributes to ableist attitudes and practices by sending a message to audiences that disabled people are unimaginable in these roles.[101] During his audition for a role as a physician on a popular television series, actor Danny Woodburn, for example, was explicitly told by the casting director that someone like him "could never be a doctor." The idea that a man with dwarfism could be a doctor or that a man with dwarfism could play a role that did not specifically relate to his dwarfism was, apparently, inconceivable.[102] Such perceptions are both created and perpetuated by popular media that rarely feature disabled people engaging in ordinary, everyday occupations and activities; instead, people with disabilities are usually assigned to roles in which their disability comprises the totality of their identity and importance to the story. While disabled actors playing disabled characters can promote more authentic representations of disability, their restriction to roles specifically coded as disabled promotes the assumption that those are the only roles for which they are suited or capable and can make it difficult for nondisabled people to see people with disabilities as anything other than simply "disabled." Furthermore, the assumption that disabled characters are more authentic when they are played by disabled people can actually work against this authenticity when these characters and the storylines they serve are stereotypical, which can legitimize the stereotypes and make it more difficult for audiences to recognize the depictions as problematic.[103]

The exclusion or underrepresentation of disabled perspectives and involvement in the creative process, Vilissa Thompson argues, "does incredible damage to our community. It fails to support the disabled artists, writers, and actors who want a seat at the table, and yet, are considered an afterthought for these entertainment projects."[104] Better and more authentic representations of disability in media, therefore, depend not only on creating greater and more subversive roles for disabled actors but also on more extensive, structural changes that work to break down barriers to the full inclusion of disabled people in every aspect of the creative process. In addition to making casting more inclusive, the spaces in which actors work must be accessible, for example. Too often, according to Danny Woodburn, audition rooms, production locations, industry offices, professional development events, and other spaces are not accessible to people with disabilities, which sends the clear message that disabled bodies and minds were not meant to inhabit those spaces. "By putting the actor with a disability in a position to ask for access," adds Woodburn, "we easily create an unconscious bias toward the actor who made a request prior to even interviewing for the job."[105] People with disabilities need to be involved in every aspect of content creation. For Judith Heumann, the role of disabled people in the creation and performance of disability stories should be equal to the number of disabled people in U.S. society, and therefore "should be one in four, in front of and behind the camera, in characters, in actors, in directors, in writers' rooms, and more."[106] Greater and more proportionate inclusion, Thompson agrees, is crucial for authentic disability representation. "[W]hether in books, comics, TV, or films," she notes, "we need actually disabled people consulted, writing, producing, directing, and casted to tell our experience the way it should be."[107]

Disability tropes in media are created by and for nondisabled people and serve ableist ends. Yet, it is important to remember that texts—that is, books, documents, films, utterances, or any medium through which meaning is constituted and cultural practices organized—have no fixed or intrinsic meanings but are polysemic and constantly shifting. The meaning of any text, in other words, is dependent on the person interpreting the text within highly specific cultural and historical contexts.[108] Produced by complex power mechanisms, multiple meanings constantly compete for authority and legitimacy, and some emerge as normative while others are rendered subordinate or deviant. Challenges to constructed norms understood as "truths" are extremely difficult, given that these challenges take place in the same discursive field as the claims to truths reside.[109] Yet, rather than passively absorbing hegemonic discourses, diverse individuals actively engage with cultural texts and meanings in ways that are shaped by their own experiences, perspectives, and historical and social locations. From these highly particular and variable standpoints, individuals and groups produce situated knowledges from which they often read texts subversively, that is, in ways that unsettle and undermine the text's hegemonic and normative discourses.[110] "Cripping" a text, for example, is to read a text in ways that destabilize its ableist messages or in ways that imaginatively inject disability into the narrative, a critical position that has tremendous transgressive potential.[111]

Cripping dominant narratives about disability is one example of the way in which media can serve not only as producers and perpetuators of stigma and oppression but also vehicles for the eradication of social injustice. Disabled actors are able to help transform perceptions of disability, for instance, not only when they play disabled characters but also when they "play across disability," that is, when they portray characters not specifically written as disabled. Disabled actors in these sorts of roles can perform a type of "subversive advocacy" by bringing creativity and fresh interpretations to established works. One notable example is the depiction of Ado Annie by Ali Stroker, a wheelchair-using actress, in the 2019 Broadway production of *Oklahoma.* Another is disabled actor Regan Linton's portrayal of Aldonza in a 2009 theatrical production of *Man of La Mancha* staged by the Physically Handicapped Actors and Musical Artists League, an ensemble of actors with physical or mental disabilities. In this version of the play, Aldonza is a wheelchair user whose chair is stolen from her during a brutal sexual assault. When Linton, a T4 paraplegic, cried out for Don Quixote to "see me as I really am . . . a creature who'll never do better than crawl," she was literally crawling on the stage, thus giving Aldonza's words a powerfully new meaning and inviting the audience to see her experience from a disability point of view.[112]

Equally powerful are the many alternative narratives of disability created by disabled people, who have been finding a larger visibility, community, and voice since the passage of the Americans with Disabilities Act, the proliferation of social media platforms, and wider opportunities for self-expression in the past few decades. Recent years have witnessed the publication of a plethora of disability memoirs that have the potential to serve as counter discourses to stereotypic portraits of disability. Authors such as Simi Linton, Eli Clare, Stephen Kuusisto, Nancy Mairs, Roxanne Gay, Naoki Higashida, Terry Galloway, and so many others have deepened my own perspectives and given me a much fuller portrait of the complexity, diversity, challenges, and richness of lived disability experiences. Writing and posting pictures and videos through social media platforms such as blogs, Facebook, Twitter, Disaboom, and YouTube is another highly important means by which people with disabilities connect to disability communities, pursue disability activism, and share information about disability experiences. Writers and activists such as Lydia X. Z. Brown, William Peace, Cara Liebowitz, Mel Baggs, Amy Sequenzia, among many others, comment on issues that rarely receive mainstream media coverage, such as the impact of the ADA, access to transportation, housing, and jobs, and the effects of violence, stigma, and discrimination.[113]

People with disabilities have long produced creative and artistic works that offer alternative narratives of disability. Discouraged by the scarcity of books that "show disability in a lighthearted way" or that depict "disability as a normal part of life," teenager Melissa Shang, for example, wrote a novel about a joyful, wheelchair-using, middle-schooler named Mia Lee, who eats lunch in the school cafeteria with her friends, takes lots of selfies, and goes to the movies on the weekend. But Shang's attempts to find a publisher for her novel were unsuccessful. As more than one editor informed her, her depiction of a character with a degenerative disease who used a wheelchair was simply "too happy" and thus contrasted too sharply with conventional narratives in which disability is portrayed as a misfortune and nondisabled characters are depicted as kind-hearted protagonists. Shang eventually used the funds from a Kickstarter campaign to self-publish her book on Amazon, where hundreds of copies of *Mia Lee is Wheeling Through Middle School* have been sold. She often spies her book on the return cart of her local library and speculates about who has read it. "Maybe it was someone who would go on to invite the special needs kid in his class over for a play date," she wonders. "Or maybe, it was another kid with a disability, who could point to the pages and say: 'She's just like me! And she's happy, too!'"[114] On Facebook, Bethany Stevens has started a visual culture campaign titled "This is What Disability

Looks Like" featuring images of people with disabilities "that do NOT pander to sentimentality, inspiration and/or paternalism like many images that have circulated around social media of late." People with disabilities submit photos of themselves and add a tagline in response to the "This is What Disability Looks Like" prompt. The campaign's Facebook page is full of images of diverse people with a wide array of disabilities who variously describe themselves as "proud," "beautiful," "tech savvy," "happily married," "unapologetic," "Christian and queer," and "irreverent." Describing the significance of the campaign and its images, Stevens writes: "Providing space for folks to come up with their own tag-line or language to go along with their images—gives disabled people that all too infrequent space to speak for themselves/ourselves! Let's tell our truths, rather than have someone else. NOTHING ABOUT US, WITHOUT US!"[115] Founded by Leroy Moore, Jr. in 2007, the group Krip-Hop Nation promotes the music of hip-hop artists with disabilities through its website, publications, radio show, performances, and other events. Its stated goals are to educate the music industry and the public at large about the history, talents, and marketability of disabled musicians and "to get the musical talents of hip-hop artists with disabilities into the hands of media outlets, educators, and hip-hop, disabled and race scholars, youth, journalists and hip-hop conference coordinators."[116] In 2017, Leroy Moore was invited to present his work titled "Black/Brown International Disability Art and Hip-Hop" at the Whitney Museum of American Art in New York City. Explaining the significance of this work, Moore noted that it demonstrated "how the state treats people with disabilities around the world and how people with disabilities are connecting through our art and music and talking about our stories through oppression, invisibility and cultural appropriation. I finally think we are coming to a place of acceptance and pride."[117]

While people with disabilities are still vastly underrepresented and mischaracterized in mainstream media, there are growing signs of progress. Major newspapers like *The New York Times* include articles about disability written by disabled people whose frank discussions of their daily lives and experiences with ableism attempt to dismantle dominant ideas about bodies and minds and to call attention to the inaccessibility of public spaces. Companies have begun to feature people with disabilities in their advertising in ways that "normalize" disability experiences. By picturing disabled and nondisabled children engaging together in typical childhood activities like trick-or-treating or posing in back-to-school clothing in its weekly circulars, the retail chain store, Target, for example, makes disability visible without othering disabled experiences. Models with paralysis, amputated limbs, and Down syndrome have started to appear more frequently in fashion advertising and even on the catwalk during New York Fashion Week, challenging traditional ideas about bodies and beauty. Remarking on the importance of disability representation in advertising, Jillian Mercado, a model with spastic muscular dystrophy who has appeared in advertising campaigns for Diesel Jeans and in merchandise ads for Beyonce's "Formation" tour, said that she initially found little support for her desire to become a fashion model "'because I didn't see anyone else like me out there.'" Disabled people need to be represented in advertising and in all forms of media, she noted, so that individuals with diverse bodies and minds can finally see themselves in cultural representations and so that images of disability will no longer be exceptional.[118]

On television, people with disabilities are becoming more visible. The show *Switched at Birth* features deaf characters played by deaf or hard of hearing actors, one of whom has a leading role, and even included one episode in which the actors communicate entirely in American Sign Language. The reality show *Born This Way* features adults with Down syndrome living independently, enjoying friendships, navigating workplaces, and experiencing romantic relationships. On the long-running children's television series, *Sesame Street*, an autistic Muppet named Julia made her debut in 2017. Created in consultation with autistic self-advocates,[119] Julia is a girl with bright red hair and green eyes whose unique way of communicating and moving about her world form part of a happy, joyful life.

One recently canceled television show that earned high praise from many within the disability community (and was a favorite in my family) is titled *Speechless*, a sitcom about a young man with cerebral palsy, J.J. DiMeo, who is nonverbal and communicates through a laser pointer and a word/alphabet board attached to his motorized wheelchair. Remarkable in a media landscape where disabled roles are played by nondisabled actors 95 percent of the time, J.J. was played by Micah Fowler, a teenage actor with cerebral palsy whose character is the focal point of the show. *Speechless* is based largely on creator Scott Silveri's experiences growing up with a brother with cerebral palsy, and members of the Cerebral Palsy Foundation were regular show consultants. Funny and irreverent, the show's storylines often focus on J.J. and his financially strapped family's attempts to make the world more accessible by calling out disabling attitudes and environments; just as often, J.J. is featured as a fairly typical teenager who attempts to navigate issues of school, romance, and family squabbles similar to other kids his age. J.J.'s disability is neither tragic nor inspirational, and characters who treat it as such appear buffoonish. In a memorable scene from the pilot episode, J.J.'s entrance into a classroom at his new mainstream school is met with a roaring standing ovation from his teacher and classmates, who quickly decide to name him class president on his very first day. In another episode, students in the school compete in an essay contest in which they are required to write about their personal hero. J.J. is disgusted to learn that a student he barely knows has chosen him as the subject of his essay based on the student's presumption that the judges will be swayed by a lachrymose tale of an inspiring disabled person. J.J. describes the story as "inspiration porn," adding "I blame Tiny Tim." In this way, *Speechless* flips the script of the traditional disability narrative by positioning the disabled character at the center of the story and using his perspective to illustrate the absurdity and artificiality of the ableist gaze. *Speechless* demonstrates what is possible when stories about disability are told with authenticity and respect for disabled lives. While stories about disability created and acted by people with disabilities are still terribly scarce in popular media, shows like *Speechless* can work to change public perceptions of disability and to promote the importance of wider and more realistic disability representations in culture. As Micah Fowler noted in a December 2016 interview with *Vulture*, "I think *Speechless* will encourage viewers to look beyond the physical or other limitations of special-needs people who come into their own lives and discover their love, personality, and even their humor!"[120]

The foregoing discussion about media representations of disability is nowhere close to exhaustive, nor does it attempt to be. It is meant merely to provide a glimpse into the most common media tropes and stereotypes and the ways in which disabled artists, writers, and activists are working to challenge them. Despite the overwhelming preponderance of negative images of disability in media, I am encouraged by narratives that push back against the damaging tropes I have come to expect nearly every time I encounter disability in a mainstream novel, movie, television show, advertisement, or Facebook post. And yet, disability stereotypes and metaphors can serve a useful, generative function. They present a "representational conundrum," as Carrie Sandahl puts it, helpful for thinking about the differences between representations of disability in narrative and the material reality of lived, disability experiences.[121] Narratives that present disability as an individual tragedy, for example, can generate useful conversations about the joy and positivity of many disabled lives and the disabling impact of environments, policies, and attitudes. Disability's representation as magical and powerful can help to highlight the precarity and disfranchisement of disabled people. Thinking of disability representation in this way allows us to move beyond the sometimes reductive project of merely identifying and judging stereotypes, Sandahl notes, and toward the more productive task of using disability tropes in popular media to analyze shifting meanings of disability and the complexity and materiality of disabled experiences within specific historical and social locations.[122] What can we learn, then, by comparing popular media's disability representation with actual disabled experiences? How can such a comparison improve the status and opportunities of people who live with disabilities? What does an examination of disability narratives from different time periods and/or cultures tell us about shifting views of disability across time and place? In short, what are the values of stereotypes as narrative devices, and how "[m]ight we harness a stereotype's power and instant recognizability to purposeful ends"?[123]

Feminist author Carolyn Heilbrun once wrote that "[p]ower consists to a large extent in deciding what stories will be told."[124] Authentic disability representation cannot be achieved, therefore, only through the multiplication of disabled characters on screen, even when they are complexly depicted. Instead, real change will come from the much harder work of "spend[ing] uncomfortable time with representational conundrums" and breaking down attitudinal and institutional barriers that have so far prevented disabled creators, writers, and actors from occupying central stage in the telling of their own stories.[125] Gaining greater access to old and new epistemological tools, people with disabilities are complicating, transgressing, and creating alternatives to the stories about disability that have heretofore dominated our media landscape. As Vilissa Thompson writes, "'Nothing about us without us' is the mantra proudly proclaimed in our community about ensuring that we are at the forefront in the way disability is understood."[126]

NOTES

1. A few portions of this chapter appear in my book chapter "'Who Has a Better Story Than Bran the Broken?' The Power of Disability Narratives," in *Behind the Throne: Essays on Power and Subversion in HBO's* Game of Thrones, ed. A. Keith Kelly (Jefferson, NC: McFarland, forthcoming).

2. Rosemarie Garland-Thomson, "Staring at the Other," *Disability Studies Quarterly* 25:4 (Fall 2005), http://dsq-sds.org/article/view/610/787.

3. Robert Bogdan, *Freakshow: Presenting Human Oddities for Amusement and Profit* (Chicago: University of Chicago Press, 1988); Rosemarie Garland-Thomson, *Freakery: Cultural Spectacles of the Extraordinary Body* (New York: New York University, 1996); Rachel Adams, *Sideshow U.S.A.: Freaks and the American Cultural Imagination* (Chicago: University of Chicago Press, 2001); Leslie Fielder, *Freaks: Myths and Images of the Secret Self* (New York: Simon and Schuster, 1979).

4. Douglas C. Baynton, "Disability and the Justification of Inequality in American History," in *The New Disability History: American Perspectives*, eds. Paul K. Longmore and Lauri Umansky (New York: New York University Press, 2001), 52.

5. In 1998, British doctor Andrew Wakefield and his colleagues published a case series in the medical journal the *Lancet* that linked autism to the MMR vaccine. The study involved only twelve children and was funded by lawyers representing parents in lawsuits against vaccine-producing companies. Charging Wakefield and his team with numerous ethical violations and scientific misconduct, the *Lancet* fully retracted the case series in 2010; Wakefield lost his medical license that same year. See T.S. Sathyanarayana Rao and Chittaranjan Andrade, "The MMR

Vaccine and Autism: Sensation, Refutation, Retraction, and Fraud," *Indian Journal of Psychiatry* 53:2 (April–June 2011): 95–96, https://doi.org/10.4103/0019-5545.82529.

6. See, for example, Frank DeStefano, et al., "Increasing Exposure to Antibody-Stimulating Proteins and Polysaccharides in Vaccines Is Not Associated with Risk of Autism," *The Journal of Pediatrics* 163:2 (August 2013): 561–567, http://www.jpeds.com/article/S0022-3476%2813%2900144-3/pdf; Anjali Jain, et al., "Autism Occurrence by MMR Vaccine Status Among US Children With Older Siblings With and Without Autism," *JAMA* 15 (2015): 1534–1540, https://doi.org/10.1001/jama.2015.3077; Kreesten Meldgaard Madsen, et al., "A Population-Based Study of Measles, Mumps, and Rubella Vaccination and Autism," *The New England Journal of Medicine* 347:19 (November 7, 2002): 1477–1482, https://www.nejm.org/doi/pdf/10.1056/NEJMoa021134.

7. Sarah Kurchak, "I'm Autistic, And Believe Me, It's A Lot Better Than Measles," *Archipelago,* February 6, 2015, https://medium.com/the-archipelago/im-autistic-and-believe-me-its-a-lot-better-than-measles-78cb039f4bea.

8. Meghan Bridgid Moran, et al., "What Makes Anti-Vaccine Websites Persuasive? A Content Analysis of Techniques Used by Anti-Vaccine Websites to Engender Anti-Vaccine Sentiment," *Journal of Communication in Healthcare* 9:3 (2016): 151–163, https://doi.org/10.1080/17538068.2016.1235531.

9. Moran, et al., "Why Makes Anti-Vaccine Websites Persuasive?"

10. World Health Organization, "Ten Threats to Global Health in 2019," accessed July 5, 2020, https://www.who.int/news-room/feature-stories/ten-threats-to-global-health-in-2019.

11. Zachary Horne, et al., "Countering Antivaccination Attitudes," *Proceedings of the National Academy of Sciences* 201504019 (August 2015), https://doi.org/10.1073/pnas.1504019112.

12. Centers for Disease Control and Prevention, "Tips from Former Smokers: About the Campaign," accessed August 8, 2017, https://www.cdc.gov/tobacco/campaign/tips/about/index.html.

13. Centers for Disease Control and Prevention, "Tips from Former Smokers: Brandon's Story," accessed August 8, 2017, https://www.cdc.gov/tobacco/campaign/tips/stories/brandon-biography.html.

14. Centers for Disease Control and Prevention, "Tips from Former Smokers: About the Campaign."

15. Dany Woodburn and Kristina Kopic, *The Ruderman White Paper on Employment of Actors with Disabilities in Television* (Ruderman Family Foundation, July 2016), 3, http://rudermanfoundation.org/wp-content/uploads/2016/07/TV-White-Paper_7-1-003.pdf.

16. Catherine Happer and Greg Philo, "The Role of the Media in the Construction of Public Belief and Social Change," *Journal of Social and Political Psychology* 1:1 (2013): 321, https://doi.org/10.5964/jspp.v1i1.96.

17. Mia Harrison, "George R.R. Martin and the Two Dwarfs," in *The Routledge Companion to Disability and Media*, eds. Katie Ellis, et al. (New York: Routledge, 2020), 115.

18. World Health Organization, "World Report on Disability," accessed September 21, 2019, https://www.who.int/disabilities/world_report/2011/repo rt/en/.

19. Centers for Disease Control and Prevention, "CDC: 1 in 4 Adults Live with a Disability," August 16, 2018, cdc.gov/media/releases/2018/po816-disability.html.

20. Baynton, "Disability and the Justification of Inequality," 52.

21. Sarah Kate Ellis, "Where We Are on TV, 2018–2019," *GLAAD Media Institute*, 7, accessed September 20, 2019, https://glaad.org/files/WWAT/WWAT_G LAAD_2018-2019.pdf.

22. Stacy Smith, et al., "Inequality in 1,200 Popular Films: Examining Portrayals of Gender, Race/Ethnicity, LGBTQ & Disability from 2007 to 2018," Annenberg Foundation and USC Annenberg, September 2019, 5, http://assets.uscannenberg.org/ docs/aii-inequality-report-2019-09-03.pdf.

23. Woodburn and Kopic, *The Ruderman White Paper*, 1.

24. Anna Landre, "Represent Disability in Media," *The Hoya*, April 12, 2019, https://thehoya.com/represent-disability-media/.

25. Javy Gwaltney, "Day In The Life: Disability and Representation in Videogames," *Paste*, March 9, 2015, https://www.pastemagazine.com/articles/2015 /03/day-in-the-life-disability-and-representation-in-v.html.

26. "Ensuring Authentic Representation of Black Disabled People in the Entertainment Industry," Webinar, *Respectability*, June 2020, https://www.respecta bility.org/2020/06/ensuring-authentic-representation-of-black-disabled-people-in -the-entertainment-industry/.

27. Judith Heumann, et al., "Road Map for Inclusion: Changing the Face of Disability in Media," *Ford Foundation*, March 26, 2019, https://www.fordfoundatio n.org/media/4276/judyheumann_report_2019_final.pdf.

28. Paul Hunt, "Discrimination: Disabled People and the Media," *Contact* 70 (Winter 1991): 45–48, https://disability-studies.leeds.ac.uk/wp-content/uploads/sites /40/library/Barnes-Media.pdf.; Colin Barnes, "Disabling Imagery and the Media: An Exploration of the Principles for Media Representations of Disabled People," The British Council of Organisations of Disabled People, 1992, https://disability-studies .leeds.ac.uk/wp-content/uploads/sites/40/library/Barnes-disabling-imagery.pdf.

29. A manic pixie dream girl is a common trope in media that depicts a vivacious and appealingly quirky female character whose main purpose within the narrative is to inspire a greater appreciation for life in a stodgy male protagonist. Examples include Holly Golightly (Audrey Hepburn) in the film *Breakfast at Tiffany's*, Sam Feehan (Natalie Portman) in the film *Garden State*, and Claire Colburn (Kirsten Dunst) in the film *Elizabethtown*.

30. A very thorough collection of criticisms of *Me Before You* from writers and activists within the disability community can be found at the blog "Crippled Scholar." See specifically "Media Roundup of Me Before You Criticism" at https://cripple dscholar.com/2016/05/28/media-roundup-of-me-before-you-criticism/.

31. Dominick Evans, "Hollywood Promotes the Idea It Is Better to Be Dead Than Disabled," *The Crip Crusader*, February 11, 2016, http://www.dominickevans.com/2 016/02/hollywood-promotes-the-idea-it-is-better-to-be-dead-than-disabled/.

32. Beth Haller, *Representing Disability in an Ableist World: Essays on Mass Media* (Louisville, KY: The Advocado Press, 2010), 78.

33. Ben Mattlin, "'Me Before You' Perpetuates the Idea that the Disabled Should Consider Suicide," *The Chicago Tribune*, May 31, 2016, http://www.chicagotribune.com/news/opinion/commentary/ct-suicide-disability-me-before-you-perspec-0601-md-20160531-story.html.

34. Kevin Irvine, "Over My Dead Body," *POZ*, January 1, 1998, https://www.poz.com/article/assisted-suicide-13730-8270.

35. Paul Longmore, *Telethons: Spectacle, Disability, and the Business of Charity* (New York: Oxford University Press, 2016), 87.

36. Jon Wiener, "The End of the Jerry Lewis Telethon—It's About Time," *The Nation*, September 2, 2011, https://www.thenation.com/article/end-jerry-lewis-telethon-its-about-time/.

37. Wiener, "The End of the Jerry Lewis Telethon."

38. Evan Kemp, Jr., "Aiding the Disabled: No Pity, Please," *The New York Times*, September 3, 1981, https://www.nytimes.com/1981/09/03/opinion/aiding-the-disabled-no-pity-please.html.

39. Laura Hershey, "From Poster Child to Protester," 1993, accessed February 9, 2018, *Independent Living Institute*, https://www.independentliving.org/docs4/hershey93.html.

40. "Jerry Lewis to Crips: 'Stay in Your House!'" *Ragged Edge Online*, accessed October 6, 2020, http://www.raggededgemagazine.com/extra/jerrylewis052401.htm.

41. "The Story," *The Kids Are All Right*, accessed September 2, 2017, http://www.thekidsareallright.org/story.html.

42. Wiener, "The End of the Jerry Lewis Telethon."

43. Muscular Dystrophy Association, "MDA History," accessed November 14, 2018, https://www.mda.org/about-mda/history.

44. Elyse Wanshel, "The MDA Telethon is Back. Many Disabled People Aren't Happy About It," *Huffpost*, October 29, 2020, https://www.huffpost.com/entry/the-mda-telethon-came-back-disabled-people-say-it-was-bad-and-always-has-been_n_5f95cf48c5b6a2e1fb626c74.

45. Dominick Evans, "Stop MDA & #EndTheTelethon Now!," *The Crip Crusader*, October 4, 2020, https://www.dominickevans.com/2020/10/stop-mda-endthetelethon-now/; Emily Wolinksy, "Dear Kevin Hart, The MDA is Heartless," *Disability Visibility Project*, October 12, 2020, https://disabilityvisibilityproject.com/2020/10/12/dear-kevin-hart-the-mda-is-heartless/.

46. Jerry's Orphan's, The Next Generation, "End the Telethon," accessed January 21, 2021, https://endthetelethon.com/faq/.

47. "Please Stop Saying 'Wheelchair Bound,'" *Free Wheelin': Life and Travel with a Disability*, November 4, 2016, http://www.freewheelintravel.org/please-stop-saying-wheelchair-bound/.

48. United States Department of Health and Human Services, "Mental Health Myths and Facts," accessed July 8, 2017, https://www.mentalhealth.gov/basics/myths-facts/.

49. Steven Hyler, "Stigma Continues in Hollywood," *Psychiatric Times*, June 1, 2003, http://www.psychiatrictimes.com/articles/stigma-continues-hollywood.

50. Camille A. Nelson, "Frontlines: Policing at the Nexus of Race and Mental Health," *Fordham Urban Law Journal* 43:4 (2016): 667, https://ir.lawnet.fordham .edu/ulj/vol43/iss3/4.

51. Amit Kama, "Supercrips versus the Pitiful Handicapped: Reception of Disabling Images by Disabled Audience Members," *Communications* 29:4 (2004): 450, https://doi.org/10.1515/comm.2004.29.4.447.

52. Sami Schalk, "Reevaluating the Supercrip," *Journal of Literary & Cultural Disability Studies* 10:1 (January 2016): 79, https://doi.org/10.3828/jlcds.2016.5.

53. Kama, "Supercrips Versus the Pitiful Handicapped," 450.

54. Schalk, "Reevaluating the Supercrip," 81.

55. Rory Conn and Dinesh Bhugra, "The Portrayal of Autism in Hollywood Films," *International Journal of Culture and Mental Health* 5:1 (2012): 54–62, https ://doi.org/10.1080/17542863.2011.553369. See also Anne-Marie Callus, "The Cloak of Incompetence: Representations of People with Intellectual Disability in Film," *Journal of Literary & Cultural Disability Studies* 13:2 (2019): 177–194, https://doi .org/10.3828/jlcds.2018.42; and John Williams, *My Son is Not Rainman: One Man, One Autistic Boy, a Million Adventures* (London: Michael O'Mara Books, 2016).

56. Sonya Loftis, *Imagining Autism: Fiction and Stereotypes on the Spectrum* (Bloomington: Indiana University Press, 2014).

57. "The Good Doctor," *IMDb*, accessed August 10, 2020, http://www.imdb .com/title/tt6470478/?ref_=nv_sr_1.

58. Loftis, *Imagining Autism*.

59. Breathingglass, "The Asperger's Geek and Why This Stereotype is Damaging," *Seeing Double, Understanding Autism*, June 18, 2015, https://seeingd oubleautismawareness.wordpress.com/2015/06/18/the-aspergers-geek-and-why-this -stereotype-is-damaging/.

60. "The Good Doctor."

61. John Duffy and Rebecca Dorner, "The Pathos of 'Mindblindness': Autism, Science, and Sadness in 'Theory of Mind' Narratives," *Journal of Literary & Cultural Disability Studies* 5:2 (2011): 201, https://doi.org/10.3828/jlcds.2011.16.

62. Simon Baron-Cohen, "Theory of Mind in Normal Development and Autism," *Prisme* 34 (2001): 174–183; See also Simon Baron-Cohen, "Autism: A Specific Cognitive Disorder of 'Mindblindness,'" *International Review of Psychiatry* 2:1 (January 1990): 81–90; and Simon Baron-Cohen, *Mindblindness: An Essay on Autism and Theory of Mind* (Boston: MIT University Press, 1995).

63. Rachel Cohen-Rottenberg, "Impaired Theory of Whose Mind (ToWM)?" *Autism and Empathy*, accessed December 20, 2020, https://autismandempathyblog.w ordpress.com/impaired-theory-of-whose-mind-towm/.

64. Baron-Cohen, "Theory of Mind in Normal Development and Autism," 174–183.

65. Melanie Yergeau, "Clinically Significant Disturbance: On Theorists Who Theorize Theory of Mind," *Disability Studies Quarterly* 33:4 (2013), https://dsq-sds .org/article/view/3876/3405.

66. Yergeau, "Clinically Significant Disturbance."

67. Matthew Hughey, "Cinethetic Racism: White Redemption and Black Stereotypes in 'Magical Negro' Films," *Social Problems* 56:3 (August 2009): 543–577, https://doi.org/10.1525/sp.2009.56.3.543.

68. "Director Spike Lee Slams 'Same Old' Black Stereotypes in Today's Films," *Yale Bulletin and Calendar* 29:21 (March 2, 2001), https://web.archive.org/web/20090121190429/http://www.yale.edu/opa/arc-ybc/v29.n21/story3.html.

69. Hughey, "Cinethetic Racism," 544.

70. Hughey, "Cinethetic Racism," 548.

71. Hughey, "Cinethetic Racism," 561–562.

72. Corrinne Duyvis, "The Mystical Disability Trope," *Disability in Kidlit*, August 1, 2014, http://disabilityinkidlit.com/2014/08/01/corinne-duyvis-the-mystical-disability-trope/.

73. Stella Young, "I'm Not Your Inspiration, Thank You Very Much," filmed April 2014 at TEDxSydney, Sydney, Australia, video, 9:04, https://www.ted.com/talks/stella_young_i_m_not_your_inspiration_thank_you_very_much?language=en.

74. Jessica Saggio, "Disabled Teen Crowned Homecoming Queen in Awesome Way," *USA Today*, November 13, 2015, https://www.usatoday.com/story/news/humankind/2015/11/13/disabled-teen-crowned-homecoming-queen-awesome-way/75658376/.

75. See for example Paul Burton, "Undefeated Norton High Wrestler Makes Opponent's Dream Come True," *CBS Boston*, January 26, 2016, http://boston.cbslocal.com/2016/01/26/norton-wrestling-deven-schuko-video/; and Johanna Li, "Man Proposes to Girlfriend and Her Sister, Who Has Down Syndrome," *Inside Edition*, July 5, 2017, http://www.insideedition.com/headlines/24315-man-proposes-to-girlfriend-and-her-sister-who-has-down-syndrome.

76. Associated Press, "Fast-Food Worker at Qdoba Praised for Feeding Disabled Customer," *Tampa Bay Times*, June 5, 2015, https://www.tampabay.com/news/humaninterest/fast-food-worker-at-qdoba-praised-for-feeding-disabled-customer-wvideo/2232544/.

77. Kim Sauder, "Disabled People Don't Exist to Make You Look Good," *crippledscholar*, May 20, 2015, https://crippledscholar.com/tag/inspiration-porn/.

78. Young, "I'm Not Your Inspiration."

79. John Altmann, "I Don't Want to Be 'Inspiring,'" *The New York Times*, October 20, 2016.

80. Schalk, "Reevaluating the Supercrip," 78–79.

81. "Caught on Camera: A Simple Act of Kindness with Big Impact," *Wave 3 News*, Louisville, Kentucky, May 11, 2015, http://www.wave3.com/story/29032820/tonight-at-6-restaurant-customer-records-random-act-of-kindness.

82. Kim Sauder, "Inspiration Porn is Not Progress, It's a New Kind of Oppression," *crippledscholar*, May 5, 2015, https://crippledscholar.com/tag/inspiration-porn/.

83. Quoted in Mark Hay, "Mat Fraser on the Future of Disability in the Media," *GOOD*, February 2, 2016, https://www.good.is/articles/mat-fraser-american-horror-story-freakshow-disability-media-oneofus.

84. Dominick Evans, "Please Stop Comparing Disabled Mimicry to Blackface," *The Crip Crusader*, July 18, 2017, https://www.dominickevans.com/2017/07/please-stop-comparing-cripping-up-to-blackface/.

85. Quoted in Evans, "Please Stop Comparing Disabled Mimicry to Blackface."

86. Quoted in Evans, "Please Stop Comparing Disabled Mimicry to Blackface."

87. The list includes (among many others) Dustin Hoffman for *Rain Man* (autism); Jessica Lange for *Blue Sky* (mental disability); Daniel Day-Lewis for *My Left Foot* (cerebral palsy); Nicole Kidman for *The Hours* (bipolar disorder); Al Pacino for *Scent of a Woman* (blindness); Hillary Swank for *Million Dollar Baby* (quadriplegia); Tom Hanks for *Philadelphia* and *Forrest Gump* (AIDS and learning disability, respectively); Julianne Moore for *Still Alice* (Alzheimer's); Jamie Foxx for *Ray* (blindness); Colin Firth for *The King's Speech* (speech impediment); and Eddie Redmayne for *The Theory of Everything* (ALS).

88. Christopher Shinn, "Disability is Not Just a Metaphor," *The Atlantic*, July 23, 2014, https://www.theatlantic.com/entertainment/archive/2014/07/why-disabled-characters-are-never-played-by-disabled-actors/374822/.

89. Shinn, "Disability is Not Just a Metaphor." See also David T. Mitchell and Sharon Snyder, *Narrative Prosthesis: Disability and the Dependencies of Discourse* (Ann Arbor: University of Michigan Press, 2001).

90. "What Disability Means," *The New York Times,* August 25, 2016.

91. Quoted in Hay, "Mat Fraser on the Future of Disability."

92. Rachel Handler, "Stop Excluding Actors with Disabilities," *Backstage*, February 9, 2016, https://www.backstage.com/magazine/article/stop-excluding-actors-disabilities-7387/.

93. Evans, "Hollywood Promotes the Idea It Is Better to Be Dead Than Disabled."

94. Ashley Spencer, "The Golden Globes Celebrated Sia's 'Music.' Autistic Activists Wish They Hadn't," *The New York Times*, February 11, 2021, https://www.nytimes.com/2021/02/11/movies/sia-music-autism-backlash.html.

95. Charlie Hancock, "Autism on Screen: Where Sia Went Wrong," *The Oxford Student*, December 6, 2020, https://www.oxfordstudent.com/2020/12/06/autism-on-screen-where-sia-went-wrong/.

96. Autistic Self Advocacy Network, "Disability Organizations: MUSIC Is Dangerous," February 3, 2021, https://autisticadvocacy.org/2021/02/disability-organizations-music-is-dangerous/.

97. Justin Curto, "Sia Criticized for Not Casting Actors With Autism, Attacks Critics on Twitter," *Vulture*, November 20, 2020, https://www.vulture.com/2020/11/sia-autism-representation-music-movie.html.

98. "Sia Talks Directing Her First Feature Film *Music*," *YouTube*, October 29, 2020, https://www.youtube.com/watch?v=SIVppt0YPio&t=1607s; Briana Lawrence, "Sia Gives a Master Class on How Not to Handle Valid Criticism From, Well, Anyone (but Especially Marginalized Groups)," *The Mary Sue*, November 20, 2020, https://www.themarysue.com/sia-music-film-critism/; Curto, "Sia Criticized for Not Casting Actors With Autism."

99. Spencer, "The Golden Globes Celebrated Sia's 'Music.'"

100. Ellise Shafer, "Sia Adds Warning Label to 'Music' Movie, Apologizes to Autism Community on Heels of Golden Globes Nominations," *Variety*, February 3, 2021, https://variety.com/2021/film/news/sia-music-warning-label-apologizes-autism -community-12.

101. Handler, "Stop Excluding Actors with Disabilities."

102. Woodburn and Kopic, *The Ruderman White Paper*, 30–31.

103. Woodburn and Kopic, *The Ruderman White Paper*, 131.

104. Vilissa Thompson, "'Nothing about Us without Us'—Disability Representation in Media," *Center for Disability Rights*, accessed October 25, 2019, http://cdrnys.org/blog/disability-dialogue/nothing-about-us-without-us-disability-rep resentation-in-media/.

105. Woodburn and Kopic, *The Ruderman White Paper*, 30.

106. Heumann, et al., *Road Map for Inclusions,* 2.

107. Thompson, "'Nothing about Us without Us'—Disability Representation in Media."

108. Stanley Fish, *Is There a Text in this Class?* (Cambridge: Harvard University Press, 1980).

109. Michel Foucault, *The History of Sexuality, Vol. 1: An Introduction* (New York: Routledge, 1978).

110. Louise Rosenblatt, *The Reader, the Text, the Poem: The Transactional Theory of the Literary Work* (Carbondale: Southern Illinois University Press, 1978).

111. Alice Hall, *Literature and Disability* (New York: Routledge, 2016), 165.

112. Richard Holicky, "The Transformation of Regan Linton," *New Mobility*, May 1, 2015, https://www.newmobility.com/2015/05/regan-linton/.

113. Haller, *Representing Disability in an Ableist World,* 126–127.

114. Melissa Shang, "Stories about Disability Don't Have to be Sad," *The New York Times*, June 21, 2017. https://www.nytimes.com/2017/06/21/opinion/stories -about-disability-dont-have-to-be-sad.html.

115. "This is What Disability Looks Like," *Facebook*, accessed July 26, 2017, https://www.facebook.com/pg/ThisIsWhatDisabilityLooksLike/about/?ref=page_i nternal.

116. Krip-Hop Nation, "What is the Krip-Hop Nation," accessed August 2, 2017, http://kriphopnation.com.

117. Kathleen Kiley, "Activist & Writer Leroy Moore Jr. Brings 'Krip-Hop' to the Whitney," *The Huffington Post*, June 5, 2017, http://www.huffingtonpost.com/ entry/activist-writer-leroy-moore-jr-brings-krip-hop_us_592e379fe4b047e77e4 c3fa1.

118. Caitlin Gibson, "Jillian Mercado Made It as a Model with a Disability. Here's What She Wants Next," *The Washington Post*, April 28, 2016. https://www.washingt onpost.com/news/arts-and-entertainment/wp/2016/04/28/jillian-mercado-made-it-as- a-model-with-a-disability-heres-what-she-wants-next/.

119. Groups such as the Autistic Self Advocacy Network broke ties with *Sesame Street* in 2019; however, when the show partnered with Autism Speaks to feature Julia in a public service campaign encouraging early screening and diagnosis of autism. See Autistic Self Advocacy Network, "ASAN Has Ended Partnership with

Sesame Street," August 5, 2019, https://autisticadvocacy.org/2019/08/asan-has-ended-partnership-with-sesame-street/.

120. E. Alex Jung, "Micah Fowler on Booking His *Speechless* Role and Playing a Character with More Severe Cerebral Palsy Than Himself," *Vulture*, December 7, 2016, http://www.vulture.com/2016/12/speechless-micah-fowler-interview.html.

121. Carrie Sandahl, "Using Our Words: Exploring Representational Conundrums in Disability Drama and Performance," *Journal of Literary & Cultural Disability Studies* 12:2 (2018): 135, https://doi.org/10.3828/jlcds.2018.11.

122. Sandahl, "Using Our Words," 135.

123. Sandahl, "Using Our Words," 133–134.

124. Carolyn Heilbrun, *Writing a Woman's Life* (New York: W.W. Norton & Company, 1988), 43–44.

125. Sandahl, "Using Our Words," 132.

126. Thompson, "'Nothing about Us without Us'—Disability Representation in Media."

Chapter 4

Disability and Inclusive Education

When she was in the fourth grade, Zoey competed in the Literature category of the annual PTA-sponsored Reflections Arts Program and ended up winning first place in the state of Oklahoma and honorable mention at the national level for her essay titled "The World Would Be a Better Place if There Were More Lalaloopsies in It." A tender homage to her then-beloved Lalaloopsy collection of rag dolls with large plastic heads and black button eyes, Zoey's essay imagined a diverse world in which every person was accepted, valued, and supported by others:

> Lalaloopsies are dolls that have neat hair and cute pets. My favorites are Jewel Sparkles and her little sister Trinket Sparkles. They are cute and nice. I also like Ribbon Slippers and Tippy Tumbelina and Twisty Tumbelina. I like Peanut Big Top and her little sister Squirt 'Lil Top. They are funny.
>
> Lalaloopsies bake lots of nice treats. They put on shows. They tell jokes and have sleepovers. They have fun.
>
> If a Lalaloopsy has a problem, the other Lalaloopsies try to help. They try to make each other feel better. They solve problems by working together.
>
> Lalaloopsies come in all different sizes and colors. You can even color on one of them and make your own Lalaloopsy. They are all different. They treat people who are different nicely. They say that it's okay to be different. Everyone deserves to be special. It doesn't matter if you have glasses, red hair, dark skin, or light skin. It doesn't matter if you have autism or OCD. It doesn't matter if you wear sneakers with dresses or tank tops. If you look different, they don't tease you. Everybody is nice to everybody else.
>
> If a Lalaloopsy walks up to a group of other Lalaloopsies and asks to play with them, they would never say, "No, go away. We don't like you." They

would not bully or tease her. They would say, "Sure, play with us. Be our
friend."

The world would be a better place if there were more Lalaloopsies in it
because the Lalaloopsies treat each other like they want to be treated. That is
the best thing of all.

In Zoey's imagined world, individuals were not left to struggle on their own
but were embraced by the entire community of friends, who understood their
connections to and responsibility for one another. In this world, differences
were not something to be feared or rejected but honored and celebrated. In
this world, no one had to worry that the expression of their authentic self
would result in marginalization, inequality, or bullying.

By imagining an ideal world of mutual dependency, acceptance, and
kindness to all, Zoey's essay offered a powerful critique of the world that
she actually inhabited. In the world of Zoey's reality, people whose bodies, minds, and behaviors differed from expected "norms" were usually
considered broken, deviant, and lesser than. In the world of reality, Zoey's
boundless energy, unique ways of thinking and learning, and quirky modes
of movement and expression were problems to be solved. In this real world,
when Zoey—my funny, smart, happy, enthusiastic, creative, loving little
girl—could not or simply would not mold or distort herself to fit into spaces
that were not made for her, she faced criticism, discrimination, punishment,
or ostracism. Nowhere did Zoey experience these things more painfully than
in the public school system.[1]

By the time that she was eight years old, Zoey had been expelled from
three private schools that lacked the resources to help her succeed socially
and academically. In the fall of 2013, we enrolled Zoey in our neighborhood
public school on the assumption that she would be supported by a range of
services and programs mandated by law. We were thus unprepared for the
school's determination to keep Zoey in a regular classroom without any
supports until the conclusion of a lengthy evaluation process despite the recommendations of our private therapists and doctors; these professionals had
already evaluated and diagnosed Zoey and had been offering her therapeutic
services since she was four years old.

By the sixth week of the semester while the evaluation continued, Zoey
was experiencing crisis in a classroom and school environment that had
failed on every level to accommodate her. Her frustration and anxiety led
to frequent, violent outbursts, which resulted in social rejection from her
peers and abandonment of all attempts at education from her teacher, who
simply allowed Zoey to wander about the classroom while the other students
participated in collaborative learning. Left largely unsupervised, Zoey often
slipped out of the classroom undetected and roamed the school hallways until

someone eventually noticed that she was missing. During one such excursion, she decided to hide in one of the empty classrooms to see how long it would take someone to find her. No one in her classroom, including her teacher, was aware of her absence until an hour later, when the principal was alerted. After several minutes of searching produced no result, the school called to tell me that they could not locate her. In a panic, I raced to the school and walked up and down the hallways calling for Zoey, who, on hearing my voice, emerged laughing from her hiding place, delighted by her trickery and completely oblivious to the chaos and panic she had caused.

My concern grew to alarm when I realized how little training and experience the principal and most staff members had in working with and responding to students with disabilities. When the school continued to insist that Zoey remain in the regular classroom without any supports, I began to suspect that the school's determination to pursue inclusion was less about Zoey's needs and more about a lack of funds. My suspicions were confirmed during a routine meeting with school administrators when the principal explicitly acknowledged that Zoey's ability to succeed in a regular classroom depended on the assistance of a full-time, one-on-one, highly trained paraprofessional but that the school district did not have the funds to provide one. When I asked what they could do to persuade the district to provide a classroom aide, the principal shrugged and suggested that I join a parents' advocacy group. It was during this same meeting that the principal felt the need to tell me that she had been fielding calls from other parents, who were concerned that their children no longer enjoyed attending school because "Zoey was ruining all of their fun."

Following a disturbing incident in which a teacher responded to Zoey's verbal and physical aggression by wrestling her to the floor and pinning her down by the arms and legs, the principal managed to produce a classroom aide who lacked any formal training or experience and was not assigned to Zoey individually but was required to float from classroom to classroom as needed. This meant that Zoey would largely remain on her own in a regular classroom with one well-meaning but completely flummoxed teacher and twenty-five terrified students with no supports or accommodations (save a scheduled, once-a-day trip to the resource room at a time that was convenient not for Zoey but for the overworked school counselor). On her second day on the job, the aide—who had not been properly apprised of Zoey's particular needs and challenges—allowed Zoey to visit the restroom on her own, something that she was never permitted to do given her habit of slipping out of her classroom and wandering the hallways. Taking full advantage of her sudden freedom, Zoey decided that she would try to find her way home. She made it all the way to the front door of the school and nearly out to the parking lot before I stopped her—I happened to be in the lobby that morning waiting for a meeting with the principal.

Determined never to return Zoey to that school environment, I began home schooling her until I managed—after a lengthy and costly battle—to have her transferred to the only elementary school in our district that provided a full-time, self-contained special education program run by a team of highly trained staff. When Zoey started the program, she attended school for only a few hours a day, regularly reacted violently to her classmates and teaching staff, cared little about her appearance, and made few if any attempts to socialize with her peers. After three years in the program, Zoey was thriving. She earned excellent grades, participated in after-school activities like honor choir and art lessons, learned to manage better her anxiety and emotions, and even made friends.

When I shared this story during a roundtable discussion at an academic conference in the spring of 2015, I was dismayed when the general consensus among the scholars present seemed to be that "inclusion is not always the best answer for students with disabilities." I am not sure that this was the moral of my story. Too often, inclusive education is narrowly understood as the education of children with disabilities in "regular" classrooms.[2] Zoey was educated in the regular classroom, but it was far from inclusive; in her situation, inclusive education meant the mere presence of a child with a disability without any real supports, no individualized attention to her particular needs, little or no training of staff, and utter failure to teach students the value of human diversity. In no way, shape, or form was this inclusive education. Moreover, the statement that "inclusive education is not always the best answer for children with disabilities" suggests that inclusive education is only about the education of students with disabilities and that the "failure" of inclusion is the responsibility of the child, not the inadequacies of the education provided. Scholars in the field of Disability Studies in Education (DSE)[3] have challenged such views by arguing that inclusive education is about the education of all students, is concerned with identifying and removing all barriers to learning, and is committed to investigating and changing cultural practices of schooling that marginalize and exclude not only on the basis of disability but also on the basis of race, class, gender, ethnicity, nationality, sexuality, and religion.[4] "Taken together," write Susan Baglieri, et al., "these departures of the DSE discourse on inclusive education from the dominant special education discourse around inclusive education are radical."[5]

In this chapter, I draw on insights from DSE and my experiences navigating the special education system to consider the most effective theories and practices for creating systems of education that are truly inclusive. Rejecting pathologizing discourses and policies that attempt to fit students with disabilities into classrooms and curricula designed for a mythical "able-bodied," neurotypical, white, male, middle-class "norm," I explore how classrooms, pedagogy, curricular materials, and cultural practices of schools can be transformed in order to accommodate all students. After analyzing the many inadequacies of so-called "inclusive education" approaches as currently practiced in American public schools, I advocate the wider application of the social interpretation of disability to education, one that sees the learning environment, not students with disabilities, as the "problem" and that works to promote an educational system based on social justice and the full and equal participation of all students.[6] As Mara Sapon-Shevin has written, "When one student is not a full participant in his or her school community, then we are all at risk. By embracing inclusion as a model of social justice, we can create a world fit for us all."[7] In the last section of the chapter, I discuss how social justice in education is achieved through Universal Design for Learning (UDL)—or the design of instructional materials and activities that allows the learning goals to be achievable by individuals with wide differences in their abilities and backgrounds—and how I have attempted to refigure my own college courses and the learning environment at my university through the application of UDL principles. Ultimately, I call on educators at every level to implement UDL, which has the potential to radically transform the meaning of inclusive education and the very concept of disability.

UNPACKING INCLUSIVE EDUCATION

In 1975, Congress enacted the Education for All Handicapped Children Act (Public Law 94–142), later renamed the Individuals with Disabilities Education Act (IDEA), which ensures that children with disabilities receive a free, appropriate education. IDEA requires that each child with a disability have an Individualized Education Program (IEP) designed by parents, teachers, and school staff to guide the delivery of special education supports and services to improve educational outcomes. By law, states are required to educate students with disabilities in the least restrictive environment and, if possible, in a "typical" education setting with nondisabled students and can remove a student with a disability from the regular educational environment only when such education "cannot be achieved satisfactorily."[8] The push for inclusive education emerged by the late 1980s and gained strength throughout the next decade in response to the disability rights movement led by self-advocates, parents' advocacy groups, and education reforms sparked by IDEA. Since then, debates have swirled over the benefits of inclusive education for children with disabilities, their classmates, and school personnel.[9]

Many proponents of inclusion argue that all children are entitled to equal participation in every aspect of the educational experience, and that all students benefit from interacting with children with a range of abilities and differences. In particular, parents want their children to form friendships with

their peers and to participate in all of the typical social activities of childhood.[10] Other supporters of inclusion stress the harmful impact of educating
children with disabilities in separate, special education classrooms, a setting
that they claim is inferior to the regular classroom environment for the following reasons: limited, less rigorous curriculum; lower expectations that can
lead to diminished academic and postsecondary opportunities; less access to
nondisabled peers; and social stigma.[11] A 2012 study from the Association
of Black Psychologists, for example, claims that for students in separate
special education programs, "the long term, detrimental effects of labeling,
stigmatization, lowered expectations, inadequate instruction, limited access
to enrichment opportunities, and special segregation can be debilitating."[12] In
an article published in the *Trotter Review*, scholars at Yale University argue
that "special education classes often become the 'dumping ground' for so-
called problem students, instead of the supportive and nurturing environment
required for students who have a genuine need for these services."[13]

Multiple accounts written by students diagnosed with various disabilities
confirm the inadequacies of many special education programs. Diagnosed
with a learning disability when she was in the third grade, Lachrista Greco,
for example, spent the majority of her elementary and middle school years in
a segregated classroom. Immediately following her diagnosis, she was placed
in special education "because that's what people do with you when they can't
figure you out."[14] While her new classroom environment allowed her to "be
myself" without the pressure of conforming to the academic performance of
her peers in the regular classroom, she nevertheless felt "stupid" and "different," particularly because her teachers lowered their expectations of her and
even explicitly told her that she would not be able to do things like the other
children because she was "not as smart." In her special education classroom,
academic standards were very low; teachers were caring, she notes, but often
at a loss for what to do with a large population of children with vastly different challenges and needs. It ended up feeling like "'The Room for the
Unwanted," Greco writes. She wanted desperately to fit in and be "normal"
but she felt like her special education placement marked her as a permanent
outsider, an object of ridicule and pity. "My time in Special Ed wasn't all
bad," she concludes, "but it seems as though some education professionals
still have no idea what to do with kids who have disabilities of any type. Not
to mention, the stigma is ever present."[15]

Several experts, however, question the effectiveness of inclusion as typically administered in U.S. public school systems. They argue that children
who struggle to learn through "traditional teaching methods" and an increasingly standardized curriculum in the regular classroom might benefit more
from individualized instruction from special education teachers.[16] Some
parents of children with disabilities are among the opponents of inclusive

education because they fear a loss of accommodations and the benefits of special education classrooms, including individual educational programming, smaller student-teacher ratios, and teachers who have special training in working with children with disabilities.[17] And as people who have experienced inclusive education firsthand rightly note, inclusive education is too often considered inclusive merely because of the physical presence of children with disabilities in the regular classroom. Cara Liebowitz writes, for example, that as the only physically disabled student in her "inclusive" classroom, she frequently felt "like an island as other students swarmed around me doing one project or another that was inaccessible to me. I had very few social interactions - no one ever asked me to join their group, and even when groups were assigned, the projects were usually motor-skill oriented, such as a poster." Time and again, she felt isolated and ignored. "No one—teachers or students—ever asked me how the classroom environment could be more accessible to me," she notes, and "[n]o one ever asked what my needs were and tried to meet them. No one knew what to do with me, so instead of asking, they simply did nothing. And yet, I'm sure if you asked any one of the administrators at my school, they would tell you that I was fully included for all six years I was at that school."[18]

Mara Sapon-Shevin argues that truly inclusive education requires planning, resources, institutional support, teacher training, staff development, and commitment. Therefore, when a student with disabilities is merely "dumped" into a regular classroom without these essentials, there is nothing inclusive about that student's education. For her, then, the problem is not with inclusion but with "irresponsible planning, irresponsible fiscal management, irresponsible teaching."[19] Such a situation is not uncommon among financially strapped school districts across the nation, according to Melinda Clayton. With IDEA's initial passage, Congress promised to provide states with an additional 40 percent of the per pupil cost of education each year to cover the higher cost of educating students with disabilities. Year after year, however, Congress has not even come close to this promised funding percentage and currently (as of 2020) covers only 13 percent of the estimated cost of educating children with disabilities in the states.[20] State and local sources, therefore, have to shoulder nearly 90 percent of the cost of special education, an expense that far outweighs the cost of including children with disabilities in regular classrooms where they are unlikely to receive the specialized services they need. As Clayton argues, "We do a disservice to these children when we cite 'equality' as the reason for removing supports when what we really mean is 'funding'. . . . If we're going to take services away from special populations, let us at least be honest about our reasons for doing so."[21]

The most ubiquitous aspect of the inclusion debates emphasizes the impact of inclusion on so-called "able-bodied" or neurotypical children. Inclusion's supporters argue that the acceptance and understanding of one another as diverse individuals with differing abilities is one of the primary goals of education. "Inclusion is consistent with multicultural educations, and [with] a world in which many more people have opportunities to know, play, and work with one another," writes Sapon-Shevin.[22] Critics of inclusion, by contrast, tend to stress the negative impact of inclusion on "regular" education students. In a briefing before the U.S. Commission on Civil Rights in 2007, for example, Abigail Thernstrom stated:

> Antisocial acts have become expressions of an illness. . . . My concern here is with the regular students eager and ready to learn in a classroom in which just a handful of kids can make schooling extremely difficult. . . . If schools try to go to bat for the regular students whose education is disrupted by trouble-makers, they risk, at best, endless hours compiling a proper paper trail, and, at worst, defeat in the courtroom many years down the road, with huge legal bills on their hands. And yet, the education of students who are ready to learn must be severely compromised when one of their peers repeatedly screams at a teacher, while another rolls around on the floor and eats paper clips and staples.[23]

Using language less explicitly disparaging of children with disabilities but no less ableist in meaning and implication, a study on inclusion published in the *Journal of the American Academy of Special Education Professionals* (JAASEP) asked:

> Do we favor the few so sensitively that we are unwilling to be concerned about the Regular Ed Students whose classrooms are being adapted to meet the needs of others? Are we truly committed to the educational experience of all students, and if so are we as educators willing to ask the frightening questions regarding the impact of Inclusion on all students? If as much as $60 billion a year is spent on the 12 percent of Students with Disabilities, do we not have an obligation to document whether that lopsided expenditure represents any benefit to Regular Ed Students?[24]

This JAASEP study reflects the widespread assumption that the so-called "regular classroom" is rightly the province of nondisabled students and a neutral, value-free space that students with disabilities invade and disrupt via their very presence and their costly needs for adaptation. What this view fails to recognize is that this space, far from neutral, is constructed for a mythical, "able-bodied," neurotypical norm that neither reflects nor accommodates the wide range of diverse learners within it, regardless of whether these learners have been diagnosed with a disability.[25]

Inclusive education, then, rarely means the full and equal participation of all students within a democratic learning environment that recognizes and accommodates multiple human diversities. Instead, inclusive education pivots around a mythical, unexamined norm against which students are measured and often labeled, marginalized, and pathologized. "Consequently," write David Mitchell, Sharon Snyder, and Linda Ware, "there is no inclusionism that does not come replete with a strategy of making estranged bodies better fit normative expectations."[26]

RACE, GENDER, AND DISPROPORTIONALITY

As many scholars have pointed out, the American public school system also makes far-reaching assumptions about racial, cultural, and gender norms that mark black and brown bodies as deviant, that marginalize or exclude cultural and ethnic differences, and that use male-centric models and criteria for diagnoses and educational placement.[27] Such assumptions have led to tremendous racial, cultural, and gender disproportionality in "judgmental" disability categories (i.e., categories that depend on professional interpretation) and special education programs and services.[28] For example, although African Americans represent only 17 percent of elementary and secondary students in the United States, they constitute 21 percent of total enrollments in special education. Black, male children comprise 80 percent of all schoolchildren labeled Emotionally Disturbed and 35 percent categorized as Learning Disabled.[29] Similarly, Latino students represent just over 20 percent of the school population but almost 24 percent of students classified with learning disabilities. American Indian/Alaska Native children are one and one-half times more likely than white students to receive services for specific learning disabilities. Of all students who currently receive special services, 54 percent come from a variety of culturally and linguistically diverse (CLD) backgrounds, and many have limited English-language proficiency.[30] And minority students—particularly Black boys—who are assigned to disability categories are more likely than their white counterparts to be disciplined, suspended, expelled, and placed into more restrictive educational settings.[31]

Reasons for the disproportionate representation of minority and CLD students in special education are numerous and varied but include cultural differences in language expression and communication styles; fewer opportunities for early exposure to school-related academic or curricular experiences; preferred learning styles, for example, learning primarily through listening or through physically interacting with learning materials; parents' inability (due to lack of time, resources, ability to communicate in English with school personnel, among others) to challenge the results of evaluations or the placement recommendations of school districts; stereotypic or lower expectations of teachers or family; and lack of culturally responsive eligibility criteria, assessments, and curricular materials that accommodate students with diverse backgrounds and learning needs.[32] Investigating the issue of racial disproportionality in special education, a report published by the U.S. Commission on Civil Rights outlined the following concerns:

- Teachers referring minority students for special education testing, but not referring similarly situated white students.
- Evaluators using different types of tests, more testing, or different interpretations of test results to determine that minority students need special education services.
- Schools placing minority special education students in self-contained classrooms, while similarly situated white students are placed in regular classrooms.
- Delays in evaluating and placing students that affect children of all races and national origins.[33]

Taken as a whole, these factors suggest that schools privilege and are structured to the advantage of the "cultural répertoire" of the white middle class. Measured against such cultural "norms," the academic performance and behaviors of minority and CLD students are much more likely to be seen as problematic and requiring the interventions of special education.[34] As Beth Ferri and David Connor note, "It is clear that special education, despite being designated to meet the needs of individual learners, has nonetheless been used to create and perpetuate the marginalization of students based on the interconnected discourses of race and ability."[35] Putting it more explicitly, Zanita Fenton concludes that "special education has been used as a tool of racial discrimination."[36]

Questions of disproportionality in special education have concentrated almost entirely on race and, in particular, on the over-representation of African American males. Yet, figures from the Department of Education demonstrate a significant disproportionality along gender lines. Approximately two-thirds of students receiving special education services under IDEA are boys, who constitute 75 percent of students assigned to Emotionally Disturbed and Learning Disability categories.[37] Since 2004, with amendments to IDEA, states are required to collect, evaluate, and report rates of disproportionality in special education, but only for racial disproportionality. States use various methods, and no single way to measure disproportionality exists. In fact, each state is allowed to decide what level of disproportionality is significant,[38] and states are not required to report rates of gender disproportionality.[39] Clearly, then, gender disparity in special education has not received the attention from states and the federal government that it seems to merit. And while scholars are increasingly paying attention to gender gaps in special education, most, according to Emily Arms, et al., tend to ask why boys are overrepresented in special education categories and programs rather than to question whether girls are underrepresented.[40]

The underrepresentation of girls in special education is related to the underrepresentation of girls in certain disability categories like autism. According to the Centers for Disease Control and Prevention, autism is four and a half times more common among boys than girls. One in forty-two boys in the United States has been diagnosed with autism, while the ratio for girls is one in 189.[41] Yet, a number of recent studies suggest that the gender gap in autism diagnoses is less the result of biology and more the product of androcentric research methods and diagnostic criteria.[42] Due to social conditioning, autistic girls sometimes develop gender-specific mechanisms for coping with challenging environments and therefore do not typically exhibit the male-associated traits and behaviors that commonly lead to a clinical diagnosis.[43] In other words, autism often presents differently in girls than it does in boys, but because researchers assume that autism is far more common in boys, they are much more likely to conduct their research using male, as opposed to female, subjects. Consequently, their understanding of autism is based on how it presents in boys, who are in turn much more likely to be diagnosed.[44]

The androcentrism that contributes to the underrepresentation of girls in autism diagnoses contributes as well to gender imbalances in special education. Across all ethnic and racial groups, twice as many boys as girls are identified as needing special education services in primary and secondary schools.[45] Research has shown that boys who are frustrated academically tend to act out negatively in class, while girls tend to internalize their frustrations and work harder to please.[46] In addition, boys are more likely to express emotions in verbal outbursts, while girls who are experiencing depression or other emotional issues tend to keep silent. Because boys are more likely than girls to exhibit behavioral characteristics associated with certain disabilities, therefore, they are more often referred to special education programs. Furthermore, girls are usually referred for special education services due to emotional disabilities only after they demonstrate behaviors typically associated with boys who already receive such services.[47] Equally troubling, boys are more likely to be classified as intellectually disabled, learning disabled, and emotionally disturbed because the threshold for achievement is higher for boys than for girls; hence, characteristics and behaviors marked as disabilities in male students are simply considered "normal" for female students.[48] These findings suggest that girls are underrepresented in disability categories and special education programs and that such underrepresentation can be explained at least in part by gender biases in assessment instruments and diagnostic criteria.[49] The consequences of such underrepresentation are potentially dramatic. Because girls have to exhibit more severe challenges in order to receive the same education supports as their male counterparts, they are likely to be diagnosed later (if at all) and hence have to wait longer to benefit from needed services.[50] They are also more likely to drop out of school, become pregnant as teenagers, and experience unemployment and poverty throughout their lives.[51]

If white, male, middle-class cultural norms are the standard by which students' abilities and behaviors are measured and if assessments and educational materials incorporate and reflect these norms, then we begin to understand disabilities, "problem" behaviors, learning "deficits," and poor student academic performance in a very different light. Thus, we need to analyze further how the culture and organization of schools constrain the achievement, overlook the needs, and pathologize the minds and bodies of students who deviate from these norms.

UNIVERSAL DESIGN FOR LEARNING

The dominant conceptualization of inclusive education in the United States is the education of children with disabilities in regular classroom settings with supports and accommodations.[52] Such a narrow view of inclusive education—as reflected in the *Journal of the American Academy of Special Education Professionals* study cited earlier—fails to acknowledge that "Regular Ed Students" might also benefit from the supports and accommodations designed to assist students with disabilities. In fact, by making a distinction between the "Regular Ed Students" and "others," the JAASEP study adheres to what Rosemarie Garland-Thomson calls the ability/disability system that creates rigid but false distinctions between bodies and minds perceived as "able" (the norm) and bodies and minds perceived as "disabled" (any and all deviations from the "norm"). As I described in chapter 1, our built environment, policies, and attitudes make little room for human variation. Instead, they are modeled on, and thus privilege, bodies and minds perceived as fit, competent, and intelligent and thus devalue, stigmatize, and subjugate bodies and minds viewed as ugly, deformed, and incompetent. When individuals "fail" to think, move, act, and look in ways that fit expected norms, they are rendered "disabled." Although this binary understanding of bodies is ideological rather than biological, Garland-Thomson notes, it nevertheless produces material results and magnifies the precarity of disabled individuals by "legitimating an unequal distribution of resources, status, and power within a biased social and architectural environment."[53]

Disability scholars challenge such hegemonic discourses by reimagining disability as a wide-ranging continuum that encompasses all minds and bodies and a product of history and culture. "Disability," writes Garland-Thomson, "is not a natural state of corporeal inferiority, inadequacy, excess, or a stroke of misfortune. Rather, disability is a culturally fabricated narrative of the body, similar to what we understand as the fictions of race and gender."[54] This social model of disability stands in stark contrast to the medical model that understands disability as an individual problem, affliction, or disease needing cure or a limitation to be overcome through hard work, pluck, and a great attitude. While acknowledging that certain impairments, including some neurological conditions and disorders that cause chronic pain, pose real difficulties, the social model of disability stresses that people are "disabled" primarily by environments, policies, and attitudes that fail to accommodate and include the vast array of human particularities. Hence, disability is not an individual problem but a human variation that needs to be accommodated through improvements in social, ideological, and economic structures. Many proponents of the social model of disability also recognize that the actual lived experiences of individuals with disabilities are multidimensional and shape the ways in which the environment is experienced. Hence, they stress the variability of the lived experiences of disabilities and their interaction with other identities such as gender, race, class, sexual orientation, age, and a host of other factors within varied environmental contexts.[55]

Applied to education, the social model of disability refuses to mark as aberrant particular students' bodies and minds but instead recognizes the variability of all students and the need to modify, adapt, and manipulate the classroom environment, curriculum, and pedagogy to accommodate this variability. The concept of UDL is the best example of the application of the social model of disability to educational approaches. Universal design involves designing products, buildings, or environments so that they can be used readily by the widest possible range of individuals. Although well established in architecture and other domains, universal design is relatively new to elementary and secondary education and even newer to higher education.[56] Based on neuroscientific evidence that individuals with varied backgrounds, abilities, and motivations have different learning needs, UDL means the creation and implementation of teaching methods and materials that reduce barriers in the learning environment and that allow learning goals to be achievable by all students.

Unlike traditional pedagogical approaches that expect diverse students to adapt to typically inflexible curricula, UDL adapts the curricula to increase access for everyone. Unlike traditional approaches that locate obstacles faced by students with disabilities, UDL understands that such obstacles are often the same obstacles encountered by students with different learning styles, backgrounds, and languages. Unlike traditional approaches that see accommodations and adaptive technologies as useful and appropriate only for students with disabilities, UDL recognizes the value and necessity of "cognitive prostheses" for enhancing the academic performance of all students.[57] Fundamentally, UDL acknowledges the unfairness of using one teaching approach, one form of assessment, or one type of curriculum that tends to privilege one type of learner. As a quotation (probably erroneously) attributed to Einstein cautions, "If you judge a fish by its ability to climb a tree, it will live its whole life believing that it is stupid."

My journey with Zoey through the murky and frustrating terrain of inclusive education has generated my outrage over how little our educational institutions, for whatever reason, truly fail to accommodate the needs of diverse learners. But it was not until I discovered UDL that I fully recognized the limits of my own teaching approaches. I had long prided myself as a disability advocate and ally, fully committed to working with individual students to ensure that they are able to access the course content. But it had never occurred to me that my view of accommodations was fundamentally flawed. It assumed that accommodations were something from which only students with disabilities benefitted. It offered accommodations on an individual, case-by-case basis. It was always an addition to existing curricular approaches, not something built into the curriculum from the start. Worst of all, my teaching methods, materials, requirements, and assessments made numerous ableist assumptions about my students' capacities to see, hear, speak, move, read, write, understand English, attend, organize, engage, and remember.

Through my exploration of UDL, I not only began to reevaluate my own narrow understanding of accommodations but also to recognize the highly medicalized, neoliberal framework that guides the policies and practices of university disability services. To access these services, federal law requires a student to self-identify as disabled and to provide sometimes extensive medical documentation to university administrators, who determine what type of accommodations are necessary and appropriate.[58] While instructors are required to provide these accommodations, it is left to the student to individually approach each instructor and to negotiate and arrange the accommodations.[59] Due to financial constraints, lack of health insurance, biases from health care professionals, and other reasons, many students are unable to obtain documentation of a medically diagnosed disability and are therefore unable to access needed services.[60] Even students who do have a medical diagnosis are frequently reluctant to self-identify due to fear of stigma, social ostracism, or not being believed.[61] This is especially true for students with invisible disabilities, who are subjected to heightened scrutiny by doctors, administrators, and professors because they do not readily fit the narrow, stereotypical portrait of what disability "should" look like.[62] "In the absence of visible signs of impairment," writes Karen Jung, those with chronic illnesses or other types of nonvisible disabilities are seen as less "legitimate" and therefore must repeatedly explain, justify, and even apologize for their need for accommodations in each course that they take.[63] Too often, students with disabilities encounter less than accommodating professors, who resent what they consider the burdensome and intrusive adjustments to their classroom policies and practices and the threat to their academic freedom and standards that adherence to disability laws and policies represent.[64] For professors who privilege traditional forms of teaching and assessment and ways of knowing, students who request accommodations seem less capable, less dedicated, or even lazy.[65] For professors who equate fairness with treating all students exactly the same, accommodations given to a few appear to be special privileges that unfairly disadvantage "the other students."[66]

The policies that guide universities' disability services are a product of the ableism that is built into the very foundations of our educational institutions.[67] By framing disability as a medical problem best solved through individual efforts, these policies tend to further pathologize, stigmatize, and marginalize the very students they are designed to aid.[68] Doctors define who is disabled, and university administrators determine what forms of accommodation are needed based on their perception of a student's level of "impairment."[69] In order to receive accommodations, disabled students are required to disclose personal information about themselves and to repeatedly negotiate and justify their access needs from vulnerable and less powerful positions within institutional spaces and relationships. Accommodations themselves are viewed narrowly as individualized adjustments to existing classroom practices. And, too often, they are treated as special exceptions to the "normal" rules that give unfair advantages to a few students at the expense of the "normal" student majority.[70]

But what if, instead, we thought of accommodations not as something that we add on to existing structures but as guiding principles for how we design all of our teaching approaches, classroom spaces, and university environments? What if we stopped expecting disabled students to expend time and energy negotiating and justifying their access needs and started "holding able-bodied individuals" and educational institutions "accountable for their role in upholding ableist systematic oppression"?[71] What if instead of assuming that accommodations for learning differences undermine equity and fairness, we recognized that equity and fairness are impossible without such accommodations? What if we understood all students as diverse learners who process, create, and communicate knowledge at different rates and through different methods and therefore benefit from flexible and varied methods of learning?[72] What if we shifted our efforts away from trying to fit disabled students into inherently ableist learning environments and worked toward reconstructing the environments themselves as inclusive and intersectional spaces where all diverse learners and their contributions to knowledge creation are accommodated and valued? How would all of these things contribute to an education system that is more equitable, kinder, and just?[73]

For me, UDL provides the most effective framework for tackling systemic ableism in education, transforming current understandings of disability and access, and putting into practice the revolutionary approaches to teaching and learning that I imagined above. The more I studied the benefits of UDL, the more I was inspired to overhaul my own teaching materials and pedagogical approaches. As a professor of gender studies, I have for some time now recognized the effectiveness of exploring gender, race, disability and other concepts through the lens of popular culture. My course on the history and culture of vampires, for example, taps into the enduring cultural fascination with all things vampiric and explores how changes over time in cultural perceptions and representations of vampires reflect shifting gender, race, class, and sexual norms and anxieties. Students who otherwise would not consider taking a class with the word "gender" in the title have proven very eager to take a course on vampires. As I grew to understand the concept of UDL, I recognized that such an approach is compatible in many ways with UDL goals to present curricular materials in ways that are familiar and engaging to students. And so, I launched my initial foray into UDL in the Fall of 2014, when I taught a class on the wildly popular Harry Potter book series—a highly familiar touchstone that perhaps more than any other aspect of popular culture captivated the imagination and influenced the coming-of-age experiences of the current generation of college students. But it would not be enough to teach a course on a theme both comfortable and familiar to my students. To truly achieve UDL, I would need to implement the core UDL principles outlined by the National Center on UDL that call for providing (1) multiple methods of representation of course content, (2) multiple means for students to express what they know, (3) and multiple methods for motivating students to learn.[74]

Multiple Methods of Representation. Students differ in the ways that they perceive and comprehend information, and all students face disability when information is presented to them in ways that they find difficult or impossible to access.[75] Following the social model of disability, such inaccessibility is the root of the problem, not the "condition" of the student. Much like a wheelchair user is disabled by the lack of ramps on buildings, a deaf student, for example, is disabled through lack of interpreters or the absence of closed captioning. Visual learners are disabled when they are offered text-exclusive formats. And students who have nominal experiences in the dominant language, cognitive strategies, and culture of the "average" classroom are disabled when information is presented in a manner that assumes a common background among all students.

Particularly at the high school and postsecondary levels, presentation often consists of text-bound information—notes on the board, worksheets, and textbooks—and teacher-centric instruction—lecture and demonstration. The goal of UDL is not to eliminate these methods but to provide additional methods and materials for diverse learners to acquire the same information and knowledge. Additionally, by providing multiple means of representation, educators are better able to construct bridges between students' culturally influenced thinking systems and those that are unfamiliar to them.[76] These forms of representation might include not only formats such as film, music, or websites but also digital texts that allow for adjustability of display, integrated highlighting, electronic note taking, audio narration, embedded prompts, linked glossaries, and background information. Providing other course materials—including syllabi, Power Point lectures, discussion questions, lecture notes, assignment guidelines, review sheets, and course calendars—in digital formats allows students to use adaptive technologies, such as text readers and closed captioning, and gives all students greater access to course materials by allowing them to navigate course content at their own speed and on their own terms. Freedom from the strictures of print, then, allows students to construct meaning actively via customization of and interactivity with the text itself.[77]

To ensure multiple means of representation in my Harry Potter course, I offered course materials—for example, syllabus, Power Point lectures, discussion questions, and study guides—in digital formats that allowed students to change font style and size, adjust volume and speed controls, and to enhance text and images through closed captioning or voice narration. Within Power Point presentations and lecture notes, I embedded support for vocabulary, unfamiliar references, jargon, colloquialisms, and symbols within the text using hyperlinks to multilingual glossaries and footnotes with definitions and explanations. I made sure that students had access to various formats of the Harry Potter books, including large print editions, text readers, digital readers, and audio books. And we analyzed the themes of the Harry Potter series primarily through individual and group exploration of the novels, movies, websites, blogs, music, and comics.

Multiple Means of Expression. Due to their wide range of physical and neurological abilities and cultural experiences and backgrounds, students differ greatly in the ways they can work within a learning environment and express what they know.[78] Yet, in most classrooms, options for the expression of knowledge are often limited to exams, essays, and class discussion. While some students effectively express their thoughts through these more traditional methods, other students better display knowledge through other means, such as performance, art projects, music, film production, digital chat rooms, and website design. A UDL approach recognizes that there is no one means of expression that will be optimal for all students, nor one kind of scaffolding or support that will help them as they learn to express themselves. Providing diverse students with a variety of options for expressing what they know, therefore, is key.

To offer multiple means of expression, I allowed students in my Harry Potter course to participate actively through a variety of means, including in-class discussions, course chat rooms, handing in written notes on course readings, and outside-of-class reflective essays. Students also demonstrated knowledge through short response papers, film reports, group teaching presentations, and a collaborative term project, which could be based on any subject relevant to Harry Potter and American culture and be submitted in any format the students chose, including film, music composition, art work, performance, or forms of written expression. I was astounded by the level of creativity and enthusiasm the students exhibited in constructing and presenting their projects. Members of Slytherin House performed a dating game called "How to Date A Slytherin"; members of Hufflepuff used drawings by creating a set of story boards that reimagined the series from Neville Longbottom's point of view; Ravenclaw House wrote a prequel to the Harry Potter series, with each member contributing a chapter to the story; and members of Gryffindor used film to create a tabloid-style newscast narrated by Rita Skeeter featuring some of the more colorful Harry Potter characters.

Multiple Means of Engagement. Students also differ markedly in the ways in which they are motivated to learn. Some students are highly engaged by spontaneity and novelty in the learning environment. While some students appreciate risk and challenge, others want certainty and clear guidelines. Group projects and collaborative learning attract some students, while others prefer individual assignments. Some students are independent learners, while others seek teacher and peer support. Hence, alternative means of engagement are crucial, as no one approach will engage all students.[79]

To offer multiple means of engagement, I gave the students opportunities to work not only independently but also collaboratively with other students and created projects and assignments that allowed for active participation, creativity, individual expression, and exploration. The second day of class, I sorted students into the four Hogwarts houses featured in the series— Gryffindor, Slytherin, Ravenclaw, and Hufflepuff—and they remained in these Houses for the rest of the semester. Students collaborated with fellow House members in discussion and study sessions and worked together on House teaching presentations and group term projects. Houses competed for the highly coveted House Cup by earning points throughout the semester for individual discussion and scores on assignments, group projects, trivia games, and our hugely successful Halloween event, to which we invited the students and teachers from a local elementary school. Dressed as characters from the series, my students served the children a colorful assortment of

Hogwarts-inspired foods and drinks (which they had worked together to prepare from scratch) and led them through a series of crafts and games, including "Pin the Tail on the Dementor" and Quidditch, of course. In order to further shift away from a teacher-centered to a student-centered approach, I attempted to include students as much as possible in course design. As Jay Dolmage notes, teachers should not be the only designers of course content but should work actively with students to develop pedagogy that is considered, flexible, and responsive to students' needs.[80] Throughout the semester, students contributed to the creation of exam questions and other assessments and engaged in self and peer evaluations. Each House was responsible for creating a teaching presentation based on materials and themes that members of the House selected. When evaluating students' work, I made sure that my comments were positive and encouraging and contained specific information for how to improve performance, and I gave students the opportunity to redo assignments using my feedback and suggestions. No in-class activity lasted longer than twenty minutes, which allowed for variation in the pace of work and gave students opportunities for breaks.

The overwhelmingly positive response, high academic performance, and enthusiasm of my students, along with the comfortable, joyful, and inclusive classroom atmosphere we worked diligently to construct, affirmed my faith in dialogic teaching and the tremendous possibilities of UDL in addressing the needs of all students.[81] Still, I encountered barriers to student learning that remained challenging to overcome through the application of existing UDL models and approaches; my exploration of the literature on UDL up to this point revealed that the "universal" part of UDL focused primarily on accommodating a variety of learning styles and much less on how UDL can accommodate a variety of behaviors or mental health needs in the classroom.[82] In other words, it seems to me that UDL experts need to address more fully how classroom spaces, teaching materials, and pedagogical approaches can be adapted to meet the needs of students at all levels with ADHD, anxiety, sensory processing disorders, depression, and mental health disabilities. How does UDL accommodate students who are too depressed to attend class, whose anxiety or distractibility prevents them from responding to any task or learning approach, or whose intense reactions to or overstimulation within certain classroom environments produce behaviors that distract or frighten their peers? How does UDL help to create an environment in which students feel safe and comfortable disclosing an "invisible" disability, including ADHD, autism, and psychiatric disabilities?

Those of us invested in truly inclusive education also need to consider more fully how a UDL approach can move beyond an emphasis on accommodations for physical and learning differences to a consideration of all constructed barriers to learning, including systemic and institutionalized racism, sexism, classism, homophobia, and religious oppression.[83] According to Heather Hackman, while existing UDL theories rightly criticize the historic exclusion of students with disabilities from educational resources, they are not as thorough in analyzing the systems of power and privilege responsible for this exclusion and how such systems operate to privilege certain ways of thinking and knowing. In other words, a truly "universal" design for learning would adequately consider how teaching materials and approaches that present heterosexuality, whiteness, maleness, ableness, or Christianity as "norms" create barriers to learning for diverse students. As Hackman writes, "whether a quiz is done individually in class, as a take home, or in small groups is irrelevant if the questions on it are inherently biased to White, male, middle-class ways of knowing, thereby making it still inaccessible to a wide range of students."[84] Hence, DSE scholars such as Mitchell, Snyder, and Ware, call for the creation and implementation of "curricular cripistemologies," which foreground the actual lived experiences of disabled and all "nonnormative" people within teaching materials and approaches regardless of the subject. Curricula that contextualize and fully integrate the history, culture, and experiences of diverse people work "to create a receptive atmosphere for productive engagements with embodied differences in school" and lessen the othering of "nonnormative" students that produces stigma and discriminatory treatment.[85]

To these suggestions for reducing the biases of curricular content, I would add that the current literature on UDL also needs to address more fully how UDL helps to dismantle the barriers created by gender and racial segregation in special education. After all, when students look around their school environment and notice that the overwhelming majority of children assigned to special education services and classrooms are Black boys, what messages about gender and race are they absorbing, and how does this awareness affect the learning of students outside of and within these classrooms? And, as Hackman notes, future scholarship needs to address more fully how UDL's emphasis on the implementation of universal design through technology interacts with issues of class, gender, age, and race. Due to generational differences, patterns of gender socialization, and the unequal distribution of economic resources in schools, students who are female, nontraditional, working-class, or persons of color, for example, are disproportionately affected by the "digital divide," that is, forms of economic and social inequality created by lack of access to, use of, or knowledge of information and communication technologies. "To assume that making classrooms accessible without attending to these issues is naive at best," Hackman writes, "and a reproduction of those very forms of oppression at worst."[86]

Relatedly, a universally designed approach to teaching and learning must also take into account the histories and experiences of trauma connected to disability or forms of structural inequality that many students bring with them to the classroom. For these students, certain course materials and discussions may invoke their memories of traumatic experiences and thus trigger anxiety, stress, and other troubling physiological responses.[87] Even within universally designed spaces and approaches, then, course content itself can create inaccessibility. Therefore, "[w]e [must] position trauma and its effects, and our responses to both, as an integral part of our" teaching and learning approaches, argues Alison Kafer, and recognize trauma as a form of disability that deserves to be accommodated in ways that enhance, not restrict, access.[88] "If students find what I bring to the room makes it hard for them to be in the room," Sara Ahmed writes, "I want to find another way to bring things in, or at least to ask myself about different ways of bringing things in."[89] Trigger warnings, for example, are one way to increase access by giving students advance notice about potentially triggering classroom materials and discussions. Such warnings can serve as a useful guide as students navigate their way through difficult material and give them more time to prepare and work through potentially distressful responses. For some students, trigger warnings alert them to the need to engage with course materials and class participation in ways that do not further traumatize them. If they believe that being physically present during a given class period would be too distressing, for example, they could attend virtually, or they could work through the course materials on their own and at a pace that they can handle. Discussion of these materials could take place during individual meetings with the professor or through the submission of a written response. Trigger warnings, then, provide "a way to 'opt in,'" Angela Carter notes, by giving students "agency to attend to the affect and effects of their trauma" and allowing them to "participate in the conversation or activity."[90] However, trigger warnings are not "end points" or simple solutions to the complex forms of trauma students bring to the classroom, as Kafer warns. Rather, they are a starting point for rethinking definitions of access and for expanding the parameters of UDL to make room for students whose ways of knowing are shaped by histories of trauma.[91]

Finally, how do we promote a universal approach to learning without collapsing important distinctions between the perceptions, treatment, and lived experiences of students categorized as disabled and students categorized as "able-bodied?" Within a UDL framework, how do we recognize that the actual lived experiences of disability give some students particular identities and narratives that allow them to make epistemological claims about ableist assumptions and policies within their educational institutions and wider communities and the need for greater social justice? And how do these sorts of situated knowledges, as well as the social locations of all students, contribute to the democratic production of knowledge in the classroom?

Again, Mitchell, Snyder, and Ware remind us of the importance of curricular reform in making the lived experiences of disability an active part of and a
source of knowledge within the UDL classroom from which all students can
learn. In such an environment, students with disabilities are not required to
adapt their minds, bodies, and ways of knowing to a hegemonic norm but can
actively draw from the authority of their personal experiences to contribute to
collective understandings.[92] According to Dene Granger, who grappled with
being labeled as learning disabled due to her dyslexia, situated knowledges
springing from the lived experiences of disability have the potential to revolutionize how students and teachers think about learning. Individuals with
disabilities, she writes, "have the power to revolutionize schools because our
bodies have been the instrument or the center, where we enact and embody
learning in beautiful, in complex, artful, tactile, and sensual ways. . . . We
know how essential this kind of creation is, how this passion can create a
powerful river."[93] As Granger acknowledges, then, disability (along with
other forms of "discredited knowing" such as gender, race, sexuality, among
others) becomes an important way for students to understand their world.
"The non-normatively embodied classroom that emerges within curricular
cripistemologies," write Mitchell, Snyder, and Ware, "becomes a place in
which diversity operates as a nuancing agent of knowledge" that "leaves no
body behind."[94]

CONCLUSION

Ultimately, Universal Design for Learning locates value in productions of
knowledge that have been traditionally ignored, marginalized, or denigrated.
I was reminded of this a few years ago while watching Zoey work on an
assessment with her speech therapist. The therapist was showing Zoey a
series of pictures and asking her to form story arcs based on the stories that
the pictures collectively illustrated. The "correct" subject of one of the pictures, for example, was a mother nervously waving goodbye to her son who
was boarding a school bus for the first time. But instead of focusing on the
picture's central subject, Zoey fixated on the lower frame of the picture where
a cat sat looking rather forlornly, in her view. To whom did the cat belong,
she wondered? Clearly, the cat was hungry—who would feed it? Where
would the cat sleep at night? Despite the therapist's insistence that her focus
was incorrect, Zoey stubbornly refused to alter her gaze and instead continued
to worry about the cat. And as the therapist grew visibly more frustrated, I
stifled my impulse to laugh. After all, why was Zoey's concern for the cat
wrong or misguided? Why was attention to the mother and her son more valued? And perhaps most importantly, who gets to make this decision? Zoey's

tendency to create knowledge from the margins led her to form new meanings about what she was seeing that necessarily disrupted and challenged the pictures' master narratives. In much the same way, UDL gives students and teachers the power to form new discourses that have the potential to radically transform restrictive ideologies and institutions and that create new, multiple understandings of the "right" way to see, hear, think, and know.

NOTES

1. This chapter is a modified and extended version of my earlier article published as "Reimagining Disability and Inclusive Education Through Universal Design for Learning," *Disability Studies Quarterly* 37:2 (2017), https://dsq-sds.org/article/view /5417/4650.

2. Mel Ainscow, et al., *Improving Schools, Developing Inclusion* (London: Routledge, 2006), 2.

3. Susan Baglieri, et al., "Disability Studies in Education: The Need for a Plurality of Perspectives on Disability," *Remedial and Special Education* 32:4 (2011): 267–278, https://doi.org/10.1177/0741932510362200.

4. Susan Baglieri, et al., "[Re]claiming 'Inclusive Education' Toward Cohesion in Educational Reform: Disability Studies Unravels the Myth of the Normal Child," *Teachers College Record* 113:10 (October 2011): 2126–2128. See also Alicia Broderick, et al., "Differentiating Instruction for Disabled Students in Inclusive Classrooms," *Theory Into Practice* 44:3 (Summer 2005): 194–202, https://doi.org/10 .1207/s15430421tip4403_3.

5. Baglieri, et al., "[Re]claiming 'Inclusive Education,'" 2128.

6. For multiple views of social justice in education, see William Ayers, et al., eds., *Handbook of Social Justice in Education* (Abingdon: Routledge, 2008).

7. Mara Sapon-Shevin, "Inclusion: A Matter of Social Justice," *Educational Leadership* 61:2 (October 2003): 28.

8. Full text of the Individuals with Disabilities Education Act, United States Department of Education, accessed March 3, 2015, http://idea.ed.gov/download/statu te.html.

9. David Connor and Beth Ferri, "The Conflict Within: Resistance to Inclusion and Other Paradoxes in Special Education," *Disability & Society* 22:1 (December 2006): 63–77, https://doi.org/10.1080/09687590601056717; Stanley Wigle and Daryl Wilcox, "Inclusion," *Remedial and Special Education* 17:5 (September 1996): 323–329, https://doi.org/0.1177/074193259601700508.

10. Laurel Garrick Duhaney and Spencer Salend, "Parental Perceptions of Inclusive Educational Placements," *Remedial and Special Education* 21 (March 2000): 124–126, https://doi.org/10.1177/074193250002100209.

11. National Education Association, "Truth in Labeling: Disproportionality in Special Education" (National Education Association, December 15, 2007), 2, http:// www.nea.org/assets/docs/HE/EW-TruthInLabeling.pdf.

12. Jamilia Codrington and Halford H. Fairchild, "Special Education and the Mis-Education of African American Children: A Call to Action" (The Association of Black Psychologists, February 13, 2012), 5, http://www.abpsi.org/pdf/specialedpositi onpaper021312.pdf.

13. Valerie Maholmes and Fay Brown, "Over-representation of African-American Students in Special Education: The Role of a Developmental Framework in Shaping Teachers' Interpretations of African-American Students' Behavior," *Trotter Review* 14 (January 1, 2002), 46. https://scholarworks.umb.edu/trotter_rev iew/vol14/iss1/6.

14. Lachrista Greco, "It Happened to Me: I Was in Special Ed," *xojane*, August 10, 2012, http://www.xojane.com/it-happened-to-me/it-happened-me-i-was-spec ial-ed.

15. Greco, "It Happened to Me."

16. Spencer Salend and Laurel Garrick Dehaney, "The Impact of Inclusion on Students With and Without Disabilities and Their Educators," *Remedial and Special Education* 20:2 (March/April 1999): 114–126, https://doi.org/10.1177/07419325990 2000209; Dev Poonam and Leslie Haynes, "Teacher Perspectives on Suitable Learning Environments for Students with Disabilities: What Have We Learned from Inclusive, Resource, and Self-Contained Classrooms?" *International Journal of Interdisciplinary Social Sciences* 9 (May 2015): 53–64.

17. Duhaney and Salend, "Parental Perceptions of Inclusive Educational Placements," 124.

18. Cara Liebowitz, "Redefining Inclusion," *That Crazy Crippled Chick*, June 20, 2011, http://thatcrazycrippledchick.blogspot.com/2011/06/redefining-inclusion.html.

19. John O'Neil, "Can Inclusion Work?" A Conversation with Jim Kauffman and Mara Sapon-Shevin," *Educational Leadership* 52 (December 1994/January 1995): 7–11, http://www.ascd.org/publications/educational_leadership/dec94/vol52/num04 /Can_Inclusion_Work¢_A_Conversation_with_Jim_Kauffman_and_Mara_Sapon -Shevin.aspx.

20. National Education Association, "Special Education," accessed January 13, 2021, https://www.nea.org/student-success/smart-just-policies/special-education.

21. Quoted in Celia R. Baker, "Teaching Students with Intellectual Disabilities in Regular Classrooms Good for Kids or Good for All?" *Deseret News,* January 7, 2013, http://www.deseretnews.com/article/865570116/.

22. O'Neil, "Can Inclusion Work?" 7–11.

23. The United States Commission on Civil Rights, "Minorities in Special Education" (December 3, 2007), 109–110, http://www.usccr.gov/pubs/Minoritie sinSpecialEducation.pdf.

24. Bonnie Dupuis, et al., "Does Inclusion Help Students: Perspectives from Regular Education and Students with Disabilities," *Journal of the American Academy of Special Education Professionals* (Summer 2006), http://aasep.org/aasep-publica tions/journal-of-the-american-academy-of-special-education-professionals-jaasep/ jaasep-summer-2006/does-inclusion-help-students-perspectives-from-regular-educat ion-and-students-with-disabilities/.

25. See Baglieri, et al., "[Re]claiming 'Inclusive Education,'" 2123–2154.

26. David Mitchell, et al., "'Every Child Left Behind': Curricular Cripistemologies and the Crip/Queer Art of Failure," *Journal of Literary & Cultural Disability Studies* 8:3 (2014): 298, https://doi.org/10.3828/jlcds.2014.24.

27. See, for example, David Connor and Beth Ferri, "Integration and Inclusion: A Troubling Nexus: Race, Disability, and Special Education," *The Journal of African American History* 90 (Winter 2005): 107–127; D. Kim Reid and Michelle Knight, "Disability Justifies the Exclusion of Minority Students: A Critical History Grounded in Disability Studies," *Educational Researcher* 35:6 (August/September 2006): 18–23; Wanda Blanchett, "Disproportionate Representation of African American Students in Special Education: Acknowledging the Role of White Privilege and Racism," *Educational Researcher* 35:6 (August/September 2006): 24–28, https://do i.org/10.3102/0013189X035006024; Carla O'Connor and Sonia DeLuca Fernandez, "Race, Class, and Disproportionality: Reevaluating the Relationship between Poverty and Special Education Placement," *Educational Researcher* 35:6 (Aug/September 2006): 6–11.

28. Many scholars have written about racial disproportionality in judgmental disability categories. See, for example, Roey Ahram et al., "Addressing Racial/Ethnic Disproportionality in Special Education: Case Studies of Suburban School Districts," *Teachers College Record* 113:10 (October 2011): 2233–2266.

29. Zanita Fenton, "Disabling Racial Repetition," in *Righting Educational Wrongs: Disability Studies in Law and Education*, eds. Beth Ferri and Arlene Kanter (Syracuse: Syracuse University Press, 2013), 113.

30. Terese C. Jimenez et al., "Gaining Access to General Education: The Promise of Universal Design for Learning," *Issues in Teacher Education* 16 (Fall 2007): 44.

31. Fenton, "Disabling Racial Repetition," 94; Maholmes and Brown, "Overrepresentation of African-American Students in Special Education," 49.

32. National Education Association, "Truth in Labeling," 14–15. See also Connor and Ferri, "Integration and Inclusion," 114.

33. The United States Commission on Civil Rights, "Minorities in Special Education."

34. O'Connor and Fernandez, "Race, Class, and Disproportionality," 8.

35. Beth Ferri and David Connor, *Reading Resistance: Discourses of Exclusion in Desegregation and Inclusion Debates* (New York: Peter Lang, 2006), 181.

36. Fenton, "Disabling Racial Repetition," 87.

37. U.S. Department of Education, Office of Special Education Programs, "IDEA Section 618 Data Products: Static Tables, Tables 1–12: Children and students served under IDEA, Part B, in the U.S. and outlying areas, by gender and age group," accessed July 15, 2016, http://www.ideadata.org/tables30th/ar_1-12.htm.

38. National Education Association, "Truth in Labeling," 14.

39. Martha Coutinho and Donald Oswald, "State Variation in Gender Disproportionality in Special Education," *Remedial and Special Education* 26:1 (January/February 2005): 8, https://doi.org/10.1177/07419325050260010201; Jennifer Tschantz and Joy Markowitz, "Gender and Special Education: Current State Data Collection," (*Project Forum*, January 2003), 2, http://www.nasdse.org/Des

ktopModules/DNNspot-Store/ProductFiles/143_49aabfa1-ef5c-4ece-9cbc-cedc6a40
5578.pdf.

40. Emily Arms et al., "Gender Bias and Imbalance: Girls in US Special Education Programmes," *Gender and Education* 20:4 (July 2008): 349–359, https ://doi.org/10.1080/09540250802190180. See also Amanda Sullivan and Aydin Bal, "Disproportionality in Special Education: Effects of Individual and School Variables on Disability Risk," *Exceptional Children* 79:4 (Summer 2013): 475–494; Martha Coutinho et al., "The Influence of Sociodemographics and Gender on the Disproportionate Identification of Minority Students as Having Learning Disabilities," *Remedial and Special Education* 23:1 (January/February 2002): 49–59; and Kathy Piechura-Couture et al., "The Boy Factor: Can Single-Gender Classes Reduce the Overrepresentation of Boys in Special Education?" *College Student Journal* 47:2 (Summer 2013): 235–243.

41. Centers for Disease Control and Prevention, "Prevalence and Characteristics of Autism Spectrum Disorder among Children Aged 8 Years — Autism and Developmental Disabilities Monitoring Network, 11 Sites, United States, 2012," *Surveillance Summaries* 65 (April 1, 2016): 1–23, http://www.cdc.gov/mmwr/volume s/65/ss/ss6503a1.htm.

42. See, for example, M. Gill, "The Other 25%: Autistic Girls and Women," *European Psychiatry* 33 (March 2016): 351–352, https://doi.org/10.1016/j.eurpsy.20 16.01.1246; Katharina Dworzynski et al., "How Different Are Girls and Boys Above and Below the Diagnostic Threshold for Autism Spectrum Disorders?" *Journal of the American Academy of Child and Adolescent Psychology* 51 (August 2012): 788–797, https://doi.org/10.1016/j.jaac.2012.05.018; and Agnieszka Rynkiewicz et al., "An Investigation of the 'Female Camouflage Effect' in Autism Using a Computerized ADOS-2 and a Test of Sex/Gender Differences," *Molecular Autism* 7 (January 21, 2016): 1–8, https://doi.org/10.1186/s13229-016-0073-0.

43. Rynkiewicz et al., "An Investigation of the 'Female Camouflage Effect' in Autism," 1–8; Radha Kothari et al., "Gender Differences in the Relationship between Social Communication and Emotion Recognition," *Journal of the American Academy of Child and Adolescent Psychology* 52 (November 2013): 1155, https://doi.org/10.1 016/j.jaac.2013.08.006.

44. Jolynn Haney, "Autism, Females, and the DSM-5: Gender Bias in Autism Diagnosis," *Social Work in Mental Health* 14:4 (2016): 396–407, https://doi.org/10.1 080/15332985.2015.1031858.

45. Donald Oswald et al., "Trends in the Special Education Identification Rates of Boys and Girls: A Call for Research and Change," *Exceptionality* 11 (2003): 223–237; Beth Ferri and David Connor, "'I Was the Special Ed Girl': Urban Working-Class Young Women of Colour," *Gender and Education* 22:1 (January 2010): 105–121, https://doi.org/10.1080/09540250802612688. See also Coutinho and Oswald, "State Variation in Gender Disproportionality in Special Education," 7–15; Sullivan and Bal, "Disproportionality in Special Education," 475–494; Coutinho et al., "The Influence of Sociodemographics and Gender," 49–59; and Piechura-Couture et al., "The Boy Factor," 235–243. Most scholars note that the underreprentation of girls in disability categories is evident across all racial and ethnic groups. But Subini Ancy Annamma

claims that while girls as a whole "are underrepresented in disciplinary actions and special education, . . . young women of color and young women who identify as queer are overrepresented in both categories." See Subini Ancy Annamma, "It Was Just Like a Piece of Gum: Using an Intersectional Approach to Understand Criminalizing Young Women of Color with Disabilities in the School to Prison Pipeline," in *Practicing Disability Studies in Education: Acting Toward Social Change*, eds. David Connor, Jan Valle, and Chris Hale (New York: Peter Lang, 2015), 84.

46. Arms et al., "Gender Bias and Imbalance," 352.

47. American Association of University Women Public Policy and Government Relations Department, "Educating Girls with Disabilities" (American Association of University Women, July 2009), 3, http://www.aauw.org/files/2013/02/position-on -disability-education-111.pdf.

48. Merle Froschl et al., "Connecting Gender and Disability," *Gender and Disability Digest* (Newton, MA: Women's Educational Equity Act Resource Center, 1999), 3, http://www2.edc.org/WomensEquity/pdffiles/disabdig.pdf.

49. Amity Noltemeyer and Caven McLoughlin, eds., *Disproportionality in Education and Special Education: A Guide to Creating More Equitable Learning Environments* (Springfield: Charles C. Thomas Publishing, 2012), 51–52.

50. Noltemeyer and McLoughlin, *Disproportionality in Education and Special Education*, 51.

51. Arms et al., "Gender Bias and Imbalance," 355; Ferri and Connor, "I Was the Special Ed Girl," 107.

52. See Baglieri et al., "[Re]claiming 'Inclusive Education' Toward Cohesion in Educational Reform," 2123–2154.

53. Rosemarie Garland-Thomson, "Integrating Disability, Transforming Feminist Theory," *National Women's Studies Association Journal* 14:3 (2002), 5–6, http:// www.jstor.org/stable/4316922. See also Rosemarie Garland-Thomson, *Extraordinary Bodies: Figuring Physical Disability in American Culture and Literature* (New York: Columbia University Press, 1997).

54. Garland-Thomson, "Integrating Disability," 5.

55. Jeanne Higbee and Emily Goff, eds., *Pedagogy and Student Services for Institutional Transformation: Implementing Universal Design in Higher Education* (Minneapolis: University of Minnesota, 2008), 14–15.

56. David Rose et al., "Universal Design for Learning in Postsecondary Education: Reflections on Principles and their Application," *Journal of Postsecondary Education and Disability* 19 (Fall 2006): 135.

57. Dave Edyburn, "Would You Recognize Universal Design for Learning if You Saw It? Ten Propositions for New Directions for the Second Decade of UDL," *Learning Disability Quarterly* 33 (Winter 2010): 39, https://doi.org/10.1177/073194 871003300103.

58. Karla McGregor et al., "The University Experience of Students with Learning Disabilities," *Learning Disabilities Research & Practice* 31:2 (2016): 90–102, https:// doi.org/10.1111/ldrp.12102.

59. Shahd Alshammari, "A Hybridized Academic Identity: Negotiating a Disability within Academia's Discourse of Ableism," in *Negotiating Disability: Disclosure and*

Higher Education, eds. Stephanie Kerschbaum, Laura Eisenmann, and James Jones (Ann Arbor: University of Michigan Press, 2017), 25–38.

60. Laura Marshak et al., "Exploring Barriers to College Student Use of Disability Services and Accommodations," *Journal of Postsecondary Education and Disability* 22:3 (2010): 151–165, http://www.eric.ed.gov/PDFS/EJ906688.pdf.

61. Karen Elizabeth Jung, "Chronic Illness and Educational Equity: The Politics of Visibility," in *Feminist Disability Studies*, ed. Kim Q. Hall (Bloomington: Indiana University Press, 2011), 263–286; Emma Cole and Stephanie Cawthon, "Self-Disclosure Decisions of University Students with Learning Disabilities," *Journal of Postsecondary Education and Disability* 28:2 (2015): 163–179, http://files.eric .ed.gov/fulltext/EJ1074663.pdf; Joyce Davidson and Victoria Henderson, "'Coming Out' on the Spectrum: Autism, Identity and Disclosure," *Social and Cultural Geography* 11:2 (2010): 155–170, https://doi.org/10.1080/14649360903525240; Andrea De Cesarei, "Psychological Factors that Foster or Deter the Disclosure of Disability by University Students," *Psychological Reports* 116:3 (2015): 665–673, https://doi.org/10.2466/15.PR0.116k26w9; Marjorie Oleny and Karin Brockelman, "Out of the Disability Closet: Strategic Use of Perception Management by Select University Students with Disabilities," *Disability & Society* 18:1 (2003): 35–50, https://doi.org/10.1080/713662200; Ellen Samuels, "Passing, Coming Out, and Other Magical Acts," in *Negotiating Disability: Disclosure and Higher Education*, eds. Stephanie Kerschbaum, Laura Eisenmann, and James Jones (Ann Arbor: University of Michigan Press, 2017), 15–24.

62. Nicole Matthews, "Teaching The 'Invisible' Disabled Students in the Classroom: Disclosure, Inclusion and the Social Model of Disability," *Teaching in Higher Education* 14:3 (2009): 229–239, https://doi.org/10.1080/13562510902 898809.

63. Jung, "Chronic Illness and Educational Equity," 278; DeAnn Lechtenberger and William Lan, "Accommodation Strategies of College Students with Disabilities," *The Qualitative Report* 15:2 (2010): 411–429, http://www.nova.edu/ssss/QR/QR15 -2/barnard-brak.pdf.

64. Stephanie Cawthon and Emma Cole, "Postsecondary Students who Have a Learning Disability: Student Perspectives on Accommodation Access and Obstacles," *Journal of Postsecondary Education and Disability* 23:2 (2010): 112–128, http:// www.eric.ed.gov/PDFS/EJ906696.pdf.

65. Tanya Osborne, "Not Lazy, Not Faking: Teaching and Learning Experiences of University Students with Disabilities," *Disability & Society* 34:2 (2019): 228–252, https://doi.org/10.1080/09687599.2018.1515724.

66. Holly Pearson and Lisa Boskovich, "Problematizing Disability Disclosure in Higher Education: Shifting towards a Liberating Humanizing Intersectional Framework," *Disability Studies Quarterly* 39:1 (2019), https://dsq-sds.org/article/vi ew/6001/5187; Jung, "Chronic Illness and Educational Equity," 274.

67. Jay Dolmage, *Academic Ableism: Disability and Higher Education* (Ann Arbor: University of Michigan Press, 2017), 3, 11; Carla Corroto and Lucinda Havenhand, "Institutional Resistance to Accessible Architecture and Design: A Collaborative Autoethnography," in *Qualitative Inquiry: Methods for Rethinking*

an Ableist World, eds. Ronald Berger and Laura Lorenz (Burlington, VT: Ashgate Publishing Company, 2015), 109–125.

68. Jung, "Chronic Illness and Educational Equity," 278; Corroto and Havenhand, 109–125; Dolmage, *Academic Ableism*, 11.

69. S. Prowse, "Institutional Construction of Disabled Students," *Journal of Higher Education Policy and Management* 31:1 (2009): 89–96, https://doi.org/10.1 080/13600800802559302.

70. Jung, "Chronic Illness and Educational Equity," 271.

71. Pearson and Boskovich, "Problematizing Disability Disclosure in Higher Education." Here, Pearson and Boskovich refer to the work of Mia Mingus and her application of her concept of access intimacy to education.

72. Pearson and Boskovich, "Problematizing Disability Disclosure in Higher Education."

73. Eduardo Barrangan and Emily Nusbaum, "Perceptions of Disability on a Postsecondary Campus: Implications for Oppression and Human Love," in *Negotiating Disability: Disclosure and Higher Education*, eds. Stephanie Kerschbaum, Laura Eisenmann, and James Jones (Ann Arbor: University of Michigan Press, 2017), 39–56.

74. National Center on Universal Design for Learning, "Universal Design for Learning Guidelines," *CAST*, accessed March 28, 2015, http://www.udlcenter.org/aboutudl/udlguidelines_theorypractice.

75. Rose et al., "Universal Design for Learning in Postsecondary Education," 136.

76. Meia Chita-Tegmark et al., "Using the Universal Design for Learning Framework to Support Culturally Diverse Learners," *Journal of Education* 192 (2011/2012): 19, https://doi.org/10.1177/002205741219200104.

77. Anne Meyer et al., *Universal Design for Learning: Theory and Practice* (Wakefield, MA: CAST, Inc., 2014), 2.

78. Rose et al., "Universal Design for Learning in Postsecondary Education," 137.

79. Rose et al., "Universal Design for Learning in Postsecondary Education," 137.

80. Jay Dolmage, "Disability Studies Pedagogy, Usability and Universal Design," *Disability Studies Quarterly* 25:4 (Fall 2005), https://doi.org/10.18061/dsq.v25i4.

81. See, for example, Stephanie Kurtts, "Universal Design for Learning in Inclusive Classrooms," *Electronic Journal for Inclusive Education* 1 (Spring 2006): 1–16, http://corescholar.libraries.wright.edu/cgi/viewcontent.cgi?article=1071&context=ejie.

82. For example, the book *Universal Design in Higher Education: From Principles to Practice* edited by Sheryl Burgstahler and Rebecca Cory (Cambridge: Harvard Education Press, 2008) devotes only one out of twenty-four chapters to how UDL can accommodate students with psychiatric disorders. Similarly, Jeanne Higbee and Emily Goff, eds., *Pedagogy and Student Services for Institutional Transformation: Implementing Universal Design in Higher Education* (Minneapolis: University of Minnesota, 2008) includes only one chapter out of thirty-eight to the issue of invisible disabilities and the need for safe environments for disclosure.

83. Kristina Knoll, for example, urges scholars "not only to take into account the many and varied bodily, mental, and psychological differences, but also to consider

how race, class, sexuality, religion, nationality, and so on, can intersect with the disability experience." Kristina Knoll, "Feminist Disability Studies Pedagogy," *Feminist Teacher* 19:2 (2009): 122.

84. Heather Hackman, "Broadening the Pathway to Academic Success: The Critical Intersections of Social Justice Education, Critical Multicultural Education, and Universal Instructional Design," in *Pedagogy and Student Services for Institutional Transformation: Implementing Universal Design in Higher Education,* eds. Jeanne Higbee and Emily Goff (Minneapolis: University of Minnesota, 2008), 39.

85. Mitchell et al., "'Every Child Left Behind,'" 302.

86. Hackman, "Broadening the Pathway to Academic Success," 36–37.

87. Sara Ahmed, "Feminist Hurt/Feminism Hurts," *feministkilljoys,* July 21, 2014, https://feministkilljoys.com/2014/07/21/feminist-hurtfeminism-hurts/.

88. Alison Kafer, "Un/safe Disclosures: Scenes of Disability and Trauma," *Journal of Literary & Cultural Disability Studies* 10:1 (March 2016): 17, https://doi .org/10.3828/jlcds.2016.1. See also Angela Carter, "Teaching with Trauma: Trigger Warnings, Feminism, and Disability Pedagogy," *Disability Studies Quarterly* 35:2 (2015), https://dsq-sds.org/article/view/4652/3935.

89. Ahmed, "Feminist Hurt/Feminism Hurts."

90. Carter, "Teaching with Trauma."

91. Kafer, "Un/safe Disclosures," 17.

92. Mitchell et al., "'Every Child Left Behind,'" 308.

93. Dene Granger, "A Tribute to My Dyslexic Body, As I Travel in the Form of a Ghost," *Disability Studies Quarterly* 30 (2010), http://dsq-sds.org/article/view/1236 /1281.

94. Mitchell et al., "'Every Child Left Behind,'" 308.

Part III

LOCATING DISABILITY

Chapter 5

Burrowing within Disability

When I was a child, I was terrified of the dark. This terror was a source of irritation for my older sister, Jill, whose need for a restful sleep was perpetually compromised by the little cat-shaped lamp with the pink and white checkered shade that illuminated our shared room every night. By contrast, my grandmother, or Grandmom, as we all called her, was deeply sympathetic to my fear and always made sure to leave on the hallway light outside of the bedroom where I slept each time that I spent the night at her house. On one particular night, long after I had finished reading the Archie and Superman comic books that Grandmom always kept for me in a little basket by the side of the bed and drifted off to sleep, my uncle arrived home. Not wanting to wake me, he shut the door to my bedroom and, consequently, closed off my light source. I awoke at some point in the night surrounded in pitch blackness. Panic set in as I stumbled out of bed and felt my way around the room, frantically searching for the door. But each step seemed only to submerge me deeper into the darkness. My heart pounded in my chest and tears streamed down my cheeks until finally I began screaming in sheer desperation. And then, Grandmom was there. She stayed with me the rest of that night, climbing into the big bed with the dark wooden headboard and squeaky springs, rubbing my arms and back while I struggled to regain control over my breathing. "Do you see that picture on the wall?" she asked. I looked up to where she was pointing and recognized the picture that I had seen many times but to which I had previously not given much thought. It was a large and apparently very old framed black-and-white photo of a baby swaddled in a fluffy white blanket sleeping peacefully under the watchful protection of a black and white dog, who was sitting directly at the baby's side. The picture had hung in the bedroom of her own grandmother's house, she explained, and when she began to grow afraid during the nights when she slept over, she would look at the faithful watchdog standing guard over the sleeping baby and immediately feel safe. There was indeed something oddly soothing about the image, I thought to myself as I stared at the picture. The longer I stared, the steadier my breathing grew and the heavier my eyelids began to feel, and sleep, when it finally came, was peaceful and uninterrupted by the insomnia that normally characterized my nights. From that night forward, the picture of the baby and the dog on my grandmother's wall became a source of comfort surpassing even that of the hallway nightlight.

My grandmother and I were organically connected on so many levels—not only by kinship, of course, but also by our deep appreciation for and implicit understanding of one another. Grandmom personified the best traits of the human spirit—kindness, gentleness, resilience, honesty, compassion, gratitude, faithfulness, and integrity. She gave so much more than she took. She found beauty, delight, and joy in such simple things. She laughed often and infectiously. She listened empathically and offered wise counsel. But it was her remarkable ability to see the best in others, to find strength in human faults, and to locate the possibilities within every problem that made her a magnet in her family and community. Children, adults, and even animals flocked to her, knowing that a moment in her company would make them feel better about themselves. In a world in which I often felt misunderstood, she was my source of unquestioning, uncritical acceptance. In my impetuousness, she found courage and daring. In my stubbornness, she located self-assuredness. With her, my hyperactivity and distractibility became creativity, enthusiasm, and boundless energy. She adored me and I her. And though I did not realize it until much later—and even then in ways I am still parsing out—my grandmother and I were also linked by trauma and disability. From the experience of trauma, we gained locations in disability from which we formed critical new insights into ourselves and the ableist society that we inhabited.

Like my grandmother, I experience disability as a form of complex embodiment, that is, as a result of both my bodymind[1] and the particular and shifting environments in which my bodymind is located. At least one of my disabilities—a significant congenital hearing loss in one ear—causes no pain or discomfort and becomes disabling only in unaccommodating environments. Diseases resulting from my genetic autoimmune disorder, however, have been sources of debilitating pain and distress, weakening, immobilizing, and scarring me with their power. And then there is my obsessive-compulsive disorder. Born from trauma when I was seven years old, my OCD remained for many years unacknowledged and unrecognized, the symptom and cause of an anxiety steadily gaining strength the more I silently fed and nurtured it even while it often tortured and exhausted me. It lives with me always, a mostly manageable condition today but one that—like my autoimmune disorders—can flicker or flare in reaction to certain triggers.

Raising Zoey gradually provided me with a disability lens through which I grew to understand my own relationship to disability. bell hooks once wrote that "I came to theory because I was hurting . . . . I came to theory desperate, wanting to comprehend—to grasp what was happening around and within me. Most importantly, I wanted to make the hurt go away. I saw in theory then a location for healing."[2] Like hooks, I came to theory because I was hurting. As I watched Zoey struggle to fit into a world that was not made for her, I turned to disability theory, "desperate, wanting to comprehend." Through theory, I found the language to contextualize Zoey's experiences and the analytical tools to make sense of them. In disability theory, I recognized my grandmother's experiences, as well as my own; I began to understand these experiences and the histories and moments from which they emerged in transformative ways. In disability theory, I found a home, a community, and a new identity. Through a disability lens, I began to reinterpret my past and ultimately to recognize how many of my disability experiences were, in turn, inextricably connected to my grandmother. Drawing from the opportunities and privileges she never had, I have been able to transform my individual experiences and perspectives into a disability standpoint. That is, I have been able to make epistemological claims about disability that are different from and in opposition to dominant claims and that call for a restructuring of institutions, environments, and attitudes so that the tremendous diversity of bodies and minds can be fully accommodated, included, and accepted. In theory, I found a location for healing. Through theory, I found a way to "confront [my] demons," as Gloria Anzuldúa once put it, to "look them in the face and live to write about them. Fear acts like a magnet; it draws the demons out of the closet and into the ink in our pens."[3]

While I easily located many of my experiences and those of my daughter and grandmother within disability theory, other aspects of our experiences were not as comfortably situated. Disability defies easy definition because it assumes a multitude of different forms and applies to a diverse array of people whose experiences of disability are highly particularized. This vastness and diversity of disability, however, are not always reflected in disability theory, which tends to highlight and even privilege certain disability identities and narratives. I have found it curious that the field of disability studies—from which I have gained such tremendous insights and new forms of knowledge—has relatively little to say about the link between disability and trauma.[4] After all, many people become disabled as a result of experiencing or witnessing traumatic events, such as war, accidents, illnesses, and physical or sexual assaults, or from experiencing the traumas of racism, poverty, or other forms of structural inequality.[5] Likewise, disability studies seems to make too little room for an acknowledgment of pain and feelings of loss and mourning that can follow disabling experiences.[6] But perhaps these relative silences in disability studies are not so curious after all, given the important and crucial work of disability studies scholars that questions and delegitimizes hegemonic understandings of disability rooted in ableism and in medical models that locate disability in bodies and minds viewed as broken, pitiable, and tragic. Such work has been essential to addressing pervasive forms of discrimination against disabled persons and to the passage of disability rights legislation. To explore the connection between disability and trauma, therefore, would be to risk underscoring the ableist narratives and tropes that disability scholars are attempting to dismantle.[7] As Daniel Morrison and Monica Casper acknowledge, "To refocus attention on the physical acts of disabling—the signal moments of bodily breach and psychic tear—feels dangerous."[8]

Disability studies' emphasis on the disabling effects of society means that too often, the sometimes disabling effects of bodies and the traumatic causes or consequences of disability remain undertheorized and even "unspeakable in disability discourse," as James Berger argues.[9] Certainly, people are disabled by unaccommodating environments and attitudes. And, certainly, even bodies and minds disabled by chronic pain, illness, injury, and neurological conditions—what Alison Kafer calls "the lived realities of impairment"—can never be understood apart from the particular histories, geographic locations, cultures, social structures, institutions, and ideologies that give them meaning.[10] But in failing to consider or acknowledge how some people experience disability through trauma or the ways in which some experience trauma as a result of disability, we are unable to understand the particular environments that give these experiences meaning and therefore seriously undermine, as Liz Crow writes, "our collective ability to conceive of, and achieve, a world which does not disable."[11] When we insist on the desirability of disability, we are unable to recognize and theorize how some experience and understand their disabilities as undesirable or painful.[12] And when we fail to emphasize all disability experiences and the intersectional nature of oppression, we risk falling into a "'disability essentialism,'" as Anna Mollow cautions, "in which the experiences, needs, desires, and aims of all disabled people are assumed to be the same and those with 'different' experiences are accommodated only if they do not make claims that undermine the movement's foundational arguments."[13] This essentialism has the effect of silencing or rendering ineligible the narratives of those whose disabilities are rooted in and/or shaped by trauma, suffering, structural inequalities, or forms of interpersonal or state-sanctioned violence, as Mia Mingus painfully acknowledges:

> In all of my work for disability justice, I always come back to the human parts
> of disability. The parts that we would rather not talk about. The parts that are not
> about the bills or budgets or laws or services. The parts that live under our skin

and inside of our bones and cells. The parts that are buried. The parts that most of us have had to learn how to navigate on our own, if we learn to navigate them at all. I love being disabled *and* my history of disability has been so drenched in trauma and sorrow, pity and isolation, silence and pain, shame and guilt, violence and abuse. I don't know how to talk about disability without talking about these parts—without pulling them out of their hiding places and holding them out to show you and asking, *where are yours?*[14]

In refuting the ableist assumption that disability is always tragic, we should not insist that disability is never tragic. For when we do so, we discredit the experiences of those with histories of trauma and violence and thus, as Mollow argues, replicate instead of repair "disability's originary violence . . . in a secondary form that we must recognize as coextensive with disability oppression."[15]

In criticizing the effort to disconnect disability from traditional narratives of pathology, tragedy, and grief, we need to analyze not only the experiences that we delegitimize but also the epistemological possibilities that we lose. Trying to "rescue" disability from an association with trauma, for example, not only contributes to pathologizing discourses that understand trauma as only undesirable and tragic; it also obscures how trauma might be a productive and even powerful location for the creation of new forms of knowledge about disability.[16] When we deny that disability is something that (sometimes tragically) happens to someone, we are unable to recognize or to understand how the origins of one's disability connect to and influence how one thinks about and experiences disability.[17] And when we refuse to acknowledge the realities of suffering and pain and the shaping influence of violence and trauma on some people's experiences of disability, as Kafer argues, we make disability studies and activism inaccessible to "people with different conceptualizations of, and relations to, disability."[18] Consequently, we exclude and fail to benefit from the valuable insights—or "criphystemologies," as Anna Mollow calls them—produced by those who "possess knowledge about our own bodies and minds that is not available to, or documentable by, those who are not disabled in the same ways."[19] Only by including these criphystemologies and treating as essential the experiences and narratives of all disabled people can we complicate, diversify, and enrichen what it means to be disabled and thus, according to Mollow, usefully illuminate "what is most disabling about disability: its unmasterability, its noncompliance, and its radical resistance to meaning."[20]

In this chapter, I draw on my grandmother's experiences and how they connect to my own to call for an expanded disability theory that makes room for the identities and experiences that sometimes push at its borders. An expanded disability theory is one that more fully acknowledges experiences of pain and trauma and the sometimes disabling effects of bodies and minds.[21] It draws wisdom from the particular experiences of those with intellectual, cognitive, and developmental disabilities and those whose disabilities are not always readily apparent. It moves beyond discussions of autonomy and independence to include issues of interdependence, vulnerability, the need for care, and corporeality, and it expands access beyond inclusion and equality into a tool of liberation for transforming and dismantling existing systems of privilege and oppression.[22]

An expanded disability theory, then, embraces the messiness, the dangers even, of actual lived disability experiences that do not fit neatly into disability studies' discourses. Such an expansion that considers and validates all disability stories does not weaken but only strengthens the mission of disability scholarship and activism—to create a world in which all bodies and minds are equally valued and accommodated. I find so much of the kind of expanded disability theory that I crave in the writings of Mia Mingus, Alison Kafer, Lydia Brown, Susan Wendell, and so many others from whose insights I have drawn to make sense of my own lived experiences of disability. In turn, those experiences have informed my particular (and partial) knowledges about what it means to live a disabled life in a world that is built for an imagined but mythical norm. And those lived experiences, in so many ways, begin with my grandmother.

CONFRONTING DISABILITY

When I was a little girl, I loved staying at my grandmother's house. There, I could always count on a full cookie jar, warm bubble baths sweetened with Chantilly Lace bath soap, and unfettered access to Grandmom's nightgowns, costume jewelry, and beautifully etched silver brush and comb set. During long summer days, Grandmom and I would rock in the swing on her back porch, sipping from tall glasses of pink lemonade, while we watched the birds and the squirrels amble across the lawn. Missy, the gentle border collie, would heave herself up from her favorite resting spot on the cool concrete floor of the work shed and pad out on her arthritic legs to greet us. Pretending that the porch was a stage, I would belt out my limited repertoire of show tunes as I skipped and danced over the hot pavement in my bare feet, Grandmom and Missy providing a captive and appreciative audience for what I confidently assumed was my budding musical talent. There on that back porch over many summer days, Grandmom would tell me stories from her past, many of them sweet and winsome and others heartbreaking in their brutality.

On Grandmom's first day of grade school in 1927 at the height of Prohibition, her teacher asked the children to introduce themselves and to describe what their father did for a living. When it was Grandmom's turn, she stood up from her chair, told the class that her name was Rose McAllister, and proudly declared that her father was a bootlegger, much to the shock of her teacher and the amusement of her classmates. She dearly loved both of her parents but was a continual witness to their violent confrontations fueled in part by poverty and alcoholism. One afternoon, she was at home playing with a friend, who started teasing Grandmom about a rather large pock mark on her nose. Overhearing the teasing, her mother—my great-grandmother, Lottie—charged into the room, wrestled the girl to the floor, and scraped away at the girl's nose until she had left a bloody wound. When Grandmom was twelve, she arrived home from school one afternoon to find her father packing a suitcase; he moved out of their home later that day even as Grandmom clung to him and begged him to stay. A few years later, her younger brother drowned while swimming with a group of older boys in a local pond.

Traumatized by her brother's death and her parents' divorce, Grandmom grew increasingly withdrawn. Like so many other Americans during the Great Depression, poverty and hunger began to wear her down. Deeply ashamed of her shabby, torn clothing, she would sit each day at the edge of the school-yard listening to the happy chatter of her classmates as they munched on sandwiches purchased from the lunch cart for a nickel a piece. One day as she saw the "lunchcart lady" heading back toward the school building at the end of the lunch period, she quickly bent her head and pretended to study a ladybug crawling over a blade of grass in an effort to avoid the woman's eye. Suddenly, she jolted in surprise when a sandwich wrapped in wax paper landed neatly in the grass by her feet. Quickly looking up, she saw the retreating figure of the lady, who had broken stride only long enough to quietly deliver what Grandmom later described as the greatest act of kindness she had theretofore experienced. I can picture her there—my grandmother as a teenager, stretched out on the pillowy lawn in her tattered dress, savoring each bite of her peanut butter sandwich, her mind momentarily liberated from the aching sadness of the past few months. That afternoon in the grass would be one of the last days of her childhood. At sixteen, she dropped out of school and married my grandfather, Robert Cunning.

Together, my grandparents worked to build a stable, loving home far different from the ones in which they had been raised. When the United States entered World War II, my grandfather felt obligated to join the military but feared that my grandmother would object to his enlistment. So, one afternoon after work, he walked to the recruiting office, signed up for the navy, and then returned home to tell Grandmom that he had been drafted—a deception to which he did not confess until years later. Finding herself alone with two small children after my grandfather shipped off to the South Pacific, my grandmother took a war job, literally transforming into Rosie the Riveter, and worked to support the Allied cause and her small family. Though she resigned her position at war's end and never worked outside of the home again, she always looked back on her time at the war plant as a period of great adventure and independence. For the first time in her adult life, she was earning her own paycheck and making every decision regarding her household and her children. If the postwar years brought any regrets, she never acknowledged them—at least not to me. My grandfather was unable to find work after the war, so he moved his young family to the country and into a rustic home with no indoor plumbing. While my mother and her younger brother relished the infinitely explorable terrain of wooded acres and stony creeks, my grandmother found little charm in hauling water from the well, using an outhouse, and warding off home invasions from snakes, mice, and other woodland creatures. Only by agreeing to have another baby did she persuade my grandfather to move back to the city a few years later. Four years after the birth of that baby, she unexpectedly became pregnant again and gave birth to her last child, sixteen years after the birth of my mother, her eldest.

And this is where the stories seemed to stop, rewind, and then repeat. These are the stories I heard over and over again on those lazy summer days on the back porch, or on cold winter mornings sitting at the round wooden table in Grandmom's kitchen, or during those sleepless nights in the big squeaky bed. The stories that she tended to repeat were those that formed not only some of the most joyful but also some of the most painful parts of her memory; always, they occurred in her childhood or young adulthood. After that, her memory grew murky and her stories less detailed, and so, she told me the same stories again and again. I never minded. With a thrill of anticipation, I would snuggle in next to her, happy to be with her and to sink once again into the comfortable familiarity of her narratives that over time I could recite by heart. Those stories from the past formed the crux of how we communicated with one another in the present and became such a regular part of our time together that it grew hard for me to imagine or to remember our times together in the years before she was grievously injured on a warm September day in 1979.

The days and weeks following what we all came to refer to as "the accident" are a bit hazy in my memory, but some things I remember vividly. I recall waking up to the sound of strange voices floating down the hallway toward my room. Rubbing the sleep from my eyes, I rolled out of bed and walked into the kitchen expecting to find my mother busily preparing breakfast and making lunches for the school day ahead. Instead, I saw my teenage sister, Julie, sitting at the table with an assortment of relatives and neighbors, all of them looking pale and stricken. My grandparents had been in a serious car accident, they explained, and my mom and dad were with them at the hospital. Your grandfather is doing well, they assured me. When I inquired after my grandmother, they fell silent, unable to meet my eyes.

On their drive to the post office the previous evening, my grandparents and their beloved chihuahua named Peanut were struck on the driver's side of their car by a man so intoxicated that he failed to brake at a four-way stop intersection. The impact of his car hitting theirs sent my grandfather's body plowing across the seat with a brute force that crushed Peanut (who later died from his injuries) and smashed my grandmother's head into the passenger side window. While my grandfather sustained only minor injuries, Grandmom suffered a traumatic brain injury that nearly ended her life.

After the accident, there followed several weeks during which my grandmother remained in the hospital, with my mother nearly constantly by her side. My mother was the bedrock of my young life, and so her sudden loss was nearly as shocking as the news of my grandmother's injury. Into the tremendous gap left by my mother's absence stepped a veritable army of relatives, neighbors, and church members who were eager and willing to help in some way—a powerful illustration of how much my grandmother was loved. My most visceral memory of that time was the food in all of its strange, unfamiliar, and abundant iterations. Because my father had to leave for work before our school bus arrived, Jill and I would walk across the street each morning to the home of one of several neighbors, who were taking turns with the "morning shift." Even though we had already eaten breakfast, we were always greeted with offers of food. At one home, we were served a heaping portion of gelatinous rice pudding teeming with plump, glistening raisins. Jill and I despised raisins. But having been taught impeccable manners, we politely accepted our bowls, carefully navigated around the raisins, and took tentative bites while casting hopeful glances out of the window for any sign of the school bus and our salvation. After school, we would board a different bus that would take us on an unfamiliar route to the home of another volunteer, who would instantly ply us with more snacks, treats, and sometimes entire meals. Always the food smelled, looked, and tasted unfamiliar, and it was quite often disagreeable, at least to my childish palate. Regardless of what we were offered, however, we ate our food and never complained. My grandmother lay grievously injured, possibly dying, in a hospital bed; the least I could do was choke down a few raisins. After work, my father would pick us up from the designated after-school location of the day, and we would return home only to be greeted by more food lovingly prepared and delivered by neighbors and friends. Most evenings, our dining room table would be laden with an assortment of differently shaped glass baking dishes, brightly colored Tupperware containers, steaming Dutch ovens, and plastic-wrapped bowls overflowing with homemade casseroles, gelatins, salads, breads, cakes, and pies. Usually joined by my grandfather and uncles, we would squeeze in around the table, fill our plates, and do our best to slog through as much of the food as possible before cramming the leftovers in our overflowing refrigerator and guiltily throwing out what we could not save.

Eventually, we were told that my grandmother would live but that she was badly injured and would have to remain in the hospital for a few more weeks. And as those weeks dragged on, I began to falter under the emotional weight of my grandmother's accident, the continued absence of my mother, and the disruption to my previously ordered life. I grew uncharacteristically quiet and withdrawn, preferring to stay indoors buried in a book while my classmates were outside for recess. As a result, my friends began to drift away and to join other peer groups. When we stayed at homes where other children our age were present, I rarely joined in their play, preferring instead to cling to the children's mother while she went about household tasks. At one home, I was thrilled when the mother asked if I wanted to help her make a cake. Proud but a bit nervous when she entrusted me with the electric mixer, an appliance that I was never permitted to use at home, I plunged the beaters into the thin cake batter and began to move them around the bottom of the bowl. When Jill and the other children banged into the kitchen from where they had been playing in the backyard, I looked up from my work to see if they were marveling at my newfound skill. In so doing, I accidentally lifted the mixers out of the bowl, which sent chocolate cake batter splattering all over the white walls and floor of the previously immaculate kitchen. The mother was extremely gracious and did not show any signs of irritation, but I was utterly and completely mortified and spent the rest of the visit crying quietly in the bathroom.

From our church community, my family I received tremendous support and sustenance during the time of my grandmother's accident. But it was also the church—its methods and messages—that fueled my growing anxiety. I grew up in a devoutly religious family and attended church services three times a week with a large group of Independent Fundamentalist Baptists who were particularly keen on emphasizing the horrors of hell, a place where unrepentant sinners burned forever in lakes of fire with no hope of redemption. To scare us into submission, the church regularly invoked the specter of Satan, who carefully monitored our actions looking for any opportunity to lead us astray and, ultimately, drag our souls down to hell's fiery pits. During vacation Bible school one summer, the church thought that it would be educational to have one of the teenagers dress up in a devil costume and randomly pop into classrooms to terrorize groups of children by chasing them around the room. To get him to disappear, we were instructed to recite James 4:7, "But resist the Devil and he will flee from you," at which he would skulk out of the room and lie in wait for his next opportunity to catch us off guard. For two weeks that summer, we joylessly made our crafts and sang our songs, always with our eyes trained on the door for the impending horror that awaited us with the Devil's reappearance. And then, of course, there were the perennial warnings about the impending "Rapture"—when Jesus Christ would return suddenly to Earth to call up to Heaven all "true" Christians—and the horrible years of war, poverty, and disease that awaited the nonbelievers who would be left behind. Such warnings were reinforced through special Sunday night church screenings of low-budget "horror" films about the "End Times" produced by evangelical film companies. The *A Thief in the Night* series of movies, for example, set the standard for the rapture-film genre and, despite their very adult content, were required viewing for young people who grew up in fundamentalist churches in the 1970s and 1980s. The first film in the series is most infamous, perhaps, for its creepy theme song "I Wish We'd All Been Ready," which featured prominently in our playlist of Sunday School hymns and made a recent comeback in a cover by singer Jordin Sparks for the 2014 apocalyptic movie *Left Behind* (based on the *Left Behind* novels by evangelical-minister-turned-author Tim LaHaye). Those left behind, the song warned, would face war, poverty, death, and overall misery. Once the rapture occurred, the unsaved would have no means of escape and no hope for redemption. "There's no time to change your mind," the song drearily concluded: "The Son has come and you've been left behind."[23]

These apocalyptic messages, while always powerful, began to assume a new level of terror for me during my grandmother's long convalescence. I began to have regular nightmares that my family was suddenly snatched up in the dead of night and that I was abandoned, left all alone to shoulder the horrors to come. Waking up from these nightmares in a pool of sweat and tears, I would clamber out of bed and feel my way down the darkened hallway, certain that at any moment the Devil would spring from the shadows and pull me down to hell. After what seemed like an eternity, I would reach my parents' bedroom and nearly weep with relief that they were still there. I would burrow in between them and pull the covers up to my chin, too petrified for sleep as images of Satan and Judgment Day continued to haunt me. After agonizing consideration, I could come to only one conclusion. I was not safe. My grandmother had been suddenly and terribly injured in an automobile accident. Satan was a constant, malignant force who was intent on stealing my soul. At any moment, the rapture would occur, and I might be left all alone. This is when my fear of the dark intensified. This is when the insomnia came. And this is what sparked my obsessions and rituals.

Several weeks after the accident, my mother decided that Grandmom had reached a point in her recovery where her grandchildren could visit her at the hospital. On the appointed day, Jill and I joined our cousins in the hospital cafeteria anxiously awaiting her arrival. Even though my mother had said that Grandmom would look and act differently, my mind could conjure up no other image than the grandmother I had always known and loved—an image that, to my great astonishment, bore no resemblance to the stranger my mother was pushing toward us in a wheelchair. The fluffy pink robe in which they had dressed her could not disguise her frail, shriveled body. The hands jutting out from her sleeves were skeletal and bruised, full of tubes and wires. Worst of all, peeking out from under the skull cap lovingly knitted by my great-grandmother was a head shorn of its once lustrous salt and pepper mane; all that remained was a bald scalp crisscrossed with angry looking scars and welts. We stared mutely at her, huddling closer together in our mutual shock. I remember my mother tapping Grandmom on the shoulder and saying, "Mom, the grandkids are here to see you." When she slowly lifted her head to peer up at us, I was horrified to notice that one of her eyes was swollen shut; the other showed no hint of recognition as it scanned our pale faces. Somehow, I ended up sitting beside Grandmom during the lunch, scared to be next to her and trying not to watch as my mom fed her spoonfuls of green gelatin. My mother had encouraged us all to talk to Grandmom, telling us that she could hear what we were saying even if she did not respond, but I could not manage more than a few words. All I wanted was to get out of the hospital and away from my grandmother. I was deeply ashamed of my reaction, but I kept telling myself that very soon, God would answer our prayers and that she would be healed, returning to the person she was before the accident. My grandmother would leave the hospital, my mother would come home, and everything would go back to normal.

But normal was a long way off and never really returned in the way that I had anticipated. Grandmom's accident left her with a severe traumatic brain injury (TBI), defined as an acquired injury to the brain caused by an external physical force that produces a diminished or altered state of consciousness and results in a diverse array of cognitive, neurological, physical, sensory, and psychosocial symptoms and impairments. The severity of TBI may range from mild (a brief change in mental status or consciousness) to severe (an extended period of unconsciousness or amnesia after the injury).[24] Those with traumatic brain injuries often experience problems with memory, learning, reasoning, and concentration; planning, organization, decision-making, and initiating and completing tasks; speaking, writing, organizing thoughts and ideas, and participating in conversations; recognizing objects, balance, and coordination; and managing emotions and behaviors.[25] Grandmom experienced difficulties in all of these areas. She relearned how to speak and to walk—although she continued to struggle with balance and coordination—but her concentration, visual perception, and abilities to process information, solve problems, plan, and organize were seriously impaired. Most challenging was the loss of her short-term memory. While she could remember in great detail events from her childhood and early adulthood, she could not recall what she had done last year, last month, last week, yesterday, or even that morning, and she was usually unable to retain new information.

Once Grandmom left the hospital, she came to live with us. My parents had our spare room installed with a hospital bed and other medical equipment, and there my mother stayed nearly constantly during the first few weeks, even sleeping on a fold-out cot next to Grandmom's bed. My grandmother required constant care and assistance with every human function from eating, to bathing, to using the bathroom. I remember my mother lifting Grandmom's frail body out of the hospital bed and carrying her to the bathroom; the strange and frightening noises that Grandmom would make when she would wake in the night and forget where she was; the sound of my mother's voice soothing her back to sleep. I remember the long train of visitors who came to call on her—relatives, friends, people from the church—and the tremendous pile of cards and flowers that began to accumulate on our kitchen table. I would hover outside of her bedroom door during these visits, still too afraid to be near her. Even as she began to recover, she remained for me a rather terrifying figure. Not only was her physical appearance frightening—her skeletal frame, shaved head, scars, and bulging eye—but also her wildly fluctuating emotional state during those first few weeks was jarring and upsetting to witness. Most difficult to witness, perhaps, was her deep sorrow at learning that so many of her loved ones had died many years before. Because she had no memory of their passing, she had to relive their deaths all over again. When she finally was able to join us in the family room in the evenings, she would sit in our big orange recliner near the television and demonstrate only marginal interest in the plot lines of our weekly programs—*Little House on the Prairie* on Mondays, *Happy Days* and *Laverne and Shirley* on Tuesdays, *The Incredible Hulk* on Fridays, and *The Love Boat* and *Fantasy Island* on Saturdays. But as soon as a news station would break in to deliver updates on the unfolding hostage crisis in Iran (where revolutionaries were holding hostage over fifty American diplomats and citizens at the U.S. embassy in Tehran), she would suddenly snap out of her reverie and stare at the screen with an almost ferocious intensity. Her difficulties with processing or making sense of information meant that she grew easily confused or frightened by things that she could not comprehend. Because the Iran hostage crisis seemed to her so incomprehensible, it became her particular fascination during those long months of her recovery, one that was fed constantly by the media's exhaustive coverage. And thus my evenings in front of the television, once a reliable source of pleasurable banality, became yet another arena in which I could not avoid the stark reality of my grandmother's injury.

During that first Christmas after Grandmom's accident, Jill kept in our shared bedroom the fourth-grade class hamster, who had been entrusted to her care during the winter break. Scamper, as he was called, was extremely somnolent during the day and barely mustered the energy to open his eyes when we would rattle his cage to ensure that he was not dead. But at night, he would suddenly spring to life. Like clockwork, once we dimmed the lights and nestled into our beds, Scamper would heave himself aboard his exercise wheel and begin to race with a ferocity that both alarmed and impressed us. Within minutes, however, Jill would be asleep, and I would lie awake listening to the continuous turning of the hamster wheel that seemed to parallel the fears and obsessions that rotated in my mind on an endless loop. I would try to read a book, but my checking and counting rituals ultimately made it difficult and sometimes impossible for me to continue on to the next page. And so, I would lie there tracing the patterns of my Peanuts bed sheets, reading and re-reading Charlie Brown and Snoopy's bubble captions as Scamper continued to race around his wheel. Over time, the reliable clicking and clacking of Scamper's tiny paws became a welcome, albeit odd, form of companionship during those long, shadowy nights. When he returned to school at the end of winter break, I genuinely mourned the loss of him.

One night, long after everyone had fallen asleep, I decided to brave the darkness of the hallway and visit the kitchen for a drink of water. As I passed by Grandmom's room, I heard her stir, and suddenly, I felt an overpowering need to be with her, even as the thought of being in close proximity to her still scared me. I tiptoed into her room, sat down in the chair by her bed, and carefully reached up to take her hand. She turned her head, and her eyes fluttered open. And then she smiled at me, and I knew that she recognized me and that she loved me. In that instant, my fear simply evaporated. I stayed with her most of that night, at one point asking her to help me finish a crossword puzzle, with me reading the questions and she just smiling and nodding as I completed the answers. I also read her a story about Franklin Roosevelt, whom I knew to be her favorite president, carefully turning the yellowed pages of my treasured children's book of U.S. presidents that had belonged to my Uncle Scott and ended abruptly with the Kennedy assassination. These activities seem a bit bizarre in hindsight, but I now realize that they were my childish attempts to connect to my grandmother in the ways that I always had—sharing with her the things that were important to me because I loved her so very much.

EXPANDING DISABILITY NARRATIVES

That quiet night of crossword puzzles and presidents was a watershed moment. Grandmom had changed, for sure, but the core traits that comprised her personality and character remained. She continued to enjoy a good meal on a scale unparalleled by anyone I have ever known and appreciated every bite of food, a lasting remnant, no doubt, of those years of poverty and hunger during the Great Depression. I can see her now, sitting with perfect contentment by herself at the dinner table long after everyone else had finished their food and moved on, making sure that she ate every last scrap of meat and gristle from the bone of her chicken leg (her favorite part of the bird) and that she had scraped every last cake crumb from her dessert plate. She loved music and seemed always to be humming or singing a happy tune as she moved about the house, substituting "do, dee, doh, doh" for lyrics that she could not remember. She had an infectious laugh and even maintained the ability to laugh at herself. Her brain injury left her with a sense of imbalance, which meant that she was very susceptible to falls and subsequent injuries. When my parents, sisters, and I came home after our first family vacation the summer following the accident, we found Grandmom sitting at her kitchen table with heavy casts on both her arm and her leg. During a late-night trip to the bathroom, she had fallen and broken both bones. In public, she always needed to hold onto someone when walking. Even now, I am amused by the memory of how my mother would walk through the mall with Grandmom on one arm and my great-grandmother, Lottie, on the other, excursions which always left Mom with a little series of bruises on the arm where Grandmom would suddenly clutch her between her thumb and forefinger as she began to lose balance. Fortunately, my mother is freakishly strong despite her small size and thus always managed to keep Grandmom and herself upright. My great-grandmother, who stood at only four feet and eleven inches, was not always so lucky. One day, while walking arm-in-arm with Grandma Lottie through an icy department store parking lot, Grandmom suddenly lost her balance and pitched backwards, dragging Grandma Lottie down with her. As my exasperated grandfather looked on, Grandmom and Grandma Lottie lay giggling in the snow with their arms still locked tightly together.

In so many ways, Grandmom remained the same, but it became increasingly apparent that the people around her had not. After the accident, I witnessed first with puzzlement and eventually with hurt and anger how differently some of her friends and even family members treated her. I watched how they dismissed or ignored her; how they infantilized and patronized her; how they spoke to her in loud, condescending, or overly cheerful tones; and how they responded to her repetitive questions with impatience or exasperation. These observations not only gave me a new yardstick for measuring human character but important, albeit painful, lessons in the sort of ableist attitudes that shape understandings of disability and the treatment of disabled people. Because Grandmom no longer fit the expectations of an ableist world, she was somehow judged less worthy of respect, attention, and dignity. In fact, her worth now seemed to be measured by her ability to inspire nondisabled people with her bravery, cheerfulness, and determination to "overcome" her injuries. Her value seemed based on the extent of her recovery, how closely she could approximate her preinjured self, and how well she could reinhabit what had become for her an often uninhabitable world.

More valuable by far than my early, inchoate lessons in ableism, however, was my mother's demonstration of respectful, ethical care. My grandmother trusted and felt safe with my mother and shared with her an almost instinctual, unspoken form of communication. My mother understood, anticipated, and fought for my grandmother's access needs. She viewed caregiving not as an act of obligation but as an expression of love and part of the large spectrum of human connection in which we variously throughout our lives give and receive the support and sustenance we each need to survive and flourish. She provided care that was respectful and loving, that safeguarded and preserved my grandmother's personhood and dignity. From my mother, I learned that a caring relationship is one of the most intimate, important, and powerful relationships we can form. A care relationship, as Eva Feder Kittay notes, demonstrates the universality of interdependency, our need for and attachments to others, and the connection between our own welfare and the well-being of others.[26] When it is given generously and received graciously, and when it is fully supported and justly compensated, caregiving is "an indispensable, and even a central good—one without which a life of dignity" and a society that supports every member are "impossible."[27] From watching the care relationship between my grandmother and my mother, I learned that "care means moving together and being limited together," as Margaret Price notes, and that it "means giving more when one has the ability to do so, and accepting help when that is needed."[28] Ethical care believes and respects a person's understanding of their own body and experiences of pain; it is participatory, "developed through the desires and needs of all participants."[29] And perhaps most of all, I learned the meaning of what Mia Mingus calls "access intimacy," or those relationships in which disabled bodies and minds can feel safe and comfortable; where no justifications or explanations of access needs are necessary; where help and support are both asked for and given without guilt or judgment; where help and support are not a form of charity or an obligation but woven into the very fabric of what it means to love and care for another person; where help and support are understood as just another form of the interdependency that characterizes all human relationships.[30]

Of course, at the age of seven, I had no way to articulate or critically analyze any of this. I knew only that my grandmother's worth was inherent, not conditional, and that her life remained meaningful and joyful. I knew only that I loved her and that where she was, I wanted to be. If she no longer easily inhabited my world, then I would enter hers by reaching deep into the spaces that she now inhabited and deeply burrowing myself within. My understanding was limited, but I now recognize that it was during these years in relationship to my grandmother that my consciousness of disability germinated. From observing how others responded to her, I began to notice how the fear and loathing of disability both results from and helps to perpetuate disability stigma and discrimination. Witnessing her struggles made me realize how little our policies, attitudes, and built environment accommodate bodies and minds that do not meet expected norms. Most importantly, watching the loving, respectful care that my mother provided her gave me a model of access intimacy that I would emulate with my daughter many years later and that would inform my thinking about the ethics of care, interdependency, and ways to practice disability justice through our most intimate, important relationships.[31] Access intimacy is the model on which we should structure not just our relationships but our ideas and institutions in order "to accommodate inevitable dependency," Kittay writes, "within a dignified, flourishing life—both for the cared for, and for the carer."[32] Only "[w]hen we recognize that dependency is an aspect of what it is to be the sorts of beings we are" and "acknowledge . . . our dependence on another," she concludes, can we "begin to confront our fear and loathing of dependency and with it, of disability" and embrace our connection with others "that makes life worthwhile."[33]

For the many ways in which it tends to disrupt existing, available narratives about disability, my grandmother's story provides an important location from which new meanings of disability can be created. My grandmother had a type of traumatic injury that has been studied almost exclusively for its impact on men; hence, her experience highlights the ongoing problem of androcentrism in medical research and treatment approaches.[34] Most moderate-to-severe brain injuries occur in men and typically result from engagement in historically male-associated, high-risk activities and occupations, such as professional contact sports, construction, or military service.[35] Hence, TBI research, treatment, and rehabilitation approaches have been modeled on male patients, particularly those injured in combat.[36] Yet, women sustain about one-third of TBIs each year, and, as recent evidence suggests, their gender creates experiences of brain injury that are distinct from those of men.[37] A team of researchers from Ontario, for example, discovered that women TBI survivors were more likely to feel patronized by family members and to have their concerns and opinions about their own health care needs disregarded by male medical personnel. The survivors also reported being negatively affected by culturally constructed standards of female appearance, specifically their loss of self-esteem when they struggled to maintain gendered expectations of feminine hygiene and beauty. Additionally, they spoke about the challenges of meeting domestic responsibilities. They were frustrated and overwhelmed by household tasks such as cooking, cleaning, and shopping that required the planning and execution skills that their injuries had impaired, and many experienced grief and guilt over their inability to deal effectively with the demands and responsibilities of motherhood. As one woman put it: "'You come out of the hospital and everything and with the injury, and you're just trying to cope with the kids. . . . the house . . . making meals. . . . With trying to cope with life . . . . It's *too* much.'"[38]

My grandmother experienced similar challenges. She married my grandfather in 1940, a time when women were expected to assume nearly sole responsibility for childcare and household tasks. Other than those years during World War II, my grandmother never entered the paid labor market, instead devoting her life to the care of her husband, children, and home. After her accident, she was unable to perform the activities that characterized society's definition of "true womanhood." She was unable to drive and so could no longer do the grocery shopping. Planning meals and cleaning her house were tasks that overwhelmed and confused her. She was happy and eager to perform simple tasks when someone else directed her, but she was unable to initiate or to execute such tasks on her own. This "failure" to live up to her own and society's gender expectations was a source of frustration and sorrow for her. And it certainly shifted her relationship with my grandfather, who had always maintained a very traditionally masculine breadwinner role in the family but was suddenly needed to assume the majority of domestic responsibilities.

Despite evidence that biological factors and gendered social norms create distinct experiences of brain injury for men and women, the relationship between gender and TBI is largely absent in the medical literature, and very few studies have focused specifically on women.[39] According to the National Institute of Health, failure to include both sexes in human subject studies undermines the rigor and applicability of research findings and results in theories and clinical practices that are ineffective or even potentially harmful for women.[40] Current understandings of the causes of and care pathways for traumatic brain injury also lack consideration for Black, Indigenous, and people of color, who are disproportionately affected by intentional TBI.[41] Black and Native American people, regardless of gender, are more likely to experience violent TBI compared to white people.[42] TBI as a result of intimate partner violence (IPV) disproportionately affects women and Native Americans, yet existing research on the connections between race, gender, TBI, and IPV is scarce.[43] Consequently, health care providers are limited in their ability to offer survivors effective supports and services.[44]

What happens, then, to a woman's identity and sense of self when a TBI undermines her ability to carry out in socially expected ways the functions— particularly mothering— that are inextricably associated with her womanhood? What is the impact on her personal relationships—with her spouse, children, friends, or colleagues? How does her gender and her race influence how she understands and experiences her injury and how others understand

and relate to her? How do her gender and race influence the type and quality of care she receives, both from family members and from medical personnel? How can we begin to answer these questions when female TBI survivors are not the subjects of medical research—when their care, treatment, needs, and experiences are viewed through the lens of the white male subject? Although the few studies that have been conducted on these issues indicate that the causes, experiences, treatment, and recovery outcomes of people with TBIs are gender and racially specific, this specificity is not adequately reflected in current medical research, policies, treatment plans, and support services. It is crucial, then, that research studies incorporate an intersectional lens to investigate the nature and incidence of TBI in order to develop tailored policy interventions that can prevent injuries, improve outcomes, and provide necessary resources and accommodations for all survivors of TBI.[45]

My grandmother's story also challenges and forces a reevaluation of some of the most foundational ideas within disability studies, particularly the privileging of certain forms of disability and the "reluctance to understand disability in terms of sickness or suffering."[46] It illustrates the need for further investigation into the particular experiences of those disabled by brain injuries, chronic conditions, cognitive disabilities, and those whose disabilities are rooted in trauma, violence, environmental hazards, or forms of structural inequality. And it reminds us that the disability studies narrative that privileges the disabling effects of society and the positive aspects of disability leaves little room for experiences—no matter how impermanent or socially constructed—of loss and sorrow and tends to ignore or even pathologize lingering and/or persistent pain or trauma.

Acknowledging the connection between disability and trauma and the suffering and grief of some disabled bodyminds is not simply something that we should do to make disability studies and communities more inclusive, as important as this goal is. Trauma, suffering, and grief should also be recognized as valuable tools for producing new identities, new communities, and new discourses about disability.[47] As many theorists have beautifully demonstrated, those "borderland" locations that seem to bind and oppress us are also the sites from which the most powerful transgressions can occur. By existing simultaneously in the border spaces that delineate and hierarchize identities, Shayda Kafai shows how we can challenge oppressive binaries and create new stories and identities that shift the meaning of what it is to be broken, mad, sick, and traumatized.[48] For Sara Ahmed, people who have been "undone by suffering can be the agents of political transformation." Instead of seeing "bad feelings" only as stifling or something to overcome, she argues, we can use them to explore "how we are affected by what comes near, which means achieving a different relationship to all our wanted and unwanted feelings as a political as well as life resource."[49] Ann Cvetkovich effectively illustrates this political potential of feelings by demonstrating that affective experiences such as grief and trauma have fueled critical aspects of queer public culture, such as lesbian activism within ACT UP. By highlighting the affective dimensions of queer activism, Cvetkovich illustrates the value and crucial role of feelings such as grief and trauma for community building, public activism, and social change.[50] For Ellen Samuels, experiences of chronic pain and illness can be an important location for the production of knowledge. Bodies disabled by chronic pain and illness do not proceed according to the demands of "normative time frames," she notes, but dwell in "a wormhole of backward and forward acceleration, jerky stops and starts, tedious intervals and abrupt endings." From their location in "crip time," she writes, these bodies are uniquely positioned to criticize the inequities created by linear, progressive time and to explore the power and possibility of time shaped by repetition, interdependence, and caregiving, a time adapted to the needs of diverse individuals whose bodies work, move, and function in a variety of ways.[51]

And yet, for all of its identificatory, epistemological, and political potential, trauma is not easily transformed into a social location. As bell hooks notes, "It is not easy to name our pain, to theorize from that location." Transforming one's trauma, pain, or grief from "a site of oppression to one of radical resistance requires sacrifice, pain, and struggle," she writes.[52] Hence, in the deployment of trauma, we risk being further traumatized. And regardless of our particular social location, forming a new, positive identity and an alternative narrative about disability while saturated in an ableist world—a world whose systems and ideologies tell you that the "condition" of your body or mind is a tragedy, a misfortune, or a pollution—is a monumental struggle, particularly for those whose economic and social resources are few.

My grandmother was located in disability but was not always able to transform this location into a site of resistance. I have often wondered how different her life would have been had she been able to live in what Alison Kafer calls a "crip future," that is, a future that accommodates and embraces "multiple ways of being."[53] In many respects, my grandmother was deeply privileged. As a working-class woman with a TBI, she experienced the intersections of gender, class, and disability discrimination, but her whiteness and the mostly invisible nature of her disability often protected her from the more overt forms of stigma experienced, for example, by people of color who are visibly disabled. While she lived in a culture that refuses to take full public responsibility for social welfare, she had the love and support of family members who provided care, advocacy, and access intimacy. Still, I cannot help but consider how different her functioning and her family dynamics might have been had she had greater access to financial resources, medical research, and practices that considered the gendered nature of TBI, paid attendant care, and adequate health insurance. How different would her self-identity have been had she lived in a culture that did not stigmatize TBIs and cognitive disabilities, that did not see disability in general as tragic, pitiful, and pathological? What if she had lived in a culture in which her pain, her sadness, and her vulnerability were just as valid as her positivity, her bravery, her likability, and her resilience? How different would her perspectives on her disabilities have been had she had access to the sort of disability theory and community that could have helped her to develop a more positive identity and an alternative vision of her world?

Grandmom lived in a world constructed not on the ideals of a crip future, but on the principles of a "cure-driven future . . . where one's life is always on hold, in limbo, waiting for the cure to arrive."[54] In a cure-driven future, Kafer explains, those with acquired disabilities often see themselves (and are seen by others) through a dual identity—the predisabled self and the postdisabled self. Like all binaric identity categories, the first half of the binary—the predisabled self—is considered the natural, normal state of being, which means that the second half of the binary—the postdisabled self—is the deviation from the norm, unnatural, and undesirable. A product of compulsory able-bodiedness, the binary reifies the discreteness of categories that are in fact fluid and mutually constituting; takes as axiomatic that disability cannot be a desirable location; and assumes that all disabled people long to return to their predisabled selves. In other words, those with disabilities are "expected to take up nostalgic positions toward our former selves, mourning what we have lost and what can now never be."[55]

This predisabled/postdisabled binary also contributes to what Kafer calls a "compulsory nostalgia," or a longing for the "normal" mind/body that perhaps never existed.[56] Compulsory nostalgia certainly framed the way in which Grandmom viewed her disability. Whenever someone asked her how she was doing, she would predictably reply, "Well, I'm grateful for where I am, but I'm not where I want to be." Her experience of disability took place within a culture in which the only acceptable future for those with disabilities is one in which they have been cured. A woman of great faith, Grandmom's version of cure was a dramatic healing from God, to whom she continually prayed, "Please, let me be me again." For many years following her accident, she fervently believed that she would one day be miraculously restored to her preinjured self; when that day never came, she continued to have faith in a just God and the attainment of perfection in Heaven. As I have argued elsewhere, mourning a loss of form, function, or identity following disability is valid and necessary. So too is longing for relief or even cure from conditions that cause pain and suffering. Ellen Samuels has written that she embraces and even celebrates her disability identity, even as she cannot fully relinquish the memory of her healthier self. While she does "not exactly" long for a cure, her impairments bring her moments of grief and suffering. "I wish to be both myself and not-myself," she acknowledges, "a state of paradoxical longing that I think every person with chronic pain occupies at some point or another."[57] While other disability scholars, such as Kafer, Price, and Alyson Patsavas, have also productively admitted to an ambivalent relationship to their disabilities and their feelings about medical interventions, they nevertheless reject what Patsavas calls "the uncomplicated quest for a medical cure [that] makes curing pain not only desirable but also compulsory."[58] I wonder, then, how Grandmom's experiences of her disability might have been different had she not lived in a culture where cure is compulsory and where the "struggle between the longed-for past . . . and the hoped-for future" is not merely validated but expected.[59]

In the multiple ways in which it is acquired, experienced, and located, disability can be the crucible that produces new, positive identities, distinct forms of resilience and agency, and deeper, more meaningful connections to individuals and communities. Disability can also be a location from which we tear down oppressive regimes and construct better ones that alter our views of what the world should be. But this location can be transformed into a site of mass-based, radical resistance only when we create theories and movements that incorporate and honor all disability experiences, even those like my grandmother's that are not always convenient. "Making this theory is the challenge before us," bell hooks reminds us, "for in its production lies the hope of our liberation."[60]

NOTES

1. Here, I draw on Margaret Price's use of "bodymind" to reflect the interdependent relationship between bodies and minds, to call attention to mental disabilities (often neglected within disability studies), and, more importantly, to describe "a socially constituted and material entity that emerges through both structural . . . contexts and also individual (specific) experience." Margaret Price, "The Bodymind Problem and the Possibilities of Pain," *Hypatia* 30:1 (Winter 2015): 271, https://doi .org/10.1111/hypa.12127.

2. bell hooks, *Teaching to Transgress: Education as the Practice of Freedom* (New York: Routledge, 1994), 59.

3. Gloria Anzaldúa, "Speaking in Tongues: A Letter to 3rd World Women Writers," in *This Bridge Called My Back: Writings by Radical Women of Color*, 2nd ed., eds. Cherríe Moraga and Gloria Anzaldúa (New York: Kitchen Table Women of Color Press, 1983), 171.

4. Daniel R. Morrison and Monica J. Casper, "Intersections of Disability Studies and Critical Trauma Studies: A Provocation," *Disability Studies Quarterly* 32:2 (2012), http://dsq-sds.org/article/view/3189/3073; James Berger, "Trauma

Without Disability, Disability Without Trauma: A Disciplinary Divide," *Journal of Advanced Composition* 24:3 (2004): 571, https://www.jstor.org/stable/20866643; Alison Kafer, "Un/Safe Disclosures: Scenes of Disability and Trauma," *Journal of Literary & Cultural Disability Studies* 10:1 (2016): 1–20, https://doi.org/10.3828/jlcds.2016.1; Anna Mollow, "Criphystemologies: What Disability Theory Needs to Know about Hysteria," *Journal of Literary & Cultural Disability Studies* 8:2 (2014): 187, 200, https://doi.org/10.3828/jlcds.2014.15; Elizabeth Donaldson and Catherine Prendergast, "Introduction: Disability and Emotion: 'There's No Crying in Disability Studies!'" *Journal of Literary & Cultural Disability Studies* 5:2 (2011): 129–135, https://doi.org/10.3828/jlcds.2011.11.

5. Berger, "Trauma Without Disability, Disability Without Trauma," 571; Irene Visser, "Trauma Theory and Postcolonial Literary Studies," *Journal of Postcolonial Writing* 47:3 (2011): 270–282, https://doi.org/10.1080/17449855.2011.569378.

6. Kafer, "Un/safe Disclosures," 6, 9; Margaret Price, *Mad at School: Rhetorics of Mental Disability and Academic Life* (Ann Arbor: University of Michigan Press, 2011): 51; Nirmala Erevelles, *Disability and Difference in Global Contexts: Enabling a Transformative Body Politic* (New York: Palgrave Macmillan, 2011).

7. See, for example, H. Rakes, "Crip Feminist Trauma Studies in Jessica Jones and Beyond," *Journal of Literary & Cultural Disability Studies* 13:1 (2019): 75–91, https://doi.org/10.3828/jlcds.2019.5; and Stephanie Kerschbaum, "On Rhetorical Agency and Disclosing Disability in Academic Writing," *Rhetoric Review* 33:1 (2014): 55–71, https://doi.org/10.1080/07350198.2014.856730.

8. Morrison and Casper, "Intersections of Disability Studies."

9. Berger, "Trauma Without Disability, Disability Without Trauma," 573.

10. Alison Kafer, *Feminist, Queer, Crip* (Bloomington: Indiana University Press, 2013), 7.

11. Liz Crow, "Including All of Our Lives: Renewing the Social Model of Disability," in *Encounters with Strangers: Feminism and Disability*, ed. Jenny Morris (London: The Women's Press, 1996), 210.

12. Price, "The Bodymind Problem," 275–276.

13. Anna Mollow, "'When Black Women Start Going on Prozac': Race, Gender, and Mental Illness in Meri Nana-Ama Danquah's *Willow Weep for Me*," *MELUS* 31:3 (Fall 2006), 70, https://doi.org/10.1093/melus/31.3.67.

14. Mia Mingus, "Access Intimacy, Interdependence, and Disability Justice," *Leaving Evidence*, accessed November 3, 2018, https://leavingevidence.wordpress.com/2017/04/12/access-intimacy-interdependence-and-disability-justice/.

15. Mollow, "Criphystemologies," 200.

16. Sara Ahmed, "Feminist Hurt/Feminism Hurts," *Feminist Killjoys*, July 21, 2014, https://feministkilljoys.com/2014/07/21/feminist-hurtfeminism-hurts/.

17. Kafer, "Un/safe Disclosures," 6.

18. Kafer, "Un/safe Disclosures," 12.

19. Mollow, "Criphystemologies," 196.

20. Mollow, "Criphystemologies," 200.

21. Morrison and Casper, "Intersections of Disability Studies."

22. Mingus, "Access Intimacy, Interdependence, and Disability Justice."

23. The song "I Wish We'd All Been Ready" was originally written and recorded by Larry Norman for his 1969 Christian rock album, *Upon this Rock*. Larry Norman, "I Wish We'd All Been Ready," recorded 1969, track 4 side 2 of *Upon this Rock*, Capitol Records.

24. Kyle C. Dennis, "Current Perspectives on Traumatic Brain Injury," *ASHA* (August 2009), https://www.asha.org/Articles/Current-Perspectives-on-Traumatic-Brain-Injury/.

25. Dennis, "Current Perspectives on Traumatic Brain Injury"; Debjani Mukherjee et al., "Women Living with Traumatic Brain Injury," *Women & Therapy* 26:1–2 (2003): 3–26, https://doi.org/10.1300/J015v26n01_01.

26. Eva Feder Kittay, "The Ethics of Care, Dependence, and Disability," *Ratio Juris* 24:1 (March 2011): 51, https://doi.org/10.1111/j.1467-9337.2010.00473.x.

27. Kittay, "The Ethics of Care," 52.

28. Price, "The Bodymind Problem," 279.

29. Price, "The Bodymind Problem," 279.

30. Mia Mingus, "Access Intimacy: The Missing Link," *Leaving Evidence*, May 5, 2011, https://leavingevidence.wordpress.com/2011/05/05/access-intimacy-the-missing-link/. See also Virginia Held, *The Ethics of Care: Personal, Political, and Global* (Oxford: Oxford University Press, 2006); Nicholas Watson et al., "(Inter)Dependence, Needs and Care: The Potential for Disability and Feminist Theorists to Develop an Emancipatory Model," *Sociology* 38:2 (2004): 331–350, https://doi.org/10.1177/0038038504040867.

31. Mingus, "Access Intimacy, Interdependence, and Disability Justice."

32. Kittay, "The Ethics of Care," 54.

33. Kittay, "The Ethics of Care," 57.

34. Canadian Institutes of Health Research, "Science Fact or Science Fiction: Traumatic Brain Injury: Does Gender Matter?" January 2015, https://cihr-irsc.gc.ca/e/documents/igh_mythbuster_january_2015_en.pdf.

35. Harvard Medical School, "Head Injury in Adults," *Harvard Health Publishing* (October 2018), https://www.health.harvard.edu/a_to_z/head-injury-in-adults-a-to-z.

36. Kim Tingley, "Do Brain Injuries Affect Women Differently?" *The New York Times Magazine*, June 26, 2019, https://www.nytimes.com/2019/06/26/magazine/do-brain-injuries-affect-women-differently-than-men.html.

37. Kamila Vagnerova et al., "Gender and the Injured Brain," *Anesthesia & Analgesia* 107:1 (July 2008): 201–214, https://doi.org/10.1213/ane.0b013e31817326a5; Angela Colantonio, "Sex, Gender, and Traumatic Brain Injury: A Commentary," *Archives of Physical Medicine and Rehabilitation* 97 (2016): S1–S4, https://www.archives-pmr.org/action/showPdf?pii=S0003-9993%2815%2901477-X.

38. Halina L. Haag et al., "Being a Woman With Acquired Brain Injury: Challenges and Implications for Practice," *Archives of Physical Medicine and Rehabilitation* 97 (2016): S67, https://www.archives-pmr.org/action/showPdf?pii=S0003-9993%2815%2900099-4.

39. Raeesa Gupte et al., "Sex Differences in Traumatic Brain Injury: What We Know and What We Should Know," *J Neurotrauma* 36:22 (November 2019): 3063–3091, https://doi.org/10.1089/neu.2018.6171.

40. Office of Research on Women's Health, "Including Women and Minorities in Clinical Research Background," National Institutes of Health, accessed September 25, 2020, https://orwh.od.nih.gov/womens-health/clinical-research-trials/nih-inclusion-policies/including-women-and-minorities; https://www.archives-pmr.org/article/S 0003-9993(15)00099-4/fulltext; Janine A. Clayton and Francis S. Collins, "Policy: NIH to Balance Sex in Cell and Animal Studies," *Nature* 509:7500 (May 14, 2014): 282–283, https://www.nature.com/news/polopoly_fs/1.15195!/menu/main/topCol umns/topLeftColumn/pdf/509282a.pdf.

41. Samira Omar et al., "Integrated Care Pathways for Black Persons with Traumatic Brain Injury: A Protocol for a Critical Transdisciplinary Scoping Review," *Systematic Reviews* 9:124 (2020): 2, https://doi.org/10.1186/s13643-020-01323-8.

42. Kristen F. Linton and Bum Jung Kim, "Traumatic Brain Injury as a Result of Violence in Native American and Black Communities Spanning from Childhood to Older Adulthood," *Brain Injury* 28:8 (2014): 1076–1081, https://doi.org/10.3109/0 2699052.2014.901558.

43. Omar et al., "Integrated Care Pathways"; Kristen Faye Linton, "Interpersonal Violence and Traumatic Brain Injuries among Native Americans and Women," *Brain Injury* 29:5 (2015): 639–643, https://doi.org/10.3109/02699052.2014.989406; Eve Valera and Aaron Kucyi, "Brain Injury in Women Experiencing Intimate Partner Violence: Neural Mechanistic Evidence of an 'Invisible' Trauma," *Brain Imaging Behav.* 11:6 (December 2017): 1664–1677, https://doi.org/10.1007/s11682-016 -9643-1.

44. Halina L. Haag et al., "Battered and Brain Injured: Assessing Knowledge of Traumatic Brain Injury among Intimate Partner Violence Service Providers," *Journal of Women's Health* 28:7 (2019): 990–996, https://doi.org/10.1089/jwh.2018.7299.

45. Tatyana Mollayeva et al., "Sex and Gender Considerations in Concussion Research," *Concussion* 3:1 (January 18, 2018), https://doi.org/10.2217/cnc-2017 -0015.

46. Mollow, "'When Black Women Start Going on Prozac,'" 71.

47. Alyson Patsavas, "Recovering a Cripistemology of Pain: Leaky Bodies, Connective Tissue, and Feeling Discourse," *Journal of Literary & Cultural Disability Studies* 8:2 (2014): 203–218, https://doi.org/10.3828/jlcds.2014.16.

48. Shayda Kafai, "The Mad Border Body: A Political In-Betweenness," *Disability Studies Quarterly* 33:1 (2013), http://dsq-sds.org/article/view/3438/3199.

49. Ahmed, "Feminist Hurt/Feminism Hurts."

50. Ann Cvetkovich, *An Archive of Feelings: Trauma, Sexuality, and Lesbian Public Cultures* (Durham, NC: Duke University Press, 2003).

51. Ellen Samuels, "Six Ways of Looking at Crip Time," *Disability Studies Quarterly* 37:3 (2017), https://dsq-sds.org/article/view/5824/4684.

52. hooks, *Teaching to Transgress*, 74; bell hooks, "Choosing the Margin as a Space of Radical Openness," *Framework: The Journal of Cinema and Media* 36 (1989): 15–23, https://www.jstor.org/stable/44111660.

53. Kafer, *Feminist, Queer, Crip*, 45.

54. Kafer, *Feminist, Queer, Crip*, 44.

55. Kafer, *Feminist, Queer, Crip*, 43.

56. Kafer, *Feminist, Queer, Crip*, 42.

57. Samuels, "Six Ways of Looking at Crip Time."

58. Patsavas, "Recovering a Cripistemology of Pain," 208.

59. Catherine Scott, "Time Out of Joint: The Narcotic Effect of Prolepsis in Christopher Reeve's *Still Me*," *Biography* 29:2 (2006): 309. Quoted in Kafer, *Feminist, Queer, Crip*, 44.

60. hooks, *Teaching to Transgress*, 75.

Chapter 6

Making Disability Home

I am a tsum tsum and I am smart and unique and talented and pretty and kind.
I wonder about what could make the world a better place and what will happen in
    Season 2 of Andi Mack.
I hear a unicorn.
I see a tsum tsum.
I want more tsum tsums and a twin sister.
I am a tsum tsum and I am smart and unique and talented and pretty and kind.
I pretend that me and my brother are tsum tsums and that I am a mermaid or a fairy
    or a princess.
I feel happy and fabulous.
I need Janet. I need for my dog Hannah to come back to life.
I worry that one day my parents will get hurt.
I cry when people I really care about die.
I am a tsum tsum and I am smart and unique and talented and pretty and kind.
I understand that my family is very kind.
I believe in everything except hell.
I dream about being a movie star, a singer, and a fashion designer.
I try to swim better and I try to be better at math even though I hate it and I try to
    stop cursing.
I hope that everyone will be very kind and nice to each other and not curse.
I am a tsum tsum and I am smart and unique and talented and pretty and kind.
                                                    —Zoey Wilson, "I am Poem," 2017

My dear Zoey, you have an insatiable enthusiasm for life, particularly its
small joys and wonders. I watch your excitement on finding a ladybug in the
grass; hearing the latest Katy Perry song on the radio; spotting your favorite Judy Moody book on the library shelf. I watch you eating a big chunk

of watermelon on the back patio in your swimsuit on a hot summer day, laughing as the juices run down your arms when you sink your teeth into the fleshy part of the fruit; you squeal with delight as you splash with a mighty cannonball into the pool. Playing with your dolls in the bathtub, you loudly belt out one song after another from your mental playlist; freshly scrubbed and smelling of lilac lotion after a day spent crunching through the brightly colored leaves that have begun to pile up in our backyard, you lie on your belly on the family room floor, your markers and colored pencils scattered about you, as you sketch out portraits of your family members and favorite toys. You spend the weekends playing dress up with your array of princess costumes, tiaras, and wigs, mostly souvenirs from Halloweens past; on wintry Saturday nights, you camp out in front of the television in your pop-up tent surrounded by your stuffed animals and munching on popcorn as you watch the latest episode of *iCarly*. Triumphantly finding a penny on the walking trail in our neighborhood, you rush home to put it in your piggy bank, gleefully splashing with your pink polka dot Hello Kitty boots in every single puddle left behind by a late spring rain shower.

Your way of seeing and interacting with your world is delightful and unique, dear Zoey. You have the remarkable ability to spot and to ascribe great importance to the tiniest, seemingly mundane, details in any text—whether it is a story, a poem, a painting, or a landscape. I marvel at your knack for memorizing rote facts and your capacity to recall events and circumstances from the time when you were a toddler. When it comes to your favorite toys or activities, you can exhibit a laser-like focus and concentration. And you are an enthusiastic and animated performer with a lovely singing voice, which you have displayed publicly during school events and in musical productions with community children's theaters. I watch proudly as you perform Taylor Swift's song "Shake It Off" for the school talent show. As soon as your name is called, you bounce onto the stage wearing your pink princess dress and tiara, pumping your fist into the air before grabbing the microphone and launching into the song. Hitting every note perfectly, you joyfully dance and jump throughout the song with an enthusiasm so infectious that the children in the audience run to the front to get closer to the stage while the adults stand to their feet and clap.

One night, I am lying next to you in your bed, smoothing your brow and trying to coax you into sleep, which has never come easily for you. As your lids grow heavier and your yawns more frequent, you mumble that you want me to sing you a lullaby. "Do you want me to sing 'Baby Mine' or 'Nothing's Gonna Harm You?'" I ask, referencing your two favorite goodnight songs. "Sing 'Home,'" you whisper, referring to the current hit single from the 2012 American Idol winner Phillip Phillips that has been playing on the radio seemly nonstop in recent weeks. "Hold on, to me as we go," I begin to sing, "as we roll down this unfamiliar road." Struggling to remember the next set of lyrics, I fumble my way through the song's middle section about scary demons and fears of getting lost, but I finish more confidently. "Just know you're not alone," I sing, "cause I'm going to make this place your home."[1] As I finish the last note, I glance down at you and see that your eyes are closed, your lips are parted slightly, and your chest is rising and falling with the deep breaths of peaceful sleep. I lie there for a few minutes more, thinking about the song I have just sung and the relevance of its message. Home is the location of wherever you happen to be, the space we will carve out and continually modify to fit who you are, and the place where, together, we will build and allocate the supports you need to thrive and flourish. Your home is not some future place away from autism, away from disability. Your home is not a goal or destination to be reached by changing who you are. Your home is right here. I will make this place your home.

In this chapter, I describe how I came to understand Zoey's autism through the lens of neurodiversity—that is, as a valid, positive, neurological difference that comprises an essential part of who she is. A term coined by sociologist Judy Singer in the late 1990s and popularized since then through the writings and activism of autistic self-advocates,[2] neurodiversity recognizes that all forms of neurological differences and disabilities are intrinsic to people's identity and personhood and should be recognized and respected as valid human variations. I gained a neurodiverse perspective from a long period of self-education during which I immersed myself in the literature of disability studies, analyzed the writings of autistic individuals, spoke with disability activists, examined the work of disability self-advocacy organizations, and, most importantly, started seeing the world from a different point of view. Using a neurodiverse viewpoint, I have learned to reject language, media representations, theories, and therapeutic approaches that frame disability as a stroke of misfortune needing to be fixed or rendered undetectable. I have fled (literally) from therapists who tried to "normalize" Zoey's behaviors and means of communication in order to make her appear more neurotypical. I have sought out therapeutic approaches and techniques that promise only to help Zoey better cope with her anxieties and that give her the tools she needs to navigate an unaccommodating and even hostile environment. I have grown to recognize that what others have called Zoey's bad or inappropriate behaviors are often the result of her frustration with moving around in a world that was not built for her. And I have learned to locate and access the supports Zoey deserves and requires so that she may fully enjoy the many gifts that her autism brings and live a happy, fulfilling life.

This neurodiverse perspective is one that I have had to struggle to achieve, for it goes against much of the established knowledge about autism constructed by the medical community, propagated by the media, and absorbed uncritically by much of the general population.³ It also goes against the knowledge created by some parents of autistic children and even some autistic people themselves, who claim that the neurodiverse perspective does not fully account for their lived realties or that it does not acknowledge the "severe" disabilities experienced by so-called "low-functioning" autistic individuals.⁴ The label "low-functioning" has typically been assigned to autistic people with "impaired" speech, social and executive functioning, or adaptive and self-care skills, those who self-harm, and/or those with intellectual disabilities. For many of these individuals and their families, autism does not seem like a neurological difference deserving validation but a debilitating disorder needing cure. Sue Rubin, a nonverbal autistic author and writer of the 2004 documentary *Autism is a World*, for example, describes her autism as "a constant struggle" and claims that "[l]ow-functioning people are just trying to get through the day without hurting, tapping, flailing, biting, screaming, etc." "As a person who lives with autism daily and will not live a normal life," she writes, "I find people who are high functioning and saying society should not look for a cure offensive. They have no idea what our lives are like."⁵

Positioning myself within these sometimes extremely contentious discourses is complicated and even risky. As a nonautistic person, I would never presume to invalidate a person's lived autism experiences, even as I recognize how our experiences—our lived realities and our perception of them—can never be fully understood apart from the context in which they take place. And while I have strongly disagreed with some of the views and methods of parents of autistic children, I realize how difficult it can be to parent a child with autism without adequate social supports, such as steady and well-compensated employment with paid family leave policies and flexible work schedules; good health insurance; access to quality and affordable medical/therapeutic/respite care; family and community support; excellent schools with lots of support and resources for autistic children; and so many other things. While I have struggled to access some of these vital resources, I have undoubtedly benefitted from most. With adequate supports, I have had the privileges of time and education to explore disability law and history, find and pay for professional services, and serve as an advocate for my daughter in our interactions with administrators, teachers, doctors, therapists, and health insurance representatives.

But this recognition of the many challenges faced by autistic people and their caregivers and the recognition of my own privileges has made me embrace the neurodiversity model more, not less. Proponents of neurodiversity do not deny the challenges that people with autism face nor reject respectful and safe therapeutic, medical, or technological interventions that can help to alleviate these challenges. My descriptions throughout this chapter of Zoey's challenges and the therapeutic interventions that I have sought are my way of affirming that the autism as difference and autism as disability positions are not mutually exclusive and can, in fact, coexist. But using a neurodiversity framework, I understand these challenges mainly as the product of an inhospitable environment that becomes less inhospitable when one has access to quality and affordable supports and services. In the low- versus high-functioning binary, functioning is reduced to a series of attributes or skills an individual either has or does not have. It does not consider that functioning is highly dependent on one's external environment and on the level of support one has for navigating that environment, as Sue Rubin's own experience demonstrates. With access to facilitated communication starting when she was thirteen, she was able to communicate with and be understood by others, attend and graduate from college, live on her own with the help of an in-home aide, and write an Oscar-nominated documentary. Too often, as autistic writer Cal Montgomery notes, we identify autism itself as a problem that limits an autistic person's "ability to function in the world" instead of recognizing "that the problem is that the world is set up for neurotypical nondisabled people."[6] When we diagnose "autistic people's failure to manage in the world as an individual medical problem," she concludes, we are unable to recognize or to challenge the many structural inequalities, environmental barriers, and stigmatizing attitudes that create and/or exacerbate this failure.[7] As Emily and Ralph Savarese ask, how do you "live in a world that aggressively prefers that you not be in it?"[8]

The categories of low and high functioning fail to capture the tremendous heterogeneity of the autism spectrum and are a product of a world that is structured according to the "norms" of neurotypical people. It privileges certain functions, such as speech, language, social interaction, and management of daily tasks, and then ranks as "low functioning" autistic people who cannot perform them in neurotypical ways. And then it decides that those who are "low functioning" are "severely impaired," that their lives have no joy or value, or that they need to be cured or prevented from being born. Juxtaposed against a neurotypical model, their lives are defined by "absence," as the late Mel Baggs, a nonverbal autistic writer, observed:

> The absence of speech. The absence of language. The absence of thought. The absence of movement. The absence of comprehension. The absence of feeling. The absence of perception.[9]

But for Baggs, what others called absence was for hir (Baggs identified as "genderless," and I am using the pronouns that sie preferred) simply a different way of communicating, moving, feeling, and thinking. "Not all of these things communicate everything that typical languages communicate, but I don't see any reason they should have to," sie wrote. "They are rich and varied forms of communication in their own right, not inadequate substitutes for the more standard forms of communication."[10] Nevertheless, "typical language takes place in the clouds," sie noted, and so sie had to "fly up there just to use and understand it" instead of remaining on the ground where sie found such richness of communication. "What has come as a surprise to me is that no matter how consistent I am on the ground, many people measure me by my ability to hurl myself into the sky."[11]

By demonstrating the richness of their engagement with the world, Baggs and so many other autistic people assigned to the "low-functioning" category of autism show us that so much of the accepted knowledge about autism is wrong, limited, or skewed. While autism creates differences in how autistic people think, move, communicate, and interact with others, as the Autistic Self Advocacy Network (ASAN) explains, "[e]very autistic person experiences autism differently."[12] Some communicate verbally, while others communicate through typing, signing, or other means. Some have attention-deficit/hyperactivity disorder (ADHD), intellectual disabilities, or mental health disabilities, and some do not. Some need a lot of help with daily tasks, while others require minimal assistance. "All of these people are autistic, because there is no right or wrong way to be autistic," ASAN correctly argues. "All of us experience autism differently, but we all contribute to the world in meaningful ways. We all deserve understanding and acceptance."[13]

This recognition that "[t]here are myriad ways to be present, connected, and alive; myriad ways to have relationships"[14] is the foundation of the neurodiversity movement, which fights for a world in which this myriad of human diversity is accommodated and valued. Neurodiversity celebrates autism's gifts and ways of being in the world, even as it recognizes the challenges faced by many autistic people. Neurodiversity validates all neurological differences, including those that "seem incapable of producing prized forms of competence,"[15] as Emily and Ralph Savarese note, and those that include experiences of pain, struggle, and even grief. Encompassing the full spectrum of autistic experiences, neurodiversity expands and deepens our knowledge of how and why autism is lived and understood in such a multitude of different ways. And from this knowledge, we are able to learn how to construct a world where these differences can find full expression.

My story of my journey with Zoey contributes a piece to this production of knowledge, but it is only a piece—partial and particular. It is told from a neurodiverse perspective but does not claim to represent the views of anyone else within the neurodiversity community, which is vast and diverse. Nor does it claim to represent Zoey's journey, for that can be told only by Zoey, whose understanding of autism comes from an intimate, experiential, and more valuable location. Rather, my story in this chapter shows how my relational position to Zoey's location has given me a revolutionary view of the world, one that I liken to the prism in one of my favorite picture books that I read over and over when I was a child. In this book, two friends live in a bleak world of black and white until one day they discover a prism. When they hold it up to the sun, light shoots through the prism and separates into the colors of the rainbow. The colors splash out over the landscape, painting every surface in brilliant hues of red, orange, yellow, green, blue, and violet. Through that prism, their world has been transformed. Zoey is my prism.

THE ZOEY PRISM

I often tell Zoey that she came out of the womb bouncing and has never stopped. Even as a newborn, she required very little sleep and rarely napped. She was an extremely alert and active baby who impressed us all with her strength when at just two weeks old, she spontaneously rolled over while lying on a bed at my mother-in-law's house. Skipping over the crawling stage entirely, she moved rapidly from sitting to standing to walking, and then to bouncing and running—everywhere. Once she became mobile, our lives changed dramatically. Engaging in exploratory or risky activities grew to be her favorite pastime, and no amount of caution, forbiddance, or even injury would dissuade her from pursuing them.

At times, Zoey's enthusiasm, energy, and obliviousness to anything but her own amusement were charming and infectious; at other times, they left me exhausted and fearful. At home, she did not hesitate to jump from the stairs, climb cabinets, and even swing from her bedroom ceiling fan. Child locks, safety gates, and awkwardly constructed barriers rarely deterred her. Excursions to the park, mall, or zoo were usually anxiety-producing affairs, as Zoey's impulsivity led her to wrestle away from my grip to run outside to the parking lot or street, to jump from swings or slides, or to climb fences or barriers. Running errands with her in tow was nearly impossible. She required my vigilant, hovering supervision in public places due to her tendency to run off and her habit of handling, breaking, or destroying merchandise. At visits to the library or video store, it was not uncommon for her to run gleefully down the aisles, knocking books or DVDs from the shelves. At department stores, she tore clothing off hangers, squirted liquid soaps, toothpaste, or lotions in her hair or onto the floor, tore magazines and greeting cards, or opened bags of candy and shoved the contents into her mouth. Fearing for her safety and wanting to stop the destruction of public property, Nathan and I began to place her in her stroller during most public outings and to avoid taking her along to any place where the use of a stroller was impossible. Once she became too big for a highchair, we stopped eating at restaurants due to her inability to sit still or to moderate her voice and actions. And we stopped taking trips or traveling to our parents' homes due to Zoey's inability to tolerate air travel or long car rides, as well as the anxiety that changes in schedule or location always brought.

Until Zoey was two years old, we lived in a small Michigan college town, where events for children Zoey's age were sporadic and tended to attract the same groups of people. I quickly became known as the mother who spent entire events chasing after her toddler, trying to prevent her from injuring herself or others with her boisterous movements and seemingly boundless energy. She was unable to sit still during story time at the local library, for example, preferring instead to run around the large recreation room and bang on the doors while the dozen or so other children sat quietly listening to the story or staring bemusedly at our antics. During group craft activities when other children dutifully created masks with glue, paint, and paper plates, Zoey soared around the room using the paper plates as skis while she smeared paint and glue on her hair, clothing, and face and sometimes the walls and carpet.

Zoey did not begin to use words until she was three years old and even then preferred singing over speaking. Shortly before her first birthday, she began to communicate her needs and desires through a pattern of classical tunes that she had learned from the Mozart, Beethoven, and Bach CDs that I regularly played in the car and from *The Little Einsteins* television show that she watched every day on the Disney Channel. For example, if she wanted a glass of milk, she would sing an enthusiastic and perfectly in tune section from Mozart's "Symphony Number 40." Her rendition of Beethoven's "Fifth Symphony" indicated that she wanted to go outside to play. I was charmed by my little girl's creative and unique means of expression but gradually became concerned that Zoey so rarely used language to communicate, preferring not only songs but also hand gestures, grunts, and, eventually, single words.

Growing up, I had little occasion to witness the behaviors of developing babies and toddlers. I was the youngest of three daughters and had little interest in playing with my younger cousins or babysitting neighborhood children. Therefore, I did not have much of a sense of what was considered "typical" childhood development and no standard against which to measure Zoey's progress. Still, as we began to take a more active role in our community and to participate more frequently in children's events, I grew increasingly aware that Zoey was different. Not only did she seem vastly more energetic and distractible than other children her age, but she also had an unusual habit of forming obsessive attachments to strange objects. For example, when she was around one year old, she began to carry a DVD case of *The Little Einsteins* television show in each hand and refused to relinquish them, even when eating, bathing, or sleeping. This lasted for several months, until she switched her allegiance to the Diddy Wishingwell figure from the Weebles Barn Dance playset that she inherited from her cousin. From there, she moved on to a small plastic pink spoon from a kitchen playset that she received for Christmas when she was two. From that time on until she was nearly four, Zoey carried the spoon constantly; every picture in our photo albums during this period depict Zoey grinning at the camera with a small pink spoon clutched firmly in her left hand. Often, she would wake up in the night screaming because she could not locate the spoon, which she had dropped during sleep. I would rush into her room, frantically crawl around on the floor until I located it, and press it back into her sweaty little palm. Often, her anxiety over losing the spoon would be so great that she would refuse to settle back down, and so I would make myself a little pallet on the floor next to her toddler bed and stay with her until the wee hours of the morning when she would finally fall into a fitful sleep.

One afternoon, I invited a colleague and her two-year-old son to our house for Zoey's first official play date. While I expected that our children would engage primarily in parallel play, showing little interest in the activities of the other, I was unprepared for how much more advanced my colleague's child seemed to be, particularly in his verbal development. Not only did he use three or four consecutive words to communicate his wants and feelings, he made eye contact with those in the room and responded well to one or two-word commands. Near the end of the visit, he plopped down in his mother's lap, looked directly at me, and said clearly, "My mommy." In that moment, I suddenly realized that Zoey rarely made eye contact and that she had never called me "mommy," even when she greeted me in the morning or needed something from me during the day.

After our move to Tulsa in July 2007, we enrolled Zoey for one day a week in a preschool across the street from the university building where my office was located. Every Wednesday, I would walk to the preschool and stand outside of the fenced-in area where the children were at recess, hoping that Zoey would not spot me as I watched her play. I had expected that Zoey's social and communication skills would develop fairly quickly once she began preschool, but after three months, she still preferred to play alone and rarely interacted with the other children. One afternoon during the chaos of school pickup time, I was helping Zoey into her coat and collecting her stuffed animal and Dora the Explorer lunchbox when one of the teachers approached me. Within full earshot of the other parents, the teacher told me that Zoey's delayed speech and "lagging" developmental skills probably indicated some sort of learning disability and suggested that I contact local agencies to inquire about early childhood services. Too stunned to upbraid her for the terribly inappropriate context and manner in which she chose to share her concerns, I scooped up Zoey into my arms and fled the building, crying during the entire drive home while Zoey happily thumbed through the latest edition of her *Highlights* magazine.

We enrolled Zoey in a different preschool in January 2008 and began working with her at home on her communication/language skills. In addition to responding to her singing or her gestures, we encouraged her to use words, and her speech began to develop gradually. Still, long after the age at which most children begin speaking in complex sentences, Zoey often pointed, grunted, or used single words to express her desires. For example, if she wanted me to hand her a doll, she would simply point at the doll or say "Doll!" She often evidenced delayed echolalia, memorizing things that others say (usually on television or in songs) and then incorporating them into her own speech. Sometimes the echoed phrases were in context and at other times, the context was not clear. I also noticed that she tended to take a literal interpretation of what was said and had little understanding of more abstract types of language, such as sarcasm or even jokes.

It was when she started her second preschool program that Zoey's impulsivity, hyperactivity, and inattentiveness truly began to concern me. She found it very difficult to sit in circle time with the other children and preferred instead to bounce about the room or to play by herself during group lessons or activities. Concentrating or staying on task for any length of time was nearly impossible for her. During a Christmas performance while the other children stood on the risers and sang "Jingle Bells," Zoey jumped on and off of the stage, laughing with delight as I—heavily pregnant with Connor at the time—struggled to contain her. At lunch time, when the other children remained in their seats and ate their food, Zoey either ran about the room or took the food from her lunch pail and threw it against the walls or at the other children. And when the other children did not engage with her in the ways that she desired, she resorted to verbal insults or to physical aggression, often hitting, pinching, kicking, or biting her classmates and sometimes even her teachers. A couple of months after Connor was born, I received a call from the preschool director asking me to come to the school to help manage Zoey, who was running throughout the building pulling artwork off the walls and kicking anyone who stood in her way. By the time I arrived, Zoey had left a trail of destruction in her wake that permitted me easily to find her whereabouts. As we made our way out of the building—me holding Connor in his carrier with one arm and a struggling Zoey with the other—the director unceremoniously instructed us not to return.

One day in the summer of 2009, Zoey and I were outside enjoying a break in what was normally the oppressive heat of Oklahoma in July. We were playing a two-person game of tag, running and laughing as we darted in and out of the shadows of our twin maple trees, hoping to catch each other vulnerable and exposed. Suddenly, Zoey looked at me and asked, "Mama, if I touch my knee, is that a song?" Thinking that she was just being silly, I laughed at her question and resumed our play. Just a couple of minutes later, she asked if touching the tree was a song. I was a bit puzzled this time but once again brushed off her question. But my bewilderment turned to concern when she continued to ask a variation of the song question repeatedly over the next hour and dozens of times throughout the afternoon and evening.

That day marked the beginning of what became for Zoey periods of weeks or even months of intense anxiety followed by periods of barely noticeable symptoms. Zoey began to exhibit unusual or illogical fears of bodily harm or contamination, especially from bodily fluids such as blood, urine, feces, or vomit. To try to ease her fears, she would engage in repeated reassurance seeking. A few entries from my "Zoey Journal" during this time period illustrate my growing concerns:

September 23, 2011

Zoey was very anxious today, both in the morning and the evening. I did not have a chance to talk to her teachers today to find out what sort of a day she had at school. Her reassurance questions have been almost continuous, and now she is starting to ask Connor the questions, which mainly relate to him. For example, she asked him a number of times today if he spit on her or touched her Pillow Pet. She asked me questions about whether Connor ate her popsicle (as she was eating it), or if he licked it or touched it.

October 22, 2011

Zoey was extremely anxious and scared most of the morning. She just had this worried expression on her face even in the midst of helping Nathan carve the Halloween pumpkin, to which she had eagerly looked forward. She is sleeping hardly at all, so I am sure that some of this is stemming from fatigue. She chose to spend most of the day in her room reading. Still, she was full of questions about the Baby Alive doll again, and she spent a great deal of time on her new obsession—coins. Nathan often leaves his change from his pockets sitting on a table in the entryway to our kitchen, and Zoey has begun obsessing over them. She has been asking constantly if she can take the change to her room, if the dime has a flower on it, if George Washington is on the quarter, if the dime is the smallest, if she can take the change to school for show and tell, if the quarter is the biggest, etc., etc., etc. These sorts of questions truly go on all day.

July 12, 2013

Zoey has begun to seek reassurance that her head will not fall off. I am not sure about the origin of this one—probably a book she read at school. Throughout a given day, she will ask repeatedly if a certain action (a nod, a twist of her neck, etc.) will result in this dreaded consequence, and no amount of reassurance will satisfy her for long. She has become so obsessed with this idea that she now refuses to play with her dolls for fear that their heads might become twisted and fall off. If I touch one of her dolls to move it from the floor to the dresser, for example, she will scream and cry and exclaim that she will "never play with that doll again."

October 7, 2014

Zoey has grown fearful that flies will enter her mouth and harm her in some way. When we go outside, she keeps her hand firmly clamped over her mouth to keep the flies out and will not remove it until she is safely inside. She will not permit us to roll down the windows when we are in the car, and I must never leave the car door open even for a moment when it is idle. If we are sitting in the car waiting for Nathan to return from a brief errand inside a store, for example, she will not permit me to leave the windows open, no matter how stuffy the car becomes. More recently, she has begun to exhibit this fear even when inside the house. If a fly or even a speck of dust that she suspects is a fly comes into her line of vision, she will immediately place her hand over her mouth and retreat to a corner while begging me to "get rid of it." Last night, she got out of bed and came downstairs to tell me that she was worried about a fly on her ceiling. When I went to her room to investigate, I saw that she was referring to a small shadow on her ceiling just above her dresser. No amount of reassurance, however, would convince her that there was not a fly in her room. After a few more trips down the stairs, I realized that I needed to appease her, and so I spent the next several minutes searching for the source of the shadow and removing it. Her fear of flies has become so acute that she refuses to play outside.

In addition to reassurance seeking, Zoey began to engage in certain rituals that involved touching, counting, repeating, or saying words in a certain pattern. During a three-month period when she was four, she began to say "one, two" in response to hearing someone speak any variation of the words "one" or "two." For example, if I asked, "Zoey, do you want one or two slices of bread," she would instantly say, "one, two," before answering my question. During another period, she insisted on touching my nose every time I entered the room. A couple of months later, she demanded that I let her touch my lips each time she believed that a speck of dust had entered her mouth. And during another stretch of a few weeks, when she provided any type of information, she would end by asking "Okay?" and if I did not say "okay" in return, she grew very agitated and kept asking "okay" again and again until I responded.

Any change of routine or stressful event heightened Zoey's anxiety and led not only to increased reassurance seeking, rituals, and tics but to her obsessive picking at the skin around her fingers and toes, resulting in bleeding, bruises, infections, and scarring.

September 24, 2013

Tonight, Zoey picked off the entire first layer of skin on her big toe. Fearing infection, I put a large dab of antibacterial cream on it and wrapped it in gauze. This might be a reaction to the stress that she is experiencing at school. She began excessive skin picking on Friday following another aggressive outburst at school, and by the end of the weekend, she had picked at the skin around her fingers and toes until they were raw and bloody. We try to convince her to stop, but she tells us that it makes her less anxious.

October 17, 2013

This afternoon, while I was outside running, Zoey picked incessantly at the skin on her big toes again and then walked down the stairs and through the front room, stood on the windowsill, and then made her way into the kitchen to the family room. Her steps were easy to retrace—she left a trail of bright red blood in her wake. Each day, I am finding new blood spots throughout the house or blood smears on the walls and furniture due to her habit of wiping the blood off on any available surface. Every time I put bandages on her wounds, she bites them off and then hides the bloody, chewed remains in various places throughout her bedroom only to be discovered by me during a routine cleaning.

Stressful situations also magnified her need for oral stimulation. She would often chew or bite her fingernails, small rubber toys, her stuffed animals, the sleeves of her shirt, and sometimes human flesh.

January 19, 2012

While I was getting Connor ready for bed, Zoey came into his room with her mouth full of what looked like white foam. I panicked and raced over to her only to discover that her mouth was full of white Styrofoam beads from the laptop desk cushion she had ripped apart in her room. I raced her to the sink and made her spit out the beads and wash her hands. When I inspected her room, I saw that the beads were all over the floor and her bed.

April 5, 2013

When I called Zoey down from her room for dinner tonight, I was alarmed to see a series of welts up and down her arms. Closer inspection revealed wet teeth marks in the center of the welts. When I asked her why she was biting herself, she shrugged and said that "my brain told me to." I have several scars on my forearms from all of the times that Zoey has suddenly clamped down on them when she is experiencing anxiety or aggression. I am dismayed that she is now beginning to target her own arms.

One of Zoey's greatest challenges was her fear of being touched, her inability to tolerate certain smells, sounds, and textures, and her difficulty transitioning between activities. Any event in Zoey's day that involved sensory output—from getting up in the morning, eating, brushing teeth, getting dressed, leaving the house, among others—was a potential trigger for anxiety, aggression, or emotional meltdowns. Zoey began to display extreme hypersensitivity to the texture, taste, and smell of certain foods and thus began to restrict her diet to bread products and most kinds of sweets. She could not tolerate certain kinds of clothing, such as stiff fabrics, pants, shirts with long sleeves, socks with seams (or socks in general), or any clothing with tags. At home and on public outings, she always wore pajamas, which she would substitute with soft, knit dresses without sleeves at school only if she wore pajama shorts underneath. Most problematic was Zoey's difficulty processing physical contact from her peers. She interpreted an accidental bump from another child walking past her as a hostile action that resulted in a defensive and usually aggressive response.

Increasingly, Zoey grew bothered by loud noises (sirens, whistles, flushing toilets, and crying babies especially trouble her) and even high-pitched remote sounds, such as the distant chiming of a clock or the tweeting of a bird. Connor, who enjoyed loud noises and rough play, was a near constant source of irritation and even anxiety. Aware of the reaction he could produce, he often drummed his fingers on the table or sang loudly just to annoy her. Sometimes, however, his actions were much more innocent. One day when Nathan arrived home with a surprise treat for the kids, Connor yelled excitedly in close proximity to Zoey; she responded by screaming in his ear, an action that resulted in his tears and her removal to a less-stimulating spot in the house.

It was in the area of peer relationships that Zoey struggled most. She usually had a strong desire to interact with others but did not do so in ways that other children considered appropriate and was often overwhelmed and confused by the process. I made a habit of lunching frequently with Zoey at school and was always struck during my visits by how little she engaged with the other students. While they had their heads close together chatting comfortably, Zoey always sat somewhat apart, swinging her legs and staring up at the ceiling seemingly oblivious to the conversation in her midst. I worried constantly about Zoey's growing social isolation and so made every effort to involve her in extracurricular activities to magnify her exposure to other children. Activities such as soccer, gymnastics, ballet, swimming, theater, and basketball, however, tended to increase her anxiety about contamination and were usually unbearable. I escorted her on class field trips, arranged play dates with kids from school, and took her to every birthday party to which she was invited. Zoey eagerly anticipated such activities but ultimately could not manage the distressful sensory, anxiety, and overstimulation issues such activities triggered.

October 26, 2012

We met Anna and her mom, Sarah,[16] at the frozen yogurt place for a quick after-school treat. Once the girls got their frozen yogurt, they sat down at a small table while Sarah and I sat on the couch and started chatting. Anna asked if she could try Zoey's yogurt, and Zoey agreed. After Anna took a bite, Zoey ran up to me and asked if she could have a different yogurt. I offered to get a different spoon or cup but she insisted on having a completely different yogurt presumably because Anna's bite had contaminated it. This comment clearly hurt Anna's feelings, but wanting to avoid a scene, I complied and bought her a new one. The next few minutes passed relatively peacefully, but then Zoey's body started spiraling out of control, and she started jumping up and down on the couch where she and Anna were sitting and purposely jumped on Anna's leg. Anna, of course, did not appreciate this but was very sweet when Zoey apologized. Zoey then began running up to the yogurt dispensing machines and sticking her fingers into the spouts and licking them and then trying to get candy out of the candy dispensers. She then ran past a table where someone had left a half-eaten cup of yogurt and knocked it to the floor. It spilled everywhere, and then Zoey began asking incessantly if it was vomit. It was at this point that I decided it was time to go. Zoey kept telling Anna that she wanted her to come to her house. I had to literally pull her off of Anna and take her by the hand to lead her out of the store. As we walked out, Anna coughed, and Zoey thought that she had coughed on her. So she got right in Anna's face and coughed on her. And she kept doing this, even wrestling out of my grasp at one point when I tried to restrain her and running up to Anna just to cough on her. She then began yelling and saying that "this was the worst day ever." I made a hasty apology to Sarah and to Anna and somehow managed to get Zoey's thrashing body into the car as people in the parking lot stared. Such scenes as the one today are becoming almost "normal," and just part of our daily routine.

March 24, 2014

I took the kids to a birthday party at Bounce-U yesterday afternoon with fairly disastrous results. There were a few incidents during the actual play period. At one point, Zoey started kicking at any child who got too close to her on the slide, and so I guided her over to another bounce area that was less populated. At another point, one of the children complained to me that Zoey was hoarding all of the flags instrumental to one of the play stations and would not share them with anyone else. So, I had to intervene in that situation. A few minutes later, four of the girls with whom Zoey had been playing ran to another play station leaving Zoey behind. When Zoey realized that they were missing, she ran after them, but came back to where I was standing a couple of minutes later. Tearfully, she told me that her friends would not play with her and that they didn't like her. I held her close and asked her why she thought that this was the case. She replied that as she approached the girls, one of them yelled out, "Oh no, here comes Zoey." Taking her hand, I led her over to the girl, who denied that she had made such a statement and invited Zoey to play with her. Things proceeded fairly well after this, until it was time to enter the party room for pizza and cake. This is when Zoey began to experience tremendous difficulties with impulse control and peer interactions. She began yelling out to the party attendants, demanding lemonade and pizza. She started obsessing about the balloons on display and asked incessantly if she could have one. As the attendants were slicing the cake, she began yelling over and over that she wanted a piece with blue icing. She was so loud that one by one, the children sitting next to her covered their ears and moved away from her and from the table altogether. I was sitting right behind her at another table trying to manage Connor, who was taking his time thoroughly enjoying his cake, and despite multiple interventions on my part, her behavior persisted. I resorted to coaxing Zoey away from the bench and having her sit next to me; at this, she began screaming and crying and telling me to let go of her—that I was "ruining her life." My plan at this point was to encourage Connor to finish as quickly as possible and usher the kids out the door before the gift opening occurred. I did not succeed. The gift opening commenced with Zoey sitting front and center. Soon, she began to complain that the boy to her right was sitting too close to her, and she began to shift to her left, effectively shoving into the girls already occupying that space. She then resorted to picking up scraps of wrapping and tissue paper and throwing them at the boy. At this, I quickly grabbed her by the hand and insisted that it was time to leave just as Connor was shoving the last forkful of cake into his mouth. As I literally pulled the kids toward the exit, Zoey began shouting that she wanted a balloon and a party bag. The host quickly untied a purple and an orange balloon and grabbed two party bags and handed them to the kids. With Zoey happily rummaging through her bag, I thought that we had made our escape; then, unexpectedly, Connor's balloon came untied and floated up to the ceiling, and he began to scream and wail. Probably less out of generosity and more out of a desire for our hasty departure, the host seized another balloon and handed it to Connor. Incredibly, as we walked out the door, one of the Bounce-U employees handed me two free passes and told us to "come again soon."

Nathan and I first sought the services of a child psychologist when it became clear that Zoey's interactions with her environment were causing her tremendous distress, severely limiting her ability to function at home and at school, and inhibiting her enjoyment of life. After a few sessions and a consideration of the results of several testing measures, the psychologist told us that Zoey presented with "textbook ADHD and obsessive-compulsive disorder (OCD)" and recommended starting her on a stimulant and a selective serotonin reuptake inhibitor (SSRI) to help manage her hyperactivity and anxiety. While these diagnoses were not entirely unexpected, I responded initially with fear, sadness, and even guilt and reacted with repulsion to the suggestion that I start my young child on medication with potentially harmful side effects. At the time, my knowledge of ADHD and OCD was limited to what I saw in various popular media sources (only later, because of Zoey's diagnosis and my subsequent research would I come to recognize the symptoms of OCD in myself and obtain my own diagnosis), whose representations were largely inaccurate, misleading, and often damaging.

In recent years, media have been saturated with stories that question the validity of the ADHD diagnosis and the use of stimulant medications to treat it.[17] Medical practitioners have been recognizing the symptoms associated with ADHD and prescribing stimulants since the 1930s. But the sizable growth in scientific knowledge about ADHD and stimulants, growing political movements advocating for children's health and welfare, and the decreasing stigma associated with mental and developmental "disorders" helped trigger a surge in ADHD diagnoses and related stimulant use by the 1990s.[18] According to CDC estimates, approximately six million, or 11 percent, of children aged four to seventeen have been diagnosed with ADHD, and school-age children in the United States are prescribed three times more psychotropic medications than children in the rest of the world combined.[19] There is no definitive medical test to detect ADHD; instead, the diagnosis depends on largely subjective determinations from practitioners based on diagnostic criteria established by the DSM, as well as observations, medical histories, and evaluations from parents and teachers. For these and other reasons, there is an intense public debate over whether the spike in ADHD diagnoses and stimulant use is the result of advances in medical understanding and treatment of the "disorder" or whether it is the consequence of various sociocultural factors, including stressful educational environments (increased academic expectations on schools with teacher shortages and overcrowded classrooms and decreasing capacity to manage productively students with learning and behavior challenges); children's growing exposure to and interaction with various media (increasing rates of screen time and use of video games and social media); poor home environments (child abuse and neglect, rising divorce rates, less-positive parental involvement, parents' use of medication to ease the stress of managing high-energy children); and the growing power of pharmaceutical companies who pay doctors to research and publicize ADHD and who aggressively promote stimulant medications to physicians, educators, and parents.[20]

While a clear public portrait of ADHD has emerged in the media in recent years, one in which children are being overdiagnosed and overmedicated as the result of lazy parents, overworked teachers, and unscrupulous doctors and pharmaceutical companies, several studies suggest that ADHD is not overdiagnosed but actually underdiagnosed in certain populations—particularly in girls, children of color, and children from lower-income families.[21] In *We've Got Issues: Children and Parents in the Age of Medication*, Judith Warner, a writer and *New York Times* contributor, details how she shifted her own media-fueled misperceptions of ADHD and other childhood disabilities after exhaustive research and dozens of interviews with medical professionals and parents of children with ADHD. She learned that racial and gender biases in diagnostic criteria and testing and unequal access to health care left countless struggling children undiagnosed and untreated, and that a mere five percent of children diagnosed with psychiatric diagnoses were treated with medication. She discovered that most parents were reluctant to seek out and to accept a psychiatric diagnosis for their children and that they resorted to medication only (if at all) after considerable struggle and thought and after trying every available alternative. And she concluded that the pervasiveness of the "lazy, neurotic parents and the overmedicated child" trope so deeply embedded in media narratives and the public imagination had little to no grounding in the actual evidence but was instead a reflection of society's collective fears, preconceptions, and prejudices about mental health.[22]

During the past couple of decades, obsessive-compulsive disorder also has been widely and inaccurately represented in several popular media, including novels, television shows, and movies. These media sources perpetuate stereotypical portraits of OCD that help to create in the public mind an image of a quirky, eccentric person who is obsessed with neatness, orderliness, and cleanliness, but whose ability to function is otherwise unimpaired. The lived reality of OCD is much more complex. OCD was once considered a rare, primarily psychological neurosis that seemed largely recalcitrant to therapy.[23] The last few decades, however, have witnessed an improved understanding of OCD as a neurobiological disorder that often responds well to a treatment approach that uses behavior therapy in combination with medications that affect serotonin levels in the brain.[24] OCD is defined by the intrusion of unwanted thoughts or images (obsessions) and the urge to diminish those thoughts or images or to prevent something dreadful from happening through the performance of rituals (compulsions). The nature of the obsessions and the compulsions vary widely from individual to individual. Common OCD obsessions include fears of contamination or disease, worries about having harmed oneself or others, a need to have things balanced or in symmetry, a fixation with certain numbers or repeating actions a certain number of times, excessive religious or moral doubts and/or intrusive sexual thoughts, and fear of losing things. Common compulsions include repeated and/or ritualized washing, checking, ordering, and arranging, touching, counting, praying, reassurance seeking, and hoarding.[25] These rituals are sometimes performed publicly (the most proverbial example is repeated hand washing) but usually in secret (such as mentally counting). What distinguishes OCD from the everyday obsessions and rituals that we all experience and perform on some level is the severity and persistence of symptoms and the amount of distress, confusion, and impairment the symptoms cause the individual.[26]

For many people, OCD is a sometimes debilitating disorder that creates significant distress and inability to engage in everyday activities. Yet, popular media have turned OCD into a punchline, a form of comic relief, or a handy catch-all phrase to describe any sort of idiosyncrasy. On television, the comedy series *Monk* featured a detective whose obsessive-compulsive disorder was the source of the show's humor, and on the hit CBS sitcom *Big Bang Theory*, a character's OCD-like characteristics were played for laughs and routinely mocked by his friends. Quizzes to test one's OCD level regularly make the round of social media platforms and are meant to be fun and humorous, not to aid those with real mental health concerns.[27] Magazines regularly offer cleaning tips "for the OCD person inside you." Twitter users adopt the hashtag #SoOCD to describe humorously their penchant for cleanliness and orderliness. And several companies use OCD to market and sell products such as mugs, makeup, action figures, and clothing, including a sweater sold by Target in 2015 that read, "OCD: Obsessive Christmas Disorder."[28] Such products commercialize and trivialize OCD and contribute to public misperception of the disorder.[29]

Zoey's early diagnoses prompted me to research exhaustively every aspect of ADHD and OCD and to develop a perspective radically different from that represented in popular media and, gradually, different from many of the psychologists and therapists whose services we sought. I found wisdom in the words of adults with ADHD, like Stephen Tonti, whose 2013 TEDx talk at Carnegie Mellon University reframed ADHD as a cognitive difference, not a disorder. "But because it's treated and misunderstood as a disorder," he noted, "it's treated as something that needs fixing. So the idea seems to be that: we need to get rid of my ADHD, but there's no getting rid of it. There's just sedating it."[30] I began to recognize that while Zoey's hyperactivity, distractibility, and especially her anxiety created significant challenges, they also contributed to her unique way of moving throughout her world and to her many gifts and talents. As clinical psychologist Lara Honos-Webb stresses, impulsivity leads one to do things that are innovative and daring and to forge new ground in areas of study or thought. Similarly, individuals who are highly distractible often have an ability to multitask and to come up with multiple ideas, which can lead to groundbreaking innovations and discoveries.[31] What is often labeled as hyperactivity is really just exuberance, characterized by high levels of energy and an abundant fascination and curiosity for one's environment.[32] And while some OCD obsessions and rituals can be debilitating and injurious, others can be a source of intense concentration and deep exploration of one's hobbies and interests.

As we met with different therapists and sought various interventions to help Zoey manage her ADHD and OCD, I grew increasingly suspicious that many of Zoey's difficulties—particularly with communication, social interactions, sensory processing, and managing the basic tasks of everyday life—could not be explained by her current diagnoses. Everything that I read and studied kept indicating that Zoey fell somewhere on the autism spectrum, but when I raised this possibility with our team of therapists, I was uniformly overruled. One child psychologist even told me that Zoey could not possibly be autistic because she did not show an unusual interest in mechanical items such as ceiling fans, vacuum cleaners, and electric trains. The self-doubt began to creep in. Everywhere I looked—medical literature, memoirs, organizational web sites, movies, television shows, and novels—the public face of autism was a white boy and sometimes a white, cisgender, heterosexual man who often possessed extraordinary, savant-like gifts or abilities. Nowhere in these images did I see Zoey's reflection. Still, my suspicions continued to mount until, finally, I located a nationally renowned therapist specializing in autism assessment and diagnosis, who recognized that Zoey's behaviors and anxieties were manifestations of or coexistent with autism and thus diagnosed Zoey accordingly. Wanting to learn everything that I could about autism, I sought out information from books and memoirs written by autistic people, autistic self-advocacy organizations, autism blogs and websites, and journal articles published by disability studies scholars. What these sources revealed was that most of what I had previously understood or been told about autism was incomplete, misleading, or simply erroneous.

Autism is a genetically based human neurological variant that produces distinctive, atypical ways of thinking, moving, social interaction, and sensory and cognitive processing.[33] As of 2020, autistic people comprise approximately 2.2 percent of the U.S. adult population, and about one in fifty-four children in the United States have an autism diagnosis. Autism is widely believed to be at least four times more common in boys than in girls.

As I have noted elsewhere throughout this book, the criteria for diagnosing autism are based on data derived largely from studies of boys, which means that girls, in whom autism presents differently, are often underdiagnosed or diagnosed much later than their male peers.[34] Some researchers believe that because girls are socially conditioned to be polite and socially adaptable, their autism-related traits and behaviors are less noticeable.[35] Often, however, the symptoms of autism in girls are ignored or dismissed due to gender biases in autism research and diagnostic criteria and the influence of socially constructed assumptions about gender.[36] The strong association between autism and maleness means that girls who display hyperactivity, distractibility, and anxiety, for example, are more likely to be diagnosed with ADHD and/or OCD instead of autism, even though the characteristics of ADHD and OCD very commonly exist as part of or in addition to autism.[37] According to Sharon daVanport, president of the Autistic Women & Nonbinary Network (AWN), different behavioral expectations for boys and girls also contribute to gender disparities in autism diagnoses. For example, a boy who shows more interest in collecting maps instead of playing outside, she argues, might be considered atypical and a cause for concern, but a girl who spends her time indoors researching an intense interest—particularly if the interest is "gender appropriate"—rarely elicits special notice.[38]

The biases in autism research, diagnostic criteria, and treatment approaches have led to the erasure and exclusion of many autistic people who are multiply located in intersecting identity categories. Influenced by Leo Kanner's theory that autism disproportionately affected hyper-ambitious, upper-middle-class families, generations of clinicians and researchers have strongly associated autism with white children. With few exceptions, autistic children of color were almost entirely absent from autism research and literature until very recently and even today are disproportionately underdiagnosed due to unequal access to health insurance and expensive diagnostic services, as well as deeply embedded racial stereotypes. This is especially true for Black boys, whose autistic traits are often attributed to intellectual or learning disabilities, conduct disorders, or ADHD.[39] The association of autism with both whiteness and maleness means that autistic girls of color are effectively erased and often misdiagnosed and thus deprived of crucial supports and resources. Morénike Giwa Onaiwu, an educator, writer, and disability rights advocate, notes that her autistic traits were for many years attributed to stereotypical ideas about her race and gender:

> Social awkwardness? Of course not; apparently I'm just rude—like all the stereotypes of 'sassy' black women rolling their heads and necks in a circle while firing off some retort. . . . Lack of eye contact? Apparently I'm a 'shy girl' or 'playing hard to get' or 'shifty.' Or maybe I'm just being respectful and

docile because I'm African and direct eye contact might be a faux pas. Sensory overload, or maybe a meltdown? Nope, more like aggression or being a drama queen. Anything but what it really is—an Autistic person being Autistic who happens to be black and happens to be a woman.[40]

While several studies and analyses today are quick to point out the prevalence of autism in communities of color, they nearly always focus on boys or do not particularize the experiences of girls. Studies of autism among girls rarely specify the experiences of girls of color. Nearly thirty years after the publication of their groundbreaking anthology on Black women's studies, Gloria T. Hull, Patricia Bell-Scott, and Barbara Smith's lament that "All the Women Are White, All the Blacks Are Men" is still entirely too relevant in the research, diagnosis, and public understanding of autism.[41]

Biases in autism-related research and literature also tend to erase and exclude autistic people who fall somewhere on the broad LGBTQ+ spectrum. Medical texts, guidebooks, educational materials, and advice manuals are overwhelmingly heteronormative in their approaches and language and rarely include or even consider the particular experiences of autistic people who identity as queer, transgender, asexual, gender fluid, bisexual, aromantic, among others.[42] Sex education materials, for example, often invalidate or fail to recognize autistic people's sexuality by emphasizing issues such as masturbation, puberty, and avoiding abuse at the neglect of issues such as dating, sexual pleasure, birth control, and marriage.[43] Within popular dating advice manuals or parents' guidebooks, the widespread assumption that autistic people are inherently heterosexual or nonsexual or that they do not have the capacity to understand gender identity has led to the invisibility of trans, genderqueer, asexual, nonbinary autists, making it difficult for them to find important sources of community and support.[44] When displayed or claimed by autistic people, identities that fall outside of heteronormative gender expectations tend to be pathologized rather than recognized as legitimate, as, for example, when gender nonconforming or asexual autists are told that their gender and/or sexual identities are simply a product of their autism and thus "not real."[45] Few resources or communities exist, then, for autistic people who do not fit or feel at home within the strictures of sexual and gender norms. And, as autistic writer Caroline Narby argues, "[w]hen the body of literature and knowledge that seeks to address autistic people leaves out discussions of gender—and accepts and reinforces sexist, heterocentric, and transphobic ideologies—it excludes and oppresses members of the very population that it purports to serve."[46]

The more I researched, the more I began to challenge my previously unexamined assumptions about what constituted "normal" or desirable forms of communication, social interaction, movement, feeling, or thinking.

Neurological and behavioral differences were not always problems, I was gradually beginning to realize—sometimes they were just differences that became problems within unaccommodating environments. And though I did not initially realize it during the early years of Zoey's diagnoses and the beginning stages of my research, I was starting to form a neurodiverse perspective. A neurodiverse perspective understands autism as a highly variable neurological difference that is just as valid and deserving of social acceptance and equal treatment as any other neurological difference within the broad landscape of human diversity. It does not deny nor minimize the challenges associated with autism and other neurological differences but recognizes that many of these challenges result from stigmatizing cultural attitudes and institutional, exclusionary barriers. Hence, while it opposes interventions that focus on cure or normalization, it recognizes the usefulness of therapeutic approaches that teach autistic people adaptive skills and promote self-advocacy and personal empowerment. And it works toward the "creation of a world in which all people can benefit from whatever supports, services, therapies, educational tools, and assistive technologies may be necessary to empower them to participate fully in society, with respect and self-determination as the guiding principles."[47]

A NEURODIVERSE APPROACH TO CARE

My research of autism led me eventually to the discovery of a thriving autism rights community of self-advocates (which I discuss extensively in chapters one and two) whose perspectives informed, enriched, and in many ways revolutionized my views of autism, developmental disabilities, and respectful and ethical care approaches. Inspired by this community and my profoundly new way of thinking, I created over time a list of nonnegotiable rules by which I evaluated the methods, rhetoric, and attitudes of potential service providers. To be deemed appropriate and safe, a therapeutic approach had to (1) respect Zoey's personhood; (2) teach Zoey skills for better coping with her environment, not focus on changing her or making her appear to be "typical"; (3) recognize Zoey as an expert of her own experience and therefore include her in the problem-solving process; (4) recognize as valuable and worthy my perspectives as Zoey's mother and include me in the problem-solving process; (5) teach me how to be a better advocate for Zoey; (6) give Zoey the tools to develop self-advocacy; (7) recommend medication only following and in conjunction with the implementation of various therapeutic approaches.[48] Weighed against these criteria, several therapies fell short. Despite our pediatrician's recommendation, I rejected applied behavior analysis with its extreme time demands on the life of our small child and its reduction of complex human motivations and responses to ticks on a time sheet and rewards for displays of acceptable (i.e., typical) behaviors. I immediately left the service of a behavioral therapist who told Zoey that she needed to stop engaging in tics and rituals because "the other kids will think that you are weird." I also decided against enlisting the services of a well-respected and highly recommended occupational therapist following my observation of her approaches during our first appointment with her. The therapist led Zoey into a room that contained a play stove and table and a full range of plates and bowls, kitchen utensils, and plastic food and invited her to begin playing. Delighted, Zoey sat on the floor and began stacking the plates and bowls, grouping the food into categories (fruits in one pile, vegetables in another, among others) and finally batting the food around the room with a rubber spatula. I smiled as I observed her, noticing nothing out of the ordinary. At home, she often categorized her toys similarly and enjoyed dressing her dolls and lining them up on the sofa according to the color of their outfits. The therapist, however, did not seem to share my pleasure in watching Zoey's play; as Zoey gleefully knocked a plastic stalk of broccoli into the corner of the room, she shook her head mournfully, leaned toward me, and whispered, "This is bad." When I gave her a confused look, she explained that presented with such items, six-year-olds are "supposed to" engage in role playing by creating detailed scenarios involving cooking or restaurants and by imagining themselves as chefs, servers, or customers. But as I returned my gaze toward Zoey's direction, I saw nothing "bad" whatsoever, only a happy little girl who was finding tremendous satisfaction in her particular style of play. We left the therapist's office that day and never returned. As ASAN argues, no one should have to "grow up constantly being told that their natural behaviors are wrong and that they cannot be accepted as they are."[49] Over the years, I have been fortunate to locate therapists who appreciate and nurture Zoey's particular ways of living and being in the world. Instead of teaching Zoey that she needs to be less autistic, they have helped her to navigate the neurotypical world in which she necessarily lives and in which she forms relationships, interacts with those who might try to abuse or take advantage of her, receives an education, and will one day seek employment. And so the skills that they are teaching her are what autist Nick Walker calls survival techniques for "navigating around an exotic foreign culture."[50]

In addition to the support and advice I have received from Zoey's team of therapists, I have gained tremendous insights from autistic adults, who, as autist Ido Kedar notes, crucially "filter the words of 'experts' through the sieve of lived experiences" and "have much to teach about the truth of disability."[51] I have drawn extensively from the recommendations of autist Judy Endow, for example, who works as a therapist for autistic children, adults, and their families. At her website "Aspects of Autism Translated," Endow posts several writings and blog posts full of helpful advice and information for autistic people and their caregivers. One of the most valuable lessons I have learned from Endow is that when autistic individuals are supported daily in sensory regulating activities, they are better able to cope with unexpected or stressful events and are thus less likely to experience explosive behaviors. Like many autistic people, Zoey has sensory processing disorder (SPD), which makes it difficult for her neurological system to receive, organize, and understand the input it receives, resulting in emotional disregulation. Sensory processing refers to how the nervous system responds to messages produced by our senses, including not only the familiar senses of sight, sound, touch, taste, and smell but also the prioceptive and vestibular senses, which produce perceptions of movement, speed, pressure on the joints and muscles, and bodily positions. As explained by Lucy Jane Miller in her book *Sensational Kids*, sensory processing disorder (SPD) exists when an individual's nervous system is unable to organize sensory signals into appropriate responses, resulting in a chronic disruption of everyday activities, routines, and social interactions. Miller likens this to a worker whose inbox keeps filling up faster than she is able to complete the work. Behavior challenges occur when the "backlog" of sensory messages accumulate and eventually overcome one's ability to cope. As Miller writes, "the cumulative effect of undisposed sensory messages is what causes children with SPD to eventually fall apart over triggering events that are minor."[52] For Ido Kedar, managing an overstimulating environment is emotionally exhausting. "The choice is to fight the intense feelings inside with so much effort (like fighting back the urge to vomit)," he writes, "or to have the feelings burst out," resulting in feelings of shame and regret. Although he has learned to exercise greater control over his emotions in response to sensory triggers, "this is still a great frustration for those of us with autism, as well as those who are with us when it happens."[53]

Zoey's particular type of SPD fits within the category of over-responsivity sensory modulation disorder, which means that she reacts to sensory messages more quickly, with more intensity, and for a longer duration than her neurotypical peers.[54] Especially affected are her senses of taste, hearing, and touch, and she therefore finds certain foods, sounds, and forms of physical contact unbearable. Interestingly, while Zoey is overreactive to sounds, physical contact, and food, she is underreactive to movement. Her proprioceptive sense—the sensory input that tells us about movement and body position—has difficulty receiving and interpreting sensory messages about her muscles, joints, and connective tissues. In practice, this means that her brain often has difficulty figuring out how to move a certain way or what type of movement and pressure are needed to complete a certain task. Because she is underresponsive to proprioceptive input, her body moves boldly through life. When she was younger, it seemed that she was perpetually running, jumping, bouncing, or turning cartwheels. She played roughly, jumped and crashed into people and objects, pushed hard on and usually broke her crayons, pens, and pencils, spoke loudly, and fidgeted constantly. Her challenges with motor planning and body awareness mean that she exhibits a certain clumsiness and often has difficulty climbing, running, hitting a ball, tying her shoes, and— when she was younger—getting dressed and undressed (particularly when buttons were involved). While she avoids many forms of human contact, she has a tendency to hug animals with an unintentional ferocity.

Occupational therapy has helped Zoey better manage her responses when she is experiencing sensory difficulties. Pediatric occupational therapy is designed to provide children with the skills necessary for managing everyday activities, tasks, and routines imperative to daily functioning and enjoyment, including eating, sleeping, playing, social interaction, self-care, and academic success at school. Zoey's therapy room is filled with slides, swings, balls, scooters, ropes, and weights, and the tables are scattered with puzzles, art supplies, and a wide array of toys. Through various forms of sensory play, her occupational therapist works to strengthen her neurological systems in order to improve her fine and gross motor abilities, reduce her sensitivity to various stimuli, and to teach her to recognize, articulate, and, ultimately, to self-regulate sensory problems.[55] Occupational therapy has also taught us how Zoey's context can influence her behavior and how to manipulate or change this context in order to improve her functioning.[56] I provide ample opportunities for Zoey to engage in heavy work activities—or whole body tasks that involve heavy resistance to the muscles and joints—such as hiking, swimming, running, and climbing, which help to decrease her sensory defensiveness and regulate her arousal levels. We equipped our large living room with a trampoline, crash pad, and small weights and designated it as an area where Zoey can engage in proprioceptive stimulation and self-regulation by moving, spinning, and jumping, and yelling. And we transformed our dining room into a sensory space full of calming activities, such as puzzles, drawing materials, play dough, books, and glue (which she used to enjoy spreading over her hands and picking off of her fingers when dry) and a pop-up tent where Zoey can retreat when she is feeling overwhelmed or anxious.

Zoey also experiences decreased sensitivity to oral sensory input. She regularly bites, chews, or mouths nonfood objects and—when she was younger—other people. We came to recognize that Zoey's chewing and biting is a form of stimming, or a repetitive body movement that self-stimulates one or more senses. Common in children with autism, stimming takes many forms, including hand flapping, rocking, and head banging, and occurs when children attempt to stimulate underactive senses or when they attempt to find ways to calm down or reduce sensory overload. While some forms of stimming are innocuous and not so different from behaviors such as toe tapping or hair twirling, they are problematic when they become destructive or self-injurious, as is often the case with Zoey. We tried to find objects on which she could bite and chew safely without damaging herself or her belongings. For a time, she used several baby teething rings made of hard, virtually indestructible BPA-free plastic. As she grew older, she began to refuse to take the baby rings with her to school or other public places. So we ordered special bracelets and necklaces designed for children with sensory processing disorder that allowed her to satisfy her need to bite and chew and that provided her with oral motor feedback.

Zoey's ability to navigate her environment has been aided tremendously by the gift of her service dog, Linda. Named for the woman who donated the funds necessary for her training by a local nonprofit group that provides service dogs to children with autism at no cost, Linda joined our family when Zoey was eleven. Her positive impact on Zoey's life has been nothing short of life-changing. Linda is able to sense when Zoey is anxious or overstimulated and will place her head or sometimes her entire body on top of Zoey to provide a comforting and calming pressure. Zoey will lie for long stretches of time with Linda curled up beside her, gently snoring while Zoey strokes her fur with one hand and reads a book with another. Especially when Zoey was younger, Linda was a constant companion in public spaces, keeping Zoey calm and focused and providing a visual clue to passersby that this is a child who needs extra support and patience. Most importantly, Zoey is able to lavish Linda with love and affection and be assured that her feelings will be reciprocated without judgment or reservation.

I encourage Zoey to embrace a positive conception of her neurological differences, to understand her autism and her ADHD as gift-conferring parts of her identity. I stress that most of her challenges come from her environment, and that the therapies and treatments that we have pursued are meant not to "fix" her but to help her better navigate a world that does not readily accommodate her. But within this ideological framework, it is difficult at times to help Zoey to situate her understanding of OCD, a neurological difference that Zoey often finds distressing and debilitating. It can result in physical damage and emotional trauma. It has prevented her from enjoying or participating in some of the great and simple pleasures of life. And adjustments to her physical environment will do little to change this.

Because I have personally experienced the distress and debilitation of OCD, witnessing Zoey's daily struggles makes it very difficult for me to understand her anxiety as just another valid and even celebratory neurological difference. But I nevertheless recognize it as a part of her personhood and one that confers particular insights about the tremendous stigma attached to mental health disabilities. And it is, in fact, within the context of how stigma affects Zoey's experiences and understanding of OCD that the social model seems most applicable. Certainly, her obsessive behaviors, ticks, and rituals by themselves can be incredibly disabling. But she is equally disabled by the unforgiving and intolerant environment in which her OCD is on such visible display, an environment that fears, misrepresents, and maligns those with neurological differences and that makes it extremely difficult for those with mental disabilities to enjoy equal social, educational, and economic opportunities. An irresponsible media incessantly perpetuate the stereotype that people with mental disabilities are violent and unstable—when in fact, they are more likely to be victims of violent crime.[57] People with mental disabilities—particularly BIPOC—are disproportionately killed by law enforcement officials and warehoused in jails and prisons,[58] and they have high rates of suicide, unemployment, and homelessness.[59]

As Zoey has grown older and as her anxieties have intensified, we have engaged the services of psychologists who are specifically trained in pediatric cognitive-behavioral therapy, and we have learned to apply the principles of this therapy at home. As its name suggests, cognitive behavioral therapy (CBT) combines behavioral and cognitive therapy to combat negative feelings by changing behaviors and thinking patterns. For people with OCD, CBT helps to reduce obsessions and rituals by teaching them to think realistically and to confront fears.[60] The cognitive aspect of CBT focuses on changing the way that children think and talk to themselves about OCD, specifically by training them to recognize OCD as a "brain hiccup" and something that can be resisted by charting and ranking one's fears and "talking back" to OCD by refusing to obey its dictates. One effective behavioral treatment for OCD is exposure and response (or ritual) prevention (ERP), which teaches children to confront what triggers their obsessions and then to resist the urge to perform the typical ritual.[61] Over time, the child begins to recognize that exposure will not result in the feared consequence and, thus, the obsessions are less likely to dominate her thoughts.[62]

I have introduced and instituted ERP very slowly, beginning with Zoey's least worrisome fears and moving gradually to more difficult exposures at a pace that Zoey controls. When she was younger, one of her recurring obsessions had to do with the "cheese touch" storyline from the *Diary of a Wimpy Kid* book series. In a revolting scenario from the first book, one of the characters is forced to eat a piece of cheese that had been casually discarded on the playground during the lunch period and left to rot and mold for several weeks. While most children would probably be disgusted and even disturbed by this description, Zoey became obsessed with it. Soon she began rejecting some of her favorite foods like pizza and fleeing the room whenever someone happened to be eating a piece of cheese. If we stopped at or even passed the cheese aisle in the grocery store, she grew very upset and sometimes explosive. One day, after she began screaming and frantically trying to escape from the shopping cart when a store employee approached us with a tray full of cheese samples, I stopped taking her on grocery trips and consulted her psychologist, who suggested that we begin incorporating ERP into Zoey's therapy. It started with short visits to the grocery store and total avoidance of the cheese section during the first few visits. This was followed by longer trips during which we inched a bit closer to the section each time until, finally, I was able to pass by and, later, even stop briefly at the section without Zoey collapsing into tears or hysterics.

Having read with Zoey the second installment in the *Diary of a Wimpy Kid* book series, I knew that there was no replication of the cheese scenario from the first book and thus allowed Zoey to watch the cinematic version one Saturday evening. While the content was age-appropriate and fairly innocuous, there was one brief scene where two of the characters watch a horror movie in which a disembodied foot terrorizes a group of travelers. In the days that followed, Zoey grew increasingly fixated on the scene and began to talk incessantly about the foot, refusing to go to sleep at night for fear that the foot would attack her in her bed. As a way of helping her to confront her fear, I encouraged her to write stories and to draw pictures of the foot, hoping that repeated exposure would dilute the power of the image in her mind. She responded with enthusiasm and began to spend hours creating elaborate horror stories with detailed plot lines and illustrations of severed feet. Proud of her artwork, she taped her illustrations to every available surface of her bedroom walls and even parts of the downstairs family room. Though such images would no doubt have appeared disturbing to those unfamiliar with their purpose, my family and I grew used to their sight and soon barely noticed them as we went about our daily affairs. Still, we were forced to confront the unique nature of Zoey's artistry when we visited her school on Parents' Day a few weeks later. On entering Zoey's classroom, Nathan and I were initially confused when we noticed the other parents whispering to each other in hushed, scandalized tones and pointing to the wall where the teacher had pinned the students' artwork. Scanning the wall, we suddenly recognized the source of their unease. Conspicuously located in the midst of the children's pictures of rainbows, fairies, and ponies was Zoey's drawing of a giant severed foot dripping with blood.

Because repeated drawings and stories about severed feet helped to ease some of Zoey's fears about attacks from bloody appendages in particular and injury and trauma in general, I began to encourage Zoey to maintain her own "Zoey Journal" where she could write and draw pictures about her anxieties, challenges, and feelings. For her, OCD is the disability that is the most tangible and immediate, and so it is the one on which she tends to reflect the most. With her permission, I am including here a passage from her Zoey Journal written in 2017 when she was twelve years old:

So, okay, you know how I have OCD. I am going to tell you how it feels for me. So, having OCD is difficult for me because it makes me worry a lot and I mean a lot. Sometimes I worry about if I have something dirty on me or if my toys are melted, but I know they are not because they are still there. I worry that my Mama and Daddy and Connor may die and I will have no family. I just worry a lot. I still worry from this day on. Me and Mama are working on how to get rid of my OCD. It takes time but we are working on it and we will never give up.

Difficulties with anxiety and with processing sensory information can have a negative impact on autistic children who want to form meaningful relationships with kids their own age. Contrary to the popular perception that autistic individuals lack interest in relating to others, many autistic people desire friendships and social connections but have unusual forms of communicating and interacting that make them stand out from their peers. When social interactions take place in overstimulating environments, especially, autistic children are often overwhelmed by sensory triggers and are unable to meet the social expectations of their nonautistic peers. This often leads to rejection, which inhibits the development of social skills and meaningful friendships. "For this reason," writes Nick Walker, "autism has been frequently misconstrued as being essentially a set of 'social and communication deficits,' by those who are unaware that the social challenges faced by autistic individuals are just by-products of the intense and chaotic nature of autistic sensory and cognitive experience."[63]

Usually, Zoey is willing and eager to interact with her peers, but because she does not always understand social norms or the unwritten rules and nuances of social engagement, she appears awkward and immature during social interactions. She has a blunt communication style and tends to take a very literal interpretation of what others say. With little understanding of or patience for the reciprocal nature of a conversation, she tends to monopolize a verbal exchange, shifting from one thought to another without allowing another person to speak. In order to strengthen Zoey's peer relationships, we enrolled her in group social skills training both at her school and in the community and practiced at home the techniques and strategies she learned in group settings. In autism-specific groups, Zoey was typically the only girl, much to her disappointment. Still, we have found a wonderful online community at the Autistic Women & Nonbinary Network, which offers articles, blogs, and other resources written by and for autistic girls and women and has provided tremendous information about the particular challenges, issues, and joys of being a female autist.[64] As Zoey gets older, it is my hope that she will be able to connect more actively with this community and even contribute to its crucial knowledge building. Enrolling Zoey in clubs and groups that allow her to pursue her interests while interacting with other kids her age—both neurodivergent and neurotypical—has offered another tremendous outlet for her talents, energies, and enthusiasms and will hopefully prove fertile ground for lasting friendships. Group activities have proven very challenging for Zoey, given her sensory challenges and OCD, but with modifications and accommodations, she has managed to find at times a comfortable space in community theater, cheerleading, voice lessons, and chess club. In fact, she has twice finished in second place in county chess tournaments involving hundreds of school-age children. Participation in these sorts of events and activities where she can shine has been one of the greatest boosters of her self-confidence and has helped her to recognize that she is an exceptional person who does many things exceptionally well.

Finally, as much as possible, I encourage Zoey to learn from the wisdom of autistic adults, many of whom have experienced her struggles, feelings of isolation, joys, and interests and have written about them from the perspective of distance and maturity. More than anything, I hope, they will help her to embrace all of the wonderful, unique things that make her who she is and to pursue unapologetically the things that fill her life with happiness. Zoey's intense, highly focused interests, for example, are a beautiful part of who she is and a source of great joy, one I never attempt to contain but only celebrate, enable, and attempt to share. When she was younger, she grew extremely attached to various objects, such as the pink plastic spoon that I described earlier. Over the years, she has cycled through periods where she is intensely focused on certain toy collections, such as Strawberry Shortcake, My Little Pony, Littlest Pet Shop, Tsum Tsums, and Num Noms. For about a two-year period, she was singularly focused on Shopkins, a range of tiny, collectible toys based on grocery items. Zoey would spend hours lining up her Shopkins into neat columns, studying her Shopkins checklists, reading her Shopkins books, watching her Shopkins movies, playing her Shopkins cards and games, and planning which of her Shopkins clothing items she would wear to school on a given day. Yet, her interests are rarely shared or tolerated by her same-age peers, and her tendency to talk incessantly about the things that she loves has made her the target of school bullies, magnified her social isolation from her peers, and subjected her to thoughtless remarks from teachers. At every turn, I encourage Zoey to disregard these soul-crushing messages that tell her that her interests are inappropriate or shameful, that try to turn her joy into something "dirty and battered."[65] I encourage her to view her interests through the lens of her fellow autists, who revel in their own "obsessive joys" and fully claim their authentic autistic selves. Gushing over her love of the television show *Glee* and sudoku puzzles, Julia Bascom notes that the best part about her autism is being "so happy, so enraptured about things no one else understands and so wrapped up in my own joy that, not only does it not matter that no one else shares it, but it can become contagious. This is the part about autism . . . I never want to lose. Without this part autism is not worth having."[66] In an August 2014 blog post, Nick Walker offered a beautiful message of hope and resiliency to young autists. Acknowledging that there will be times of sorrow, frustration, and even anger, Walker promised that living an unapologetically autistic life ultimately brings fulfillment, inner peace, and love:

> And although it took some time and involved some major struggles, and although there are still plenty of struggles, I eventually ended up becoming a happy adult with an awesome life where I spend much of my time doing things that I love—a life full of good friendships, good community, and those simple moments of joy, grace, kindness, and connection that make a life worthwhile. I'm glad I stuck around long enough to get this far. The hard parts were worth it.[67]

For autistic writer Amy Sequenzia, autism is life, humanity, family, and community. Autism is "living, learning, growing" through "good times and bad times." It is struggling together for rights, respect, and recognition. And, perhaps most of all, "Autism is joy":

> We enjoy our lives, we celebrate our successes.
> We learn and we share. We are everywhere. . . .
> We spin and flap and jump and we smile.[68]

A CONCLUSION, OF SORTS

My dear Zoey, I sit here just a couple of weeks before I have to submit the final version of this manuscript, agonizing over and second-guessing every line of this chapter. I started the "Zoey Journal" that evolved into this chapter when you were just four years old. By the time this book is published, you will have turned sixteen. Twelve years ago, I could not have imagined where you are now—your self-confidence; your wide circle of friends; your school for kids on the autism spectrum where you are fully supported and valued; all of the amazing people who have come to comprise our support network; and your ability to engage with your environment in ways that you find satisfying and joyful. I sit here on an uncharacteristically warm late January night, pleasantly distracted by the sound of hip-hop music and the bursts of laughter coming from your room as you chat over the computer with your friends and plan what you will do when you return to school next week after a long period of distance learning due to the ongoing COVID-19 crisis. As I read over this chapter, I am struck again by how my description of your interests now seems outdated. When you come into the room to show me a picture you have drawn, I ask you if you would be willing to write a paragraph describing the things that make you happy and whether I can incorporate it into the conclusion to this chapter. You return a few moments later with a sheet of lined notebook paper on which you have scrawled in your characteristically large, enthusiastic handwriting:

> I love anime and cosplaying. These things make me happy because in anime there are all different kinds of it, it's not just one thing that will get boring eventually. I've always loved dressing up as my favorite characters. I cosplay almost all of the boys from my hero academia. I also cosplay characters from naruto and stranger things. I enjoy this because it makes me feel happy and excited.

You have changed and matured so much, Zoey, but the core of you remains the same. You still have passionate, intense interests, but they have shifted from Shopkins to anime. You still love costumes and wigs, but instead of playing dress up, you "cosplay." Instead of using glue to make slime, you use latex to create elaborate scars and wounds to transform into the characters from your favorite shows. You still love to read, but the Judy Moody books on your shelves have been replaced by manga comics and graphic novels.

Sitting here thinking about the last twelve years, I realize that what has changed the most is me. Twelve years ago, things seemed bleak. Saturated in a medical model of disability, I met each new diagnosis, each new school expulsion, each new dire prognosis or predication with increasing despair and uncertainty about the future. Through our journey together, my viewpoint has been transformed. Suddenly, a memory from the past surfaces, one that brings a smile to my face. You were six, and we were at a Blockbuster video store searching for a Dora the Explorer movie. Full of joy, you skipped and jumped through the aisles, singing tunes from the Dora show and shouting with enthusiasm each time you spotted a video that sparked your interest. After just a few minutes in the store, we were the recipients of the usual stares and disapproving gazes. Catching up with you, I leaned down and whispered, "Zoey, you are bothering the other people in the store because you are being too loud." At this, you looked around for a few seconds, shrugged, and then turned to me and said, "No, the other people are just being too quiet." How right you were, Zoey, and how much you have been the prism through which I began to see my world differently. And while my view is still limited, partial, and constantly evolving, it is the location from which I will continue to fight for a world where you no longer have to "hurl yourself into the sky" just to be seen but where you can live, and laugh, and thrive, and love, and be loud—just by being exactly who you are.

NOTES

1. Phillip Phillips, "Home," track 2 on *The World from the Side of the Moon*, Interscope Records, 2012.

2. See Judy Singer, *NeuroDiversity: The Birth of an Idea* (Judy Singer, 2017); Harvey Blume, "Neurodiversity: On the Neurological Underpinnings of Geekdom," *The Atlantic*, September 1998, https://www.theatlantic.com/magazine/archive/1998/09/neurodiversity/305909/; Steve Silberman, *Neurotribes: The Legacy of Autism and the Future of Neurodiversity* (New York: Avery Books, 2015); and Dawn Prince-Hughes, *Songs of the Gorilla Nation: My Journey Through Autism* (New York: Three Rivers Press, 2004).

3. See, for example, Stuart Murray, "Autism Functions/The Function of Autism," *Disability Studies Quarterly* 30:1 (2010), https://dsq-sds.org/article/view/1048/1229.

4. Ginny Russell provides a thorough, if not exhaustive, discussion of some leading criticisms of the neurodiversity movement in Ginny Russell, "Critques of the Neurodiversity Movement," in *Autistic Community and the Neurodiversity Movement*, ed. Steven Kapp (Singapore: Palgrave Macmillan, 2020), 287–303, https://doi.org/10.1007/978-981-13-8437-0_21.

5. Sue Rubin, "Acceptance versus Cure," *CNN*, 2005, accessed January 30, 2021, https://www.cnn.com/CNN/Programs/presents/shows/autism.world/notebooks/sue/notebook.html.

6. Cal Montgomery, "Defining Autistic Lives," *Ragged Edge Online*, June 30, 2005, http://www.raggededgemagazine.com/reviews/ckmontrubin0605.html.

7. Montgomery, "Defining Autistic Lives."

8. Emily Thornton Savarese and Ralph James Savarese, "The Superior Half of Speaking: An Introduction," *Disability Studies Quarterly* 30:1 (2010), https://dsq-sds.org/article/view/1062/1230.

9. Mel Baggs, "Cultural Commentary: Up in the Clouds and Down in the Valley: My Richness and Yours," *Disability Studies Quarterly* 30:1 (2010), https://dsq-sds.org/article/view/1052/1238.

10. Baggs, "Cultural Commentary."

11. Baggs, "Cultural Commentary."

12. Autistic Self Advocacy Network, "Position Statements," accessed January 5, 2018, http://autisticadvocacy.org/about-asan/position-statements/.

13. Autistic Self Advocacy Network, "Position Statements."

14. Savarese and Savarese, "The Superior Half of Speaking."

15. Savarese and Savarese, "The Superior Half of Speaking."

16. Names have been changed to ensure confidentiality.

17. Judith Warner, *We've Got Issues: Children and Parents in the Age of Medication* (New York: Riverhead Books, 2010), 1–17; Jane McLeod, et al., "Public Knowledge, Beliefs, and Treatment Preferences Concerning Attention-Deficit Hyperactivity Disorder," *Psychiatric Services* 58:5 (2007): 626–631.

18. Guifeng Xu, et al., "Twenty-Year Trends in Diagnosed Attention-Deficit/Hyperactivity Disorder Among US Children and Adolescents, 1997–2016," *JAMA*

Netw Open 1:4 (August 2018): 1–9, https://jamanetwork.com/journals/jamanetworko
pen/fullarticle/2698633.

19. Centers for Disease Control and Prevention, "Attention-Deficit/Hyperactivity
Disorder," accessed March 17, 2019, https://www.cdc.gov/ncbddd/adhd/data.html.

20. Michael Davidovitch et al., "Challenges in Defining the Rates of ADHD
Diagnosis and Treatment: Trends Over the Last Decade," *BMC Pediatr.* 17:218
(December 2017), https://doi.org/10.1186/s12887-017-0971-0; Alan Schwarz, "The
Selling of Attention Deficit Disorder," *The New York Times*, December 14, 2013,
http://www.nytimes.com/2013/12/15/health/the-selling-of-attention-deficit-disorder.
html?pagewanted=all.

21. Tumaini Coker et al., "Racial and Ethnic Disparities in ADHD Diagnosis
and Treatment," *Pediatrics* 138:3 (2016): e20160407, https://doi.org/10.1542/peds
.2016-0407; Rick Mayes et al., "Medicating Children: The Enduring Controversy
over ADHD and Pediatric Stimulant Pharmacotherapy," *Child and Adolescent
Psychopharmacology News* 13:5 (2008): 1–5, 9, https://scholarship.richmond.edu/cg
i/viewcontent.cgi?article=1063&context=polisci-faculty-publications; Devon Frye,
"Children Left Behind," *Attitude*, accessed November 8, 2019, https://www.additude
mag.com/race-and-adhd-how-people-of-color-get-left-behind/.

22. Warner, *We've Got Issues*, 1–17.

23. Christopher Pittenger et al., "Clinical Treatment of Obsessive Compulsive
Disorder," *Psychiatry* 2:11 (2005): 34–43, https://www.ncbi.nlm.nih.gov/pmc/article
s/PMC2993523/?report=classic.

24. Jon E. Grant and Samuel R. Chamberlain, "Exploring the Neurobiology of
OCD: Clinical Implications," *The Psychiatric Times*, March 2, 2020, https://www.psy
chiatrictimes.com/view/exploring-neurobiology-ocd-clinical-implications.

25. Daniel A. Drubach, "Obsessive-Compulsive Disorder," *Continuum* 21:3
Behavioral Neurology and Neuropsychiatry (2015): 783–788, https://doi.org/10.1212
/01.CON.0000466666.12779.07.

26. John S. March et al., "Cognitive-Behavioral Psychotherapy for Pediatric
Obsessive-Compulsive Disorder," *Journal of Clinical Child & Adolescent Psychology*
30:1 (2001): 8–18, https://doi.org/10.1207/S15374424JCCP3001_3.

27. Arshia Dhar, "Pop Culture Has Reduced OCD to Quirks and Punchlines,"
Firstpost, October 12, 2019, https://www.firstpost.com/living/pop-culture-has-reduce
d-ocd-to-quirks-and-punchlines-making-a-mockery-of-those-who-live-with-the-
condition-7472891.html.

28. Maru Gonzalez, "Attention Hipsters: OCD is Not a Joke," *HuffPost*, June 16,
2015, https://www.huffingtonpost.com/maru-gonzalez/attention-hipsters-ocd-is-not-a
-joke_b_7581942.html.

29. Rachelle Pavelko and Jessica Myrick, "Tweeting and Trivializing: How the
Trivialization of Obsessive–Compulsive Disorder via Social Media Impacts User
Perceptions, Emotions, and Behaviors," *Imagination, Cognition and Personality* 36:1
(2016): 41–63, https://doi.org/10.1177/0276236615598957.

30. Stephen Tonti, "ADHD as a Difference in Cognition, Not a Disorder," Filmed
April 11, 2013 at TEDxCMU, Carnegie Mellon University, Pittsburgh, PA, video,
13:37, https://www.youtube.com/watch?v=uU6o2_UFSEY.

31. Lara Honos-Webb, *The Gift of ADHD: How to Transform Your Child's Problems into Strengths* (Oakland: New Harbinger Publications, 2007), 95–97.

32. Honos-Webb, *The Gift of ADHD*, 149.

33. Nick Walker, "What is Autism?" *Neurocosmopolitanism*, March 1, 2014, https ://neurocosmopolitanism.com/what-is-autism/.

34. Svenny Kopp and Christopher Gillberg, "The Autism Spectrum Screening Questionnaire (ASSQ)-Revised Extended Version (ASSQ-REV): An Instrument for Better Capturing the Autism Phenotype in Girls?" *Research in Developmental Disabilities* 32:6 (November-December, 2011): 2875–2888, https://doi.org/10.1 016/j.ridd.2011.05.017; Simon Baron-Cohen, "The Extreme Male Brain Theory of Autism," *Trends in Cognitive Sciences* 6:6 (2002): 248–254, https://doi.org/10.1016/ S1364-6613(02)01904-6.

35. Agnieszka Rynkiewicz et al., "An Investigation of the 'Female Camouflage Effect' in Autism Using a Computerized ADOS-2 and a Test of Sex/Gender Differences," *Molecular Autism* 7 (January 21, 2016): 1–8, https://doi.org/10.1186/s 13229-016-0073-0; Clare Sarah Allely, "Understanding and Recognising the Female Phenotype of Autism Spectrum Disorder and the 'Camouflage' Hypothesis: A Systematic PRISMA Review," *Advances in Autism* 5:1 (March 2019): 14–37, https:/ /doi.org/10.1108/AIA-09-2018-0036; Michelle Dean, et al., "The Art of Camouflage: Gender Differences in the Social Behaviors of Girls and Boys with Autism Spectrum Disorder," *Autism* 21:6 (2017): 678–689, https://doi.org/10.1177/13623613166 71845; National Autistic Society, "Gender and Autism," accessed October 4, 2018, https://www.autism.org.uk/about/what-is/gender.aspx.

36. Jolynn Haney, "Autism, Females, and the DSM-5: Gender Bias in Autism Diagnosis," *Social Work in Mental Health* 14:4 (2016): 396–407, https://doi.org/10.1 080/15332985.2015.1031858.

37. Matthew Rozsa, "Gender Stereotypes Have Made Us Horrible at Recognizing Autism in Women and Girls," *Quartz*, October 12, 2016, https://qz.com/804204/asd -in-girls-gender-stereotypes-have-made-us-horrible-at-recognizing-autism-in-women -and-girls/.

38. Judith Gould and Jacqui Ashton-Smith, "Missed Diagnosis or Misdiagnosis: Girls and Women on the Autism Spectrum," *Good Autism Practice* 12:1 (2011): 34–41, https://doi.org/10.1177/1362361317706174; Tyler McFayden, et al., "Brief Report: Sex Differences in ASD Diagnosis—A Brief Report on Restricted Interests and Repetitive Behaviors," *Journal of Autism and Developmental Disorders* 49:4 (April 2019): 1693–1699, https://doi.org/10.1007/s10803-018-3838-9; Allison Ratto, et al., "What About the Girls? Sex-Based Differences in Autistic Traits and Adaptive Skills," *Journal of Autism and Developmental Disorders* 48:5 (2018): 1698–1711, https://doi.org/10.1007/s10803-017-3413-9; Rozsa, "Gender Stereotypes."

39. Jason Travers et al., "A Multiyear National Profile of Racial Disparity in Autism Identification," *Journal of Special Education* 47:1 (2013): 41–49, https://doi .org/10.1177/0022466911416247; David S. Mandell, et al., "Racial/Ethnic Disparities in the Identification of Children with Autism Spectrum Disorders," *American Journal of Public Health* 99:3 (2009): 493–498, https://doi.org/10.2105/AJPH.2007.131243; John Constantino and Tony Charman, "Gender Bias, Female Resilience, and the

Sex Ratio in Autism," *Journal of the American Academy of Child and Adolescent Psychiatry* 51:8 (August 2012): 756–758, https://doi.org/10.1016/j.jaac.2012.05.0 17; Centers for Disease Control and Prevention, "Racial and Ethnic Differences in Children Identified with Autism Spectrum Disorder," *Community Report on Autism*, 2018, https://www.cdc.gov/ncbddd/autism/addm-community-report/documents/diff erences-in-children-addm-community-report-2018-h.pdf; Steve Silberman, "The Invisibility of Black Autism," *UNDARK*, May 17, 2016, https://undark.org/2016/05 /17/invisibility-black-autism/.

40. Quoted in Rozsa, "Gender Stereotypes."

41. Gloria T. Hull et al., *But Some Of Us Are Brave: All the Women Are White, All the Blacks Are Men: Black Women's Studies* (New York: The Feminist Press, 1982). See also, Lydia X. Z. Brown et al., eds., *All the Weight of Our Dreams: On Living Racialized Autism* (Lincoln, NE: DragonBee Press, 2017).

42. Caroline Narby, "Double Rainbow: Asperger's and Girls," *Bitch Media*, February 7, 2012, https://www.bitchmedia.org/post/double-rainbow-aspergers-and -girls-feminism-autism-books.

43. Alyssa Hillary, "The Erasure of Queer Autistic People," in *Criptiques*, ed. Caitlin Wood (May Day Press, 2014), 127.

44. Hillary, "The Erasure of Queer Autistic People," 124–126.

45. Lydia X. Z. Brown, "Gendervague: At the Intersection of Autistic and Trans Experiences," *Asperger/Autism Network*, June 22, 2016, https://www.aane.org/gend ervague-intersection-autistic-trans-experiences/.

46. Caroline Narby, "Double Rainbow: Parent Guides, Part 1," *Bitch Media*, February 17, 2012, https://www.bitchmedia.org/post/double-rainbow-parent-guides -part-1-feminism.

47. Autistic Self Advocacy Network, "Position Statements."

48. My ideas about ethical therapeutic interventions come from autistic self-advo-cates. See, for example, Julia Bascom, ed., *Loud Hands: Autistic People, Speaking* (Washington, DC: The Autistic Press, 2012).

49. Autistic Self Advocacy Network, "Position Statements."

50. Nick Walker, "Advice to Young Autistics: Stick Around and Be Awesome," *Neurocosmopolitanism*, August 21, 2014, http://neurocosmopolitanism.com/advice-t o-young-autistics-stick-around-and-be-awesome/.

51. Ido Kedar, "No, I'm Not a Horse: A Refutation of the Clever Hans Comparison to Autistic Typers," *Ido in Autismland*, April 21, 2016, http://idoinautismland.com/ ?cat=9.

52. Lucy Jane Miller, *Sensational Kids: Hope and Help for Children with Sensory Processing Disorder* (New York: Perigee, 2014), 105.

53. Ido Kedar, "Struggling for Self Control in a Sensory Overwhelming World," *Ido in Autismland*, April 2, 2012, http://idoinautismland.com/?cat=106.

54. Miller, *Sensational Kids*, 23.

55. Miller, *Sensational Kids*, 52, 62–63.

56. Miller, *Sensational Kids*, 64.

57. David M. Perry and Lawrence Carter-Long, *The Ruderman White Paper on Media Coverage of Law Enforcement Use of Force and Disability: A Media Study*

(2013–15) and Overview (Ruderman Foundation, March 2016): 5–7, https://ruderma nfoundation.org/wp-content/uploads/2017/08/MediaStudy-PoliceDisability_final-fin al.pdf; Erika Harrell, *Crimes Against Persons with Disabilities: 2009–2015 Statistical Tables* (U.S. Department of Justice Bureau of Justice Statistics, NCJ No. 250632, July 2017): 1–17, https://www.bjs.gov/content/pub/pdf/capd0915st.pdf; Rachel Morgan and Jennifer Truman, *Criminal Victimization, 2019* (U.S. Department of Justice Bureau of Justice Statistics, NCJ No. 255113, September 2020): 1–51, https://www .bjs.gov/content/pub/pdf/cv19.pdf.

58. John Swaine et. al., "The Counted: People Killed by Police in the U.S., Recorded by the Guardian- With your Help," *The Guardian*, accessed September 10, 2020, https://www.theguardian.com/us-news/series/counted-us-police-killings; John Swaine, et. al., "The Counted: About the Project," *The Guardian*, accessed September 10, 2020, https://www.theguardian.com/us-news/ng-interac- tive/2015/jun/01/about- the-counted; Autistic Self Advocacy Network, "Autism and Safety Toolkit: Research Overview on Autism and Safety," 1–28, accessed September 10, 2020, https://autisti cadvocacy.org/wp-content/uploads/2017/11/Autism-and-Safety-Pt-1.pdf.

59. Autistic Self Advocacy Network, "Autism and Safety Toolkit"; National Alliance on Mental Illness, "Mental Health by the Numbers," *NAMI*, accessed April 22, 2019, https://www.nami.org/Learn-More/Mental-Health-By-the-Numbers.

60. Aureen Pinto Wagner, *What to Do When your Child has Obsessive-Compulsive Disorder: Strategies and Solutions* (Mobile, AL: Lighthouse Press, 2002), 119–120.

61. Brian A. Boyd et al., "Modified Exposure and Response Prevention to Treat the Repetitive Behaviors of a Child with Autism: A Case Report," *Case Reports in Psychiatry* 2011 (2011): 241095, https://doi.org/10.1155/2011/241095.

62. John March, *Talking Back to OCD: The Program That Helps Kids and Teens Say "No Way"—and Parents Say "Way to Go"* (New York: The Guilford Press, 2006), 61–62; 68–69.

63. Walker, "What is Autism?"

64. Jean Widegardner, "The Onus of Acceptance," *Autistic Women & Nonbinary Network*, October 7, 2013, https://autismwomensnetwork.org/the-onus-of-accept ance/.

65. Julia Bascom, "The Obsessive Joy of Autism," *Just Stimming*, accessed December 1, 2013, https://juststimming.wordpress.com/2011/04/05/the-obsessive- joy-of-autism/.

66. Bascom, "The Obsessive Joy of Autism."

67. Nick Walker, "Advice to Young Autistics."

68. Amy Sequenzia, "This is Autism," *Ollibean*, accessed June 3, 2018, https:// ollibean.com/autism/.

Part IV

MOTHERING DISABILITY

Chapter 7

Disability and the Constructs of Motherhood

In the spring of 2016, I traveled for the first time to Copenhagen, Denmark, to evaluate a university study abroad program in gender studies. My first full day touring the city, I marveled at the curved, cobblestone streets lined with historic buildings, squares, fountains, and brightly colored shops. As I strolled down Vesterbro in the city center searching for a place where I could enjoy a cup of coffee and a pastry, I stopped short at the sight of a long row of baby carriages parked by the windows outside of a cafe. Within the carriages, much to my astonishment, babies bundled snugly in snowsuits and woolen blankets napped peacefully while their caregivers sat inside, leisurely sipping coffee and chatting with friends.

At dinner that evening with a group of Danish professors from the university, I recounted my surprise at finding babies left unsupervised in the chilly March air outside of several cafes and shops that I had passed during my exploration of the city. My dinner companions seemed amused by my reaction, quite common among Americans they noted, and went on to tell me that children in Denmark, from babies to school-age children, spend a great deal of time outdoors regardless of the temperature. Children playing in the fresh air instead of indoors at a daycare or in a classroom have less exposure to germs and risk of infection, they noted, and babies sleep longer and more comfortably bundled up outside in the cold. Cafes lined with rows of sleeping babies, they added, indicate that groups of mothers are gathering inside for community and support during the sometimes stressful months of new parenthood. This led to a conversation during which I learned that new mothers in Denmark are entitled to nearly a year of paid parental leave and regular home visits from nurses, who provide postpartum care (including treatment for postpartum depression), conduct baby wellness checks, offer advice and answer questions, and oversee arrangements for playgroups into which all new mothers are assigned by the Danish government. By the age of one, approximately 98 percent of Danish children are part of the government-subsidized daycare system for which families pay very little out-of-pocket expense, giving their mothers time and social permission to pursue their professional and personal ambitions. Returning to the subject of my astonishment over the napping babies outside of the shops and cafes, I asked whether unsupervised children led to incidents of child abduction. They sat for a moment in silence while they thought about this until one woman managed to recall an incident "about six years ago" in which a man snatched a bicycle parked outside of a Copenhagen store and peddled off, only to realize a few moments later that three young children were napping in the attached cargo bay. The man gently roused the oldest child and asked for her home address, which she sleepily recited. He then biked the children to their home, helped them out of the cargo bay, and waited until they were safely inside before riding away.

While I was aware that Danish attitudes and policies regarding parenting and children were very different from those in the United States, this dinner conversation taught me that the differences were much more far-reaching and consequential than I had assumed. Around the same time that the Copenhagen bike thief was safely delivering home the three children he had unwittingly kidnapped, an American mother from Chicago, Kim Brooks, was arrested for leaving her four-year-old son, Felix, alone in a car. They were on their way to the airport to catch a flight home following a visit with family in Richmond, Virginia, when Brooks pulled into a local Target store for a quick errand. Felix, happily absorbed in a game he was playing on his iPad, began to protest loudly when Brooks tried to get him out of the car. So she decided to leave him where he was with the car locked and alarmed and the windows slightly cracked. It was a cool day—barely fifty degrees—and she would be in the store for only about five minutes, she reasoned. But while she was gone, a bystander recorded a video of Felix alone in the back seat and sent it to the police. Brooks was charged with "contributing to the delinquency of a minor," but due to some skillful maneuvering from her lawyer, she received a relatively lenient sentence of mandatory parenting classes and performance of community service. A white, married, educated woman, Brooks was "not the kind of mom they'll throw the book at," her lawyer had correctly assured her.[1]

By contrast, the kinds of moms they *will* throw the book at do not share Brooks's privileges and thus face even harsher penalties for their parenting choices. In 2014, Debra Harrell, an African American single mom, was arrested for allowing her nine-year-old daughter to play alone at a park a mile from the McDonald's where she was working. Unable to afford adequate childcare, Harrell often resorted to bringing her daughter to work—where the nine-year old would sit in a restaurant booth for hours, bored and listless—but occasionally allowed her to play at the park while she finished her shift. One afternoon, after someone at the park called the police, her daughter was sent to a foster care facility for fourteen days, and Harrell was charged with unlawful conduct toward a child, a felony punishable by up to ten years in jail.[2]

Parents in the United States today raise children in a pervasive culture of fear.[3] We are bombarded by warnings from experts about the hazards to our children from peanuts, glucose, chemicals, artificial colors, faulty car seats, junk food, cyberbullying, violent media, too much screen time, and overexposure to sunlight. Warned constantly by the media about the dangers of child murder and abduction, we consider it abnormal and even criminal in some circumstances to leave children unattended, even for a few minutes. And so, few children today are permitted to walk to school, to ride their bicycles, to attend a friend's birthday party, to go to the park, or even to play in their own backyards without a parent directly and constantly supervising them. "The downside for parents," Kim Brooks notes, "is that unless you are extremely wealthy and can pay a professional to help keep adult eyes on your child around-the-clock, it is very difficult and maybe impossible to live a full, balanced life while watching and supervising children every second. It's hard to meet today's standards of 'good' parenting and still be a good friend, a good employee, a good sibling, a good member of your community. Parenthood becomes all-consuming."[4]

Daily across the United States, mothers who break from rigid parenting norms and expectations are surveilled, harassed, called out, shamed, demonized, and arrested. From the moment they become a parent, mothers are simply expected to know instinctively their child's needs and how to provide for them. Held to an impossible standard of perfection, they are expected to cheerfully assume the majority of parenting responsibilities and to selflessly advance their child's interests by subsuming completely their own.[5] Those who cannot live up to these expectations earn their society's wrath. As Brooks argues, "We're contemptuous of 'lazy' poor mothers, . . . 'distracted' working mothers, . . . 'selfish' rich mothers, . . . of mothers who have no choice but to work, but also of mothers who don't need to work and still fail to fulfill an impossible ideal of selfless motherhood. You don't have to look very hard to see the common denominator."[6] Always, it seems, U.S. society places the responsibility for child welfare almost entirely on the shoulders of American mothers even as it fails to give mothers and families the provisions that would vastly improve the health and safety of their children, including subsidized childcare, paid family leave, flexible working schedules (especially those that accommodate children's school schedules), shorter work weeks, a decent minimum wage, family wages paid directly to caregivers, universal preschool, affordable and universal healthcare—including mental healthcare—and stricter gun laws.

Before I became a parent, I had only a vague, mostly theoretical under-standing of how society monitors, judges, and sometimes criminalizes mothering and, consequently, how women hold themselves and other moth-ers to impossible, unachievable standards. My experiences of pregnancy, childbirth, and mothering made my understanding intimate and personal, even as I grew to recognize that my privileges insulated me from the level of surveillance experienced by women of color, women with certain dis-abilities, poor women, and LGBTQ+ women. And it was not until Zoey was diagnosed with several neurodiversities that I began to experience and explore how societal and personal expectations for mothering magnify exponentially when parenting a child with disabilities. Like all mothers, mothers of children with disabilities are expected to foster their children's growth through unlimited time, energy, and resources.[7] But they are also expected to be what sociologist Amy Sousa calls "warrior-heroes" who tire-lessly battle educational, political, medical, and social institutions in order to obtain needed services for their children regardless of the financial and personal costs.[8] So pervasive is the "warrior-hero" ideology, Sousa notes, that few cultural alternatives exist for those mothers who lack the finances, time, and education required to fulfill it.[9] For many years, I bought into the ideology and judged my mothering and that of others according to its tenets. There are times that I still do. But, as I hope to demonstrate in the next two chapters, I have learned that the heroic mothering paradigm is damaging because its definition of good mothering is tied to and actually constructed from hegemonic ideas of class, race, gender, and ability. It tends to medi-calize children's disabilities by presenting them as something that can and should be "fixed." It assumes that good mothering requires only an individ-ual woman's efforts and perseverance. And it requires, and in fact demands, that a woman sacrifice not only her time and energies but her care of self at the altar of her child's well-being. Disrupting the "good mother" and "heroic mothering" paradigms requires that we keep offering up cultural alternatives of motherhood, ones that demonstrate that good mothering does not depend on wealth, whiteness, ability, and heteronormativity; that encourage moth-ers to help their children develop eventually into self-advocates equipped to fight the obstacles of disabling environments, structures, and attitudes; that recognize that good mothering depends largely on family and community support, state resources, and public responsibility for social welfare; and that acknowledge that a mother's self-care is not an act of indulgence but is in fact crucial both to her ability to care for others and to her own happiness and well-being.

MOTHERING ZOEY

I had never really planned to be a mother. The youngest of three girls, I was the baby of the family, perhaps a bit spoiled by my loving parents, who applauded my scholastic achievements and, later, supported my desire to eschew marriage and motherhood in favor of graduate school and a career in academia. Unmarried and childless throughout my twenties, my time was my own. I could rise at whatever hour suited me, eat meals hunched over the computer as I answered e-mails or hacked away at my PhD dissertation, spend hours thumbing through philosophy texts while sitting on the floor of the used bookstore, or stay up until 2:00 a.m. watching classic horror movies on television.

Following the birth of my sister's first child, my thoughts increasingly drifted toward marriage and motherhood. Holding my newborn nephew in my arms, I began to imagine the joy that a family of my own could bring. Still, I was determined to postpone such plans until I could finish school and establish myself in my profession. It wasn't until three years later, when I met Nathan, the man who would become my husband, while teaching at a small university in Hays, Kansas, that I seriously revisited my desire to start a family. Nathan and I married a few months after we began dating, and a little over a year following our wedding, we were delighted to discover that we would soon be parents.

To prepare for my impending motherhood, I exhaustively pored through books on parenting and childcare, including the proverbial *What to Expect When You're Expecting*, read dozens of consumer reports on the safest cribs, car seats, and strollers, and converted my study into a nursery with soft yellow paint and a Pooh Bear and Friends mural dancing happily across the walls. I went to each prenatal checkup armed with information and full of questions. Unfortunately, my obstetrician—only one of two in our tiny Kansas town—had little tolerance for my attempts to be an active partner in my pregnancy and birth experience. After giving me a perfunctory examination, he would stride toward the door as I began to ask questions, with one hand resting impatiently on the door handle. When I presented him with my birthing plan, on which I had devoted hours of consideration based in large part on the advice in the feminist classic *Our Bodies, Ourselves*, he gave it a glance, scoffed loudly, and handed it back to me. "Your birthing plan should have only one sentence," he said. "'Come home with a healthy baby.'" Patting me on the knee as if to suggest that this neatly solved the matter, he rose from his chair and walked out the door, glancing over his shoulder only long enough to add, "Oh, and you should just trust your doctor."

My pregnancy was somewhat difficult due to intermittent flare ups of my chronic spondylitis—one manifestation of my autoimmune disorder—and the near crippling sciatica that left me unable to walk for days at a stretch; hence, my lifestyle grew increasingly sedentary. A constant worry was a recurrence of my iritis, another painful, chronic condition resulting from my autoimmune disorder that had already negatively affected my vision and caused photophobia and anterior synechia. Taking corticosteroid drugs while pregnant could pose a (relatively small) risk to my baby, but lack of treatment could result in further eye damage and even vision loss. Fortunately, I carried Zoey to term with no serious complications and went into labor two weeks ahead of schedule when my water broke unexpectedly one late afternoon as I was grading final exams. My bag had been packed for weeks, and so Nathan and I left abruptly for the short trip to the hospital, calling our family members on the way. A few hours after my arrival at the hospital, I had quickly dilated to ten centimeters but was unable to deliver Zoey vaginally, even with the use of forceps. Worried about Zoey's heart rate, the doctor ordered an emergency Cesarean section, and the nurses began to prepare me for surgery. Everything after that point began to move in slow motion. I remember seeing the fear in Nathan's eyes as he hastily donned a pair of scrubs, the metallic taste of blood on my lips that I had bitten while bearing down in my delivery attempts, the antiseptic smell of the nurse's uniform as she bent over me to insert an IV into my arm, and the searing pain in my abdomen as the doctor cut, pulled, and tugged at my skin—there had been no time for a spinal block. At 12:48 a.m. on May 13, 2005, the doctor pulled Zoey from my body and handed her to Nathan, who knelt beside me so that I could see her. Exhausted from the ordeal of delivery, she was lying contentedly in Nathan's arms, and I strained to raise myself up a bit from the gurney where I was strapped down by multiple attachments to plant a kiss on her soft cheek. I was relieved by my baby's safe arrival—which is what my doctor had told me was my only concern—but I was shocked by the unexpected trauma of the birth and nursed lingering doubts about whether the C-section had been absolutely necessary.

Like many women, everything about my birthing experience was consistent with my society's highly medicalized view of childbearing as a painful, risky process best managed in a hospital with the use of drugs and other interventionist procedures.[10] Pregnancy and birth are normal, healthy processes for most women, the vast majority of whom have healthy pregnancies and babies. While maternity care interventions, such as artificial induction, episiotomies, epidurals, and Cesarean sections, are sometimes medically justified, they are used far too often and unnecessarily on healthy women and can lead to serious health risks and complications. At over 30 percent as of 2020, the current C-section rate in the United States is more than seven times the rate in 1970 and more than three times the ideal rate for C-section births as determined by the World Health Organization (WHO).[11] Cesarean sections have the potential to save lives, but C-section rates higher than 10 percent are not related to reductions in maternal and newborn mortality rates, according to WHO.[12] Rather, they are associated with the shorter duration, lower legal risk, and higher profits associated with Cesarean births, particularly in fee-for-service hospitals where the highest number of C-sections are performed.[13]

Waiting for a woman's labor to take its natural course, then, is neither convenient nor profitable for the majority of doctors and hospitals.[14] Nor are procedures that are shown to improve birth outcomes and women's satisfaction with the birthing process, such as continuous and individual care from an experienced caregiver (such as a midwife or doula); walking during labor (untethered to monitors and machines); use of comfort measures, such as massage and warm baths; the use of warm compresses on the perineum (that can help prevent the need for an episiotomy); and the ability to use various positions during labor (such as standing or squatting instead of illogically lying flat on one's back).[15] Such practices convenience a woman and her baby but not necessarily her doctor and are thus routinely underused and even actively resisted, even when women request them.[16] When pregnant women's birthing plans are ignored, when their right to have a say in how and when they deliver is denied, and when they are prosecuted for refusing medical interventions that they do not want or need, they are victims of what Loretta Ross and Rickie Solinger call "obstetric violence."[17] Those most vulnerable to obstetric violence are poor women, disabled women, women of color, and immigrant women, who, historically, have been denied the right to control their bodies, make their own reproductive decisions, or parent without surveillance, judgment, and criminalization.[18]

Despite all of my careful research, I was not at all prepared for how I—with all of my privileges—would be subject to a sort of disciplinary gaze from the moment I became a parent. It started during my hospital stay. Just minutes after enduring a major surgical procedure, the nurses brought Zoey to me for breastfeeding, which I gamely attempted despite the throbbing pain in my abdomen and waves of nausea. My sharpest memory of those first few moments after giving birth was of holding Zoey to my breast as I continuously vomited over her little head into a blue plastic bucket. That bucket would have come in handy when a few hours after delivery, I stood up for the first time on a nurse's order and blood and other mysterious fluids came rushing out of my vagina and landed with an audible plop onto the floor of my hospital room. The nurse who was supporting me by the arms looked down at the fluids rapidly absorbing into the carpet with palpable disgust and actually chastised me for the mess I had created. I longed to sleep, but the nurses frowned at my suggestion that perhaps Zoey could rest in the nursery for a couple of hours. That my baby needed to be with me every moment, with me providing all of the necessary care, seemed to them unquestionable. Zoey cried every time that I attempted to place her in her hospital crib, so I held her in my arms continuously. On the second night of my hospital stay, I had reached a point of exhaustion from not having slept for about forty-eight hours and simply could not bear the thought of enduring the pain associated with heaving myself and Zoey out of bed to change her diaper. Around 2:00 a.m., I hit the call button on my hospital bed. When the nurse poked her head in the door, I described my pain and exhaustion and, despite the exasperated look she was giving me, asked her almost sheepishly if she would change Zoey's diaper. She let out an audible sigh of disgust, snatched Zoey from my arms, expertly cleaned and diapered her, and then handed her back to me all without an encouraging word or even a smile.[19] During the rest of my stay, I never again asked for her help, nor did I call on the assistance of any of the other medical staff. To admit that I needed help was clearly a sign of my incompetence as a mother.

I instantly adored my new baby girl and eagerly and lovingly tended to her, but no amount of reading could have prepared me for how exhausted, inadequate, and isolated I would feel those first few days and weeks after bringing Zoey home from the hospital. Films, television shows, and novels usually depict cherubic, peaceful, newborn babies wrapped snuggly in eiderdown blankets cradled in the arms of smiling mothers with perfectly coiffed hair and clean, thin, well-groomed bodies. Magazine articles regularly applaud the "impressive" self-discipline of celebrities, who miraculously bounce back to their perfect, pre-pregnancy bodies mere weeks after giving birth. Nothing could have been further from my reality. Zoey was a difficult, colicky baby who cried nearly nonstop most evenings and still refused to sleep in her crib. Each night, after giving Zoey a final breastfeeding and rocking her to sleep, I would carefully rise from the armchair and silently tiptoe across the room, where, as gently as possible, I would lower her onto the bassinet. Holding my breath, I would begin slowly to edge away, but inevitably, her eyes would pop open and she would begin to wail. At this, I would scoop her back up and attempt to rock her to sleep and to place her in her bed once more, but always to no avail. Finally, I conceded defeat and began to sleep propped up in a chair holding Zoey in my arms. Exhausted and overwhelmed, I found that simple, everyday things such as eating regular meals, bathing, and deciding what to wear required too much effort. One morning, a couple of weeks after giving birth, I dragged myself to the bathroom for a shower, and as I was getting undressed, I glanced in the mirror, something that I had not bothered to do for several days. I was shocked to see staring back at me an unkempt, sallow-faced woman with dark circles under her eyes, cracked and sore nipples, and a lumpy, misshapen body.

My life had become nearly as unrecognizable as my body. I had always been a confident, capable, independent person who welcomed professional and personal challenges and boldly navigated my way around unfamiliar places and situations. Now, holding my newborn daughter in my arms, I felt frightened by the daunting responsibilities of motherhood and overwhelmed by the interminable length of days that seemed to merge together without beginning or end. Due no doubt to fatigue, hormone changes, and the abrupt upheaval of my previous life, my emotions those first few weeks oscillated between intense joy and overwhelming moments of sadness. While expert advice and friends and family assured me that such feelings were normal, that fully 80 percent of women experience the "baby blues" in the days immediately following childbirth, I was often confused and upset by the range of emotions I was feeling during what should have been the happiest time of my life. Deepening my melancholy was the pediatrician's concern that Zoey was not gaining weight as rapidly as she should have a week after her birth and his recommendation that I begin supplementing breastfeeding with formula. For me, the sacrifices of time and mobility that breastfeeding represented were the epitome of a mother's heroic commitment to her child's health and well-being. And those moments in the stillness of the night or the early hours of the morning when it was just Zoey and me, she sucking insistently on my breast with her tiny fist curled up against her cheek as I stroked her downy head, were the most tender, precious, and memorable of my life. Formula delivered in a bottle seemed a terrible intrusion on these moments and a tacit indictment of my body that had failed to provide Zoey with adequate nourishment. With a little more time, patience, and greater support from the medical staff, Zoey probably would have begun to thrive from breastfeeding alone, but as a new, inexperienced mom, I panicked and started supplementing with formula even as my disappointment and sense of failure deepened.[20] I obtusely believed that in order to prove my worthiness as a mother, I had to singularly provide all of her care, including feedings, diaper changes, and baths. I refused offers from family to hold her at night while I got some rest and gently turned away friends who volunteered to sit with her while I ran errands or enjoyed an evening out with Nathan. To ask for help would mean that I was weak, incompetent, that I had failed as a mother; worse, to acknowledge feelings of sadness and isolation would be to suggest that I did not love my daughter or my new role as a mother, neither of which was remotely true.

One night when Zoey was eight weeks old, I decided once again to try placing her in her bassinet after nursing her and rocking her to sleep. As before, I skulked away from her crib, not daring to breathe, expecting to hear at any moment an indignant wail of abandonment, but this time, her eyes remained closed, her little chest rising and falling as she slept contentedly. It was a strange sort of freedom; I tried to sleep in my bed that night, but it had become an unfamiliar terrain, oddly unsettling in its comfort. I finally opted to sit in a chair next to her crib where I kept myself in a state of catlike readiness, prepared to spring at the first hint of wakefulness. But the weeks of sleepless nights finally caught up to me, and when several hours later I awoke groggy and disoriented, I was alarmed to discover that Zoey was no longer in her bed. Horrified that I had forsaken my vigil, I nearly leapt out of the chair and sprinted down the hallway to the living room where I found Nathan sitting in the armchair feeding Zoey a bottle. When he insisted that I go back to sleep, I did not argue and stumbled back down the hallway, too tired at that moment to contemplate the awesome fact that my daughter had just slept through the night in her own bed.

For me, that was a watershed moment. With more rest, my strength and confidence grew, and the turbulence of my emotions subsided. I suddenly cared again about regular showers, clean clothes, and well-groomed hair. I found time again for house cleaning, baking, and e-mail correspondence. I rediscovered the pleasure of reading, listening to music, and watching movies. I realized that I did not have to remain a virtual prisoner in my home and began taking Zoey with me on errands, visits to friends' homes, or long strolls through the neighborhood. And I finally drew on my support network, leaving Zoey with my mother-in-law for a couple of hours at least once a week while Nathan and I enjoyed some time to ourselves.

Two months after Zoey was born, we moved to Michigan, where I had accepted a professorship at a large, public university. Many times, Nathan and I have looked back on those two years that we spent in Michigan and marveled that we managed to survive relatively unscathed. Within the space of a few months, we had experienced fully eight of the most stressful life events identified by psychiatrists Thomas Holmes and Richard Rahe on their famous Social Readjustment Rating Scale. We had a new baby, geographic location, job, and house. Nathan had finished school and had begun his teaching career. And we both experienced the loss of our beloved grandfathers before the end of our first year in Michigan. For me, one of the most vivid aspects of that time was how I struggled constantly to balance my home and working lives and the guilt I experienced when I felt that I was not able to do my best in either area. Before Zoey, I was fully dedicated to my teaching and research, spending hours each week reading, writing, and preparing for classes, staying late in my office most afternoons chatting with students, and volunteering for numerous service duties. After Zoey, I remained passionate about my career but found that I lacked the time and energy to maintain my previous standards or to devote most of my out-of-class hours to student meetings or committee work. Still, I was an unproven entity in my new job and was thus determined to demonstrate my worth despite the tug of my new parenting role. My colleagues' failure to understand or to sympathize with the demands of being a mother to a newborn baby certainly complicated my situation. The week before the beginning of the fall semester of my first year at the university, the chair of my department announced that he had managed to secure funding for the entire department to attend a two-day working retreat at a luxury hotel on the coast, some 150 miles away. While my colleagues cheered at his news, I sat contemplating wearily how I would manage to leave Zoey for two days while I was still breastfeeding. I could pump and store my milk, of course, but pumping had proven difficult and cumbersome. It was odd. My breasts released milk unreservedly when Zoey was attached to them, but confronted with an uncomfortable, plastic cone, they balked and stubbornly clammed up like an uncooperative witness. There was nothing to be done, I concluded. Nathan and Zoey would have to come with me. When I informed my chair that not only would my husband and baby be accompanying me on the trip but that I would need frequent breaks during the meetings to breastfeed Zoey, he seemed taken aback. Clearly, it had never occurred to him that gallivanting off to a weekend retreat might prove difficult for some members of his department. And then there were the actual logistics of the trip. I had quickly learned that taking a newborn any-where for an extended period of time was a significant production involving a lot of advance preparation and multiple pieces of equipment. Into the trunk of our car, Nathan and I loaded the portable crib, stroller, blankets and sheets, diapers and wipes, baby bath, bottles, burp cloths, breast pads, baby clothes, toys, and white noise machine (without which Zoey would not be able to sleep), along with our suitcase and my laptop. Once we arrived, everything had to be unpacked and assembled, and so by the time Zoey was bathed, fed, rocked, and tucked in for the night, I was exhausted and collapsed on the bed next to Nathan, listening somewhat wistfully to the sounds of clinking wine glasses and laughter from my colleagues who were socializing on the patio directly below my open window.

The next two days were some of the longest and dreariest I have ever expe-rienced. While I sat through endless presentations and tedious discussions of department business, Nathan sat in our room watching over Zoey and waiting for my intermittent breastfeeding visits. No one had thought to order meals for him, and so during lunches and dinners, I shared my food while holding Zoey on my lap in an effort to squeeze in some mom time before dashing off to the next session. On the second day, we were dismayed to discover that Nathan would have to check out of our hotel room before noon, as we would be leaving for home that evening. With no room and no place to go, really, Nathan resorted to strolling Zoey up and down the sidewalks while I looked on from the windows of the conference room, envious of his company and access to fresh air.

Even after classes began, I maintained a strict, albeit scaled down, breastfeeding schedule consisting of a morning, bedtime, and two daytime feedings with Nathan supplementing with formula as needed when I was on campus. My breasts quickly adapted to the regimen, predictably letting down at the designated hour. One afternoon, I fell behind schedule, and as I was hastily preparing to leave for home in time for the third feeding of the day, I was delayed in the department office by a senior colleague known for his verbosity. As he droned on and on about some committee matter, I suddenly detected the familiar swelling sensation of my breasts, which were dutifully ready to release despite the absence of a baby at the helm. It was then that I remembered that I was not wearing my breast pads, and just as my breasts let down, I quickly hugged the binder I was holding against my chest just in case the milk leaked beyond my suit jacket, which luckily was black and not likely to display a stain. After a few more minutes, my colleague began to wind down and concluded our conversation by asking me to sign a committee form. Without thinking, I placed my binder on the counter in front of us and leaned over to my left to grab a pen and sign the document. When I rose up to hand it back, I was startled to see that my colleague was not looking at me or at the document but grimacing instead at my binder, which to my great mortification now had rivulets of my breast milk cascading down its front cover. Without another word, my colleague abruptly turned and exited the office and did not speak to me or look me in the eye again for the two years that I remained at the university. I did not mourn the loss of his company.

Without our support network and in the absence of colleagues who shared our experiences of new parenting, those two years in Michigan were often isolating and lonely. Still, we had the joy of watching Zoey grow and develop into an active, healthy, happy, quirky toddler who navigated and explored her world in unique and enthusiastic ways. And we were excited when I was offered a position as director of the women's and gender studies program at the University of Tulsa. The job was a better fit for my teaching and research interests, and Tulsa represented easier access to Nathan's family, most of whom lived in Kansas and Colorado.

About a year and a half following our arrival in Tulsa, our son, Connor, was born. This time, my Cesarean delivery was carefully planned and prepared for, with relatives streaming into town days before Connor's arrival to help with last-minute details and to assist with his care following the birth. Considering myself a seasoned professional in the motherhood department, I was much calmer and relaxed during my hospital stay and felt no guilt about keeping Connor in the nursery at night while I caught a couple of hours of much-needed sleep in between breast feedings. I unreservedly welcomed help from nurses—who were tremendously skilled and compassionate—in changing and bathing him, and I willingly allowed relatives to hold him while I showered or took walks around the maternity wing. I was delighted when my milk came in three days after giving birth and experienced no difficulties at all with latching or milk production.

Fortunately, in the days following Connor's arrival, I did not have to anticipate an upcoming move across the country or prepare for a new teaching position; instead, thanks to the university's parental leave policy, I was able to spend that spring semester and the summer months concentrating solely on caring for Connor and Zoey without the additional pressure of work commitments. Such a "luxury" is not universal at my university, where full-time hourly staff are eligible only for six weeks of unpaid parental and family leave. This situation is typical of the vast majority of workers in the United States, which is the only country among the forty-one nations included in the Organization for Economic Cooperation and Development (OECD) that does not mandate paid parental leave. Among the other forty OECD nations, nearly half offer up to ten months of paid parental leave, and approximately 66 percent mandate at least twenty weeks; in no nation is required paid leave less than two months.[21] In some countries—such as Finland, Japan, Korea, Portugal, Norway, Luxembourg, Sweden, and Iceland—a generous portion of paid leave is earmarked for new fathers.[22] Such policies help to promote gender equality in the labor force, the trend toward equal sharing of childcare responsibilities, and the breakdown of gender stereotypes.[23]

By the time Connor was eight weeks old, he was sleeping for five or six hour stretches at night; hence, I had more energy for daily activities and for playing with Zoey. But it was by the summer of 2009, when Connor was just a few months old, that Zoey began to exhibit increasing signs of anxiety and obsessive behaviors. Her behavioral challenges began to mount that fall both at home and at school. After she was expelled from her preschool for aggressive actions toward her peers, we decided to seek the help of a child psychologist.

With each passing year, as we sought the services of numerous therapists and tried multiple treatment strategies, I became more and more absorbed in Zoey's care while attempting to carve out time each day for Connor as well. The crumbs of me that remained were divided among my husband, my teaching, and my research. I allowed old friendships to lapse and simply did not bother with forming new ones. My child seemed to be unraveling before my eyes on a daily basis, and so social interactions with colleagues felt wearisome, and conversations or disagreements about department business seemed petty and trite. Spending time with mothers who eagerly shared news about their neurotypical children's activities and accomplishments soon became unbearable; while their children attended ballet lessons and soccer games, my child was attending psychiatry and therapy appointments. I began to turn down nearly all invitations to lunches and social gatherings until finally there were no more invitations to refuse. Nathan and I stopped watching the nightly news and avoided reading books or watching movies with any sort of disturbing, serious subject matter, opting instead for silly, light-hearted comedies or escapist fantasies. Eating at restaurants, going to the movie theater, or visiting the mall were far too triggering to Zoey's multiple sensory issues; traveling long distances in the car or any activity that required Zoey to remain seated and calm were Herculean efforts usually not worth the trouble. Leaving both Connor and Zoey with a sitter seemed out of the question, and so Nathan and I had a night out only during those sporadic occasions when our parents were in town to watch the kids. And that sense of isolation and loneliness that had pervaded our time in Michigan began to return.

I had grown up in a home that resembled those of 1950s television shows. Although she worked outside of the home as a registered nurse, my mother maintained a spotless household, changed the sheets on all of the beds once a week, and served home-cooked meals complete with dessert each night. My father spent his evenings reading, drawing, or helping us with our various school projects. We attended church every Wednesday evening and twice on Sunday. Voices were rarely raised in anger, and my sisters and I were, for the most part, obedient, easy-going children who, apart from the occasional fight and flares of sibling rivalry, got along well, had a wide network of friends, and excelled academically. Family vacations were fun-filled, memorable events, and on holidays, our home overflowed with good food, laughter, and dozens of relatives, almost all of whom lived nearby. While the life I had created resembled that of my childhood in some respects, it was also very different, and for a time, it was difficult to reconcile my expectations and ideals with my reality. Those early years, while I was grappling with Zoey's diagnoses and managing my family dynamics, were challenging. But my sense of isolation lifted a bit as, gradually, I grew more comfortable sharing some of my family's struggles with friends and colleagues, most of whom now had a better understanding of why I appeared so infrequently at department-sponsored events, why I declined most social invitations, and why I had resigned my position as director of the gender studies program. I embraced the support and generosity of colleagues who cared more about my well-being than that of the gender studies program and learned to tune out the criticism of those who did not. Although I still found it difficult to summon the time, energy, or motivation for socializing, I worked on expanding my circle of friends and drawing on the wisdom and support of other parents who were raising neurodiverse children. Most helpful was my growing education in disability studies. I transitioned from reading books written by medical professionals to reading books, articles, blogs, and websites written by disabled scholars and activists who revolutionized my understanding of disability, my role as the mother of a disabled child, and my own relationship to disability. And, eventually, I located therapists who shared my delight in Zoey's energy, creativity, and intellect, helped us to discover strategies and tools through which

Zoey could better navigate her environment, and contributed meaningfully to my parenting journey.

Still, my time never felt as if it belonged to me. When I was not on campus, I was home with one or both of the kids and committed to spending my time playing and interacting with them. It wasn't until I tucked them into bed at night that I could begin preparing for classes or marking student papers, activities that I nearly always had to cram into the three or four hours between the kids' bedtime and my own. Weekends were similarly devoted to family time and to squeezing in a couple of hours with Nathan in the evenings. Leaving Zoey for any significant period of time to travel to archives or to attend academic conferences was impossible, and so my research, writing, and professional networking began to suffer. I honestly did not resent nor truly mourn these limits on my professional or social opportunities. Caring for Zoey and Connor was my highest priority, and there were many, many joyful and happy moments mixed in with the more challenging ones. But this nearly constant care with very little time for rest or recreation began to sap my energy and to affect my health.

THE GOOD MOTHER/BAD MOTHER BINARY
AND THE HEROIC MOTHERING PARADIGM

Like so many other mothers, I often measure my maternal fitness according to the socially constructed idea of the "good mother," defined generally as a mother who vigilantly safeguards her children's health and happiness, actively intervenes in her children's educational and social activities, religiously studies and follows the advice of childcare experts, and, of course, selflessly places her family's needs before her own.[24] The good mother is the linchpin of a larger cultural ideal surrounding motherhood, an ideal that has been not only shaped by long-standing ideas of good mothering[25] but also formed by new, modern standards that comprise what Susan Douglas and Meredith Michaels call "the New Momism." These include "the insistence that no woman is truly complete or fulfilled unless she has kids, that women remain the best primary caretakers of children, and that to be a remotely decent mother, a woman has to devote her entire physical, psychological, emotional, and intellectual being, 24/7, to her children."[26] In many ways, Douglas and Michaels write, the New Momism creates standards more impossible to meet than those promulgated during the June Cleaver-era. Today's good mothers must enroll their children in every possible extracurricular activity, transform pinecones and wire hangers into festive decorations, feed their kids only home-cooked, organic food, spend hundreds of dollars on each birthday party, and construct funhouses in the backyard all while maintaining a clean home and a great sex life with their husbands.[27]

The good mother, of course, is a social construct formed in opposition to its evil counterpart—the "bad mother." While good mothers are charged with safeguarding the health of families, future citizens, and the nation, bad mothers get pregnant before marriage, bear crack babies, and burden the community with their exploitation of the welfare system.[28] Both halves of the binary are constructed from and judged by the hegemonic ideals of white, heteronormative, middle-class, able-bodiedness. While the motherhood of women who seem to embody these ideals is valorized, expected, and even compulsory, the motherhood of women who do not is immediately suspect, subject to scrutiny, surveillance, and disciplinary controls. The good mother/bad mother binary, then, categorizes all mothers as either "good" or "bad" and presents the women within these categories as a singular, indistinguishable mass.[29] It thus not only reinforces the "Otherness" of traditionally marginalized groups by positioning women on the good mother/bad mother binary according to their race, class, ability, age, gender identity, and sexual orientation but also collapses important distinctions within identity categories (variations in skin color, type of disability, level of conformity to gender norms, among others)[30] and obscures the variability and intersectionality of women's identities and experiences.

The bad mother construct imposes severe penalties that bring potentially serious material consequences on women who are located within marginalized groups. Lesbian, nonbinary, and transgender mothers are discriminated against in the adoption system and often denied custody. Poor, single, teenage moms are accused of making bad choices when in fact they often have few choices to make due to a lack of good educational and occupational opportunities and punitive social policies, such as the Personal Responsibility and Work Opportunity Act.[31] Asylum-seeking immigrant women are sometimes cruelly separated from their children at the border due to U.S. immigration policies that devalue and disregard their motherhood and their children's welfare. Incarcerated mothers are regularly shackled and chained to hospital beds during labor and delivery, separated from their children after birth, and face termination of their parental rights.[32] And mothers of color are regularly surveilled, called out, and punished by members of the public and criminalized by the state. Black and Native American women, for example, have disproportionally been subjected to involuntary sterilization and Cesarean sections, drug testing during pregnancy, prosecution for drug use, and the removal of their children.[33]

The bad mother construct has been particularly damaging to disabled women.[34] The inexhaustive, expert care of one's children that characterizes the crux of the good mothering ideal expects and demands "able" bodies.

Because they "are viewed as dependent, in need of protection, and incompetent, rather than capable, strong, and nurturing,"[35] women with disabilities are understood narrowly as the recipients, not the providers, of care and are therefore automatically disqualified from the good mother category.[36] Consequently, disabled mothers—especially those with psychiatric, intellectual, or developmental disabilities—are much more likely than nondisabled mothers to have their children removed from their homes or to lose custody of their children.[37]

The compulsory able-bodiedness at the center of the mothering ideal has not only denied disabled women's capacity for childcare but also deprived them of their basic right to reproduce.[38] Rooted in and justified by the widespread popularity of ableist and racist eugenic discourses, fears that genetic "deficiencies" would pass from one generation to the next resulted in the forced sterilization and institutionalization of disabled women throughout the nineteenth and twentieth centuries.[39] Today, people with disabilities who want to become parents continue to face tremendous medical, legislative, judicial, and attitudinal obstacles.[40] For example, they often contend with coercive tactics from medical professionals designed to encourage sterilization or abortions and experience significant barriers to accessing assistive reproductive services or to adopting children.[41] With the growing availability and sophistication of prenatal screening, disabled women are pressured to "ensure the infallibility of their offspring" through genetic testing and to choose abortion if such testing detects "negative" fetal anomalies.[42] Those who refuse to do so, and even those who dare to get pregnant at all, face public denunciation.[43] The very definition of the "bad" mother, women with disabilities are accused of "inflicting" their conditions on their offspring and burdening their communities with the (expensive) care and support of disabled children.[44] Framed by historical understandings that view disabled women's sexuality, reproduction, and mothering as deviant and dangerous, this sort of reproductive coercion that steers disabled women away from pregnancy and condemns disabled women who exercise their reproductive rights is a modern form of eugenics, writes Judith Daar, one that does tremendous harm to women, children, and to society.[45] And by reading the body of a disabled woman "as a threat to established social norms by virtue of its capacity to propagate itself," writes Terri Beth Miller, this reproductive coercion magnifies the stigma and precarity of disabled lives.[46]

In addition to constructing and reifying ableist, sexist, racist, and classist ideals, the good mother/bad mother binary is both a product and perpetuator of gender inequality. It perpetuates the idea that women are meant to be mothers, assumes that childrearing is mostly a mother's responsibility, and both obscures and glorifies the role of fathers. The way in which our society demands so much of its mothers while expecting so little of its fathers is often the source of my bewilderment and frustration. While men are still expected to sacrifice themselves on the altar of family responsibility and are still identified largely through the outdated idea of the family breadwinner, they also receive an outsized form of social validation when they play a role, no matter how minimal, in their child's life. During our first year in Michigan, Nathan put aside his own career aspirations in order to stay home with Zoey full time. While I was at the university, he would often take Zoey to the park or to the library, where he was usually the only dad in a sea of mothers on outings with their children. Simply for spending time with his child, he became the recipient of tremendous social approval, characterized by warm nods and glances and multiple comments from other mothers and even strangers about the excellence of his parenting. Yet, during my excursions with Zoey, I rarely if ever received similar praise. Spending time with my daughter was something that, as her mother, I was simply expected to do. As Douglas and Michaels point out, "a dad who knows the name of his kids' pediatrician and reads them stories at night is still regarded as a saint; a mother who doesn't is a sinner."[47] But the good mother/bad mother binary is not simply a social ideal that shapes expectations for women and men and performances of motherhood and fatherhood; it is also constructed and maintained by laws and economic institutions, such as sex-segregation in the workforce and the gender wage gap, that contribute to systemic forms of gender inequality.[48]

Inevitably, the good mother/bad mother binary imposes standards by which all women discipline themselves in order to avoid being deemed incompetent, egocentric, unnatural, or, worst of all, the root cause of all of their child's current or future problems.[49] Mothers of neurodiverse children, especially, have good reason to fear "mother blame," given the pervasiveness of so-called "scientific theories" that locate the origins of children's "disorders" in the personalities and behaviors of their mothers. In the early twentieth century, for example, Sigmund Freud blamed what he called castrating or schizophrenogenic mothers for producing neurotic or schizophrenic sons. By the mid-twentieth century, psychologists such as Leo Kanner and Bruno Bettelheim attributed troubling or "deviant" behavior among children to "refrigerator mothers," whose coldness and subconscious rejection of motherhood, they claimed, had caused their offspring's developmental and behavioral troubles.[50] By the 1960s, psychologists like Irving Bieber were arguing that possessive and "overintimate" mothers were likely to turn their male children into homosexuals.[51] Today, research from the relatively new field of epigenetics (that analyzes the impact of environmental influences on gene expression) has been used to demonstrate the influence of a mother's actions on her child's health histories as early as the womb.[52] Members of the National Scientific Council on the Developing Child (NSCDC), for example, warn that a woman's emotional and physical experiences both during pregnancy and during her child's early formative years can cause epigenetic changes in her child's brain cells, ultimately affecting the systems that manage the child's response to illness and adversity later in life.[53] "The epigenetic changes that occur in the fetus during pregnancy," they conclude, affect not just the developing child, but "can be passed on to later generations, affecting the health and welfare of children, grandchildren, and their descendants."[54]

Not all research on child development inevitably blames mothers for childhood "disorders," of course. In fact, the NSCDC has connected fetal and child development to the biological and social role of the father and, crucially, environmental factors, including lack of access to nutritious foods, exposure to toxic chemicals, and the effects of racial, class, and gender discrimination.[55] When epigenetic research recognizes wider environmental influences on fetal and child development, notes Harvard professor Sarah Richardson, et al., it can be used to make a strong argument for the need for social, as opposed to individual, changes and even guide policies that support parents and children. Frequently, however, this research is taken out of context, exaggerated, and oversimplified in irresponsibly titled news stories that tend to emphasize a mother's individual influence while minimizing or even ignoring other important, environmental factors. "Pregnant women's high-fat, high-sugar diets may affect future generations," cautioned the title of a 2016 article in *Science Daily* that cited a study linking pregnant women's poor eating habits to obesity, heart disease, and diabetes in "multiple generations."[56] An article in *Healthline* from 2014 titled "Study: Depression During Pregnancy Increases a Child's Risk of Mood Disorders" warned that according to published research, a mother's depression "can pass through the placenta and may influence the fetus' brain development." *Parents Magazine* asked: "Could Too Much Stress During Pregnancy Harm the Baby?" in a 2018 article that discussed the implications of a study connecting a woman's stress during pregnancy to alterations in the fetus's brain development and gut microbiome. "Scientists believe that the altered gut microbiota is linked to a greater risk of neurodevelopmental disorders, including autism and schizophrenia," the article cautioned.[57] Hence, epigenetic research with so much potential to create real, structural changes for improving the lives of women and children has been deployed to "scapegoat mothers" and to magnify the surveillance and regulation of pregnant bodies.[58]

Historically, mothers of neurodiverse children have been particularly vulnerable to mother blame, which not only punishes and regulates motherhood but stigmatizes and pathologizes neurodiversity.[59] While few current medical studies or popular advice books "blame" women directly for their children's "disorders," most tend to treat neurodiversities as something needing cure through a mother's diligent efforts. A popular guide for parenting children with OCD written by Dr. John March, for example, assures parents that they are not to blame for their child's OCD but cautions that they are nevertheless responsible for addressing the disorder skillfully and aggressively.[60] Authors of *A Parent's Guide to Asperger Syndrome and High-Functioning Autism* urge mothers to become "expert[s] in your child's abilities and disabilities, making decisions about which of the treatments to try, and educating teachers, service providers, and others about your child. . . . You are the consistent thread from one classroom to another, from one intervention to another, from one therapist to another, who manages all the details, remembers all the important facts, and knows what worked and what didn't."[61] Mothering a neurodiverse child, then, demands an even higher set of expectations than the sort of "intensive mothering" described by Susan Douglas and others. To meet such high standards of maternal fitness, mothers of neurodiverse children must be well versed in pedagogical approaches, health care provisions, pharmacology, nutrition, and psychiatry as they valiantly navigate the dense bureaucracies of the educational, medical, and insurance systems.[62] Maternal fitness, therefore, is usually measured by how actively a mother intervenes in her child's institutional life, dynamically pursues therapeutic and social opportunities, and selflessly pushes aside her own needs, especially when they conflict with the needs of her child. As a result, many mothers continue to experience guilt or stigma when they fall short of the heroic, selfless, and labor-intensive care expected of mothers raising children with disabilities.[63]

Exacerbating mothers' guilt and feelings of inadequacy are the descriptions of heroic mothering in memoirs primarily written by middle- or upper-class women whose children live with neurological disabilities or whose children have "overcome" such disabilities due to their mothers' courageous actions. In her discourse analysis of thirty-three mothers' memoirs published between 1988 and 2009, Amy Sousa discovered that mothers of children with intellectual disabilities often employ quest-driven language and imagery to present themselves as warrior heroes, becoming the primary advocates, researchers, and representatives for their children and taking on the responsibility for finding the best therapies using valiant, exhaustive, and costly measures.[64] Indeed, my own examination of mothers' memoirs illustrates the pervasiveness of the heroic mothering paradigm. When her son Nat was diagnosed with autism, Susan Senator, for example, describes her "ravenous need for action" as she pored over scientific studies and diagnostic manuals in search of answers and treatments, refusing to accept the bleak outcomes they portended; her moment of "angry disbelief," she writes, was her first step toward advocacy and "the start of the new path we would blaze for Nat."[65] Beth Alison Maloney writes that despite her exhaustion and sadness over her son's debilitating obsessive-compulsive disorder, she needed always to remain in motion, constantly dispensing or ordering medications, e-mailing doctors with questions, reading articles and reports, and guiding her son through his endless rituals and compulsions.[66] Coral Bergmann recounts how she would lie in bed each morning and envision herself as Mel Gibson in *Braveheart*, brandishing a sword above her head as she charged into battle "to slay the invisible dragon called autism." A self-described "warrior mom," Bergmann outlines how her days were devoted to her son's regimen, which consisted of eighty supplements a day, special exercises and baths, applied kinesiology treatments, Cranial Sacral therapy, cold laser treatments, and a strict diet consisting of no wheat, milk, sugar, soy, eggs, yeast, and fruit—interventions that added up to $70,000 a year. "I am my son's full time researcher, biochemist, pharmacist, educator, doctor, nutritionist, and chef," she proclaims. "I control all aspects of his environment down to the smallest detail."[67]

Inevitably, the heroic mothering paradigm contributes to the medical model of disability and the tremendous social expectations placed on all mothers of neurodiverse children. For Sousa, the paradigm perpetuates the idea that while mothers are no longer the cause of their children's disabilities, they are nevertheless responsible for curing them or at least discovering the best medical, educational, and social services through which to treat them. As so many parenting memoirs suggest, if mothers do not act heroically, if they do not exhaust every possibility on behalf of their child, then they have failed. Consequently, "the idealized notion of mother-valor quickly shifts back to mother-blame in which mothers are viewed as proximate causes of prolonged or exacerbated disability."[68] Additionally, mothers who actively employ the heroic mothering paradigm unwittingly reinforce rather than challenge the cultural assumption that disability is an undesirable state demanding forceful intervention through a mother's individual, heroic efforts. As Sousa points out, by characterizing their efforts as heroic, they are suggesting that their children are nearly insurmountable problems that require extraordinary valiance. Such an implication, Sousa argues, creates another artificial binary of the normal/abnormal child and thus perpetuates the "othering" of children with neurological or developmental disabilities.[69]

Finally, the heroic mothering paradigm is dangerous not only because it reinforces an artificial good mother/bad mother binary, vilifies mothers who do not meet the impossible standards of the good mother model, and disciplines and polices women's lives, but because it advances a neoliberal model of mothering and care. Such a model, according to Lisa Duggan, "promotes the privatization of the costs of social reproduction, along with the care of human dependency needs, through personal responsibility exercised in the family and civil society—thus shifting costs from state agencies to individuals and households."[70] Within a neoliberal model, women's association with and relegation to care work and reproductive labor have led to women's economic dependency and inability to achieve full social equality. Consequently, much feminist theorizing and activism have focused on rescuing women from networks of family, care, and dependency, while championing ideals of autonomy and individual-ism.[71] This emphasis, however, tends to perpetuate individualistic, "norma-tive"—that is, white, heteronormative, ableist, middle-class—constructs of personhood and "actively obscures" the sociopolitical roots of inequality.[72] Likewise, the heroic mothering paradigm problematically frames mothering as an individual responsibility requiring individual approaches. In this scenario, disability is overcome through the individual actions of heroic mothers; the persistence of disability, therefore, is the result of a mother who simply fell short of her heroic responsibilities. What this scenario fails to acknowledge is that one's ability to be a "good" mother depends largely on a complex web of supports that are accessible only to the most privileged members of society. Getting needed services for a child requires multiple doctors' appointments; expensive testing; comprehensive insurance; a detailed knowledge of the inner workings of the health care and educational systems; an understanding of various laws and regulations; a team of well-paid therapists; and people in positions of authority who listen, communicate, and collaborate respectfully, expertly, and compassionately.[73] To be the sort of advocate valorized in media and in the popular imagination, then, a mother needs an abundance of time, wealth, energy, support, validation, education, and a host of other resources not readily available to women outside of the white, middle-to-upper-class, "able-bodied," heteronormative, English-speaking ideal.

In rejecting a neoliberal model of mothering and care, then, the task before us is not to "reinstate compulsory motherhood, nor tie an ethic of care to female subjectivity alone," as Cynthia Lewiecki-Wilson argues. Nor is it to rescue marginalized individuals with the most privileges from subjugated identities and categories, which benefits the few and does nothing to chal-lenge systemic and institutionalized forms of oppression. Rather, our task is "to build, instead, a global ethic of and commitment to mutual interdepen-dence, social justice, and personal possibility."[74] And it is to this task that I turn in the next and final chapter.

NOTES

1. Kim Brooks, "Motherhood in the Age of Fear," *The New York Times*, July 27, 2018, https://www.nytimes.com/2018/07/27/opinion/sunday/motherhood-in-the-age -of-fear.html?auth=login-email&login=email.

2. Kelly Wallace, "Mom Arrested for Leaving 9-Year-Old Alone at Park," *CNN*, July 21, 2014, https://www.cnn.com/2014/07/21/living/mom-arrested-left-girl-park -parents/index.html.

3. Judith Warner, *Perfect Madness: Motherhood in the Age of Anxiety* (New York: Riverhead Books, 2005).

4. John Brodie, "5 Questions for Kim Brooks," *Maisonette*, accessed June 1, 2019, https://www.maisonette.com/le_scoop/5-questions-for-kim-brooks. See also Kim Brooks, *Small Animals: Parenthood in the Age of Fear* (New York: Flatiron Books, 2018).

5. Robyn Powell, "How We Treat Disabled Mothers," *Medium*, May 11, 2017, https://medium.com/the-establishment/how-we-treat-disabled-mothers-a76 5ed94e95a.

6. Brooks, "Motherhood in the Age of Fear."

7. Amy Sousa, "From Refrigerator Mothers to Warrior-Heroes: The Cultural Identity Transformation of Mothers Raising Children with Intellectual Disabilities," *Symbolic Interaction* 34:2 (Spring 2011): 239, https://doi.org/10.1525/si.2011.34. 2.220.

8. Sousa, "From Refrigerator Mothers to Warrior-Heroes," 220.

9. Sousa, "From Refrigerator Mothers to Warrior-Heroes," 239.

10. Richard Johanson et al., "Has the Medicalisation of Childbirth Gone Too Far?," *BMJ* 324 (2002): 892–895, https://doi.org/10.1136/bmj.324.7342.892.

11. World Health Organization, "WHO Statement on Caesarean Section Rates," April 2015, https://www.who.int/reproductivehealth/publications/maternal_perinatal _health/cs-statement/en/. See also Michelle Osterman and Joyce Martin, "Trends in Low-risk Cesarean Delivery in the United States, 1990–2013," *National Vital Statistics Reports* 63:6 (November 5, 2014): 1–15, https://www.cdc.gov/nchs/data/ nvsr/nvsr63/nvsr63_06.pdf.

12. World Health Organization, "WHO Statement on Caesarean Section Rates."

13. Gerard H. A. Visser et al., "FIGO Position Paper: How to Stop the Caesarean Section Epidemic," *The Lancet* 392:10155 (October 13, 2018): 1286–1287, https:// doi.org/10.1016/S0140-6736(18)32113-5; Stephanie Teleki, "Birthing A Movement To Reduce Unnecessary C-Sections: An Update From California," *Health Affairs,* October 31, 2017, https://www.healthaffairs.org/do/10.1377/hblog20171031.709216/ full/.

14. Tina Rosenberg, "Reducing Unnecessary C-Section Births," *The New York Times*, January 19, 2016, https://opinionator.blogs.nytimes.com/2016/01/19/arsdarian -cutting-the-number-of-c-section-births/.

15. Judy Norsigian, "Our Bodies, Ourselves: Pregnancy and Birth," *Our Bodies, Ourselves*, accessed December 12, 2018, https://www.ourbodiesourselves.org/publi cations/pregnancy-and-birth/; Katie Cook and Colleen Loomis, "The Impact of Choice and Control on Women's Childbirth Experiences," *The Journal of Perinatal Education* 21:3 (2012): 158–68, https://doi.org/10.1891/1058-1243.21.3.158; Johanson et al., "Has the Medicalisation of Childbirth Gone Too Far?," 892–895.

16. Norsigian, "Our Bodies, Ourselves: Pregnancy and Birth."

17. Loretta Ross and Rickie Solinger, *Reproductive Justice* (Oakland: University of California Press, 2017), 188.

18. Ross and Solinger, *Reproductive Justice,* 10.

19. This narrative of my experience is not meant as an indictment of nurses or other health care professionals. My mother is a registered nurse, and so I grew up admiring and respecting the work that nurses do, and I have received excellent health

care from the members of other nursing staffs throughout my life. I am especially grateful to the skilled, caring, and compassionate nurses at St. John Hospital in Tulsa, Oklahoma, who took such excellent care of me during my delivery and postnatal recovery in January 2009 when my son Connor was born.

20. See Linda Blum, *At the Breast: Ideologies of Breastfeeding and Motherhood in the Contemporary United States* (Boston: Beacon Press, 1999) and Pam Carter, *Feminism, Breasts and Breast-Feeding* (New York: St. Martin's Press, 1995).

21. Estonia offers more than a year and a half of paid leave to new parents—by far the highest benefit mandated by any of the countries represented in the OECD. Gretchen Livingston and Deja Thomas, "Among 41 Countries, Only U.S. Lacks Paid Parental Leave," *Pew Research Center*, December 16, 2019, https://www.pewresea rch.org/fact-tank/2019/12/16/u-s-lacks-mandated-paid-parental-leave/.

22. Livingston and Thomas, "Among 41 Countries."

23. Bjorn Thor Arnarson and Aparna Mitra, "The Paternity Leave Act in Iceland: Implications for Gender Equality in the Labour Market," *Applied Economics Letters* 17 (2010): 677–680, https://doi.org/10.1080/13504850802297830.

24. Ann Crittenden, *The Price of Motherhood: Why the Most Important Job in the World is Still the Least Valued* (New York: Henry Holt and Company, 2001); Sharon Hays, *The Cultural Contradictions of Motherhood* (New Haven: Yale University Press, 1996).

25. Molly Ladd-Taylor and Lauri Umansky, eds., *"Bad" Mothers: The Politics of Blame in Twentieth-Century America* (New York: New York University Press, 1988); Rima Apple, *Perfect Motherhood: Science and Childbearing in America* (New Brunswick: Rutgers University Press, 2006); Kathleen Jones, "'Mother Made Me Do It': Mother-Blaming and the Women of the Child Guidance Movement," in *"Bad" Mothers: The Politics of Blame in Twentieth-Century America*, eds. Molly Ladd-Taylor and Lauri Umansky (New York: New York University Press, 1998), 99–126.

26. Susan Douglas and Meredith Michaels, *The Mommy Myth: The Idealization of Motherhood and How It Has Undermined All Women* (New York: Free Press, 2004), 4.

27. Douglas and Michaels, *The Mommy Myth,* 1–27.

28. Ladd-Taylor and Umansky, eds., *"Bad" Mothers*, 1–23.

29. Corbett Joan O'Toole, "Sex, Disability and Motherhood: Access To Sexuality For Disabled Mothers," *Disability Studies Quarterly* 22:4 (2002), http://dsq-sds.org/article/view/374/495.

30. O'Toole, "Sex, Disability and Motherhood."

31. Susan Chase and Mary Rogers, eds., *Mothers and Children: Feminist Analyses and Personal Narratives* (New Brunswick: Rutgers University Press, 2001), 46; Gwendolyn Mink, *Welfare's End* (Ithaca, NY: Cornell University Press, 1998), 58; Anna Marie Smith, *Welfare Reform and Sexual Regulation* (Cambridge: Cambridge University Press, 2007), 77; Shawn A. Cassiman, "Mothering, Disability, and Poverty: Straddling Borders, Shifting Boundaries, and Everyday Resistance," in *Disability and Mothering: Liminal Spaces of Embodied Knowledge*, eds. Cynthia Lewiecki-Wilson and Jen Cellio (Syracuse: Syracuse University Press, 2011), 289.

32. Jennifer G. Clarke and Rachel E. Simon, "Shackling and Separation: Motherhood in Prison," *AMA Journal of Ethics*, September 2013, https://journalofeth ics.ama-assn.org/article/shackling-and-separation-motherhood-prison/2013-09.

33. Ross and Solinger, *Reproductive Justice,* 49–54; Cassiman, "Mothering, Disability, and Poverty," 291.

34. O'Toole, "Sex, Disability And Motherhood."

35. Powell, "How We Treat Disabled Mothers."

36. O'Toole, "Sex, Disability and Motherhood."

37. National Council on Disability, "Rocking the Cradle: Ensuring the Rights of Parents with Disabilities and Their Children," September 27, 2012, 72, https://www .ncd.gov/sites/default/files/Documents/NCD_Parenting_508_0.pdf.

38. Cynthia Lewiecki-Wilson and Jen Cellio, "Introduction: On Liminality and Cultural Embodiment," in *Disability and Mothering: Liminal Spaces of Embodied Knowledge*, eds. Cynthia Lewiecki-Wilson and Jen Cellio (Syracuse: Syracuse University Press, 2011), 8.

39. Terri Beth Miller, "Stalking Grendel's Mother: Biomedicine and the Disciplining of the Deviant Body," in *Disability and Mothering: Liminal Spaces of Embodied Knowledge*, eds. Cynthia Lewiecki-Wilson and Jen Cellio (Syracuse: Syracuse University Press, 2011), 50–52.

40. Samantha Walsh, "'What Does It Matter?' A Meditation on the Social Positioning of Disability and Motherhood," in *Disability and Mothering: Liminal Spaces of Embodied Knowledge*, eds. Cynthia Lewiecki-Wilson and Jen Cellio (Syracuse: Syracuse University Press, 2011), 85–86.

41. Judith F. Daar, "Accessing Reproductive Technologies: Invisible Barriers, Indelible Harms," *Berkeley Journal of Gender, Law, and Justice* 23:1 (2008): 77, https://doi.org/10.15779/Z38K93156H.

42. Ora Prilletensky, "A Ramp to Motherhood: The Experiences of Mothers with Physical Disabilities," *Sexuality and Disability* 21:1 (2003): 22–23, https://doi.org /10.1023/A:1023558808891; Marsha Saxton, "Born and Unborn: The Implications of Reproductive Technologies for People with Disabilities," in *Test-Tube Women: What Future For Motherhood?*, eds. Rita Arditti, Renate Duelli-Klein, and Shelley Minden (London: Pandora Press, 1984), 298–312; Felicity Boardman, "Negotiating Discourses of Maternal Responsibility, Disability, and Reprogenetics: The Role of Experiential Knowledge," in *Disability and Mothering: Liminal Spaces of Embodied Knowledge*, eds. Cynthia Lewiecki-Wilson and Jen Cellio (Syracuse: Syracuse University Press, 2011), 35.

43. Boardman, "Negotiating Discourses of Maternal Responsibility, Disability, and Reprogenetics," 36–37.

44. Boardman, "Negotiating Discourses of Maternal Responsibility, Disability, and Reprogenetics," 36–37. See also Gail Landsman, *Reconstructing Motherhood and Disability in an Age of "Perfect" Babies* (New York City: Routledge, 2009).

45. Daar, "Accessing Reproductive Technologies," 80; Nikolas Rose, *The Politics of Life Itself: Biomedicine, Power, and Subjectivity in the Twenty-First Century* (Princeton: Princeton University Press, 2007).

46. Miller, "Stalking Grendel's Mother," 52.

47. Douglas and Michaels, *The Mommy Myth*, 8.

48. Julie Maybee, "The Political Is Personal: Mothering at the Intersection of Acquired Disability, Gender, and Race," in *Disability and Mothering: Liminal Spaces of Embodied Knowledge*, eds. Cynthia Lewiecki-Wilson and Jen Cellio (Syracuse: Syracuse University Press, 2011), 253.

49. Linda Blum, "'Not This Big, Huge, Racial-Type Thing, but . . . ': Mothering Children of Color with Invisible Disabilities in the Age of Neuroscience," *Signs: Journal of Women in Culture and Society* 36:4 (Summer 2011): 941–967, https://doi .org/10.1086/658503; Douglas, 20.

50. See Leo Kanner, "Autistic Disturbances of Affective Contact," *Nervous Child* 2 (1943): 217–250; Leo Kanner, "Problems of Nosology and Psychodynamics of Early Infantile Autism," *American Journal of Orthopsychiatry* 19 (1949): 416–426; Leo Kanner, "To What Extent Is Early Infantile Autism Determined by Constitutional Inadequacies?" *Research Publications-Association for Research in Nervous and Mental Disease* 33 (1954): 378; and Bruno Bettelheim, *The Empty Fortress: Infantile Autism and the Birth of the Self* (New York: The Free Press, 1967). See also Jordynn Jack, *Autism and Gender: From Refrigerator Mothers to Computer Geeks* (Urbana: University of Illinois Press, 2014) and Josje Weusten, "Narrative Constructions of Motherhood and Autism: Reading Embodied Language beyond Binary Oppositions," *Journal of Literary & Cultural Disability Studies* 5:1 (2011): 53–69, https://doi.org /10.3828/jlcds.2011.4.

51. Irving Bieber et al., *Homosexuality: A Psychoanalytic Study* (New York: Basic Books, 1962).

52. Victoria Pitts-Taylor, "The Plastic Brain: Neoliberalism and the Neuronal Self," *Health* 14:6 (2010): 635–652, https://doi.org/10.1177/1363459309360796; Glenda Wall, "Mothers' Experiences with Intensive Parenting and Brain Development Discourse," *Women's Studies International Forum* 33:3 (2010): 253–263, https://doi .org/10.1016/j.wsif.2010.02.019.

53. National Scientific Council on the Developing Child, *Early Experiences Can Alter Gene Expression and Affect Long-Term Development: Working Paper No. 10* (Harvard University: Center on the Developing Child, 2010), 1–10, https:/ /developingchild.harvard.edu/wp-content/uploads/2010/05/Early-Experiences-Can-Alter-Gene-Expression-and-Affect-Long-Term-Development.pdf.

54. National Scientific Council on the Developing Child, "Early Experiences."

55. National Scientific Council on the Developing Child, "Early Experiences."

56. "Pregnant Women's High-Fat, High-Sugar Diets May Affect Future Generations," *Science News*, June 16, 2016, https://www.sciencedaily.com/releases /2016/06/160616141336.htm.

57. Lauren Wiener and Whitney C. Harris, "Could Too Much Stress During Pregnancy Harm the Baby?" *Parents*, accessed July 6, 2019, https://www.par ents.com/pregnancy/my-body/can-too-much-stress-during-pregnancy-be-bad-for-my -baby/.

58. Sarah Richardson et al., "Don't Blame the Mothers," *Nature* 512 (August 14, 2014): 131, https://j.mp/2ozaF9A.

59. Sara Ryan and Katherine Runswick-Cole, "Repositioning Mothers: Mothers, Disabled Children, and Disability Studies," *Disability & Society* 23:3 (2008): 199–210, https://doi.org/10.1080/09687590801953937.

60. John March, *Talking Back to OCD* (New York: The Guilford Press, 2007), 12.

61. Sally Ozonoff, *A Parent's Guide to Asperger Syndrome and High-Functioning Autism* (New York: The Guilford Press, 2002), 75.

62. Linda Blum, "Mother-Blame in the Prozac Nation: Raising Kids with Invisible Disabilities," *Gender and Society* 21:2 (April 2007): 212, 222, https://doi.org/10.1177/0891243206298178.

63. Blum, "Mother-Blame in the Prozac Nation," 211.

64. Sousa, "From Refrigerator Mothers to Warrior-Heroes," 227–228.

65. Susan Senator, *Making Peace with Autism: One Family's Story of Struggle, Discovery, and Unexpected Gifts* (Boston: Trumpeter Books, 2005), 41–42.

66. Beth Alison Maloney, *Saving Sammy: A Mother's Fight to Cure Her Son's OCD* (New York: Three Rivers Press, 2009), 138–139.

67. Jenny McCarthy, ed., *Mother Warriors: A Nation of Parents Healing Autism Against All Odds* (New York: Penguin Group, 2008), 185–188.

68. Sousa, "From Refrigerator Mothers to Warrior-Heroes," 235.

69. Sousa, "From Refrigerator Mothers to Warrior-Heroes," 237.

70. Lisa Duggan, *The Twilight of Equality?: Neoliberalism, Cultural Politics, and the Attack on Democracy* (Boston: Beacon Press, 2003), 14.

71. Cynthia Lewiecki-Wilson, "Uneasy Subjects: Disability, Feminism, and Abortion," in *Disability and Mothering: Liminal Spaces of Embodied Knowledge*, eds. Cynthia Lewiecki-Wilson and Jen Cellio (Syracuse: Syracuse University Press, 2011), 77; Eva Feder Kittay, "The Ethics of Care, Dependence, and Disability," *Ratio Juris* 24:1 (March 2011): 52–53, https://doi.org/10.1111/j.1467-9337.2010.00473.x.

72. Duggan, *The Twilight of Equality?* 3; Lewiecki-Wilson, "Uneasy Subjects," 67.

73. Ruth Colker, "Blaming Mothers: A Disability Perspective," *Boston University Law Review* 95:3 (April 2015): 1205–1224, https://doi.org/10.2139/ssrn.2604972.

74. Lewiecki-Wilson, "Uneasy Subjects," 78.

Chapter 8

Refiguring Motherhood through a Disability Lens

I experienced what I now recognize as an "aha moment" on the last day of a week that had been filled with shuttling Zoey to various therapy appointments, taking Connor to gymnastics and birthday parties, mulling over the latest troubling report from Zoey's psychologist, phone calls to the health insurance company that had rejected payment for a new round of medication, and attempts to navigate the public school system in an effort to secure the resources that Zoey would need to survive in a mainstream classroom environment. It had proven to be another long, exhausting day helping Zoey to control her emotions and to manage the meltdown that had resulted in her dumping out the contents of her dresser drawers, destroying several of her books, tearing the sheets from her bed, and punching a hole in her bedroom wall. I felt physically and emotionally depleted, even a bit hopeless. For years, I had watched my child struggle, and despite multiple interventions, nothing seemed to be working. As I so often did in the evening once I got the kids settled into their beds, I headed toward the family room eager to collapse into a chair and flick on the television set, too tired to read or to write, hoping to escape for an hour or so into the banality of a dance competition or a teen comedy from the 1980s. On my way, I glanced out the windows and spotted the neighborhood park just outside of our backyard fence that features a quarter mile gravel track. I could hear the buzzing of a lawnmower next door and detect the scent of freshly mown grass, which, for me, always conjures such pleasant memories of childhood when my sister, Jill, and I would run barefoot through neighborhood lawns at dusk, delaying in every way we knew how the moment when we would have to go inside and get ready for bed. I watched a family of four gliding past on their bicycles as children in the park whooped and hollered with delight. A sudden, unexpected sorrow swept over me, and choking back the sob I felt rising in my throat, I quickly ran up the stairs to my bedroom, fell to my knees on the floor, and allowed myself to weep as I hadn't wept in years—that sort of deep, agonizing form of weeping that burns your lungs and produces alarming, guttural sounds from your mouth. At one point, I grabbed a pillow from the bed and buried my face in it, fearful that the kids or Nathan would hear me. I must not allow them to see me cry, I thought. I am supposed to be the strong one. I cried until my entire body ached, until my face was bloated and red, and until I simply did not have the strength to cry anymore. I lay on the floor for a few more minutes contemplating my next move. I considered calling my mother to whom I always turned for support and solace, but I was not sure that I was ready to relive the emotional pain of the last few minutes. For reasons that are still not entirely clear, I abruptly stood up, entered my closet, and rummaged around until I located a long-abandoned pair of jogging pants and running shoes. I needed to run, I thought to myself as I changed, to sweat, to gasp, to feel something other than this creeping despair.

But once I was outside standing on the track, this idea that had seemed so attractive in theory now seemed only daunting. It was 8:30 p.m. but still over ninety degrees, extreme even for Tulsa in June. And while I had long been intrigued by the idea of running, I had never been a runner, even when I was at my fittest. At most, I could manage a good power walk followed by some strength training. Squinting against the lowering sun, I sighed heavily and began to stretch, every muscle in my body groaning in silent protest. Deciding that I was sufficiently warmed up after a few minutes, I took a deep breath and began to run, moving one foot in front of the other slowly and deliberately. If only I could make it once around the track, I would be satisfied, I told myself. After all, it was only a quarter mile. But within a matter of seconds, I was panting, burdened by the heat and by a body that had not experienced this sort of punishment since my days in gym class when laps around the outdoor track were excruciatingly routine. Still, I kept plodding along, swiping my arm across my sweaty brow every so often and ignoring the growing fatigue in my legs, which by the last turn felt absolutely leaden. Would they continue to support my weight, I vaguely wondered, or suddenly fold under me like those of a newborn colt taking her first steps? Gasping loudly, I spotted my back gate, which had been my starting point. Ten more steps at most, I assured myself, and then I could stop. Never had a few seconds passed so slowly, and despite my pain, I chuckled inwardly as I pictured myself moving in slow motion to the iconic strains of the theme song from *Chariots of Fire*. At last, I reached the gate, and ignoring my temptation simply to collapse in a little heap and hibernate for the next twelve hours or so, I kept walking at a swift pace, afraid that if I allowed myself to sit down, I would not be able to find the strength to get back up. Still breathing heavily, I wound my way around the track an additional three laps, intermittently jogging and walking.

Near the end of the mile, I placed my hands on my chest and was curiously reminded of the time when I was eleven years old and my pet goldfish leapt suddenly out of its bowl to land with a splat on the kitchen floor; similar to the furious thumping of the goldfish against my cupped hands as I scooped it up and returned it to its bowl, my heart was pounding insistently against my outstretched palms. Unfortunately, the goldfish did not survive the trauma—I hoped that my heart would fare better.

I reentered my house triumphantly that evening. Though tired in body, I felt a surge of mental and emotional well-being stemming from the endorphin boost and the momentary distraction from life's worries. During those thirty minutes, I was concentrating almost singularly on the movement of my body, the rhythms of my pacing, and the air flowing in and out of my lungs. In other words, I had carved out a small space in the midst of my stressful day in which I could focus entirely on me. This realization was startling and unfamiliar.

SELF-CARE AS AN ACT OF POLITICAL WARFARE

As I discussed in chapter 7, mothers in the United States are expected to neglect their own needs, desires, and even health in service to their children. Those few, brave mothers who dare to intimate publicly that they might be deserving of a bit of self-care often face swift social punishment. Cheryl Richardson, a life coach who appeared on the *Oprah Winfrey Show* in 1992, for example, was literally booed by the studio audience when she stated that women should put themselves first on their list of priorities.[1] Recalling this incident several years later, Oprah Winfrey remembered her surprise at the audience's outrage and her attempts to cool things down. "She's not saying that by putting yourself first, you're abandoning everything else," Winfrey assured her audience. "She didn't say leave your children in the streets. She just said put yourself on the list. It was a strange concept."[2]

Having been trained my entire life and particularly since the birth of my children that women should be the epitome of generosity and self-sacrifice, taking time that evening of my first official run to focus on my own needs was a "strange concept" indeed and one that I tentatively and uneasily approached. Each night, I forced myself to head outside after the kids were settled for the evening and make a single, grueling lap around the track. By the second week, I had worked up to four laps, intermittently running and walking. I was delighted when, after the third week, I was able to run a consistent mile without walking breaks. Within six weeks, I was able to run a continuous four miles with ease and decided to begin training for a half marathon race in the spring.

I do not think that it is possible for me to overstate the impact that running had and continues to have on my body, mind, and emotions. During each run, I was moving, taking up space, sweating, grunting—things that, historically, women have been prohibited or discouraged from doing. As Laura Argintar writes, "We have been socialized to feel unentitled to our own space, to shrink our presence. To be feminine is to be small and contained. By contrast, to exude masculinity is to recline or spread out to assert power."[3] All of my life I had been a cerebral being, finding power in words, reading, studying, and writing. From childhood to adulthood, books have been a primary source of wisdom, solace, enjoyment, and escape, forming the backdrop of so many of my life's major events. In second grade, when my loneliness and anxiety reached a peak following my grandmother's accident, my friends became Ramona Quimby and the Boxcar Children. Judy Blume's *Are You There, God, It's Me, Margaret*; *Tales of a Fourth Grade Nothing*; and *Tiger Eyes* guided me through the trials and embarrassments of puberty and adolescence. High school was marked by my journey through Shakespeare and the literary classics; by college and graduate school, I had gained an entirely new perspective on power, privilege, and oppression through my reading of theorists such as Michel Foucault, bell hooks, Audre Lorde, and Judith Butler. During the early days of Zoey's diagnoses, I once again turned to books for wisdom and support, poring through advice from therapists, practical suggestions from parents and caregivers, and, later, memoirs, novels, and blogs written by individuals with neurological diversities and other disabilities. And keeping my journal about Zoey provided me with a safe space of sorts to tease out and to make sense of my tangled thoughts and emotions through the transformative power of words. But now, I was finding a new source of power rooted in the physical realm. I never appreciated how deeply intertwined were my mind and my body, how the strengthening of the latter could generate such powerful moments of clarity and feelings of serenity, well-being, and confidence. Those runs gave me a quiet space to breathe deeply, to think clearly, to stomp out my frustrations, and to approach the many roles of my life—mother, partner, daughter, friend, professor, colleague—with much more appreciation, humility, and joy. So many of the ideas that eventually comprised the substance of this book were formed while I was running alone in the woods, on a nature trail, or on the little track outside of my back door. For the first time in years, I was taking care of me and in so doing was making myself more capable of caring for those I love. I recalled the words of one of Zoey's therapists, who stressed how important it was for me to cultivate my own well-being in order to tend properly to Zoey's needs. It's like on the airplane, she had noted, when the flight attendant tells you to secure your own oxygen mask before assisting your child. Having heard this well-worn analogy many times, I impatiently dismissed her concern and inwardly marveled at how little she grasped the realities of my situation. Now I understood the wisdom in her platitude.

The ability to practice self-care has been used as a sort of litmus test in America for determining who is entitled to full citizenship. Douglas Baynton writes that the inability to care for one's self as the result or the cause of disability has been used throughout history to justify the exclusion of and discrimination against people with disabilities, women, people of color, and immigrants. A common argument for slavery, for example, drew on the opinions of medical authorities, who claimed that African Americans were mentally deficient and thus incapable of taking care of themselves.[4] Opponents of women's suffrage argued that women's weaker mental and physical constitutions rendered them unfit to exercise full equality and that the demands of political participation would lead to further disabilities.[5] U.S. immigration policies denied entry to any "lunatic, idiot, or any person unable to take care of himself or herself without becoming a public charge" or anyone with a "mental or physical defect being of a nature which *may affect* the ability of such alien to earn a living."[6] Today, open hostility and discrimination against fat people are based largely on the assumption that such individuals are lazy and self-indulgent, lacking in self-discipline and self-care. One's access to full citizenship in America, then, has been linked solidly to the ability to exercise self-care; as Baynton notes, the attributions of disease and impairment to oppressed groups have been effective and "powerful tools for inequality," telling us much about historical attitudes toward disability in the process.[7]

During the 1950s, a new iteration of self-care emerged within the health care community when patients in institutionalized settings began to use self-care practices as a way of developing their sense of autonomy and self-worth. But it was people of color within activist spaces who, by the 1970s, transformed self-care from a litmus test of social equality into a tool of social justice. Members of the Black Panther Party (BPP), for example, politicized the concept of self-care when they connected it to the well-being and survival of the Black community.[8] Facing the continual onslaught of systemic racism, Black people suffered disproportionately from the effects of poverty, discrimination, and violence and from a health care system that ignored, pathologized, or even tried to exterminate them. Black, queer women within the BPP were among the first to assert that self-care was both a form of community survival within an inequitable sociopolitical system and an everyday revolutionary practice.[9] Angela Davis and Ericka Huggins, for example, recognized that the self-care practices—such as yoga and meditation—that they developed to manage better their exhaustion and trauma made them more resilient and useful within activist spaces, which, in turn, benefitted the entire Black community. Practicing radical self-care "means we're able to bring our entire selves into the movement," Davis remarked in a 2018 interview with AFROPUNK. "It means we incorporate into our work as activists ways of acknowledging and hopefully moving beyond trauma. It means a holistic approach."[10] Recognizing that wellness was crucial to fighting systemic racism, Davis and several other Black queer women were essential to the creation and implementation of BPP "survival programs" that established health care clinics, education programs, and food distribution centers for the Black community.[11] For them, self-care and community care were inextricably connected. As Davis argues, "[a]nyone who's interested in making change in the world also has to learn how to take care of . . . themselves."[12]

The African American poet, essayist, and activist Audre Lorde extended, perhaps most famously, the idea of self-care as revolutionary practice when she wrote, "Caring for myself is not self-indulgence. It is self-preservation, and that is an act of political warfare."[13] For Lorde, self-care was about self-preservation in a world that values some lives over others and about centering her own needs within a community in which Black women are often expected to "shoulder the burdens of others with little concern for [their] own health and happiness."[14] By directing care away from bodies deemed more valuable and toward herself, Lorde was insisting that she mattered. When we insist that we matter, notes Sara Ahmed, we are "transforming what matters. Women's lives matter; black lives matter; queer lives matter; disabled lives matter; trans lives matter; the poor; the elderly; the incarcerated, matter. For those who have to insist they matter to matter: selfcare is warfare."[15]

Lorde's message continues to resonate with the members of marginalized communities, who have had to look after themselves and others in the face of an indifferent or even malignant medical and social system. Since the 1970s, groups of radical feminists have established their own journals, books, and health care centers to combat the paternalism, misinformation, and judgment they received from male doctors and to provide female-centered health and reproductive care to women and girls.[16] Decimated by the AIDS crisis and enraged by the callous indifference of government leaders to queer lives, members of the LGBTQ+ community throughout the 1980s and 1990s created a dynamic network of self-help and patient advocacy groups to provide aid to the sick and dying and their families and to fight for the research, development, and availability of vital medical information and safe and effective drug treatments.[17] As marginalized groups have become more vocal and visible in their demands for justice and fair treatment in the last couple of decades, they have faced intensified forms of violence and discrimination, such as police violence, deportation, incarceration, gun violence, environmental hazards, and attacks on reproductive rights that have imperiled their health and safety. Hence, members of BIPOC, disabled, queer, trans, and feminist communities continue to cultivate self and community care through engagement in activist groups, community centers, self-help organizations, and social media platforms. Within these spaces, they have been able to share knowledge, support each other, and participate in ongoing struggles to demonstrate the value of their lives.

But the concept of self-care has in recent years been coopted by the particular forces of American neoliberalism and capitalism, who have reduced self-care to an individual goal achievable by anyone who can afford to purchase it. A plethora of books, magazines, and social media sites targeting a largely female audience promise happiness, wellness, and empowerment through the buying of consumer goods. Probably the most ubiquitous and successful (as well as widely lampooned) example of wellness for purchase is the company Goop, founded by actress-turned-lifestyle-guru Gwyneth Paltrow. Drawing on mythical notions of an idyllic, romanticized premodern past, as well as exoticized visions of Eastern mysticism, Goop's website encourages the purchase of products promising to restore women's health, empower their minds and bodies, and return them to a state of natural femininity.[18] In one of Goop's most infamous posts, for example, readers were introduced to an "ancient Chinese" practice of inserting jade eggs into the vagina in order to cleanse the womb and restore sexual energy and satisfaction. Available for purchase on the Goop website for $66, "this nephrite jade stone," the post claimed, "helps connect the second chakra (the heart) and yoni for optimal self-love and well-being." For a mere $2,800, customers can also purchase a hand-engraved spirit animal signet ring, which Shamanic healer and intuitive, Colleen McCann, explains "can be harnessed for help in life" and guide the wearer to mental, emotional, spiritual, and physical well-being.[19] The hefty price tag associated with most Goop products clearly signals that Paltrow and her team have targeted an audience of white, wealthy women and have developed products meant to appeal to that particular demographic.[20] And judging from the company's $250 million value, it is also clear that Goop's consumers are buying into the site's brand of wellness and empowerment, despite its specious and even potentially harmful claims. (In 2018, a California prosecution team slapped Goop with a $145,000 fine for misleading customers by making claims not backed by scientific evidence.[21])

Goop's promotion of health and empowerment through the purchase of expensive vaginal jade eggs and gold spirit-animal rings was probably not what Audre Lorde had in mind when she described self-care as an act of political warfare. It is hard to imagine that the type of consumer-driven individualism (or even narcissism) that Goop's brand so aggressively markets is what Lorde envisioned when she argued that self-care is an important weapon in the fight against oppression.[22] Unharnessed from rampant consumerism, self-care can be a simple, accessible act, as activist Aimaloghi Eromosele reminds us. It can mean resting without apology or justification, feeding your body, reading a book for pleasure, walking through the woods, or sitting quietly with your thoughts. It can be anything that brings you clarity, peace, and joy. It can be reconnecting with friends, drawing on supportive relationships, asking for help, and setting boundaries. Self-care is the idea of valuing one's needs and health in order to continue to be able to contribute to society and the needs of others. "Self-care," Eromosele writes, "is anything that gives you a way to reconnect with yourself and your community in meaningful, long-term ways that nurture our individual welfare and gives us the power to survive and continue to do the collective work."[23]

Yet, even this noncommercialized version of self-care dips into neoliberal rhetoric when it leaves unquestioned the assumption that self-care and empowerment are attainable through individual action, a message popularized in the recent spate of bestselling "feminist" self-help guides written by celebrity personalities, such as Facebook CEO Sheryl Sandberg, who encourage women to take responsibility for their own well-being. By focusing on upward mobility and individual self-improvement, writes sociologist Catherine Rottenberg, this sort of neoliberal feminism obscures the structural forces that produce intersectional inequalities. And it tends to reify ableism, "white and class privilege, and heteronormativity"[24] by alienating disabled, LGBTQ+, BIPOC, low-income, and other marginalized communities, who often lack not only the finances but the time and social resources required to practice many forms of self-care.[25] Within this framework, then, self-care once again functions as a type of disciplinary mechanism; if self-care and happiness are products of individual striving, then the lack of self-care and happiness signals individual, not structural, failure. The problem, once again, is yours.

Perhaps most problematic of all, a neoliberal vision of self-care fails to recognize that self-care can occur only within networks of support. Too often, notes artist and educator Abeni Jones, we tell someone who is struggling to "take care of yourself," thereby suggesting that care is an individual responsibility, when we should be asking, "How can I support you?," which is a recognition that our health and wellness depend on the care and support we receive from others.[26] As a disabled trans woman of color, Jones knows full well how difficult and depleting it is to face constant attacks on your very right to exist and how inapplicable the ideal of rugged individualism is to "those of us with brains or bodies that require other people's support in order to make it through this world."[27] For her, self-care consists of "a strong, tight-knit community of caring folks" who care for her when she cannot care for herself and who anticipate and tend to even her most intimate needs without being asked and without the expectation of reimbursement or reciprocation.[28] While community and institutional supports prop up all members of society, the supports of the most marginalized—those who need extra help with daily tasks, who use visible forms of accommodation, who have formed "chosen" families, who rely on self-help organizations, who receive forms of government assistance, and who ask for help when they cannot help themselves—are most visible and thus more highly stigmatized within a society that "demonizes the burdensome" and prizes autonomy and self-reliance above all else.[29] By championing individualism, consumerism, and personal growth, then, neoliberal self-care culture contributes to the stigma of dependency and, therefore, the precarity of disabled people and other marginalized groups. And by obscuring the universality and beauty of interdependency, it helps to stymie the expansion of public resources that value and care for all members of society.

MOTHERS' WELFARE AS SOCIAL WELFARE

Feminist author Jill Filopovic has written that "it's time we decided that female pleasure isn't an indulgence or a privilege but a social good—and that women deserve more than just equality."[30] This idea of women's wellness and pleasure as a public good that bears public responsibility is revolutionary. Too often, we tend to think of equality as a goal achievable by individual will and adjustment rather than a project that requires the dismantling and reconstruction of entire economic, social, and political systems in order to make these systems work for the greatest diversity of human beings. The result is that women—particularly women whose gender intersects with other marginalized identities—are haplessly trying to compete within institutions that were not built for them and that have little regard for the particularity of their lives, needs, and happiness. Like an old garment, institutions acquire the shape of the person who most inhabits them, as Sara Ahmed writes.[31] The garment is worn easily and unconsciously by those who fit this shape but uncomfortably and highly self-consciously by those who do not. Like the wearer of the ill-fitting garment, women historically have had to rearrange their bodies—their lives, their schedules, their attitudes, and their needs—and to minimize their visible signs of difference from institutional norms in order to pass through and to survive within the institutions.[32] Survival is self-preservation, and self-preservation is self-care. Passing is a form of survival.

Institutions like the home and the workplace are constituted by and serve as prime mechanisms for the reproduction of gender norms. One vivid illustration of the power of gender as an organizing force is the extent to which one's sex determines how much and what type of unpaid work one performs.[33] While the time spent on household chores has declined for both men and women in recent decades, for example, women still perform considerably more household work than their husbands do, even when they work full time. Total hours spent on unpaid household work, much of it childcare, amount to at least half of the hours of paid work in the labor market, and about 80 percent of this labor is performed by women.[34] Women also tend to assume a disproportionate share of routine, repetitive housecleaning and childcare tasks, while men tend to take on less frequent, flexible tasks, such as outdoor chores, repairs, bills, and reading or playing with the children.[35]

For most women, becoming a mother dramatically increases the work that they perform in the home while it has a chilling effect on their participation in the paid labor force. The rigid structure of the workplace is still largely modeled after the stereotypic man and is therefore not built to accommodate workers who are expected to assume primary responsibility for the care of children and other family members.[36] The predominant cultural belief that women should always put family first conflicts directly with the image of the ideal male worker, who is expected to devote himself to work even if this devotion means the sacrifice of family time. Women who reduce their working hours or leave their jobs temporarily to care for their children usually do so because of the prejudice and inflexibility they encounter from their employers; the result can be a lifetime disadvantage in income, promotion, and overall career success.[37] And the deeply embedded cultural connection between women and motherhood affects the status of all female workers, who are often seen as less valuable and less competent than their male counterparts.[38] "Unpaid female caregiving is not only the lifeblood of families," writes Ann Crittenden, "it is the very heart of the economy." By some estimates, women's unpaid contributions total over $500,000 in real wages, she notes. "This huge gift of unreimbursed time and labor explains, in a nutshell, why adult women are so much poorer than men—even though they work longer hours than men in almost every country in the world."[39]

With little public provision for childcare, American society disproportionately assigns the responsibility for raising the nation's future citizens to individual women.[40] If and when a woman returns to work after having a baby, she must confront the difficult task of securing quality care for her child and the often exorbitant cost such care will incur. In more than half of U.S. states, childcare costs exceed public university tuition.[41] Currently in the United States, there is no federally subsidized childcare, but this was not always so. When the surge of working mothers during World War II created an urgent need for childcare on a nationwide scale, the federal government quickly passed the Lanham Act, which provided for the creation of federally subsidized childcare centers across the country. Some of the new centers were affordable, innovative, and comprehensive in their approach to childcare. For example, the Kaiser Centers in Portland, Oregon—what historian Sonya Michel calls "the jewels of wartime childcare"—offered children's play spaces, medical clinics that provided vaccinations and routine health care, and even personal assistants, who shopped for groceries from a woman's customized grocery list and had her items bagged and ready when she came to pick up her children at the end of her work day.[42] But many wartime public childcare facilities, as Michel acknowledges, were uneven in quality, sometimes inconvenient in hours and location, and often racially discriminatory. Despite evidence of the program's popularity and benefits—particularly for some of the most economically disadvantaged families—funding was cut after the end of the war, and the centers closed shortly thereafter.[43] American mothers' mixed experience with child daycare, as well as the strengthening "discourse of the democratic family," Michel writes, help to explain why there were not more forceful demands for the continuation of state-subsidized childcare in the postwar period.[44]

In 1971, organized feminists spearheaded a second attempt to create a nationwide, federally subsidized system of childcare, which resulted in Congressional passage of the bipartisan Comprehensive Child Development Act (CCDA). Described by its Congressional supporters as "the most significant proposal on childcare ever introduced in Congress," the CCDA was a marked departure from previous government approaches toward early childhood services in that it was not framed as a temporary wartime emergency (like the Lanham Act) or applicable exclusively to low-income families (as were programs like Head Start). Rather, it offered a "permanent commitment by the federal government to better the lives of all children."[45] The CCDA's potential to produce real change in the lives of working mothers and their children meant that it came under heavy fire from its opponents, who denounced the bill as nothing short of an attack on the traditional gender relations of the family at the center of American society. Removing children from their mothers' influence by putting them in daycare centers, they argued, would weaken the mother-child bond, disrupt children's development during the most formative years, and lead to a breakdown of the family unit.[46] The prominence of organized feminists among the bill's most ardent supporters and the overt framing of the bill as a women's equality measure made the CCDA an easy target for critics of women's liberation. The act was harmful not only to the nation's children, they insisted, but also to the vast majority of American women who found their spiritual and emotional fulfillment through their roles as mothers.[47] Finally, many of the bill's most vocal detractors drew on the bugaboo of socialism and the dangers of an overreaching federal government to create public fear and suspicion of the bill—a tactic with a long history of success in defeating social reform measures in the United States and one still commonly employed today. As the mayor of Belle Glade, Florida warned, the bill was "designed to destroy the family and the home, place our children in government institutions, and lead us into a totalitarian state."[48] Ultimately, President Richard Nixon vetoed the CCDA. While he acknowledged the need for daycare services in the United States, he criticized the bill and its supporters for weakening the family through government intrusion into the private realm of childcare and advancing a communal, as opposed to a family-centered, approach to child rearing.[49]

More recent attempts to provide public support for working families have been equally vulnerable to opposition and delay. After years of debate and political resistance, President Bill Clinton signed into law the Family and Medical Leave Act (FMLA) in February 1993. The FMLA allows up to twelve weeks of unpaid, job-protected leave to workers in order to recover from a serious medical condition, provide care for a seriously ill family member, or care for a new child. But because it is unpaid, many workers— nearly half of those qualified—cannot afford to take the leave. And approximately 40 percent of workers do not even qualify for FMLA, given that it is restricted to workers who have been employed at their current job for at least a year, have worked a minimum of 1,250 hours in the twelve months before their leave is to begin, and who work for an employer with at least fifty employees.[50] To this day, the United States remains the only nation within the Organization for Economic Cooperation and Development that does not mandate paid parental leave.

Three years after the passage of the FMLA, Hillary Rodham Clinton wrote a child advocacy book titled *It Takes a Village* in which she argued that children's development and success were inextricably connected to how well the society in which they live sustains and supports families. American conservatives swiftly condemned the book as an attack on the nuclear family, parental rights, and women's "traditional" roles as housewives and mothers. Senator and presidential hopeful Bob Dole best expressed conservative outrage, perhaps, in his acceptance speech at the 1996 Republican National Convention. "And after the virtual devastation of the American family, the rock upon which this country was founded," he said, "we are told that it takes a village, that is collective, and thus the state, to raise a child. . . . And with all due respect, I am here to tell you it does not take a village to raise a child. It takes a family to raise a child," he declared, as the crowd cheered and applauded.[51]

The consistent failure of the United States to understand childcare as a public rather than an individual responsibility best meted out by mothers in the privacy of their own homes has resulted in the sorts of dangers to women, families, and children that the opposition to federally subsidized childcare was supposed to prevent. Evidence from numerous studies demonstrates that it is the quality, not the location, of childcare that is most crucial to children's healthy development. As the American Academy of Pediatrics notes, high-quality childcare can exist in a variety of places, including the home, a daycare facility, or a preschool. "When care is consistent, emotionally supportive, and appropriate to the child's age, development, and temperament," it stresses, "there is a positive effect on children and families."[52] Quality childcare helps children to learn and prepare for school and leads to better outcomes later in life. Families with access to affordable, quality childcare are more financially stable, with parents able to pursue careers and obtain steady income.[53] Yet, affordable, quality childcare is out of reach for most families. The absence of a coherent, subsidized, federally regulated daycare system results in a patchwork quilt of daycare institutions and providers across the states that are wildly uneven in quality and availability. While children under the age of five spend an average of thirty-six hours per week in childcare settings, nearly 42 percent live in "child-care deserts," or rural areas where no childcare centers are located or where childcare centers are so scarce that they cannot meet the demand.[54] And because childcare work is so poorly compensated and, in many states, requires minimal or no training in safety, health, or child development, childcare has high turnover rates and varies widely in quality and expertise.[55] Because childcare work is associated with women and the private sphere, it is performed by women workers (94 percent of all childcare workers), many of them women of color (40 percent), and—like most jobs associated with women—is undervalued and grossly underpaid. In 2018, childcare workers earned an average of $11.17 per hour; today, 40 percent of childcare workers live below 200 percent of the federal poverty line.[56] And so, the caretakers of the nation's children earn wages lower than any other occupational group in the United States. The same system that exploits its workers demands an exorbitant price from American families, who spend on average over 25 percent of their income on childcare, a percentage that soars to over 52 percent for single parents.[57] Today, families spend more on childcare than any other household expense—more, even, than the average amount spent on housing and transportation combined.[58] The consequences of families' inability to access quality, affordable childcare disproportionately affect American mothers, who are usually the ones forced to quit their jobs or to scale back their working hours to care for their children at home. This results in lost wages and benefits for women workers and less financial stability for families. Like so many other social services that in other countries are considered a universal human right, quality childcare in the United States and its many associated benefits for children, women workers, and families are accessible only to those who can afford them.

Even more challenging is providing quality and affordable care for children with disabilities. In the United States, public provisions designed to assist families with care of their disabled children is woefully inadequate. Parents can apply for Supplemental Security Income (SSI) benefits for their children through the federal Social Security system or for federal and state programs like Medicaid, the Children's Health Insurance Program (CHIP), or Temporary Assistance for Needy Families (TANF) that provide family support and community-based services. However, these programs are difficult to access. Families who apply for the services provided by these programs—ranging from personal assistance to respite care and housing—face a lengthy approval process, sometimes as much as five years.[59] And because these programs require strict low-income and asset requirements for eligibility, many families—particularly those with medium incomes—are not able to benefit from them. Yet, these families—even those with private insurance—often cannot afford the tremendous costs associated with some disabilities (e.g., medication, medical equipment, therapy, doctor or hospital visits, transportation, and housing modifications). In fact, most private insurance plans do not cover services that would contribute greatly to families' caregiving efforts, such as in-home health aides and respite care providers, who offer assistance with activities of daily living (such as meal preparation, dressing, grooming, medication monitoring, transportation, and light housekeeping).[60]

In a system where public provisions are limited and difficult to obtain, the care of children with disabilities is largely a private, unpaid endeavor that can take a tremendous financial, physical, and emotional toll on American families. A large national study led by researchers from Boston Children's Hospital (BCH) and the University of Southern California (USC) determined that parents—particularly mothers—provide nearly $36 billion annually in uncompensated medical care at home to children with disabilities, including those with chronic health conditions.[61] Another study by The Arc—an advocacy group for people with intellectual and developmental disabilities—found that nearly 60 percent of families caring for children with intellectual and/or developmental disabilities spent more than forty hours per week providing unpaid caregiving, with 40 percent spending more than eighty hours a week.[62] The often time-intensive and expensive forms of disability care can result in heavy financial burdens. Out-of-pocket health care costs for a disabled child are three times more expensive than the out-of-pocket costs for children without disabilities or chronic health conditions.[63] And yet, many caregivers—particularly women—cannot reconcile the hours that they devote to unpaid care work with their paid employment situations that fail to offer flexible work schedules, shared-leave programs, or paid family leave. As a result, many women resort to part-time employment, cutting back on their hours, taking leaves of absence, seeking less demanding or more flexible jobs, or leaving the paid workforce entirely.[64] Consequently, their families lose approximately $17.6 billion in income each year, the BCH and USC researchers estimated.[65] And without adequate social, economic, and community supports, female caregivers are susceptible to physical and mental health challenges caused by stress, anxiety, and feelings of isolation.[66]

Parental happiness depends largely on the extent to which parents feel adequately supported by the social system of which they are a part. A collaborative study by researchers at the University of Texas, Wake Forest

University, and Baylor University, for example, analyzed the happiness gap between parents and nonparents in twenty-two nations, all wealthy countries with similar birth rates. The study revealed that in the United States, parents are 13 percent less happy than nonparents, the largest gap in all of the countries surveyed and one explained entirely by the absence of social policies allowing parents to better combine paid work with family obligations.[67] In the United States, the inherent challenges of raising children are compounded by a system that provides parents with little to no support. It is unsurprising, then, that countries with wide social safety nets and generous family policies had reverse gaps, with parents identifying as happier than those without children.[68] And American unhappiness is not restricted to citizens with children. Since 2012, the United Nations has published an annual World Happiness Report that ranks the world's nations according to the happiness of their citizens based on factors such as economic wealth, life expectancy, social support, freedom to make life choices, and levels of government corruption. Except for its tenth-place ranking for income, the United States did not crack the top ten on any category in 2019, coming in thirty-seventh for social support and sixty-first for freedom, for example. Overall, the United States came in nineteenth place, dropping a total of five spots since Donald Trump took office. The largest factor in the nation's relatively low ranking is its lack of a strong welfare state common in many European countries, including Denmark, Finland, Norway, Iceland, and Sweden. Without a strong social welfare system, most Americans experience stress and anxiety over low wages, dead-end jobs, the rising costs of education, childcare, health care (including the exorbitant price of many prescription drugs), and housing, and the looming threat of unexpected expenses or even financial disaster due to illness or injury, unemployment, and many other factors. Meanwhile, the gap between the richest and the poorest Americans continues to widen.[69]

In light of the foregoing discussion about America's woefully inadequate social support system, it seems fitting to circle back to where I began my exploration of disability and mothering at the start of the previous chapter—Denmark, a nation that sits at or near the top of the World Happiness Report every year.[70] A central aspect of Danish national character is the concept of *hygge*, a term associated with contentment, relaxation, and well-being. Hygge means enjoying the things that bring happiness, comfort, and nourishment usually in fellowship with friends and loved ones in a relaxed and intimate atmosphere. Whether they are sharing a coffee or pastry with a friend, curling up with a good book in front of a roaring fireplace, playing games with their children, or going for a walk in the fresh air, hygge is essentially about making time throughout the day to appreciate and share simple pleasures. It might be tempting to stop there—to focus merely on the Danes' individual efforts to savor the things that make them happy. But the key to understanding the high levels of happiness in Denmark—like other nations that rank in the top ten of the World Happiness report—is the country's understanding of individual happiness as a public good and therefore its assumption of public responsibility for individual welfare. In turn, Danes understand their individual responsibility for the collective well-being. They pay approximately 45 percent in income taxes, one of the highest tax rates in the world, but receive for their investment an incredible return—freedom from anxiety about the future. In a country with free university education, universal health care, paid family leave, subsidized childcare, and generous vacation, pension, unemployment, and disability policies, the Danish are free to focus less of their attention on sustaining life and more on the things that make life worthwhile.[71] These benefits are not the exclusive province of a handful of wealthy elites or bestowed as a form of charity upon the neediest citizens. Rather, they are universal, human rights generating social harmony and personal happiness—as well as some of the highest levels of income and gender equality in the world.

CONCLUSION: CRIPPING TIME

Happiness and well-being are public, not solely private, responsibilities. Yet, in the United States, we continue to insist that happiness, success, and well-being are products of individual striving and that children's welfare is best promoted by nuclear families and self-sacrificing mothers. And so, we are all the bird in Marilyn Frye's allegorical cage, blaming ourselves for our failure to free ourselves by stepping around the wire right in front of us and thus not recognizing the wider system of intersecting wires that, together, comprise the cage that traps us.[72] I also think that those with more privileges, who face fewer of these intersecting wires and thus more easily navigate the strictures of the birdcage, often fail to recognize their own interdependence— how their individual achievements are dependent on a multitude of external supports. The sense of wellness and empowerment I obtain from running, for example, is made possible not only by my own determination but by my access to flexible work hours, leisure time, healthy food, and decent health care. It is possible because I have a marital partner who assumes his share of household and childcare responsibilities so that I can carve out time for my own well-being. And it is possible because, for the most part, it fits neatly into contemporary social narratives that equate wellness, good citizenship, and even human worth with particular visible performances of self-care. As disability scholars have long recognized, and as my own story demonstrates, self-sufficiency is an illusion, a myth; interdependence is the actual human condition.[73] We flourish only when we are amply supported by the structures, discourses, and individuals who surround us. As Kim Q. Hall notes, "flourishing . . . is made possible by our complex enmeshment in community with human and nonhuman others."[74]

But our flourishing is also highly dependent on the type of community in which we are complexly enmeshed. This community must be flexible and expandable enough to meet our particular needs, not require that we manipulate ourselves to fit its strictures. In her stage show turned 2018 Netflix special, *Nanette*, Australian comedian Hannah Gadsby—who is autistic and identifies as queer—described how her mother recently apologized to her for trying to "normalize" her. "I knew . . . . well before you did . . . that your life was going to be so hard," her mother told her. "I knew that, and I wanted it more than anything in the world not to be the case. And I know I made it worse, because I wanted you to change because I knew the world wouldn't."[75] Ever since I first saw *Nanette*, that line has stuck with me—"I wanted you to change because I knew the world wouldn't." Countless therapists and teachers have shared this view—Zoey has to modify herself to fit into the world because it is terribly, terribly difficult to navigate a world that was not built for you. I cannot deny that this is true, that those who do not easily inhabit cultural norms face ridicule, marginalization, abuse, and extermination. As Zoey's mother, I would give anything to protect her from those who would silence her. But the attempt to contort oneself to fit social expectations is in itself a form of silencing, a denial of self, a self-annihilation. At what cost does one survive in the world? Audre Lorde wrote that we render ourselves invisible and remain silent in the hope that we will be safe—safe from contempt, judgment, challenge, or erasure. But "we can sit in our corners mute forever . . . and we will still be no less afraid," she argues, because "we were never meant to survive. . . . Because the machine will try to grind you into dust anyway, whether or not we speak. . . . Your silence will not protect you."[76] Nor will silence help to alter or tear down those structures and ideologies that privilege only certain bodies and minds and that assume that there are correct ways of knowing, thinking about, and interacting with the world. Individual flourishing, then, takes place in a community that recognizes, values, and supports the multiple pathways and timelines through which we move about our world.

I am in bed thinking about this in the wee hours of the morning on the day of the half marathon. Like the race that I am about to run that demands a certain pace, progression, and endpoint as markers of success, the current constitution of the world marks success by our seamless movement through a linear progression of time. From the moment we are born, we are weighed, measured, and judged against a set of constructed norms that are deeply ableist—Apgar scales, weight and height percentiles, developmental milestones, IQ scores, and standardized test results carefully monitor and evaluate our progress throughout our childhood and teenage years. From there, we are expected to move from dependence to self-reliance as we graduate from college and launch lucrative careers in our twenties and establish heteronormative families through marriage, children, and home ownership by our thirties. If we do not meet these expected milestones in the prescribed way and at the prescribed time, we are labeled, marginalized, stigmatized, left behind. We have failed to achieve success. In an ableist world, disability is defined not only by the failure to keep pace with this linear progression but also by the assumption that for disabled people, the milestones are and in fact should be out of reach. But viewed through the lens of disability, it is clear that it is the timeline and the milestones themselves—not the bodies who fail to meet them—that are the problem. Similar to many LGBTQ+ individuals who "queer" time by producing alternative temporalities that question and challenge hegemonic models of family, sexuality, and reproduction,[77] disabled individuals refuse an ableist temporality, even as they demand the unfettered and equal right to pursue education, jobs, romance, sexuality, reproduction, and housing. By cripping time, we create our own timelines; we recognize and value the nonlinear, meandering, stumbling, dawdling, circuitous ways by which many of us move through life; and we call into question the traditional beats and rhythms by which we measure success.[78] I am reminded of all of the many doctors, therapists, teachers, and family members—most of them well meaning—who have told me what Zoey is, should be, could be, and will not be. As Robert McRuer has written, "the sites or locations where disability identities emerge will always be interrogated and transformable, sustaining and understanding that who we are or might be can only have meaning in relation to who we are not (yet)."[79] As Zoey and I have cripped our own trajectory, we have left some of them behind and incorporated others into our village as we have zigzagged on and off of the path of "should, could, and will not be." Throughout this journey, I have come to stop navigating toward the known and to trust in the unseen; to value the reality and sustenance of community and interdependence; and, most of all, to embrace and even treasure our collective lived messiness.

My alarm suddenly blares to attention at 5:00 a.m. Avoiding the temptation to hit the snooze button and to nestle further into my comforter, I drag myself out of bed and make my way downstairs on legs shaky from the cold and from the nerves that have suddenly overcome me. I flick on the television to hear the weather report and listen to the forecaster predict a frigid start to what is going to be a cold, windy, cloudy day. As I make a bowl of oatmeal into which I slice a banana and pour a couple of teaspoons of honey, I chuckle to myself. I had begun my journey to the half marathon in the oppressive Oklahoma heat of mid-June, and I will conclude my journey on an unusually blustery day near the middle of March. After eating, I hastily dress, rouse the kids and prepare their breakfast, and wait for our sitter, Jenny, to arrive.

A couple of hours later, I stand at the start line as Nathan looks on from the sidelines; he is proud of me. At the sound of the gun, I give him a small wave and begin to move. The throngs of people surrounding me make it difficult to begin running, but soon I am able to weave my way through the crowd and work up to race speed. I avoid the temptation to keep pace with the faster runners and instead fall into a steady rhythm, which I hope to maintain to the end. As I work up a sweat, I am grateful for the cloudy sky and chilly temperature. We approach the first hill, and the people around me begin to move faster; contrarily, I follow the advice from the dozen or so books that I have read in preparation for the race and drop to a slower pace, swinging my arms lower and quicker. Oh, wow, this is steep. When I reach the top of the hill, I pass the runners who expended too much energy during the uphill climb and resume my normal pace, making sure to reduce the pressure on my legs on the downhill by taking short, quick strides. I'm glad that's over.

As the miles click by, I concentrate on the music from my iPod. For my running playlist, I have chosen songs of strength, perseverance, courage, and hope. During practice runs, they motivated and inspired me, they spoke back to and defied my doubts, and they warded off my frustrations. These lyrics conjure up so many images and memories—of Zoey's struggles and diagnoses; my long and ongoing process to educate myself about disabilities; our many battles against economic, social, and educational institutions; balancing work and home while trying to find a space that is mine; the sweet, precious moments I have shared with my children; and the unimaginable joys of this life that I never anticipated but would never relinquish—they flash through my mind like a movie reel. Rounding the last turn, I finally spot the finish line in the distance. Suddenly, I am no longer tired. I quicken my pace, spurred on by my fellow runners and by the cheers of the thickening spectators. I do not see Nathan in the crowd, but I know he is there, watching and applauding me. My arms pump faster, my breaths are deeper, my legs are working at maximum capacity. I take my final steps and raise my arms as I cross the finish line.

I have participated in a radical act, and not just because I ran over thirteen miles without stopping. I directed attention and care toward my own body and spirit and thus made myself—a woman, a mother, a person with a disability, a mother of a child with a disability—someone worthy of care. In my assertion of self, in my visibility, in my body that takes up space, in my words on this page, I insist that I matter. I insist that Zoey matters. In so doing, I hope that I am making her path more manageable, that maybe I am clearing enough debris so that when one day I am gone, she can better navigate her journey in concert with and deeply enmeshed in her community, to boldly and unapologetically take up her own space on her own terms remaining exactly who she is. By insisting that we matter, we are able to transform what matters.[80]

On the way home, we pick up bagels for the kids and Jenny. As I enter the house, the beautiful chaos resumes. Connor and Jenny are laughing together at the kitchen table, which is littered with crayons, paste, scissors, and construction paper; they are creating a picture book about a dragon in a sailboat. Connor squeals when he sees me and jumps into my arms. As I pull him close to me and plant a kiss on his head, I notice that his hair is covered in paste. While happily munching on a bagel, he proudly shows me his illustrations, and I praise his creativity. I walk up the stairs in search of Zoey and notice the little pools of water on each step. She has been playing in the sink again. As I approach her bedroom, I hear the Tinkerbell movie soundtrack that she has been listening to over and over again for the past few months. I crack open her bedroom door. Dressed in her favorite purple nightgown with a bright pink flowerpot hat that we bought at the ice rink a few months ago perched on her head, she is stomping about the room in time to the music, pausing every now and then to fling water from the cup she is holding onto the walls, the floor, and her stuffed animals, who are dutifully lined up on her bed. Outside, the temperature slowly warms and the budding trees give evidence of the approaching spring. But in Zoey's room, spring has already arrived, and the world needs watering. When she spots me watching her, she flashes me an impish smile but then impatiently waves me away. There is much work to be done, after all.

NOTES

1. Cheryl Richardson, *The Art of Extreme Self-Care: Transform Your Life One Month at a Time* (Carlsbad, CA: Hay House, Inc, 2009), 44.

2. Quoted in "Live Fully," *Weight Watchers*, accessed June 10, 2017, https://www.weightwatchers.com/us/article/live-fully.

3. Laura Argintar, "The Proliferation of the Shrinking Woman: How Women Are Taught to Grow Inward," *Elite Daily*, December 30, 2013, http://elitedaily.com/women/growth-proliferation-shrinking-woman-taking-space-woman/.

4. Douglas Baynton, "Disability and the Justification of Inequality in American History," in *The New Disability History: American Perspectives*, eds. Paul K. Longmore and Lauri Umansky (New York: New York University Press, 2001), 36–40.

5. Baynton, "Disability and the Justification of Inequality," 41–44.

6. Baynton, "Disability and the Justification of Inequality," 45–48. See also Matthew Frye Jacobsen, *Barbarian Virtues: The United States Encounters Foreign Peoples at Home and Abroad, 1876–1917* (New York: Hill and Wang, 2000).

7. Baynton, "Disability and the Justification of Inequality," 34.

8. Ryan J. Kirkby, "'The Revolution Will Not Be Televised': Community Activism and the Black Panther Party, 1966–1971," *Canadian Review of American Studies* 41:1 (2011): 25–62, https://doi.org/10.3138/cras.41.1.25.

9. Robyn Ceanne Spencer, "Engendering the Black Freedom Struggle: Revolutionary Black Womanhood and the Black Panther Party in the Bay Area, California," *Journal of Women's History* 20:1 (Spring 2008): 90–113, https://doi.org /10.1353/jowh.2008.0006.

10. "Radical Self-Care: Angela Davis," *AFROPUNK*, December 17, 2018, https:/ /www.youtube.com/watch?v=Q1cHoL4vaBs.

11. Aimaloghi Eromosele, "There is No Self-Care without Community Care," *URGE*, November 10, 2020, https://urge.org/there-is-no-self-care-without-community-care/.

12. "Radical Self-Care: Angela Davis."

13. Audre Lorde, *A Burst of Light and Other Essays* (Mineola, New York: Ixia Press, 2017), 130.

14. Evette Dionne, "For Black Women, Self-Care is a Radical Act," *Ravishly*, March 9, 2015, https://ravishly.com/2015/03/06/radical-act-self-care-black-women -feminism.

15. Sara Ahmed, "Selfcare as Warfare," *feministkilljoys*, August 25, 2014, https:// feministkilljoys.com/2014/08/25/selfcare-as-warfare/comment-page-1/.

16. Jennifer Nelson, *More than Medicine: A History of the Feminist Women's Health Movement* (New York: New York University Press, 2015); Wendy Kline, *Bodies of Knowledge: Sexuality, Reproduction, and Women's Health in the Second Wave* (Chicago: University of Chicago Press, 2010).

17. Deborah Gould, *Moving Politics: Emotion and ACT UP's Fight Against AIDS* (Chicago: University of Chicago Press, 2009); David France, *How to Survive a Plague: The Story of How Activists and Scientists Tamed AIDS* (New York: Vintage Books, 2016).

18. Stassa Edwards, "Wellness, Womanhood, and the West: How Goop Profits from Endless Illness," *Jezebel*, April 28, 2017, https://jezebel.com/wellness-womanh ood-and-the-west-how-goop-profits-fro-1793674265.

19. "A Guide to Spirit Animals: A Q&A with Colleen McCann," *Goop*, accessed June 28, 2019, https://goop.com/style/trends/guide-spirit-animals/.

20. Edwards, "Wellness, Womanhood, and the West."

21. Jessica Ravitz, "Gwyneth Paltrow's Goop Brand Hit with Penalties for 'Unsubstantiated Claims,'" *CNN*, September 5, 2018, https://www.cnn.com/2018/09 /05/health/goop-fine-california-gwyneth-paltrow/index.html.

22. Jordan Kisner, "The Politics of Conspicuous Displays of Self-Care," *The New Yorker*, March 14, 2017, https://www.newyorker.com/culture/culture-desk/the-politic s-of-selfcare.

23. Eromosele, "There is No Self-Care without Community Care."

24. Catherine Rottenberg, "How Neoliberalism Colonised Feminism—And What You Can Do about It," *The Conversation*, May 23, 2018, https://theconversation .com/how-neoliberalism-colonised-feminism-and-what-you-can-do-about-it-94856. See also Catherine Rottenberg, *The Rise of Neoliberal Feminism* (London: Oxford University Press, 2018).

25. Abeni Jones, "How to Take Care of Each Other: Community Care in Times of Crisis," *Autostraddle*, June 8, 2020, https://www.autostraddle.com/how-to-take-care -of-each-other-community-care-in-times-of-crisis-425239/.

26. Abeni Jones, "Beyond Self-Care Bubble Baths: A Vision for Community Care," *Autostraddle*, July 20, 2017, https://www.autostraddle.com/on-being-a-burde n-whats-missing-from-the-conversation-around-self-care-385525/comment-page-1/ #comment-1093748.

27. Jones, "Beyond Self-Care Bubble Baths."

28. Jones, "Beyond Self-Care Bubble Baths."

29. Jones, "Beyond Self-Care Bubble Baths."

30. Jill Filipovic, *The H-Spot: The Feminist Pursuit of Happiness* (New York: Nation Books, 2017), 10.

31. Sara Ahmed, *Living a Feminist Life* (Durham: Duke University Press, 2017), 125.

32. Ahmed, *Living a Feminist Life*, 131.

33. Cecilia Ridgeway, *Framed by Gender: How Gender Inequality Persists in the Modern World* (New York: Oxford University Press, 2011), 139.

34. Ann Crittenden, *The Price of Motherhood: Why the Most Important Job in the World is Still the Least Valued* (New York: Henry Holt and Company, 2001), 8.

35. Ridgeway, *Framed by Gender,* 140–141.

36. Ridgeway, *Framed by Gender,* 95.

37. Ridgeway, *Framed by Gender,* 150–151.

38. Ridgeway, *Framed by Gender,* 117–118.

39. Crittenden, *The Price of Motherhood,* 8.

40. Ridgeway, *Framed by Gender,* 131.

41. Child Care Aware of America, "The U.S. and the High Price of Child Care: An Examination of a Broken System," 2019, https://cdn2.hubspot.net/hubfs/3957809/2 019%20Price%20of%20Care%20State%20Sheets/Final-TheUSandtheHighPriceofC hildCare-AnExaminationofaBrokenSystem.pdf?utm_referrer=https%3A%2F%2Fw ww.childcareaware.org

42. Sonya Michel, *Children's Interests/Mothers' Rights: The Shaping of America's Childcare Policy* (New Haven: Yale University Press, 1999), 142–143; "We Have a Childcare Crisis in this Country. We Had the Solution 78 Years Ago?" *The Washington Post*, July 23, 2018, https://www.washingtonpost.com/news/postevery thing/wp/2018/07/23/we-have-a-childcare-crisis-in-this-country-we-had-the-solution -78-years-ago/?utm_term=.82618698c4a0.

43. Chris Herbst, "Universal Child Care, Maternal Employment, and Children's Long-Run Outcomes: Evidence from the U.S. Lanham Act of 1940," *Journal of Labor Economics* 35:2 (April 2017): 519–564, https://doi.org/10.1086/689478.

44. Michel, *Children's Interests/Mothers' Rights,* 147.

45. Andrew Karch, *Early Start: Preschool Politics in the United States* (Ann Arbor: University of Michigan Press, 2013), 71.

46. Karch, *Early Start,* 74.

47. Karch, *Early Start,* 74.

48. Karch, *Early Start,* 74.

49. Karch, *Early Start,* 83.

50. United States Department of Labor, "Health Benefits, Retirement Standards, and Workers' Compensation: Family and Medical Leave," accessed May 31, 2019, https://webapps.dol.gov/elaws/elg/fmla.htm.

51. "Text of Robert Dole's Speech to the Republican National Convention, August 15, 1996," *CNN*, accessed July 20, 2019, http://www.cnn.com/ALLPOLITICS/1996/conventions/san.diego/transcripts/0815/dole.fdch.shtml.

52. American Academy of Pediatrics, "Quality Checklist for Choosing Child Care," accessed April 30, 2019, https://www.aap.org/en-us/advocacy-and-policy/aap-health-initiatives/healthy-child-care/Pages/Choosing-Child-Care.aspx.

53. Child Care Aware of America, "The U.S. and the High Price of Child Care."

54. Child Care Aware of America, "The U.S. and the High Price of Child Care"; Rasheed Malik et al., "Child Care Deserts: An Analysis of Child Care Centers by ZIP Code in 8 States," *Center for American Progress*, October 27, 2016, https://www.americanprogress.org/issues/early-childhood/reports/2016/10/27/225703/child-care-deserts/.

55. U.S. Department of Health and Human Services, National Institutes of Health, and National Institute of Child Health and Human Development, "The NICHD Study of Early Child Care and Youth Development," 2006, http://www.nichd.nih.gov/sites/default/files/publications/pubs/documents/seccyd_06.pdf; Brigid Schulte et al, "The Care Report," *New America*, September 2016, https://www.newamerica.org/in-depth/care-report/.

56. Child Care Aware of America, "The U.S. and the High Price of Child Care."

57. James Browne and Dirk Neumann, "OECD Tax Wedge and Effective Tax Rates on Labour," *OECD*, 2017, https://taxben.oecd.org/tax-ben-resources/Childcare-costs-in-2015.pdf.

58. Child Care Aware of America, "The U.S. and the High Price of Child Care"; "We Have a Childcare Crisis in this Country"; Browne and Neumann, "OECD Tax Wedge."

59. The Arc, "Still in the Shadows with Their Future Uncertain: A Report on Family and Individual Needs for Disability Supports (FINDS), Summary of Key Findings and a Call to Action," June 2011, 7, https://www.thearc.org/document.doc?id=3672.

60. John A. Romley et al., "Family-Provided Health Care for Children With Special Health Care Needs," *Pediatrics* 139:1 (January 2017): 6–7, https://doi.org/10.1542/peds.2016-1287.

61. Romley et al., "Family-Provided Health Care," 3.

62. The Arc, "Still in the Shadows," 6.

63. Romley et al., "Family-Provided Health Care," 4.

64. National Alliance for Caregiving, "Caregivers of Children: A Focused Look at Those Caring for A Child with Special Needs under the Age of 18," November 2009, 8, http://www.caregiving.org/data/Report_Caregivers_of_Children_11-12-09.pdf.

65. Romley et al., "Family-Provided Health Care," 4.

66. Romley et al., "Family-Provided Health Care," 2, 5; Michelle Diament, "Disability Caregivers Struggling Financially, Emotionally," *Disability Scoop*, June 15, 2011, https://www.disabilityscoop.com/2011/06/15/disability-caregivers-struggling/13339/.

67. KJ Dell'Antonia, "For U.S. Parents, a Troubling Happiness Gap," *The New York Times*, June 17, 2016, https://well.blogs.nytimes.com/2016/06/17/for-u-s-parents-a-troubling-happiness-gap/.

68. Jennifer Glass et al., "Parenthood and Happiness: Effects of Work-Family Reconciliation Policies in 22 OECD Countries,' *American Journal of Sociology* 122:3 (November 2016): 886–929, https://doi.org/10.1086/688892.

69. Organisation for Economic Cooperation and Development, *OECD Economic Surveys: United States 2018* (Paris: OECD Publishing, 2018), 12, https://doi.org/10.1 787/eco_surveys-usa-2018-en.

70. John F. Helliwell et al., eds., *World Happiness Report 2019* (New York: Sustainable Development Solutions Network, 2019), https://s3.amazonaws.com/ happiness-report/2019/WHR19.pdf.

71. Anna Altman, "The Year of Hygge, the Danish Obsession with Getting Cozy," *The New Yorker*, December 18, 2016, https://www.newyorker.com/culture/culture -desk/the-year-of-hygge-the-danish-obsession-with-getting-cozy.

72. Marilyn Frye, *The Politics of Reality* (New York: Crossing Press, 1983), 1–16.

73. See Lennard Davis, *Bending Over Backwards: Disability, Dismodernism, and Other Difficult Positions* (New York: New York University Press, 2002), 31.

74. Kim Q. Hall, "Toward a Queer Crip Feminist Politics of Food," *philoSOPHIA* 4:2 (Summer 2014), 178, https://muse.jhu.edu/article/565882.

75. Hannah Gadsby, *Nanette*, directed by John Olb and Madeleine Parry (Netflix, 2018).

76. Audre Lorde, *Sister Outsider* (New York: Crossing Press, 1984), 41–42.

77. For more on "queer time," see Lee Edelman, *No Future: Queer Theory and the Death Drive* (Durham: Duke University Press, 2004); J. Jack Halberstam, *In a Queer Time and Place: Transgender Bodies, Subcultural Lives* (New York: New York University Press, 2005); J. Jack Halberstam, *The Queer Art of Failure* (Durham: Duke University Press, 2011); José Esteban Muñoz, *Cruising Utopia: The Then and There of Queer Futurity* (New York: New York University Press, 2009); Heather Love, *Feeling Backward: Loss and the Politics of Queer History* (Cambridge: Harvard University Press, 2007); Elizabeth Freeman, *Time Binds: Queer Temporalities, Queer Histories* (Durham: Duke University Press, 2010); and Sara Ahmed, *Queer Phenomenology: Orientations, Objects, Others* (Durham: Duke University Press, 2006).

78. For more on "crip time," see Alison Kafer, *Feminist, Queer, Crip* (Bloomington: Indiana University Press, 2013); Ellen Samuels, "Six Ways of Looking at Crip Time," *Disability Studies Quarterly* 37:3 (2017), https://dsq-sds.org/article/view/58 24/4684; Jasbir Puar, "Prognosis Time: Towards a Geopolitics of Affect, Debility, and Capacity," *Women and Performance: A Journal of Feminist Theory* 19:2 (2009): 161–172, https://doi.org/10.1080/07407700903034147; Adam W. Davidson, "Stasis-Maintenance-(Un)productive-Presence: Parenting a Disabled Child as Crip Time," *Disability Studies Quarterly* 40:3 (2020), https://dsq-sds.org/article/view /6693; Sarah E. Stevens, "Care Time," *Disability Studies Quarterly* 38:4 (2018), https://dsq-sds.org/article/view/6090/5136; Petra Kuppers, "Crip Time," *Tikkun* 29:4 (2014): 29–31, https://doi.org/10.1215/08879982-2810062; Michael Flaherty, *The Textures of Time: Agency and Temporal Experience* (Temple University Press, 2011); and Michael Flaherty, *A Watched Pot: How We Experience Time* (New York: New York University Press, 1999).

79. Robert McRuer, *Crip Theory: Cultural Signs of Queerness and Disability* (New York: New York University Press, 2006), 72.

80. Ahmed, "Selfcare as Warfare."

Epilogue

Zoey is the prism through which I have gained a disability view of the world, one that has given me tremendous insights into my own personal history and has brought into sharp relief the way in which disability—both the lived experience and the category of analysis—connects me back toward my grandmother and forward toward my daughter. Because of my disability view of the world, I became disabled. Becoming disabled has taught me to value the many ways of being in the world. It has led me to recognize the power, wisdom, beauty, and delight of the margins, the corners, the chaos, and the skewed perspectives. It has allowed me to embrace, to cherish even, a lived messiness. It has shifted my sense and use of time by infusing my days with new gratitude and purpose and altering the way that I measure progress and success. And it has magnified my outrage over continued structural inequalities and social and economic injustices—the lack of universal health insurance, government-subsidized childcare, paid family leave and flexible work policies for all employees, decent wages and housing, well-funded public schools that can provide academic excellence along with a full range of services for the children who need them—and the hypocrisy of a nation that celebrates family values but does so little to actually support families.

We live in a society that places a premium on independence, the idea that the value of our lives is directly correlated to our ability to do things on our own without the help of others. Not only is independence an impossibility—each person's ability to survive, function, and flourish depends on a multitude of others—it is a deeply ableist concept that privileges seemingly nondisabled bodies and minds and deeply stigmatizes bodies and minds for which assistance is an apparent necessity. In the ableist framework of independence, writes Mia Mingus, dependence "will always get framed as 'burden,' and disability will always get framed as 'inferior.'"[1] Because the ableist myth of independence is so pervasive in our culture, many disabled people have measured and articulated their own experiences within it instead of against it. Too often, independence is hailed as the goal, the indicator of equality and justice achieved. Even the need for personal assistance, writes Eva Feder Kittay, is often framed in terms of a type of prosthesis that allows one to achieve independence.[2] The legitimacy of independence itself, then, is rarely questioned, making it extremely difficult to recognize or promote the value of interdependency. "To actively work to build something that is thought of as undeniably undesirable and to try and reframe it to others as liberatory," Mingus writes, "is no small task."[3]

Yet, it is only through the recognition of interdependency as a necessary, universal, positive feature of the human experience can we begin to understand and appreciate our connections to one another; to recognize that the disabled person receiving assistance is not the exception, but the rule; to develop relationships between carers and recipients of care that are genuinely respectful, dignified, visible, and fairly compensated; to embrace the diverse experiences and contributions we each bring to the human collective; and to demand a society that recognizes its public responsibility for enabling and supporting the dependency work that occurs in the private realm. As Kittay argues: "When we recognize that dependency is an aspect of what it is to be the sorts of beings we are, we, as a society, can begin to confront our fear and loathing of dependency and with it, of disability. When we acknowledge how dependence on another saves us from isolation and provides the connections to another that makes life worthwhile, we can start the process of embracing needed dependencies."[4]

In December 2019, a novel strain of coronavirus disease (a severe, acute respiratory syndrome) was first identified in Wuhan, China, and quickly spread around the world, infecting more than 100 million people in more than 215 countries and territories and resulting in more than two million deaths (as of January 2021). With an incompetent and dysfunctional administration in the White House, along with the absence of a robust public health care system and social safety net, the COVID-19 pandemic devastated the United States. Throughout 2020, while much of the rest of the world saw steep declines in new cases, the numbers in the United States continued to soar, resulting in over 26 million infections and over 430,000 deaths (as of January 2021). People in countries with high levels of public responsibility for social welfare, like Denmark and the Netherlands, looked on in horror at overflowing American emergency rooms; hospital staff forced to work without personal protective equipment; essential workers who risked their lives by returning to jobs for which they are miserably remunerated; parents who clamored for affordable childcare; people standing in massive unemployment lines; and a president who dismissed, disregarded, and even publicly ridiculed the advice of scientific experts.

The COVID-19 pandemic has exposed some of the greatest weaknesses of the United States and laid bare long-standing inequalities of race, gender, class, and disability. Years of discriminatory treatment and unequal access to jobs, health care, education, and housing have resulted in a disproportionate impact of the pandemic on the nation's most marginalized and vulnerable citizens. Yet, with tens of millions of Americans working and attending school remotely, trying to juggle professional and private responsibilities, and paying enormous out-of-pocket expenses for health care and treatment, the pandemic has suddenly called mainstream attention to issues for which the disability community has long been campaigning—the need for greater accessibility in education, flexibility in work schedules and patterns, universal and affordable health care, income equality, and expansion of the welfare state. Such measures, if universally and permanently enacted, have the potential to improve not only the lives of people with disabilities but the lives of all Americans. Perhaps out of the darkness of our current historical moment will emerge a transformative understanding of what it means to need accommodations, of our interconnectedness and reliance on a complex web of familial and community support, and of the responsibility of our government to ensure the safety and well-being of all of its citizens. This starts with a disability view of the world.

NOTES

1. Mia Mingus, "Access Intimacy, Interdependence and Disability Justice," *Leaving Evidence*, April 12, 2017, https://leavingevidence.wordpress.com/2017/04/12/access-intimacy-interdependence-and-disability-justice/.

2. Eva Feder Kittay, "The Ethics of Care, Dependence, and Disability," *Ratio Juris* 24:1 (March 2011): 50, https://doi.org/10.1111/j.1467-9337.2010.00473.x.

3. Mingus, "Access Intimacy, Interdependence and Disability Justice."

4. Kittay, "The Ethics of Care," 57.

Bibliography

Adams, Rachel. *Sideshow U.S.A.: Freaks and the American Cultural Imagination.* Chicago: University of Chicago Press, 2001.

Ahern, Laurie. "Torture Not Treatment: Electric Shock and Long-Term Restraint in the United States on Children and Adults with Disabilities at the Judge Rotenberg Center." Disability Rights International, 2010. https://www.driadvocacy.org/wp-content/uploads/USReport-accessible.doc.

Ahmed, Sara. "Feminist Hurt/Feminism Hurts." *feministkilljoys*, July 21, 2014. https://feministkilljoys.com/2014/07/21/feminist-hurtfeminism-hurts/.

Ahmed, Sara. *Living a Feminist Life.* Durham: Duke University Press, 2017.

Ahmed, Sara. *Queer Phenomenology: Orientations, Objects, Others.* Durham: Duke University Press, 2006.

Ahmed, Sara. "Selfcare as Warfare." *feministkilljoys*, August 25, 2014. https://feministkilljoys.com/2014/08/25/selfcare-as-warfare/comment-page-1/.

Ahram, Roey, Edward Fergus, and Pedro Noguera. "Addressing Racial/Ethnic Disproportionality in Special Education: Case Studies of Suburban School Districts." *Teachers College Record* 113:10 (October 2011): 2233–2266.

Ainscow, Mel, Tony Booth, and Alan Dyson. *Improving Schools, Developing Inclusion.* London: Routledge, 2006.

Allely, Clare Sarah. "Understanding and Recognising the Female Phenotype of Autism Spectrum Disorder and the 'Camouflage' Hypothesis: A Systematic PRISMA Review." *Advances in Autism* 5:1 (March 2019): 14–37. https://doi.org/10.1108/AIA-09-2018-0036.

Alshammari, Shahd. "A Hybridized Academic Identity: Negotiating a Disability within Academia's Discourse of Ableism." In *Negotiating Disability: Disclosure and Higher Education*, edited by Stephanie Kerschbaum, Laura Eisenmann, and James Jones, 25–38. Ann Arbor: University of Michigan Press, 2017.

Altman, Anna. "The Year of Hygge, the Danish Obsession with Getting Cozy." *The New Yorker*, December 18, 2016. https://www.newyorker.com/culture/culture-desk/the-year-of-hygge-the-danish-obsession-with-getting-cozy.

Altmann, John. "I Don't Want to Be 'Inspiring.'" *The New York Times*, October 20, 2016.

American Academy of Pediatrics. "Quality Checklist for Choosing Child Care." Accessed April 30, 2019. https://www.aap.org/en-us/advocacy-and-policy/aap-health-initiatives/healthy-child-care/Pages/Choosing-Child-Care.aspx.

The American Association of People with Disabilities and the Leadership Conference Education Fund. "Equity in Transportation for People with Disabilities." *The Leadership Conference on Civil and Human Rights.* Accessed July 20, 2018. http://www.civilrightsdocs.info/pdf/transportation/final-transportation-equity-disability.pdf.

American Association of University Women Public Policy and Government Relations Department. "Educating Girls with Disabilities." American Association of University Women, July 2009. http://www.aauw.org/files/2013/02/position-on-disability-education-111.pdf.

American Disabled for Attendant Programs Today (ADAPT). "Judge Rotenberg Center: A History of Torture." Accessed July 31, 2019. https://adapt.org/jrc/.

American Psychiatric Association. "DSM-5 Development, Neurodevelopmental Disorders." Accessed June 3, 2017. http://www.dsm5.org/meetus/pages/neurodevelopmental%20disorders.aspx.

Annamma, Subini Ancy. "It Was Just Like a Piece of Gum: Using an Intersectional Approach to Understand Criminalizing Young Women of Color with Disabilities in the School to Prison Pipeline." In *Practicing Disability Studies in Education: Acting Toward Social Change*, edited by David Connor, Jan Valle, and Chris Hale, 83–102. New York: Peter Lang, 2015.

Anzaldúa, Gloria. *Borderlands/La Frontera: The New Mestiza.* San Francisco: Aunt Lute Books, 1987.

Anzaldúa, Gloria. "Speaking in Tongues: A Letter to 3rd World Women Writers." In *This Bridge Called My Back: Writings by Radical Women of Color*, 2nd ed., edited by Cherríe Moraga and Gloria Anzaldúa. New York: Kitchen Table Women of Color Press, 1983.

Apple, Rima. *Perfect Motherhood: Science and Childbearing in America.* New Brunswick: Rutgers University Press, 2006.

The Arc. "Still in the Shadows with Their Future Uncertain: A Report on Family and Individual Needs for Disability Supports (FINDS), Summary of Key Findings and a Call to Action." June 2011. https://www.thearc.org/document.doc?id=3672.

Argintar, Laura. "The Proliferation of the Shrinking Woman: How Women Are Taught to Grow Inward." *Elite Daily*, December 30, 2013. http://elitedaily.com/women/growth-proliferation-shrinking-woman-taking-space-woman/.

Arms, Emily, Jill Bickett, and Victoria Graf. "Gender Bias and Imbalance: Girls in U.S. Special Education Programmes." *Gender and Education* 20:4 (July 2008): 349–359. https://doi.org/: 10.1080/09540250802190180.

Arnarson, Bjorn Thor and Aparna Mitra. "The Paternity Leave Act in Iceland: Implications for Gender Equality in the Labour Market." *Applied Economics Letters* 17 (2010): 677–680. https://doi.org/: 10.1080/13504850802297830.

Arnold, Carrie. "Autism's Race Problem." *Pacific Standard*, May 25, 2016. https://ps mag.com/news/autisms-race-problem.

Associated Press. "Fast-Food Worker at Qdoba Praised for Feeding Disabled Customer." *Tampa Bay Times*, June 5, 2015. https://www.tampabay.com/news/humaninterest/f ast-food-worker-at-qdoba-praised-for-feeding-disabled-customer-wvideo/2232544/.

Autism Science Foundation. "Beware of Non-Evidence-Based Treatments." Accessed May 4, 2019. https://autismsciencefoundation.org/what-is-autism/beware-of-non-evidence-based-treatments/.

Autism Speaks. *Autism Every Day*. Milestone Video, 2006. https://www.youtube.com /watch?v=O0vCz2KWMM0.

Autistic Self Advocacy Network. "ASAN Has Ended Partnership with Sesame Street." August 5, 2019. https://autisticadvocacy.org/2019/08/asan-has-ended-par tnership-with-sesame-street/.

Autistic Self Advocacy Network. "Autism and Safety Toolkit: Research Overview on Autism and Safety." Accessed September 10, 2020. https://autisticadvocacy.org/w p-content/uploads/2017/11/Autism-and-Safety-Pt-1.pdf.

Autistic Self Advocacy Network. "Before You Donate to Autism Speaks, Consider the Facts." Accessed November 22, 2018. https://autisticadvocacy.org/wp-content/ uploads/2017/04/AutismSpeaksFlyer_color_2017.pdf.

Autistic Self Advocacy Network. "Disability Organizations: MUSIC Is Dangerous." February 3, 2021. https://autisticadvocacy.org/2021/02/disability-organizations -music-is-dangerous/.

Autistic Self Advocacy Network. "Horrific Autism Speaks 'I am Autism' Ad Transcript." September 23, 2009. https://autisticadvocacy.org/2009/09/horrific-auti sm-speaks-i-am-autism-ad-transcript/.

Autistic Self Advocacy Network. "Position Statements." Accessed January 5, 2018. http://autisticadvocacy.org/about-asan/position-statements/.

Autistic Self Advocacy Network. "Statement on Autism Speaks Board Appointments." December 7, 2015. https://autisticadvocacy.org/2015/12/statement-on-autism-spe aks-board-appointments/.

Ayers, William, Therese Quinn, and David Sovall, eds. *Handbook of Social Justice in Education*. Abingdon: Routledge, 2008.

Baggs, Mel. "Cultural Commentary: Up in the Clouds and Down in the Valley: My Richness and Yours." *Disability Studies Quarterly* 30:1 (2010). https://dsq-sds.org/ article/view/1052/1238.

Baglieri, Susan, Jan W. Valle, David J. Connor, and Deborah J. Gallagher. "Disability Studies in Education: The Need for a Plurality of Perspectives on Disability." *Remedial and Special Education* 32:4 (2011): 267–278. https://doi .org/: 10.1177/0741932510362200.

Baglieri, Susan, Lynne Bejoian, Alicia Broderick, David Connor, and Jan Valle. "[Re]claiming 'Inclusive Education' Toward Cohesion in Educational Reform: Disability Studies Unravels the Myth of the Normal Child." *Teachers College Record* 113:10 (October 2011): 2122–2154.

Baio, Jon, Lisa Wiggins, Deborah Christensen, Matthew J. Maenner, Julie Daniels, Zachary Warren, Margaret Kurzius-Spencer, Walter Zahorodny,

Cordelia Robinson Rosenberg, Tiffany White, et al. "Prevalence of Autism Spectrum Disorder Among Children Aged 8 Years—Autism and Developmental Disabilities Monitoring Network, 11 Sites, United States, 2014." *MMWR Surveillance Summaries* 67 (April 27, 2018): 1–23. http://doi.org/10.15585/mmwr.ss6706a1.

Baker, Celia R. "Teaching Students with Intellectual Disabilities in Regular Classrooms Good for Kids or Good for All?" *Deseret News,* January 7, 2013. http://www.deseretnews.com/article/865570116/.

Barnes, Colin. "Disabling Imagery and the Media: An Exploration of the Principles for Media Representations of Disabled People." The British Council of Organisations of Disabled People, 1992. https://disability-studies.leeds.ac.uk/wp-content/uploads/sites/40/library/Barnes-disabling-imagery.pdf.

Baron-Cohen, Simon. "Autism: A Specific Cognitive Disorder of 'Mindblindness.'" *International Review of Psychiatry* 2:1 (January 1990): 81–90.

Baron-Cohen, Simon. "The Extreme Male Brain Theory of Autism." *Trends in Cognitive Sciences* 6:6 (2002): 248–254. https://doi.org/10.1016/S1364-6613(02)01904-6.

Baron-Cohen, Simon. *Mindblindness: An Essay on Autism and Theory of Mind.* Boston: MIT University Press, 1995.

Baron-Cohen, Simon. "Theory of Mind in Normal Development and Autism." *Prisme* 34 (2001): 174–183.

Barrangan, Eduardo and Emily Nusbaum. "Perceptions of Disability on a Postsecondary Campus: Implications for Oppression and Human Love." In *Negotiating Disability: Disclosure and Higher Education,* edited by Stephanie Kerschbaum, Laura Eisenmann, and James Jones, 39–56. Ann Arbor: University of Michigan Press, 2017.

Barrett, Michèle and Anne Phillips. *Destabilizing Theory: Contemporary Feminist Debates.* Stanford: Stanford University Press, 1992.

Bascom, Julia, ed. *Loud Hands: Autistic People, Speaking.* Washington, DC: The Autistic Press, 2012.

Bascom, Julia. "The Obsessive Joy of Autism." *Just Stimming.* Accessed December 1, 2013. https://juststimming.wordpress.com/2011/04/05/the-obsessive-joy-of-autism/.

Baynton, Douglas. "Disability and the Justification of Inequality in American History." In *The New Disability History: American Perspectives,* edited by Paul K. Longmore and Lauri Umanski, 33–57. New York: New York University Press, 2001.

Bell, Christopher, ed. *Blackness and Disability: Critical Examinations and Cultural Interventions.* Germany: LIT Verlag, 2011.

Beresford, Peter. "'Mad,' Mad Studies and Advancing Inclusive Resistance." *Disability & Society* 35:8 (2020): 1337–1342. https://doi.org/10.1080/09687599.2019.1692168.

Berger, James. "Trauma Without Disability, Disability Without Trauma: A Disciplinary Divide." *Journal of Advanced Composition* 24:3 (2004): 563–582. https://www.jstor.org/stable/20866643.

Berlant, Lauren. "Slow Death: Sovereignty, Obesity, Lateral Agency." *Critical Inquiry* 33 (2007): 754–780. https://doi.org/10.1086/524831.

Berne, Patty. "Disability Justice—A Working Draft by Patty Berne." *Sins Invalid*, June 9, 2015. https://www.sinsinvalid.org/blog/disability-justice-a-working-draft -by-patty-berne.

Bérubé, Michael. Blog. Accessed June 13, 2019. http://www.michaelberube.com/i ndex.php/weblog/comments/877/.

Bettelheim, Bruno. *The Empty Fortress: Infantile Autism and the Birth of the Self.* New York: The Free Press, 1967.

Bieber, Irving, Harvey J. Dain, Paul R. Dince, Marvin G. Drellich, Henry G. Grand, Ralph H. Gundlach, Malvina W. Kremer, Alfred H. Rifkin, Cornelia B. Wilbur, and Tony Bieber. *Homosexuality: A Psychoanalytic Study.* New York: Basic Books, 1962.

Black, Emily Rapp. "Why is Our Existence as Humans Still Being Denied?" *The New York Times*, July 26, 2017. https://www.nytimes.com/2017/07/26/opinion/why-is-our-existence-as-humans-still-being-denied.html.

Blanchett, Wanda. "Disproportionate Representation of African American Students in Special Education: Acknowledging the Role of White Privilege and Racism." *Educational Researcher* 35:6 (August/September 2006): 24–28. https://doi.org/10 .3102/0013189X035006024.

Block, Laurie. "Stereotypes about People with Disabilities." *Disability History Museum.* Accessed July 31, 2019. https://www.disabilitymuseum.org/dhm/edu/ essay.html?id=24.

Blum, Linda. *At the Breast: Ideologies of Breastfeeding and Motherhood in the Contemporary United States.* Boston: Beacon Press, 1999.

Blum, Linda. "Mother-Blame in the Prozac Nation: Raising Kids with Invisible Disabilities." *Gender and Society* 21:2 (April 2007): 202–226. https://doi.org/10.1 177/0891243206298178.

Blum, Linda. "'Not This Big, Huge, Racial-Type Thing, but . . . ': Mothering Children of Color with Invisible Disabilities in the Age of Neuroscience." *Signs: Journal of Women in Culture and Society* 36:4 (Summer 2011): 941–967. https:// doi.org/10.1086/658503.

Blume, Harvey. "Neurodiversity: On the Neurological Underpinnings of Geekdom." *The Atlantic*, September 1998. https://www.theatlantic.com/magazine/archive/ 1998/09/neurodiversity/305909/.

Boardman, Felicity. "Negotiating Discourses of Maternal Responsibility, Disability, and Reprogenetics: The Role of Experiential Knowledge." In *Disability and Mothering: Liminal Spaces of Embodied Knowledge*, edited by Cynthia Lewiecki-Wilson and Jen Cellio, 34–48. Syracuse: Syracuse University Press, 2011.

Bogdan, Robert. *Freakshow: Presenting Human Oddities for Amusement and Profit.* Chicago: University of Chicago Press, 1988.

Boyd, Brian A., Cooper R. Woodard, and James W. Bodfish. "Modified Exposure and Response Prevention to Treat the Repetitive Behaviors of a Child with Autism: A Case Report." *Case Reports in Psychiatry* 2011 (2011): 241095. https://doi.org/10 .1155/2011/241095.

Breathingglass. "The Asperger's Geek and Why This Stereotype Is Damaging." *Seeing Double, Understanding Autism*, June 18, 2015. https://seeingdoubleautis mawareness.wordpress.com/2015/06/18/the-aspergers-geek-and-why-this-stereot ype-is-damaging/.

Broderick, Alicia, Heeral Mehta-Parekh, and D. Kim Reid. "Differentiating Instruction for Disabled Students in Inclusive Classrooms." *Theory Into Practice* 44:3 (Summer 2005): 194–202. https://doi.org/10.1207/s15430421tip4403_3.

Brodie, John. "5 Questions for Kim Brooks." *Maisonette*. Accessed June 1, 2019. https://www.maisonette.com/le_scoop/5-questions-for-kim-brooks.

Bronson, Jennifer, Laura M. Maruschak, and Marcus Berzofsky. *Disabilities Among Prison and Jail Inmates, 2011–2012*. Washington: Bureau of Justice Statistics, 2015. http://www.bjs.gov/content/pub/ pdf/dpji1112.pdf.

Bronstein, Scott and Jessi Joseph. "Therapy to Change 'Feminine' Boy Created a Troubled Man, Family Says." *CNN*, June 10, 2011. http://www.cnn.com/2011/US /06/07/sissy.boy.experiment/index.html.

Brooks, Kim. "Motherhood in the Age of Fear." *The New York Times*, July 27, 2018. https://www.nytimes.com/2018/07/27/opinion/sunday/motherhood-in-the-age-of-fear.html?auth=login-email&login=email.

Brooks, Kim. *Small Animals: Parenthood in the Age of Fear*. New York: Flatiron Books, 2018.

Brown, Keah. "Love, Disability, and Movies." *Catapult,* April 27, 2016. https://ca tapult.co/stories/love-disability-and-movies.

Brown, Lydia X. Z. "Disability is a Social Construct: A Sociological Perspective on Autism and Disability." *Autistic Hoya*, November 1, 2011. http://www.autistichoya .com/2011/11/disability-is-social-construct.html.

Brown, Lydia X. Z. "Gendervague: At the Intersection of Autistic and Trans Experiences." *Asperger/Autism Network*, June 22, 2016. https://www.aane.org/ gendervague-intersection-autistic-trans-experiences/.

Brown, Lydia X. Z. "The Significance of Semantics." *Autistic Hoya*, August 4, 2011. http://www.autistichoya.com/2011/08/significance-of-semantics-person-first.html? m=1.

Brown, Lydia X. Z., E. Ashkenazy, and Morénike Giwa Onaiwu, eds. *All the Weight of Our Dreams: On Living Racialized Autism*. Lincoln: DragonBee Press, 2017.

Brown, S. E. "Super Duper? The (Unfortunate) Ascendancy of Christopher Reeve." *Independent Living Institute*, October 1996. http://independentliving.org/docs3/ brown96c.html.

Browne, James and Dirk Neumann. "OECD Tax Wedge and Effective Tax Rates on Labour." OECD, 2017. https://taxben.oecd.org/tax-ben-resources/Childcare-costs -in-2015.pdf.

Brune, Jeffrey and Daniel Wilson. "Introduction." In *Disability and Passing: Blurring the Lines of Identity*, edited by Jeffrey A. Brune and Daniel Wilson, 1–12. Philadelphia: Temple University Press, 2013.

Buck v. Bell, 274 U.S. 200 (1927).

Burton, Paul. "Undefeated Norton High Wrestler Makes Opponent's Dream Come True." *CBS Boston*, January 26, 2016. http://boston.cbslocal.com/2016/01/26/norton-wrestling-deven-schuko-video/.

Butler, Judith. *Gender Trouble: Feminism and the Subversion of Identity*. New York: Routledge, 1990.

Butler, Judith. "Imitation and Gender Insubordination." In *Inside/Out: Lesbian Theories, Gay Theories*, edited by Diana Fuss, 13–31. New York: Routledge, 1991.

Callus, Anne-Marie. "The Cloak of Incompetence: Representations of People with Intellectual Disability in Film." *Journal of Literary & Cultural Disability Studies* 13:2 (2019): 177–194. https://doi.org/10.3828/jlcds.2018.42.

Canadian Institutes of Health Research. "Science Fact or Science Fiction: Traumatic Brain Injury: Does Gender Matter?" January 2015. https://cihr-irsc.gc.ca/e/documents/igh_mythbuster_january_2015_en.pdf.

Carter, Angela. "Teaching with Trauma: Trigger Warnings, Feminism, and Disability Pedagogy." *Disability Studies Quarterly* 35:2 (2015). https://dsq-sds.org/article/view/4652/3935.

Carter, Pam. *Feminism, Breasts and Breast-Feeding*. New York: St. Martin's Press, 1995.

Casey, Bryan. "Uber's Dilemma: How the ADA May End the on Demand Economy." *UMass Law Review* 12:1 (2017). https://scholarship.law.umassd.edu/umlr/vol12/iss1/3.

Cassiman, Shawn A. "Mothering, Disability, and Poverty: Straddling Borders, Shifting Boundaries, and Everyday Resistance." In *Disability and Mothering: Liminal Spaces of Embodied Knowledge*, edited by Cynthia Lewiecki-Wilson and Jen Cellio, 289–301. Syracuse: Syracuse University Press, 2011.

"Caught on Camera: A Simple Act of Kindness with Big Impact." *Wave 3 News*, Louisville, Kentucky, May 11, 2015. http://www.wave3.com/story/29032820/tonight-at-6-restaurant-customer-records-random-act-of-kindness.

Cawthon, Stephanie and Emma Cole. "Postsecondary Students Who Have a Learning Disability: Student Perspectives on Accommodation Access and Obstacles." *Journal of Postsecondary Education and Disability* 23:2 (2010): 112–128. http://www.eric.ed.gov/PDFS/EJ906696.pdf.

Centers for Disease Control and Prevention. "Attention-Deficit/Hyperactivity Disorder." Accessed March 17, 2019. https://www.cdc.gov/ncbddd/adhd/data.html.

Centers for Disease Control and Prevention. "CDC: 1 in 4 Adults Live with a Disability." August 16, 2018. cdc.gov/media/releases/2018/po816-disability.html.

Centers for Disease Control and Prevention. "Disability Impacts All of Us." Accessed July 31, 2019. https://www.cdc.gov/ncbddd/disabilityandhealth/infographic-disability-impacts-all.html.

Centers for Disease Control and Prevention. "Prevalence and Characteristics of Autism Spectrum Disorder Among Children Aged 8 Years—Autism and Developmental Disabilities Monitoring Network, 11 Sites, United States, 2012." *Surveillance Summaries* 65 (April 1, 2016): 1–23. http://www.cdc.gov/mmwr/volumes/65/ss/ss6503a1.htm.

Centers for Disease Control and Prevention. "Racial and Ethnic Differences in Children Identified with Autism Spectrum Disorder." Community Report on Autism, 2018. https://www.cdc.gov/ncbddd/autism/addm-community-report/docu ments/differences-in-children-addm-community-report-2018-h.pdf.

Centers for Disease Control and Prevention. "Tips from Former Smokers: About the Campaign." Accessed August 8, 2017. https://www.cdc.gov/tobacco/campaign/tip s/about/index.html.

Centers for Disease Control and Prevention. "Tips from Former Smokers: Brandon's Story." Accessed August 8, 2017. https://www.cdc.gov/tobacco/campaign/tips/sto ries/brandon-biography.html.

Cepko, Roberta. "Involuntary Sterilization of Mentally Disabled Women." *Berkeley Journal of Gender, Law, and Justice* 8:1 (September 1993): 121–165. https://doi .org/10.15779/Z38729X.

Chainey, Naomi. "Passing Is Not a Privilege." *Ramp Up*, June 6, 2014. https://www .abc.net.au/rampup/articles/2014/06/06/4018773.htm.

Chambers, Bethan, Clodagh M. Murray, Zoe V. R. Boden, and Michelle P. Kelly. "'Sometimes Labels Need to Exist': Exploring How Young Adults with Asperger's Syndrome Perceive Its Removal from the *Diagnostic and Statistical Manual of Mental Disorders* Fifth Edition." *Disability & Society* 35:4 (2020): 589–608. https ://doi.org/10.1080/09687599.2019.1649121.

Chase, Susan and Mary Rogers, eds. *Mothers and Children: Feminist Analyses and Personal Narratives*. New Brunswick: Rutgers University Press, 2001.

Child Care Aware of America. "The U.S. and the High Price of Child Care: An Examination of a Broken System." 2019. https://cdn2.hubspot.net/hubfs/3957809 /2019%20Price%20of%20Care%20State%20Sheets/Final-TheUSandtheHighPri ceofChildCare-AnExaminationofaBrokenSystem.pdf.

Chita-Tegmark, Meia, Jenna Gravel, Maria de Lourdes B. Serpa, Yvonne Domings, and David Rose. "Using the Universal Design for Learning Framework to Support Culturally Diverse Learners." *Journal of Education* 192 (2011/2012): 17–22. https ://doi.org/10.1177/002205741219200104.

Clare, Eli. "Sex, Celebration and Justice." Queerness and Disability Conference, 2002. Accessed June 2, 2018. https://eliclare.com/what-eli-offers/lectures/queer -disability.

Clarke, Jennifer G. and Rachel E. Simon. "Shackling and Separation: Motherhood in Prison." *AMA Journal of Ethics*, September 2013. https://journalofethics.ama-assn .org/article/shackling-and-separation-motherhood-prison/2013-09.

Clayton, Janine A. and Francis S. Collins. "Policy: NIH to Balance Sex in Cell and Animal Studies." *Nature* 509:7500 (May 14, 2014): 282–283. https://www.nature .com/news/polopoly_fs/1.15195!/menu/main/topColumns/topLeftColumn/pdf/50 9282a.pdf.

Codrington, Jamila and Halford H. Fairchild. "Special Education and the Mis-Education of African American Children: A Call to Action." The Association of Black Psychologists, February 13, 2012. http://www.abpsi.org/pdf/specialedpositi onpaper021312.pdf.

Cohen-Rottenberg, Rachel. "Doing Social Justice: Thoughts on Ableist Language and Why It Matters." *Disability and Representation*, September 14, 2013. http://www.disabilityandrepresentation.com/2013/09/14/ableist-language/.

Cohen-Rottenberg, Rachel. "Impaired Theory of Whose Mind (ToWM)?" *Autism and Empathy*. Accessed December 20, 2020. https://autismandempathyblog.wordpress.com/impaired-theory-of-whose-mind-towm/.

Cohen-Rottenberg, Rachel. "On Normalcy and Identity Politics." *Disability and Representation*, March 24, 2014. http://www.disabilityandrepresentation.com/?s=language.

Coker, Tumaini R., Marc N. Elliot, Sara L. Toomey, David C. Schwebel, Paula Cuccaro, Susan Tortolero Emery, Susan Davies, Susanna N. Visser, and Mark A. Schuster. "Racial and Ethnic Disparities in ADHD Diagnosis and Treatment." *Pediatrics* 138:3 (2016): e20160407. https://doi.org/10.1542/peds.2016-0407.

Colantonio, Angela. "Sex, Gender, and Traumatic Brain Injury: A Commentary." *Archives of Physical Medicine and Rehabilitation* 97 (2016): S1–S4. https://www.archives-pmr.org/action/showPdf?pii=S0003-9993%2815%2901477-X.

The Colbert Report. Comedy Central, April 15, 2010. https://www.cc.com/episodes/ktt9wb/the-colbert-report-april-15-2010-aimee-mullins-season-6-ep-52.

Cole, Emma and Stephanie Cawthon. "Self-Disclosure Decisions of University Students with Learning Disabilities." *Journal of Postsecondary Education and Disability* 28:2 (2015): 163–179. http://files.eric.ed.gov/fulltext/EJ1074663.pdf.

Colker, Ruth. "Blaming Mothers: A Disability Perspective." *Boston University Law Review* 95:3 (April 2015): 1205–1224. https://doi.org/10.2139/ssrn.2604972.

Collins, Patricia Hill. *Black Feminist Thought: Knowledge, Consciousness, and the Politics of Empowerment*. New York: Routledge, 1990.

Conn, Rory and Dinesh Bhugra. "The Portrayal of Autism in Hollywood Films." *International Journal of Culture and Mental Health* 5:1 (2012): 54–62. https://doi.org/10.1080/17542863.2011.553369.

Connor, David, and Beth Ferri. "The Conflict Within: Resistance to Inclusion and Other Paradoxes in Special Education." *Disability & Society* 22:1 (December 2006): 63–77. https://doi.org/10.1080/09687590601056717.

Connor, David and Beth Ferri. "Integration and Inclusion: A Troubling Nexus: Race, Disability, and Special Education." *The Journal of African American History* 90 (Winter 2005): 107–127.

Constantino, John and Tony Charman. "Gender Bias, Female Resilience, and the Sex Ratio in Autism." *Journal of the American Academy of Child and Adolescent Psychiatry* 51:8 (August 2012): 756–758. https://doi.org/10.1016/j.jaac.2012.05.017.

Cook, Katie and Colleen Loomis. "The Impact of Choice and Control on Women's Childbirth Experiences." *The Journal of Perinatal Education* 21:3 (2012): 158–168. https://doi.org/10.1891/1058-1243.21.3.158.

Cooper, Chet. "The Road I Have Taken: Christopher Reeve and the Cure; An Interview with Christopher Reeve and Fred Fay." *ABILITY Magazine*. Accessed August 1, 2019. https://www.abilitymagazine.com/reeve_interview.html.

Corroto, Carla and Lucinda Havenhand. "Institutional Resistance to Accessible Architecture and Design: A Collaborative Autoethnography." In *Qualitative*

Inquiry: Methods for Rethinking an Ableist World, edited by Ronald Berger and Laura Lorenz, 109–125. Burlington, VT: Ashgate Publishing Company, 2015.

Coutinho, Martha and Donald Oswald. "State Variation in Gender Disproportionality in Special Education." *Remedial and Special Education* 26:1 (January/February 2005): 7–15. https://doi.org/10.1177/07419325050260010201.

Coutinho, Martha, Donald Oswald, and Al Best. "The Influence of Sociodemographics and Gender on the Disproportionate Identification of Minority Students as Having Learning Disabilities." *Remedial and Special Education* 23:1 (January/February 2002): 49–59.

Crittenden, Ann. *The Price of Motherhood: Why the Most Important Job in the World is Still the Least Valued.* New York: Henry Holt and Company, 2001.

Crow, Liz. "Including All of Our Lives: Renewing the Social Model of Disability." In *Encounters with Strangers: Feminism and Disability*, edited by Jenny Morris, 206–226. London: The Women's Press, 1996.

Cuomo, Chris. *Feminism and Ecological Communities: An Ethic of Flourishing.* New York: Routledge, 1998.

Curto, Justin. "Sia Criticized for Not Casting Actors with Autism, Attacks Critics on Twitter." *Vulture*, November 20, 2020. https://www.vulture.com/2020/11/sia-auti sm-representation-music-movie.html.

Cvetkovich, Ann. *An Archive of Feelings: Trauma, Sexuality, and Lesbian Public Cultures.* Durham, NC: Duke University Press, 2003.

Daar, Judith F. "Accessing Reproductive Technologies: Invisible Barriers, Indelible Harms." *Berkeley Journal of Gender, Law, and Justice* 23:1 (2008): 18–82. https://doi.org/10.15779/Z38K93156H.

Davidovitch, Michael, Gideon Koren, Naama Fund, Maayan Shrem, and Avi Porath. "Challenges in Defining the Rates of ADHD Diagnosis and Treatment: Trends over the Last Decade." *BMC Pediatric* 17:218 (December 2017). https://doi.org/10.1186/s12887-017-0971-0.

Davidson, Adam W. "Stasis-Maintenance-(Un)productive-Presence: Parenting a Disabled Child as Crip Time." *Disability Studies Quarterly* 40:3 (2020). https://dsq-sds.org/article/view/6693.

Davidson, Joyce and Victoria Henderson. "'Coming Out' on the Spectrum: Autism, Identity and Disclosure." *Social and Cultural Geography* 11:2 (2010): 155–170. https://doi.org/10.1080/14649360903525240.

Davies, Quentin. "'Prisoners of the Apparatus': The Judge Rotenberg Center." *Autistic Self Advocacy Network*, August 9, 2014. https://autisticadvocacy.org/2014/08/prisoners-of-the-apparatus/.

Davis, Lennard. *Bending Over Backwards: Disability, Dismodernism, and Other Difficult Positions.* New York: New York University Press, 2002.

Davis, Lennard. *Enforcing Normalcy: Disability, Deafness, and the Body.* London: Verso, 1995.

Dean, Michelle, Robin Harwood, and Connie Kasari. "The Art of Camouflage: Gender Differences in the Social Behaviors of Girls and Boys with Autism Spectrum Disorder." *Autism* 21:6 (2017): 678–689. https://doi.org/10.1177/136236 1316671845.

De Cesarei, Andrea. "Psychological Factors that Foster or Deter the Disclosure of Disability by University Students." *Psychological Reports* 116:3 (2015): 665–673. https://doi.org/10.2466/15.PR0.116k26w9.

"Definition of Disability." *Google.* Accessed January 15, 2017. https://www.google.c om/search?source=hp&ei=ORFCXc_GO6GzggeAu6G4BQ&q=definition+of+dis ability.

Dell'Antonia, K. J. "For U.S. Parents, a Troubling Happiness Gap." *The New York Times*, June 17, 2016. https://well.blogs.nytimes.com/2016/06/17/for-u-s-parents -a-troubling-happiness-gap/.

Dennis, Kyle C. "Current Perspectives on Traumatic Brain Injury." *ASHA* (August 2009). https://www.asha.org/Articles/Current-Perspectives-on-Traumatic-Brain-Injury/.

Denzin, Norman and Yvonna Lincoln. *The Sage Handbook of Qualitative Research.* Thousand Oaks: Sage Publications, 2005.

DeStefano, Frank, Cristofer S. Price, and Eric S. Weintraub. "Increasing Exposure to Antibody-Stimulating Proteins and Polysaccharides in Vaccines Is Not Associated with Risk of Autism." *The Journal of Pediatrics* 163:2 (August 2013): 561–567. http://www.jpeds.com/article/S0022-3476%2813%2900144-3/pdf.

Devita-Raeburn, Elizabeth. "The Controversy over Autism's Most Common Therapy." *Spectrum*, August 10, 2016. https://www.spectrumnews.org/features/de ep-dive/controversy-autisms-common-therapy/.

Dhar, Arshia. "Pop Culture Has Reduced OCD to Quirks and Punchlines." *Firstpost*, October 12, 2019. https://www.firstpost.com/living/pop-culture-has-reduced-ocd -to-quirks-and-punchlines-making-a-mockery-of-those-who-live-with-the-condi tion-7472891.html.

Diament, Michelle. "Disability Caregivers Struggling Financially, Emotionally." *Disability Scoop*, June 15, 2011. https://www.disabilityscoop.com/2011/06/15/di sability-caregivers-struggling/13339/.

Diament, Michelle. "Groups Outraged Over Video Released By Autism Speaks." *Disability Scoop*, September 25, 2009. https://www.disabilityscoop.com/2009/09/ 25/autism-speaks-video/5541/.

Dionne, Evette. "For Black Women, Self-Care Is a Radical Act." *Ravishly*, March 9, 2015. https://ravishly.com/2015/03/06/radical-act-self-care-black-women-feminism.

"Director Spike Lee Slams 'Same Old' Black Stereotypes in Today's Films." *Yale Bulletin and Calendar* 29:21 (March 2, 2001). https://web.archive.org/web/20 090121190429/http://www.yale.edu/opa/arc-ybc/v29.n21/story3.html.

Disability Justice. "*Olmstead v. L.C.*" Accessed December 11, 2016. http://disabili tyjustice.org/olmstead-v-lc/.

Dolmage, Jay. *Academic Ableism: Disability and Higher Education.* Ann Arbor: University of Michigan Press, 2017.

Dolmage, Jay. "Disability Studies Pedagogy, Usability and Universal Design." *Disability Studies Quarterly* 25:4 (Fall 2005). http://doi.org/10.18061/dsq.v25i4.

Donaldson, Elizabeth and Catherine Prendergast. "Introduction: Disability and Emotion: 'There's No Crying in Disability Studies!'" *Journal of Literary & Cultural Disability Studies* 5:2 (2011): 129–135. https://doi.org/10.3828/jlcds.

Doucette, Luticha. "If You're in a Wheelchair, Segregation Lives." *The New York Times*, May 17, 2017. https://www.nytimes.com/2017/05/17/opinion/if-youre-in-a-wheelchair-segregation-lives.html.

Douglas, Susan and Meredith Michaels. *The Mommy Myth: The Idealization of Motherhood and How It Has Undermined All Women.* New York: Free Press, 2004.

Drescher, Jack. "Out of DSM: Depathologizing Homosexuality." *Behavioral Sciences* 5:4 (December 2015): 565–575. https://doi.org/10.3390/bs5040565.

Drew, Julia Rivera. "Disability, Poverty, and Material Hardship since the Passage of the ADA." *Disability Studies Quarterly* 35:3 (2015). https://dsq-sds.org/article/view/4947/4026.

Drubach, Daniel A. "Obsessive-Compulsive Disorder." *Continuum* 21:3 *Behavioral Neurology and Neuropsychiatry* (2015): 783–788. https://doi.org/10.1212/01.CON.0000466666.12779.07.

Duffy, John and Rebecca Dorner. "The Pathos of 'Mindblindness': Autism, Science, and Sadness in 'Theory of Mind' Narratives." *Journal of Literary & Cultural Disability Studies* 5:2 (2011): 201–215. https://doi.org/10.3828/jlcds.2011.16.

Duggan, Lisa. *The Twilight of Equality?: Neoliberalism, Cultural Politics, and the Attack on Democracy.* Boston: Beacon Press, 2003.

Duhaney, Laurel Garrick and Spencer Salend. "Parental Perceptions of Inclusive Educational Placements." *Remedial and Special Education* 21 (March 2000): 121–128. https://doi.org/10.1177/074193250002100209.

Dusenbery, Maya. *Doing Harm: The Truth about How Bad Medicine and Lazy Science Leave Women Dismissed, Misdiagnosed, and Sick.* New York: HarperOne, 2018.

Duyvis, Corrinne. "The Mystical Disability Trope." *Disability in Kidlit*, August 1, 2014. http://disabilityinkidlit.com/2014/08/01/corinne-duyvis-the-mystical-disability-trope/.

Dworzynski, Katharina, Angelica Ronald, Patrick Bolton, and Francesca Happe. "How Different Are Girls and Boys Above and Below the Diagnostic Threshold for Autism Spectrum Disorders?" *Journal of the American Academy of Child and Adolescent Psychology* 51 (August 2012): 788–797. https://doi.org/10.1016/j.jaac.2012.05.018.

Eagleton, Terry. *The Illusions of Postmodernism.* Oxford: Blackwell, 1996.

Edelman, Lee. *No Future: Queer Theory and the Death Drive.* Durham: Duke University Press, 2004.

Edwards, Stassa. "Wellness, Womanhood, and the West: How Goop Profits from Endless Illness." *Jezebel*, April 28, 2017. https://jezebel.com/wellness-womanhood-and-the-west-how-goop-profits-fro-1793674265.

Edyburn, Dave. "Would You Recognize Universal Design for Learning If You Saw It? Ten Propositions for New Directions for the Second Decade of UDL." *Learning Disability Quarterly* 33 (Winter 2010): 33–41. https://doi.org/10.1177/073194871003300103.

Ellis, Carolyn. *The Ethnographic I: A Methodological Novel about Autoethnography.* Walnut Creek, CA: AltaMira, 2004.

Ellis, Sarah Kate. "Where We Are on TV, 2018–2019." *GLAAD Media Institute.* Accessed September 20, 2019. https://glaad.org/files/WWAT/WWAT_GLAAD_2018-2019.pdf.

Eltagouri, Maria. "'The View's' Joy Behar Calls Mike Pence to Apologize for Calling His Christian Faith a 'Mental Illness.'" *The Washington Post*, March 8, 2018. https://www.washingtonpost.com/news/acts-of-faith/wp/2018/03/08/joy-behar-called-mike-pences-faith-a-mental-illness-then-she-called-to-apologize/.

"Ensuring Authentic Representation of Black Disabled People in the Entertainment Industry." Webinar. *Respectability*, June 2020. https://www.respectability.org/2020/06/ensuring-authentic-representation-of-black-disabled-people-in-the-entertainment-industry/.

Erevelles, Nirmala. *Disability and Difference in Global Contexts: Enabling a Transformative Body Politic.* New York: Palgrave Macmillan, 2011.

Eromosele, Aimaloghi. "There is No Self-Care without Community Care." *URGE*, November 10, 2020. https://urge.org/there-is-no-self-care-without-community-care/.

Evans, Dominick. "Hollywood Promotes the Idea It Is Better to Be Dead Than Disabled." *The Crip Crusader*, February 11, 2016. http://www.dominickevans.com/2016/02/hollywood-promotes-the-idea-it-is-better-to-be-dead-than-disabled/.

Evans, Dominick. "Please Stop Comparing Disabled Mimicry to Blackface." *The Crip Crusader*, July 18, 2017. https://www.dominickevans.com/2017/07/please-stop-comparing-cripping-up-to-blackface/.

Evans, Dominick. "Stop MDA & #EndTheTelethon Now!" *The Crip Crusader*, October 4, 2020. https://www.dominickevans.com/2020/10/stop-mda-endthetelethon-now/.

Fenton, Zanita. "Disabling Racial Repetition." In *Righting Educational Wrongs: Disability Studies in Law and Education*, edited by Beth Ferri and Arlene Kanter, 174–206. Syracuse: Syracuse University Press, 2013.

Ferri, Beth and David Connor. "'I Was the Special Ed Girl': Urban Working-Class Young Women of Colour." *Gender and Education* 22:1 (January 2010): 105–121. https://doi.org/10.1080/09540250802612688.

Ferri, Beth and David Connor. *Reading Resistance: Discourses of Exclusion in Desegregation and Inclusion Debates.* New York: Peter Lang, 2006.

Fielder, Leslie. *Freaks: Myths and Images of the Secret Self.* New York: Simon and Schuster, 1979.

Filipovic, Jill. *The H-Spot: The Feminist Pursuit of Happiness.* New York: Nation Books, 2017.

Fish, Stanley. *Is There a Text in this Class?* Cambridge: Harvard University Press, 1980.

Flaherty, Michael. *The Textures of Time: Agency and Temporal Experience.* Temple University Press, 2011.

Flaherty, Michael. *A Watched Pot: How We Experience Time.* New York: New York University Press, 1999.

Foucault, Michel. *The History of Sexuality, Volume 1.* New York: Pantheon Books, 1978.

France, David. *How to Survive a Plague: The Story of How Activists and Scientists Tamed AIDS*. New York: Vintage Books, 2016.

Freeman, Elizabeth. *Time Binds: Queer Temporalities, Queer Histories*. Durham: Duke University Press, 2010.

Froschl, Merle, Ellen Rubin, and Barbara Sprung. "Connecting Gender and Disability." *Gender and Disability Digest* (Newton, MA: Women's Educational Equity Act Resource Center, 1999): 1–12. http://www2.edc.org/WomensEquity/pdffiles/disabdig.pdf.

Frye, Devon. "Children Left Behind." *Attitude*. Accessed November 8, 2019. https://www.additudemag.com/race-and-adhd-how-people-of-color-get-left-behind/.

Frye, Marilyn. *The Politics of Reality*. New York: Crossing Press, 1983.

Gadsby, Hannah. *Nanette*. Directed by John Olb and Madeleine Parry. Netflix, 2018.

Garland-Thomson, Rosemarie. "Becoming Disabled." *The New York Times*, August 19, 2016. https://www.nytimes.com/2016/08/21/opinion/sunday/becoming-disabled.html.

Garland-Thomson, Rosemarie. *Extraordinary Bodies: Figuring Physical Disability in American Culture and Literature*. New York: Columbia University Press, 1997.

Garland-Thomson, Rosemarie. "First Person: Rosemarie Garland-Thomson." *Emory Report* 56 (July 6, 2004). http://www.emory.edu/EMORY_REPORT/erarchive/2004/July/er%20july%206/7_6_04firstperson.html.

Garland-Thomson, Rosemarie. *Freakery: Cultural Spectacles of the Extraordinary Body*. New York: New York University Press, 1996.

Garland-Thomson, Rosemarie. "Integrating Disability, Transforming Feminist Theory." *NWSA Journal* 14:3 (Autumn 2002): 1–32. http://www.jstor.org/stable/4316922.

Garland-Thomson, Rosemarie. "Re-shaping, Re-thinking, Redefining: Feminist Disability Studies." *Center for Women Policy Studies*, 2001. https://www.womenenabled.org/pdfs/Garland-Thomson,Rosemarie,RedefiningFeministDisabilitiesStudiesCWPR2001.pdf.

Garland-Thomson, Rosemarie. "Staring at the Other." *Disability Studies Quarterly* 25:4 (Fall 2005). http://dsq-sds.org/article/view/610/787.

Garland-Thomson, Rosemarie. *Staring: How We Look*. Oxford: Oxford University Press, 2009.

Garland-Thomson, Rosemarie. "The Story of My Work: How I Became Disabled." *Disability Studies Quarterly* 34:2 (2014). https://dsq-sds.org/article/view/4254.

Gibson, Caitlin. "Jillian Mercado Made It as a Model with a Disability. Here's What She Wants Next." *The Washington Post*, April 28, 2016. https://www.washingtonpost.com/news/arts-and-entertainment/wp/2016/04/28/jillian-mercado-made-it-as-a-model-with-a-disability-heres-what-she-wants-next/.

Gill, M. "The Other 25%: Autistic Girls and Women." *European Psychiatry* 33 (March 2016): 351–352. https://doi.org/10.1016/j.eurpsy.2016.01.1246.

Glass, Jennifer, Robin W. Simon, and Matthew A. Andersson. "Parenthood and Happiness: Effects of Work-Family Reconciliation Policies in 22 OECD Countries." *American Journal of Sociology* 122:3 (November 2016): 886–929. https://doi.org/10.1086/688892.

Gonnerman, Jennifer. "The School of Shock." *Mother Jones*, August 20, 2007. https ://www.motherjones.com/politics/2007/08/school-shock/.

Gonzalez, Maru. "Attention Hipsters: OCD is Not a Joke." *HuffPost*, June 16, 2015. https://www.huffingtonpost.com/maru-gonzalez/attention-hipsters-ocd-is-not-a -joke_b_7581942.html.

"The Good Doctor." *IMDb*. Accessed August 10, 2020. http://www.imdb.com/title/ tt6470478/?ref_=nv_sr_1.

Gould, Deborah. *Moving Politics: Emotion and ACT UP's Fight against AIDS*. Chicago: University of Chicago Press, 2009.

Gould, Judith and Jacqui Ashton-Smith. "Missed Diagnosis or Misdiagnosis: Girls and Women on the Autism Spectrum." *Good Autism Practice* 12:1 (2011): 34–41. https://doi.org/10.1177/1362361317706174.

Gourdine, Ruby M., Tiffany D. Baffour, and Martell Teasley. "Autism and the African American Community." *Social Work in Public Health* 26:4 (2011): 454– 470. https://doi.org/10.1080/19371918.2011.579499.

Granger, Dene. "A Tribute to My Dyslexic Body, As I Travel in the Form of a Ghost." *Disability Studies Quarterly* 30 (2010). http://dsq-sds.org/article/view/1236/1281.

Grant, Jon E. and Samuel R. Chamberlain. "Exploring the Neurobiology of OCD: Clinical Implications." *The Psychiatric Times*, March 2, 2020. https://www.psy chiatrictimes.com/view/exploring-neurobiology-ocd-clinical-implications.

Greco, Lachrista. "It Happened to Me: I Was in Special Ed." *xojane*, August 10, 2012. http://www.xojane.com/it-happened-to-me/it-happened-me-i-was-special-ed.

Groopman, Jerome. "The Reeve Effect." *The New Yorker*, November 2, 2003. https:/ /www.newyorker.com/magazine/2003/11/10/the-reeve-effect.

"A Guide to Spirit Animals: A Q&A with Colleen McCann." *Goop*. Accessed June 28, 2019. https://goop.com/style/trends/guide-spirit-animals/.

Gupte, Raeesa, William Brooks, Rachel Vukas, Janet Pierce, and Janna Harris. "Sex Differences in Traumatic Brain Injury: What We Know and What We Should Know." *J Neurotrauma* 36:22 (November 2019): 3063–3091. https://doi.org/10 .1089/neu.2018.6171.

Gwaltney, Javy. "Day in the Life: Disability and Representation in Videogames." *Paste*, March 9, 2015. https://www.pastemagazine.com/articles/2015/03/day-in-t he-life-disability-and-representation-in-v.html.

Haag, Halina L., Michiko Caringal, Sandra Sokoloff, Pia Kontos, Karen Yoshida, and Angela Colantonio. "Being a Woman with Acquired Brain Injury: Challenges and Implications for Practice." *Archives of Physical Medicine and Rehabilitation* 97 (2016): S67. https://www.archives-pmr.org/action/showPdf?pii=S0003-9993% 2815%2900099-4.

Haag, Halina L., Sandra Sokoloff, Nneka MacGregor, Shirley Broekstra, Nora Cullen, and Angela Colantonio. "Battered and Brain Injured: Assessing Knowledge of Traumatic Brain Injury among Intimate Partner Violence Service Providers." *Journal of Women's Health* 28:7 (2019): 990–996. https://doi.org/10.1089/jwh .2018.7299.

Hackman, Heather. "Broadening the Pathway to Academic Success: The Critical Intersections of Social Justice Education, Critical Multicultural Education, and

Universal Instructional Design." In *Pedagogy and Student Services for Institutional Transformation: Implementing Universal Design in Higher Education*, edited by Jeanne Higbee and Emily Goff, 25–48. Minneapolis: University of Minnesota, 2008.

Halberstam, J. Jack. *In a Queer Time and Place: Transgender Bodies, Subcultural Lives*. New York: New York University Press, 2005.

Halberstam, J. Jack. *The Queer Art of Failure*. Durham: Duke University Press, 2011.

Hall, Alice. *Literature and Disability*. New York: Routledge, 2016.

Hall, Kim Q. "Toward a Queer Crip Feminist Politics of Food." *philoSOPHIA* 4:2 (Summer 2014): 177–196. https://muse.jhu.edu/article/565882.

Haller, Beth. *Representing Disability in an Ableist World: Essays on Mass Media*. Louisville, KY: The Advocado Press, 2010.

Hamer, Fannie Lou. "Testimony before the Credentials Committee at the Democratic National Convention, Atlantic City, New Jersey, August 22, 1964." In *The Speeches of Fannie Lou Hamer: To Tell It Like It Is*, edited by Maegan Parker Brooks and Davis W. Houck, 42–45. Jackson: University Press of Mississippi, 2011.

Hamilton, Anna. "30 Years after the ADA, It's Time to Imagine a More Accessible Future." *Bitch Media*, July 20, 2020. https://www.bitchmedia.org/article/reima gining-americans-with-disabilities-act-anniversary.

Hancock, Charlie. "Autism on Screen: Where Sia Went Wrong." *The Oxford Student*, December 6, 2020. https://www.oxfordstudent.com/2020/12/06/autism-on-screen -where-sia-went-wrong/.

Handler, Rachel. "Stop Excluding Actors with Disabilities." *Backstage*, February 9, 2016. https://www.backstage.com/magazine/article/stop-excluding-actors-disab ilities-7387/.

Haney, Jolynn. "Autism, Females, and the DSM-5: Gender Bias in Autism Diagnosis." *Social Work in Mental Health* 14:4 (2016): 396–407. https://doi.org /10.1080/15332985.2015.1031858.

Happer, Catherine and Greg Philo. "The Role of the Media in the Construction of Public Belief and Social Change." *Journal of Social and Political Psychology* 1:1 (2013): 321–336. https://doi.org/10.5964/jspp.v1i1.96.

Harding, Sandra. *The Science Question in Feminism*. Ithaca: Cornell University Press, 1986.

Harrell, Erika. *Crimes Against Persons with Disabilities: 2009–2015 Statistical Tables* (U.S. Department of Justice Bureau of Justice Statistics, NCJ No. 250632, July 2017): 1–17. https://www.bjs.gov/content/pub/pdf/capd0915st.pdf.

Harrison, Mia. "George R.R. Martin and the Two Dwarfs." In *The Routledge Companion to Disability and Media*, edited by Katie Ellis, Gerard Goggin, Beth Haller, and Rosemary Curtis, 113–121. New York: Routledge, 2020.

Harvard Medical School. "Head Injury in Adults." *Harvard Health Publishing*, October 2018. https://www.health.harvard.edu/a_to_z/head-injury-in-adults-a-to-z.

Hay, Mark. "Mat Fraser on the Future of Disability in the Media." *GOOD*, February 2, 2016. https://www.good.is/articles/mat-fraser-american-horror-story-freakshow -disability-media-oneofus.

Hays, Sharon. *The Cultural Contradictions of Motherhood.* New Haven: Yale University Press, 1996.

Heilbrun, Carolyn. *Writing a Woman's Life.* New York: W.W. Norton & Company, 1988.

Heilker, Paul. "Autism, Rhetoric, and Whiteness." *Disability Studies Quarterly* 32:4 (2012). https://dsq-sds.org/article/view/1756.

Held, Virginia. *The Ethics of Care: Personal, Political, and Global.* Oxford: Oxford University Press, 2006.

Helliwell, John F., Richard Layard, and Jeffrey D. Sachs, eds. *World Happiness Report 2019.* New York: Sustainable Development Solutions Network, 2019. https ://s3.amazonaws.com/happiness-report/2019/WHR19.pdf.

Henry, Elsa. "Autism Speaks Does Not Speak For Me." *Feminist Sonar,* November 13, 2013. http://feministsonar.com/2013/11/autism-speaks-does-not-speak-for -me/.

Herbst, Chris. "Universal Child Care, Maternal Employment, and Children's Long-Run Outcomes: Evidence from the U.S. Lanham Act of 1940." *Journal of Labor Economics* 35:2 (April 2017): 519–564. https://doi.org/10.1086/689478.

Herman, Aaron. "Ableism at Tufts and the 'Life, Animated' Screening." *The Tufts Daily,* March 13, 2017. https://tuftsdaily.com/opinion/2017/03/13/op-ed-ableism -at-tufts-and-the-life-animated-screening/.

Hershey, Laura. "From Poster Child to Protestor." *Independent Living Institute.* Accessed August 1, 2019. https://www.independentliving.org/docs4/hershey93. html.

Hesse-Biber, Sharlene Nagy, ed. *Handbook of Feminist Research: Theory and Praxis.* 2nd edition. Thousand Oaks, CA: Sage Publications, 2012.

Heumann, Judith, Katherine Salinas, and Michellie Hess. *Road Map for Inclusions: Changing the Face of Disability in Media.* Ford Foundation, March 26, 2019. https://www.fordfoundation.org/media/4276/judyheumann_report_2019_final .pdf.

Higbee, Jeanne and Emily Goff, eds. *Pedagogy and Student Services for Institutional Transformation: Implementing Universal Design in Higher Education.* Minneapolis: University of Minnesota, 2008.

Hillary, Alyssa. "The Erasure of Queer Autistic People." In *Criptiques,* edited by Caitlin Wood, 121–146. Portland, OR: May Day Press, 2014.

Hillsburg, Heather. "Mental Illness and the Mad/woman: Anger, Normalcy, and Liminal Identities in Mary McGarry Morris's *A Dangerous Woman.*" *Journal of Literary & Cultural Disability Studies* 11:1 (2017): 1–16. https://doi.org/10.3828 /jlcds.2017.1.

Holicky, Richard. "The Transformation of Regan Linton." *New Mobility,* May 1, 2015. https://www.newmobility.com/2015/05/regan-linton/.

Honos-Webb, Lara. *The Gift of ADHD: How to Transform Your Child's Problems into Strengths.* Oakland: New Harbinger Publications, 2007.

hooks, bell. "Choosing the Margin as a Space of Radical Openness." *Framework: The Journal of Cinema and Media* 36 (1989): 15–23. https://www.jstor.org/stable /44111660.

hooks, bell. *Teaching to Transgress: Education as the Practice of Freedom.* New York: Routledge, 1994.

Horne, Zachary, Derek Powell, John E. Hummel, and Keith J. Holyoak. "Countering Antivaccination Attitudes." *Proceedings of the National Academy of Sciences* 201504019 (Aug 2015). https://doi.org/10.1073/pnas.1504019112.

"H.R.620—115th Congress (2017–2018)." *Congress.gov.* Accessed July 27, 2020. https://www.congress.gov/bill/115th-congress/house-bill/620/text.

Hughey, Matthew. "Cinethetic Racism: White Redemption and Black Stereotypes in 'Magical Negro' Films." *Social Problems* 56:3 (August 2009): 543–577. https://doi.org/10.1525/sp.2009.56.3.543.

Hull, Gloria T., Patricia Bell-Scott, and Barbara Smith. *But Some of Us Are Brave: All the Women Are White, All the Blacks Are Men: Black Women's Studies.* New York: The Feminist Press, 1982.

Hunt, Paul. "Discrimination: Disabled People and the Media." *Contact* 70 (Winter 1991): 45–48. https://disability-studies.leeds.ac.uk/wp-content/uploads/sites/40/library/Barnes-Media.pdf.

Hyler, Steven. "Stigma Continues in Hollywood." *Psychiatric Times*, June 1, 2003. http://www.psychiatrictimes.com/articles/stigma-continues-hollywood.

"Individuals with Disabilities Education Act." United States Department of Education. Accessed March 3, 2015. http://idea.ed.gov/download/statute.html.

Inskeep, Steve. "How Police Handled Pro-Trump Mob Compared with Protesters for Black Racial Justice." *NPR*, January 7, 2021. https://www.npr.org/sections/insurrection-at-the-capitol/2021/01/07/954410419/how-the-u-s-capitol-mob-was-treated-differently-than-earlier-black-protesters.

Irvine, Kevin. "Over My Dead Body." *POZ*, January 1, 1998. https://www.poz.com/article/assisted-suicide-13730-8270.

Jack, Jordynn. *Autism and Gender: From Refrigerator Mothers to Computer Geeks.* Urbana: University of Illinois Press, 2014.

Jacobsen, Matthew Frye. *Barbarian Virtues: The United States Encounters Foreign Peoples at Home and Abroad, 1876–1917.* New York: Hill and Wang, 2000.

Jain, Anjali, Jaclyn Marshall, and Ami Buikema. "Autism Occurrence by MMR Vaccine Status Among U.S. Children with Older Siblings with and without Autism." *JAMA* 313:15 (2015): 1534–1540. https://doi.org/10.1001/jama.2015.3077.

"Jerry Lewis to Crips: 'Stay in Your House!'" *Ragged Edge Online.* Accessed October 6, 2020. http://www.raggededgemagazine.com/extra/jerrylewis052401.htm.

"Jerry's Orphans Protest the MDA Telethon." *The Kids are All Right.* Accessed September 20, 2017. http://www.thekidsareallright.org/story.html.

Jerry's Orphan's, The Next Generation. "End the Telethon." Accessed January 21, 2021. https://endthetelethon.com/faq/.

Jimenez, Terese C., Victoria I. Graf, and Ernest Rose. "Gaining Access to General Education: The Promise of Universal Design for Learning." *Issues in Teacher Education* 16 (Fall 2007): 41–54.

Johanson, Richard, Mary NewBurn, and Alison Macfarlane. "Has the Medicalisation of Childbirth Gone too Far?" *BMJ* 324 (2002): 892–895. https://doi.org/10.1136/bmj.324.7342.892.

Jones, Abeni. "Beyond Self-Care Bubble Baths: A Vision for Community Care." *Autostraddle*, July 20, 2017. https://www.autostraddle.com/on-being-a-burden -whats-missing-from-the-conversation-around-self-care-385525/comment-page-1/ #comment-1093748.

Jones, Abeni. "How to Take Care of Each Other: Community Care in Times of Crisis." *Autostraddle*, June 8, 2020. https://www.autostraddle.com/how-to-take -care-of-each-other-community-care-in-times-of-crisis-425239/.

Jones, Kathleen. "'Mother Made Me Do It': Mother-Blaming and the Women of the Child Guidance Movement." In *"Bad" Mothers: The Politics of Blame in Twentieth-Century America*, edited by Molly Ladd-Taylor and Lauri Umansky, 99–126. New York: New York University Press, 1998.

Jones, Monique. "Exclusive Interview: #DisabilityTooWhite Creator Vilissa Thompson." *Just Add Color*, May 24, 2016. http://colorwebmag.com/2016/05/24/ exclusive-interview-disabilitytoowhite-creator-vilissa-thompson/.

Jung, E. Alex. "Micah Fowler on Booking His *Speechless* Role and Playing a Character with More Severe Cerebral Palsy Than Himself." *Vulture*, December 7, 2016. http://www.vulture.com/2016/12/speechless-micah-fowler-interview. html.

Jung, Karen Elizabeth. "Chronic Illness and Educational Equity: The Politics of Visibility." In *Feminist Disability Studies*, edited by Kim Q. Hall, 263–286. Bloomington: Indiana University Press, 2011.

Kafai, Shayda. "The Mad Border Body: A Political In-betweenness." *Disability Studies Quarterly* 33:1 (2013). http://dsq-sds.org/article/view/3438/3199.

Kafer, Alison. *Feminist, Queer, Crip.* Bloomington: Indiana University Press, 2013.

Kafer, Alison. "Un/safe Disclosures: Scenes of Disability and Trauma." *Journal of Literary & Cultural Disability Studies* 10:1 (March 2016): 1–20. https://doi.org/10 .3828/jlcds.2016.1.

Kama, Amit. "Supercrips versus the Pitiful Handicapped: Reception of Disabling Images by Disabled Audience Members." *Communications* 29:4 (2004): 447–466. https://doi.org/10.1515/comm.2004.29.4.447.

Kanner, Leo. "Autistic Disturbances of Affective Contact." *Nervous Child: Journal of Psychopathology, Psychotherapy, Mental Hygiene, and Guidance of the Child* 2 (1943): 217–250.

Kanner, Leo. "Problems of Nosology and Psychodynamics of Early Infantile Autism." *American Journal of Orthopsychiatry* 19 (1949): 416–426.

Kanner, Leo. "To What Extent Is Early Infantile Autism Determined by Constitutional Inadequacies?" *Research Publications-Association for Research in Nervous and Mental Disease* 33 (1954): 378–385.

Karch, Andrew. *Early Start: Preschool Politics in the United States.* Ann Arbor: University of Michigan Press, 2013.

Kedar, Ido. "No, I'm Not a Horse: A Refutation of the Clever Hans Comparison to Autistic Typers." *Ido in Autismland*, April 21, 2016. http://idoinautismland.com/ ?cat=9.

Kedar, Ido. "Struggling for Self Control in a Sensory Overwhelming World." *Ido in Autismland*, April 2, 2012. http://idoinautismland.com/?cat=106.

Kemp, Jr., Evan. "Aiding the Disabled: No Pity, Please." *The New York Times*, September 3, 1981. https://www.nytimes.com/1981/09/03/opinion/aiding-the-d isabled-no-pity-please.html.

Kerschbaum, Stephanie. "On Rhetorical Agency and Disclosing Disability in Academic Writing." *Rhetoric Review* 33:1 (2014): 55–71. https://doi.org/10.1080 /07350198.2014.856730.

Kiley, Kathleen. "Activist & Writer Leroy Moore Jr. Brings 'Krip-Hop' to the Whitney." *The Huffington Post*, June 5, 2017. http://www.huffingtonpost.com/ entry/activist-writer-leroy-moore-jr-brings-krip-hop_us_592e379fe4b047e77e4 c3fa1.

Kirkby, Ryan J. "'The Revolution Will Not Be Televised': Community Activism and the Black Panther Party, 1966–1971." *Canadian Review of American Studies* 41:1 (2011): 25–62. https://doi.org/10.3138/cras.41.1.25.

Kisner, Jordan. "The Politics of Conspicuous Displays of Self-Care." *The New Yorker*, March 14, 2017. https://www.newyorker.com/culture/culture-desk/the-poli tics-of-selfcare.

Kittay, Eva Feder. "The Ethics of Care, Dependence, and Disability." *Ratio Juris* 24:1 (March 2011): 49–58. https://doi.org/10.1111/j.1467-9337.2010.00473.x.

Kittay, Eva Feder. "Forever Small: The Strange Case of Ashley X." *Hypatia* 26:3 (Summer 2011): 610–612. https://doi.org/10.1111/j.1527-2001.2011.01205.x.

Kleege, Georgina. *Sight Unseen*. New Haven and London: Yale University Press, 1999.

Kline, Wendy. *Bodies of Knowledge: Sexuality, Reproduction, and Women's Health in the Second Wave*. Chicago: University of Chicago Press, 2010.

Kluchin, Rebecca. *Fit to Be Tied: Sterilization and Reproductive Rights in America, 1950–1980*. New Jersey: Rutgers University Press, 2009.

Knoll, Kristina. "Feminist Disability Studies Pedagogy." *Feminist Teacher* 19:2 (2009): 122–133.

Kopp, Svenny and Christopher Gillberg. "The Autism Spectrum Screening Questionnaire (ASSQ)-Revised Extended Version (ASSQ-REV): An Instrument for Better Capturing the Autism Phenotype in Girls?" *Research in Developmental Disabilities* 32:6 (November-December, 2011): 2875–2888. https://doi.org/10.1 016/j.ridd.2011.05.017.

Kothari, Radha, David Skuse, Justin Wakefield, and Nadia Micali. "Gender Differences in the Relationship between Social Communication and Emotion Recognition." *Journal of the American Academy of Child and Adolescent Psychology* 52 (November 2013): 1148–1157. https://doi.org/10.1016/j.jaac.2013 .08.006.

Kras, Joseph. "The Ransom Notes Affair: When the Neurodiversity Movement Came of Age." *Disability Studies Quarterly* 30:1 (2010). http://dsq-sds.org/article/view /1065.

Krauthammer, Charles. "Restoration, Reality and Christopher Reeve." *Time*, February 14, 2000. http://content.time.com/time/magazine/article/0,9171,996064,00.html.

Krip-Hop Nation. "What is the Krip-Hop Nation?" Accessed August 2, 2017. http:// kriphopnation.com.

Kuppers, Petra. "Crip Time." *Tikkun* 29:4 (2014): 29–31. https://doi.org/10.1215/0 8879982-2810062.

Kurchak, Sarah. "I'm Autistic, and Believe Me, It's a Lot Better Than Measles." *Archipelago*, February 6, 2015. https://medium.com/the-archipelago/im-autistic -and-believe-me-its-a-lot-better-than-measles-78cb039f4bea.

Kurtts, Stephanie. "Universal Design for Learning in Inclusive Classrooms." *Electronic Journal for Inclusive Education* 1 (Spring 2006): 1–16. http://corescho lar.libraries.wright.edu/cgi/viewcontent.cgi?article=1071&context=ejie.

Ladd-Taylor, Molly. "Contraception or Eugenics? Sterilization and 'Mental Retardation' in the 1970s and 1980s." *CBMH/BCHM* 31:1 (2014): 192–193. https://doi.org/10.3138/cbmh.31.1.189.

Ladd-Taylor, Molly. *Fixing the Poor: Eugenic Sterilization and Child Welfare in the Twentieth Century*. Baltimore: Johns Hopkins University Press, 2017.

Ladd-Taylor, Molly and Lauri Umansky, eds. *"Bad" Mothers: The Politics of Blame in Twentieth-Century America*. New York: New York University Press, 1988.

Lamm, Nomy. "This is Disability Justice." *The Body is Not an Apology*, September 2, 2015. https://thebodyisnotanapology.com/magazine/this-is-disability-justice/.

Lamp, Sharon. "'It is for the Mother': Feminists' Rhetorics of Disability during the American Eugenics Period." *Disability Studies Quarterly* 26:4 (2006). https://dsq -sds.org/article/view/807.

Landsman, Gail. *Reconstructing Motherhood and Disability in an Age of "Perfect" Babies*. New York City: Routledge, 2009.

Langan, Mary. "Parental Voices and Controversies in Autism." *Disability & Society* 26:2 (2011): 193–205. https://doi.org/10.1080/09687599.2011.544059.

Lawrence, Briana. "Sia Gives a Master Class on How Not to Handle Valid Criticism From, Well, Anyone (but Especially Marginalized Groups)." *The Mary Sue*, November 20, 2020. https://www.themarysue.com/sia-music-film-criticism/.

Lechtenberger, DeAnn and William Lan. "Accommodation Strategies of College Students with Disabilities." *The Qualitative Report* 15:2 (2010): 411–429. http:// www.nova.edu/ssss/QR/QR15-2/barnard-brak.pdf.

Lee, Chana Kai. *For Freedom's Sake: The Life of Fannie Lou Hamer*. Urbana: University of Illinois Press, 1999.

Leigh, Vanessa. "Critical Conversations: Lydia X. Z. Brown on Ableism and the New Anthology *All the Weight of Our Dreams*." *Adios Barbie*, July 18, 2016. http: //www.adiosbarbie.com/2016/07/critical-conversations-lydia-x-z-brown-on-abl eism-and-the-new-anthology-all-the-weigh-of-our-dreams/.

Lewiecki-Wilson, Cynthia. "Rethinking Rhetoric through Mental Disabilities." *Rhetoric Review* 22:2 (2003): 156–167.

Lewiecki-Wilson, Cynthia. "Uneasy Subjects: Disability, Feminism, and Abortion." In *Disability and Mothering: Liminal Spaces of Embodied Knowledge*, edited by Cynthia Lewiecki-Wilson and Jen Cellio, 63–78. Syracuse: Syracuse University Press, 2011.

Lewiecki-Wilson, Cynthia and Jen Cellio. "Introduction: On Liminality and Cultural Embodiment." In *Disability and Mothering: Liminal Spaces of Embodied*

Knowledge, edited by Cynthia Lewiecki-Wilson and Jen Cellio, 1–15. Syracuse: Syracuse University Press, 2011.

Lewis, Talila. "Emmett Till and the Pervasive Erasure of Disability in Conversations about White Supremacy and Police Violence." *Talila A. Lewis*, January 28, 2017. https://www.talilalewis.com/blog/emmett-till-disability-erasure.

Li, Johanna. "Man Proposes to Girlfriend and Her Sister, Who Has Down Syndrome." *Inside Edition*, July 5, 2017. http://www.insideedition.com/headlines/24315-man-p roposes-to-girlfriend-and-her-sister-who-has-down-syndrome.

Liebowitz, Cara. "Redefining Inclusion." *That Crazy Crippled Chick*, June 20, 2011. http://thatcrazycrippledchick.blogspot.com/2011/06/redefining-inclusion.html.

Linton, Kristen Faye. "Interpersonal Violence and Traumatic Brain Injuries among Native Americans and Women." *Brain Injury* 29:5 (2015): 639–643. https://doi.org /10.3109/02699052.2014.989406.

Linton, Kristen F. and Bum Jung Kim. "Traumatic Brain Injury as a Result of Violence in Native American and Black Communities Spanning from Childhood to Older Adulthood." *Brain Injury* 28:8 (2014): 1076–1081. https://doi.org/10.3109 /02699052.2014.901558.

Linton, Simi. *Claiming Disability*. New York: New York University Press, 1998.

Little People of America. "What is LPA?" Accessed August 1, 2019. https://www .lpaonline.org/about-lpa_.

"Live Fully." *Weight Watchers*. Accessed June 10, 2017. https://www.weightwatcher s.com/us/article/live-fully.

Livingston, Gretchen and Deja Thomas. "Among 41 Countries, Only U.S. Lacks Paid Parental Leave." *Pew Research Center*, December 16, 2019. https://www.pewresea rch.org/fact-tank/2019/12/16/u-s-lacks-mandated-paid-parental-leave/.

Loftis, Sonya. *Imagining Autism: Fiction and Stereotypes on the Spectrum*. Bloomington: Indiana University Press, 2014.

Longmore, Paul. *Telethons: Spectacle, Disability, and the Business of Charity*. New York: Oxford University Press, 2016.

Longmore, Paul K. and David Goldberger. "The League of the Physically Handicapped and the Great Depression: A Case Study in the New Disability History." *The Journal of American History* 87:3 (December 2000): 888–922. https://doi.org/10 .2307/2675276.

Lorde, Audre. *A Burst of Light and Other Essays*. Mineola, NY: Ixia Press, 2017.

Lorde, Audre. *Sister Outsider*. New York: Crossing Press, 1984.

Lovaas, O. Ivar, Benson Schaeffer, and James Q. Simmons. "Building Social Behavior in Autistic Children by Use of Electric Shock." *Journal of Experimental Research in Personality* 1 (1965): 99–109.

Love, Heather. *Feeling Backward: Loss and the Politics of Queer History*. Cambridge: Harvard University Press, 2007.

Lynn, Mahdia. "Here's What Transgender People with Disabilities Want You to Know." *BuzzFeed*, August 19, 2017. https://www.buzzfeed.com/mahdialynn/heres -what-disabled-transgender-people-want-you-to-know.

Madsen, Kreesten Meldgaard, Anders Hviid, Mogens Vestergaard, Diana Schendel, Jan Wohlfahrt, Poul Thorsen, Jørn Olsen, and Mads Melbye. "A Population-Based

Study of Measles, Mumps, and Rubella Vaccination and Autism." *The New England Journal of Medicine* 347:19 (November 7, 2002): 1477–1482. https://ww w.nejm.org/doi/pdf/10.1056/NEJMoa021134.

Maholmes, Valerie and Fay Brown. "Over-representation of African-American Students in Special Education: The Role of a Developmental Framework in Shaping Teachers' Interpretations of African-American Students' Behavior." *Trotter Review* 14 (January 1, 2002): 45–59. https://scholarworks.umb.edu/trotte r_review/vol14/iss1/6.

Mairs, Nancy. *Plaintext*. Tucson: University of Arizona Press, 1986.

Malik, Rasheed, Katie Hamm, Maryam Adamu, and Taryn Morrissey. "Child Care Deserts: An Analysis of Child Care Centers by ZIP Code in 8 States." *Center for American Progress*, October 27, 2016. https://www.americanprogress.org/issues/ early-childhood/reports/2016/10/27/225703/child-care-deserts/.

Maloney, Beth Alison. *Saving Sammy: A Mother's Fight to Cure Her Son's OCD*. New York: Three Rivers Press, 2009.

Mandell, David S., John Listerud, Susan Levy, and Jennifer A. Pinto-Martin. "Race Differences in the Age at Diagnosis among Medicaid-Eligible Children with Autism." *Journal of the American Academy of Child and Adolescent Psychiatry* 41:12 (December 2002): 1447–1453. https://doi.org/10.1097/00004583-2002120 00-00016.

Mandell, David S., Lisa D. Wiggins, Laura Arnstein Carpenter, Julie Daniels, Carolyn DiGuiseppi, Maureen S. Durkin, Ellen Giarelli, Michael J. Morrier, Joyce S. Nicholas, Jennifer A. Pinto-Martin, et al. "Racial/Ethnic Disparities in the Identification of Children with Autism Spectrum Disorders." *American Journal of Public Health* 99:3 (2009): 493–498. https://doi.org/10.2105/AJPH.2007.131243.

March, John. *Talking Back to OCD: The Program That Helps Kids and Teens Say "No Way"—and Parents Say "Way to Go."* New York: The Guilford Press, 2006.

March, John S., Martin Franklin, Aimee Nelson, and Edna Foa. "Cognitive-Behavioral Psychotherapy for Pediatric Obsessive-Compulsive Disorder." *Journal of Clinical Child & Adolescent Psychology* 30:1 (2001): 8–18. https://doi.org/10.1 207/S15374424JCCP3001_3.

Marshak, Laura, Todd Van Wieren, Dianne Ferrell, Lindsay Swiss, and Catherine Dugan. "Exploring Barriers to College Student Use of Disability Services and Accommodations." *Journal of Postsecondary Education and Disability* 22:3 (2010): 151–165. http://www.eric.ed.gov/PDFS/EJ906688.pdf.

Matthews, Malcolm. "Why Sheldon Cooper Can't Be Black: The Visual Rhetoric of Autism and Ethnicity." *Journal of Literary & Cultural Disability Studies* 13:1 (2019): 57–74. https://doi.org/10.3828/jlcds.2019.4.

Matthews, Nicole. "Teaching the 'Invisible' Disabled Students in the Classroom: Disclosure, Inclusion and the Social Model of Disability." *Teaching in Higher Education* 14:3 (2009): 229–239. https://doi.org/10.1080/13562510902898809.

Mattlin, Ben. "Cure Me? No, Thanks." *The New York Times*, March 22, 2017. https://www.nytimes.com/2017/03/22/opinion/cure-me-no-thanks.html.

Mattlin, Ben. "'Me Before You' Perpetuates the Idea That the Disabled Should Consider Suicide." *The Chicago Tribune*, May 31, 2016. http://www.chicagotr

ibune.com/news/opinion/commentary/ct-suicide-disability-me-before-you-perspec
-0601-md-20160531-story.html.

Maybee, Julie. "The Political Is Personal: Mothering at the Intersection of Acquired Disability, Gender, and Race." In *Disability and Mothering: Liminal Spaces of Embodied Knowledge*, edited by Cynthia Lewiecki-Wilson and Jen Cellio, 245–259. Syracuse: Syracuse University Press, 2011.

Mayes, Rick, Jennifer L. Erkulwater, and Catherine Bagwell. "Medicating Children: The Enduring Controversy over ADHD and Pediatric Stimulant Pharmacotherapy." *Child and Adolescent Psychopharmacology News* 13:5 (2008): 1–5, 9. https:// scholarship.richmond.edu/cgi/viewcontent.cgi?article=1063&context=polisci-fac ulty-publications.

McCarthy, Jenny, ed. *Mother Warriors: A Nation of Parents Healing Autism against All Odds*. New York: Penguin Group, 2008.

McFayden, Tyler, Jordan Albright, Ashley Muskett, and Angela Scarpa. "Brief Report: Sex Differences in ASD Diagnosis—A Brief Report on Restricted Interests and Repetitive Behaviors." *Journal of Autism and Developmental Disorders* 49:4 (April 2019): 1693–1699. https://doi.org/10.1007/s10803-018 -3838-9.

McGregor, Karla, Natalie Langenfeld, Sam Van Horne, Jacob Oleson, Matthew Anson, and Wayne Jacobson. "The University Experience of Students with Learning Disabilities." *Learning Disabilities Research & Practice* 31:2 (2016): 90–102. https://doi.org/10.1111/ldrp.12102.

McLeod, Jane, Danielle L. Fettes, Peter S. Jensen, Bernice A. Pescosolido, and Jack K. Martin. "Public Knowledge, Beliefs, and Treatment Preferences Concerning Attention-Deficit Hyperactivity Disorder." *Psychiatric Services* 58:5 (2007): 626–631.

McPartland, James C., Brian Reichow, and Fred R. Volkmar. "Sensitivity and Specificity of Proposed DSM-5 Diagnostic Criteria for Autism Spectrum Disorder." *Journal of the American Academy of Child & Adolescent Psychiatry* 51:4 (April 2012): 368–383. https://doi.org/10.1016/j.jaac.2012.01.007.

McRuer, Robert. *Crip Theory: Cultural Signs of Queerness and Disability*. New York: New York University Press, 2006.

McRuer, Robert. *Crip Times: Disability, Globalization, and Resistance*. New York: New York University Press, 2018.

Meyer, Anne, David Rose, and David Gordon. *Universal Design for Learning: Theory and Practice*. Wakefield, MA: CAST, Inc., 2014.

Michel, Sonya. *Children's Interests/Mothers' Rights: The Shaping of America's Childcare Policy*. New Haven: Yale University Press, 1999.

Miller, Andrew. "Personalising Ethnography: On Memory, Evidence, and Subjectivity: The Writing and Learning Journey." *New Writing* 5:2 (September 2008): 89–113. https://doi.org/10.1080/14790720802209971.

Miller, Lucy Jane. *Sensational Kids: Hope and Help for Children with Sensory Processing Disorder*. New York: Perigee, 2014.

Miller, Terri Beth. "Stalking Grendel's Mother: Biomedicine and the Disciplining of the Deviant Body." In *Disability and Mothering: Liminal Spaces of Embodied*

Knowledge, edited by Cynthia Lewiecki-Wilson and Jen Cellio, 49–62. Syracuse: Syracuse University Press, 2011.

Milner, Paul and Berni Kelly. "Community Participation and Inclusion: People with Disabilities Defining Their Place." *Disability & Society* 24:1 (2009): 47–62. https://doi.org/10.1080/09687590802535410.

Mingus, Mia. "Access Intimacy, Interdependence, and Disability Justice." *Leaving Evidence*. Accessed November 3, 2018. https://leavingevidence.wordpress.com/2017/04/12/access-intimacy-interdependence-and-disability-justice/.

Mingus, Mia. "Access Intimacy: The Missing Link." *Leaving Evidence*, May 5, 2011. https://leavingevidence.wordpress.com/2011/05/05/access-intimacy-the-missing-link/.

Mingus, Mia. "Changing the Framework: Disability Justice." *Leaving Evidence*, February 12, 2011. https://leavingevidence.wordpress.com/2011/02/12/changing-the-framework-disability-justice/.

Minh-ha, Trinh T. *Framer Framed*. New York: Routledge, 1991.

Mink, Gwendolyn. *Welfare's End*. Ithaca, NY: Cornell University Press, 1998.

Mitchell, David and Sharon Snyder. *The Biopolitics of Disability: Neoliberalism, Ablenationalism, and Peripheral Embodiments*. Ann Arbor: University of Michigan Press, 2015.

Mitchell, David and Sharon Snyder. *Narrative Prosthesis: Disability and the Dependencies of Discourse*. Ann Arbor: University of Michigan Press, 2001.

Mitchell, David, Sharon Snyder, and Linda Ware. "'Every Child Left Behind': Curricular Cripistemologies and the Crip/Queer Art of Failure." *Journal of Literary & Cultural Disability Studies* 8:3 (2014): 295–313. https://doi.org/10.3828/jlcds.2014.24.

Mollayeva, Tatyana, Graziella El-Khechen-Richandi, and Angela Colantonio. "Sex and Gender Considerations in Concussion Research." *Concussion* 3:1 (January 18, 2018). https://doi.org/10.2217/cnc-2017-0015.

Mollow, Anna. "Criphystemologies: What Disability Theory Needs to Know about Hysteria." *Journal of Literary & Cultural Disability Studies* 8:2 (2014): 185–201. https://doi.org/10.3828/jlcds.2014.15.

Mollow, Anna. "Identity Politics and Disability Studies: A Critique of Recent Theory." *Michigan Quarterly Review* 43:2 (Spring 2004). http://hdl.handle.net/2027/spo.act2080.0043.218.

Mollow, Anna. "'When Black Women Start Going on Prozac': Race, Gender, and Mental Illness in Meri Nana-Ama Danquah's *Willow Weep for Me*." *MELUS* 31:3 (Fall 2006): 67–99. https://doi.org/10.1093/melus/31.3.67.

Montgomery, Cal. "Defining Autistic Lives." *Ragged Edge Online*, June 30, 2005. http://www.raggededgemagazine.com/reviews/ckmontrubin0605.html.

Moran, Meghan Bridgid, Melissa Lucas, Kristen Everhart, Ashley Morgan, and Erin Prickett. "What Makes Anti-Vaccine Websites Persuasive? A Content Analysis of Techniques Used by Anti-Vaccine Websites to Engender Anti-Vaccine Sentiment." *Journal of Communication in Healthcare* 9:3 (2016): 151–163. https://doi.org/10.1080/17538068.2016.1235531.

Morgan, Rachel and Jennifer Truman. *Criminal Victimization, 2019* (U.S. Department of Justice Bureau of Justice Statistics, NCJ No. 255113, September 2020): 1–51. https://www.bjs.gov/content/pub/pdf/cv19.pdf.

Morrison, Daniel R. and Monica J. Casper. "Intersections of Disability Studies and Critical Trauma Studies: A Provocation." *Disability Studies Quarterly* 32:2 (2012). http://dsq-sds.org/article/view/3189/3073.

Mukherjee, Debjani, Judy Panko Reis, and Wendy Heller. "Women Living with Traumatic Brain Injury." *Women & Therapy* 26:1–2 (2003): 3–26. https://doi.org/10.1300/J015v26n01_01.

Mulderink, Elizabeth. "The Emergence, Importance of #DisabilityTooWhite Hashtag." *Disability Studies Quarterly* 40:2 (2020). https://dsq-sds.org/article/view/6484/5565.

Muncey, Tessa. "Doing Autoethnography." *International Journal of Qualitative Methods* 4:3 (2005): 69–86. https://doi.org/10.1177/160940690500400105.

Muñoz, José Esteban. *Cruising Utopia: The Then and There of Queer Futurity*. New York: New York University Press, 2009.

Murray, Stuart. "Autism Functions/The Function of Autism." *Disability Studies Quarterly* 30:1 (2010). https://dsq-sds.org/article/view/1048/1229.

Muscular Dystrophy Association. "MDA History." Accessed November 14, 2018. https://www.mda.org/about-mda/history.

Narby, Caroline. "Double Rainbow: Asperger's and Girls." *Bitch Media,* February 7, 2012. https://www.bitchmedia.org/post/double-rainbow-aspergers-and-girls-feminism-autism-books.

Narby, Caroline. "Double Rainbow: Parent Guides, Part 1." *Bitch Media*, February 17, 2012. https://www.bitchmedia.org/post/double-rainbow-parent-guides-part-1-feminism.

National Alliance for Caregiving. "Caregivers of Children: A Focused Look at Those Caring for A Child with Special Needs Under the Age of 18." November 2009. http://www.caregiving.org/data/Report_Caregivers_of_Children_11-12-09.pdf.

National Alliance on Mental Illness. "Mental Health by the Numbers." Accessed April 22, 2019. https://www.nami.org/Learn-More/Mental-Health-By-the-Numbers.

National Autistic Society. "Gender and Autism." Accessed October 4, 2018. https://www.autism.org.uk/about/what-is/gender.aspx.

National Center on Universal Design for Learning. "Universal Design for Learning Guidelines." *CAST.* Accessed March 28, 2015. http://www.udlcenter.org/aboutudl/udlguidelines_theorypractice.

National Council on Disability. "Rocking the Cradle: Ensuring the Rights of Parents with Disabilities and Their Children." September 27, 2012. https://www.ncd.gov/sites/default/files/Documents/NCD_Parenting_508_0.pdf.

National Education Association. "Special Education." Accessed January 13, 2021. https://www.nea.org/student-success/smart-just-policies/special-education.

National Education Association. "Truth in Labeling: Disproportionality in Special Education." December 15, 2007. http://www.nea.org/assets/docs/HE/EW-TruthInLabeling.pdf.

National Scientific Council on the Developing Child. *Early Experiences Can Alter Gene Expression and Affect Long-Term Development: Working Paper No. 10.* Harvard University: Center on the Developing Child, 2010. https://developingch ild.harvard.edu/wp-content/uploads/2010/05/Early-Experiences-Can-Alter-Gene -Expression-and-Affect-Long-Term-Development.pdf.

Ne'eman, Ari. "The Future (and the Past) of Autism Advocacy, Or Why the ASA's Magazine, *The Advocate*, Wouldn't Publish This Piece." *Disability Studies Quarterly* 30:1 (2010). http://dsq-sds.org/article/view/1059/1244.

Nelson, Camille A. "Frontlines: Policing at the Nexus of Race and Mental Health." *Fordham Urban Law Journal* 43:4 (2016): 615–684. https://ir.lawnet.fordham.edu/ ulj/vol43/iss3/4.

Nelson, Jennifer. *More Than Medicine: A History of the Feminist Women's Health Movement.* New York: New York University Press, 2015.

Neuman, William. *Social Research Methods: Qualitative and Quantitative Approaches.* Needham Heights, MA: Allyn and Bacon, 1994.

Noltemeyer, Amity and Caven McLoughlin, eds. *Disproportionality in Education and Special Education: A Guide to Creating More Equitable Learning Environments.* Springfield: Charles C. Thomas Publishing, 2012.

Norman, Larry. "I Wish We'd All Been Ready." Track 4 side 2 of *Upon this Rock.* Capitol Records, 1969.

Norsigian, Judy. "Our Bodies, Ourselves: Pregnancy and Birth." *Our Bodies, Ourselves.* Accessed December 12, 2018. https://www.ourbodiesourselves.org/ publications/pregnancy-and-birth/.

Not Dead Yet. "Who We Are." Accessed August 1, 2019. http://notdeadyet.org/ about.

O'Connor, Carla and Sonia DeLuca Fernandez. "Race, Class, and Disproportionality: Reevaluating the Relationship between Poverty and Special Education Placement." *Educational Researcher* 35:6 (Aug/September 2006): 6–11.

Office of Research on Women's Health. "Including Women and Minorities in Clinical Research Background." National Institutes of Health. Accessed September 25, 2020. https://orwh.od.nih.gov/womens-health/clinical-research-trials/nih-inc lusion-policies/including-women-and-minorities.

Office of the Surgeon General (U.S.), Office of Disease Prevention and Health Promotion (U.S.), Centers for Disease Control and Prevention (U.S.), National Institutes of Health (U.S.). "The Surgeon General's Call To Action To Prevent and Decrease Overweight and Obesity." Office of the Surgeon General, 2001. Accessed July 31, 2019. https://www.ncbi.nlm.nih.gov/books/NBK44210/.

Oleny, Marjorie and Karin Brockelman. "Out of the Disability Closet: Strategic Use of Perception Management by Select University Students with Disabilities." *Disability & Society* 18:1 (2003): 35–50. https://doi.org/10.1080/713662200.

Oliver, Michael. *The Politics of Disablement: A Sociological Approach.* New York: St. Martin's, 1990.

Olmstead v. L.C. 527 U.S. 581 (1999).

Omar, Samira, Llana James, Angela Colantonio, and Stephanie A. Nixon. "Integrated Care Pathways for Black Persons with Traumatic Brain Injury: A Protocol for a

Critical Transdisciplinary Scoping Review." *Systematic Reviews* 9:124 (2020): 1–12. https://doi.org/10.1186/s13643-020-01323-8.

O'Neil, John. "Can Inclusion Work?" A Conversation with Jim Kauffman and Mara Sapon-Shevin." *Educational Leadership* 52 (December 1994/January 1995): 7–11. http://www.ascd.org/publications/educational_leadership/dec94/vol52/num04/Can_Inclusion_Work¢_A_Conversation_with_Jim_Kauffman_and_Mara_Sapon-Shevin.aspx.

Opar, Alisa. "The Seekers: Why Parents Try Fringe Therapies for Autism." *Spectrum*, September 21, 2016. https://www.spectrumnews.org/features/deep-dive/the-seekers-parents-who-find-fringe-therapies-for-autism/.

Organisation for Economic Cooperation and Development. *OECD Economic Surveys: United States 2018.* Paris: OECD Publishing, 2018. https://dx.doi.org/10.1787/eco_surveys-usa-2018-en.

Osborne, Tanya. "Not Lazy, Not Faking: Teaching and Learning Experiences of University Students with Disabilities." *Disability & Society* 34:2 (2019): 228–252. https://doi.org/10.1080/09687599.2018.1515724.

Osterman, Michelle and Joyce Martin. "Trends in Low-risk Cesarean Delivery in the United States, 1990–2013." *National Vital Statistics Reports* 63:6 (November 5, 2014): 1–15. https://www.cdc.gov/nchs/data/nvsr/nvsr63/nvsr63_06.pdf.

Oswald, Donald, Al Best, Martha Coutinho, and Heather Nagle. "Trends in the Special Education Identification Rates of Boys and Girls: A Call for Research and Change." *Exceptionality* 11 (2003): 223–237.

O'Toole, Corbett Joan. "Disclosing Our Relationships to Disabilities: An Invitation for Disability Studies Scholars." *Disability Studies Quarterly* 33:2 (2013). http://dsq-sds.org/article/view/3708/3226.

O'Toole, Corbett Joan. "Sex, Disability and Motherhood: Access to Sexuality for Disabled Mothers." *Disability Studies Quarterly* 22:4 (2002). http://dsq-sds.org/article/view/374/495.

Otterman, Sharon. "New Library Is a $41.5 Million Masterpiece. But about Those Stairs." *The New York Times*, November 5, 2019. https://www.nytimes.com/2019/11/05/nyregion/long-island-city-library.html.

Ozonoff, Sally. *A Parent's Guide to Asperger Syndrome and High-Functioning Autism.* New York: The Guilford Press, 2002.

"Passing for Neurotypical." *Learn from Autistics*, October 27, 2015. https://www.learnfromautistics.com/passing-for-neurotypical/.

Patsavas, Alyson. "Recovering a Cripistemology of Pain: Leaky Bodies, Connective Tissue, and Feeling Discourse." *Journal of Literary & Cultural Disability Studies* 8:2 (2014): 203–218. https://doi.org/10.3828/jlcds.2014.16.

Pavelko, Rachelle and Jessica Myrick. "Tweeting and Trivializing: How the Trivialization of Obsessive–Compulsive Disorder via Social Media Impacts User Perceptions, Emotions, and Behaviors." *Imagination, Cognition and Personality* 36:1 (2016): 41–63. https://doi.org/10.1177/0276236615598957.

Peace, William. Blog Posts on Christopher Reeve. *Bad Cripple.* Accessed August 1, 2019. http://badcripple.blogspot.com/search?q=christopher+reeve.

Pearson, Holly and Lisa Boskovich. "Problematizing Disability Disclosure in Higher Education: Shifting Towards a Liberating Humanizing Intersectional Framework." *Disability Studies Quarterly* 39:1 (2019). https://dsq-sds.org/article/view/6001/51 87.

Perry, David M. and Lawrence Carter-Long. *The Ruderman White Paper on Media Coverage of Law Enforcement Use of Force and Disability: A Media Study (2013–2015) and Overview.* Newton, MA: Ruderman Family Foundation, 2016. http://www. rudermanfoundation.org/news-and-events/ruderman- white-paper.

Phillips, Phillip. "Home." Track 2 on *The World from the Side of the Moon.* Interscope Records, 2012.

Piechura-Couture, Kathy, Elizabeth Heins, and Mercedes Tichenor. "The Boy Factor: Can Single-Gender Classes Reduce the Overrepresentation of Boys in Special Education?" *College Student Journal* 47:2 (Summer 2013): 235–243.

Piepmeier, Alison. "Saints, Sages, and Villains: Endorsement of and Resistance to Cultural Stereotypes in Memoirs by Parents of Children with Disabilities." *Disability Studies Quarterly* 32:1 (2012). http://doi.org/10.18061/dsq.v32i1 .3031.

Piepmeier, Alison, Amber Cantrell, and Ashley Maggio. "Disability Is a Feminist Issue: Bringing Together Women's and Gender Studies and Disability Studies." *Disability Studies Quarterly* 34:2 (2014). http://dsq-sds.org/article/view/4252/3592.

Pittenger, Christopher, Ben Kelmendi, Michael Bloch, John H. Krystal, and Vladimir Coric. "Clinical Treatment of Obsessive Compulsive Disorder." *Psychiatry* 2:11 (2005): 34–43. https://www.ncbi.nlm.nih.gov/pmc/articles/PMC2993523/?report =classic.

Pitts-Taylor, Victoria. "The Plastic Brain: Neoliberalism and the Neuronal Self." *Health* 14:6 (2010): 635–652. https://doi.org/10.1177/1363459309360796.

"Please Stop Saying 'Wheelchair Bound.'" *Free Wheelin': Life and Travel with a Disability,* November 4, 2016. http://www.freewheelintravel.org/please-stop-sayin g-wheelchair-bound/.

Plous, Scott and Tyrone Williams. "Racial Stereotypes from the Days of American Slavery: A Continuing Legacy." *Journal of Applied Social Psychology* 25:9 (1995): 795–817. https://doi.org/10.1111/j.1559-1816.1995.tb01776.x.

Poonam, Dev and Leslie Haynes. "Teacher Perspectives on Suitable Learning Environments for Students with Disabilities: What Have We Learned from Inclusive, Resource, and Self-Contained Classrooms?" *International Journal of Interdisciplinary Social Sciences* 9 (May 2015): 53–64.

Powell, Robyn. "How We Treat Disabled Mothers." *Medium,* May 11, 2017. https ://medium.com/the-establishment/how-we-treat-disabled-mothers-a765ed94e95a.

Powell, Robyn. "The Women with Disabilities Who Fought for Your Health Care This Year." *Vice,* December 20, 2017. https://broadly.vice.com/en_us/article/w jp5px/the-women-with-disabilities-who-fought-for-your-health-care-this-year.

"Pregnant Women's High-Fat, High-Sugar Diets May Affect Future Generations." *Science News,* June 16, 2016. https://www.sciencedaily.com/releases/2016/06 /160616141336.htm.

Prendergast, Catherine. "On the Rhetorics of Mental Disability." In *Towards a Rhetoric of Everyday Life*, edited by Martin Nystrand and John Duffy, 189–207. Madison: The University of Wisconsin Press, 2003.

Price, Margaret. "The Bodymind Problem and the Possibilities of Pain." *Hypatia* 30:1 (Winter 2015): 268–284. https://doi.org/10.1111/hypa.12127.

Price, Margaret. *Mad at School: Rhetorics of Mental Disability and Academic Life.* Ann Arbor: University of Michigan Press, 2011.

Prilletensky, Ora. "A Ramp to Motherhood: The Experiences of Mothers with Physical Disabilities." *Sexuality and Disability* 21:1 (2003): 21–47. https://doi.org/10.1023/A:1023558808891.

Prince-Hughes, Dawn. *Songs of the Gorilla Nation: My Journey through Autism.* New York: Three Rivers Press, 2004.

"Proceedings: Panel: Closing Plenary." *Disability History*. Accessed June 2, 2018. http://www.disabilityhistory.org/dwa/queer/panel_closing.html.

Prowse, S. "Institutional Construction of Disabled Students." *Journal of Higher Education Policy and Management* 31:1 (2009): 89–96. https://doi.org/10.1080/13600800802559302.

Puar, Jasbir. "Prognosis Time: Towards a Geopolitics of Affect, Debility, and Capacity." *Women and Performance: A Journal of Feminist Theory* 19:2 (2009): 161–172. https://doi.org/10.1080/07407700903034147.

Puar, Jasbir. *The Right to Maim: Debility, Capacity, Disability.* Durham: Duke University Press, 2017.

"Radical Self-Care: Angela Davis." *AFROPUNK*, December 17, 2018. https://www.youtube.com/watch?v=Q1cHoL4vaBs.

Rakes, H. "Crip Feminist Trauma Studies in Jessica Jones and Beyond." *Journal of Literary & Cultural Disability Studies* 13:1 (2019): 75–91. https://doi.org/10.3828/jlcds.2019.5.

Ramos, Eli. "Autism Speaks Doesn't Speak for Me." *Odyssey*, September 18, 2017. https://www.theodysseyonline.com/autism-speaks-doesnt-speak.

Rao, T.S. Sathyanarayana and Chittaranjan Andrade. "The MMR Vaccine and Autism: Sensation, Refutation, Retraction, and Fraud." *Indian Journal of Psychiatry* 53:2 (April-June 2011): 95–96. https://doi.org/10.4103/0019-5545.82529.

Ratto, Allison B., Lauren Kenworthy, Benjamin E. Yerys, Julia Bascom, Andrea Trubanova Wieckowski, Susan W. White, Gregory L. Wallace, Cara Pugliese, Robert T. Schultz, Thomas H. Ollendick, et al. "What About the Girls? Sex-Based Differences in Autistic Traits and Adaptive Skills." *Journal of Autism and Developmental Disorders* 48:5 (2018): 1698–1711. https://doi.org/10.1007/s10803-017-3413-9.

Ravitz, Jessica. "Gwyneth Paltrow's Goop Brand Hit with Penalties for 'Unsubstantiated Claims.'" *CNN*, September 5, 2018. https://www.cnn.com/2018/09/05/health/goop-fine-california-gwyneth-paltrow/index.html.

Rayne, Robyn. "Unlocked: The Lois Curtis Story." *Robin Rayne*, November 27, 2010. https://assignmentatlanta.wordpress.com/2010/11/27/unlocked-the-lois-curtis-story/.

Reid, D. Kim and Michelle Knight. "Disability Justifies the Exclusion of Minority Students: A Critical History Grounded in Disability Studies." *Educational Researcher* 35:6 (August/September 2006): 18–23.

Rekers, George and O. Ivar Lovaas. "Behavioral Treatment of Deviant Sex-Role Behaviors in a Male Child." *Journal of Applied Behavior Analysis* 7:2 (1974): 173–190. https://doi.org/10.1901/jaba.1974.7-173.

Renfrow, Daniel G. "A Cartography of Passing in Everyday Life." *Symbolic Interaction* 27:4 (2004): 485–506. https://doi.org/10.1525/si.2004.27.4.485.

Reynolds, Dave. "'Ashley Treatment Was Illegal,' Watchdog Group Says." *Inclusion Daily Express*, May 8, 2007. http://www.inclusiondaily.com/archives/07/05/09/05 0807waashleyx.htm.

Richardson, Cheryl. *The Art of Extreme Self-Care: Transform Your Life One Month at a Time.* Carlsbad, CA: Hay House, Inc, 2009.

Richardson, Sarah S., Cynthia R. Daniels, Matthew W. Gillman, Janet Golden, Rebecca Kukla, Christopher Kuzawa, and Janet Rich-Edwards. "Don't Blame the Mothers." *Nature* 512 (2014): 131–132. https://j.mp/2ozaF9A.

Ridgeway, Cecilia. *Framed by Gender: How Gender Inequality Persists in the Modern World.* New York: Oxford University Press, 2011.

Ridgway, Andrea. "A Response to 'The Controversy over Autism's Most Common Therapy.'" *Autism Spectrum Therapies*, August 29, 2016. http://autismtherapies.co m/blog/a-response-to-the-controversy-over-autisms-most-common-therapy/.

Roberts, Dorothy. *Killing the Black Body: Race, Reproduction, and the Meaning of Liberty.* New York: Pantheon Books, 1999.

Robison, John Elder. "I Resign My Roles at Autism Speaks." *Look Me in the Eye*, November 13, 2013. http://jerobison.blogspot.com/2013/11/i-resign-my-roles-at-a utism-speaks.html.

Robison, John Elder. "What is Neurodiversity?" *Psychology Today*, October 7, 2013. https://www.psychologytoday.com/blog/my-life-aspergers/201310/what-is-neuro diversity.

Romley, John A., Aakash K. Shah, Paul J. Chung, Marc N. Elliot, Katherine D. Vestal, and Mark A. Schuster. "Family-Provided Health Care for Children with Special Health Care Needs." *Pediatrics* 139:1 (January 2017): 1–10. https://doi.org /10.1542/peds.2016-1287.

Rose, David, Wendy Harbour, Catherine Sam Johnston, Samantha Daley, and Linda Abarbanell. "Universal Design for Learning in Postsecondary Education: Reflections on Principles and Their Application." *Journal of Postsecondary Education and Disability* 19 (Fall 2006): 135–151.

Rose, Nikolas. *The Politics of Life Itself: Biomedicine, Power, and Subjectivity in the Twenty-First Century.* Princeton: Princeton University Press, 2007.

Rosenberg, Tina. "Reducing Unnecessary C-Section Births." *The New York Times*, January 19, 2016. https://opinionator.blogs.nytimes.com/2016/01/19/arsdarian-c utting-the-number-of-c-section-births/.

Rosenblatt, Louise. *The Reader, the Text, the Poem: The Transactional Theory of the Literary Work.* Carbondale: Southern Illinois University Press, 1978.

Ross, Loretta and Rickie Solinger. *Reproductive Justice*. Oakland: University of California Press, 2017.

Rottenberg, Catherine. "How Neoliberalism Colonised Feminism—And What You Can Do About It." *The Conversation*, May 23, 2018. https://theconversation.com/how-neoliberalism-colonised-feminism-and-what-you-can-do-about-it-94856.

Rottenberg, Catherine. *The Rise of Neoliberal Feminism*. London: Oxford University Press, 2018.

Rozsa, Matthew. "Gender Stereotypes Have Made Us Horrible at Recognizing Autism in Women and Girls." *Quartz*, October 12, 2016. https://qz.com/804204/asd-in-girls-gender-stereotypes-have-made-us-horrible-at-recognizing-autism-in-women-and-girls/.

Rubin, Sue. "Acceptance versus Cure." *CNN*, 2005. Accessed January 30, 2021. https://www.cnn.com/CNN/Programs/presents/shows/autism.world/notebooks/sue/notebook.html.

Russell, Ginny. "Critques of the Neurodiversity Movement." In *Autistic Community and the Neurodiversity Movement,* edited by Steven Kapp, 287–303. Singapore: Palgrave Macmillan, 2020. https://doi.org/10.1007/978-981-13-8437-0_21.

Ryan, Sara and Katherine Runswick-Cole. "Repositioning Mothers: Mothers, Disabled Children, and Disability Studies." *Disability & Society* 23:3 (2008): 199–210. https://doi.org/10.1080/09687590801953937.

Rynkiewicz, Agnieszka, Erik Marchi, Björn Schuller, Stefano Piana, Antonio Camurri, Amandine Lassalle, and Simon Baron-Cohen. "An Investigation of the 'Female Camouflage Effect' in Autism Using a Computerized ADOS-2 and a Test of Sex/Gender Differences." *Molecular Autism* 7 (January 21, 2016): 1–8. https://doi.org/10.1186/s13229-016-0073-0.

Saggio, Jessica. "Disabled Teen Crowned Homecoming Queen in Awesome Way." *USA Today*, November 13, 2015. https://www.usatoday.com/story/news/humankind/2015/11/13/disabled-teen-crowned-homecoming-queen-awesome-way/75658376/.

Salend, Spencer and Laurel Garrick Dehaney. "The Impact of Inclusion on Students with and without Disabilities and Their Educators." *Remedial and Special Education* 20:2 (March/April 1999): 114–126. https://doi.org/10.1177/074193259902000209.

Samuels, Ellen. "My Body, My Closet: Invisible Disability and the Limits of Coming-Out Discourse." *GLQ: A Journal of Lesbian and Gay Studies* 9:1–2 (2003): 233–255.

Samuels, Ellen. "Passing, Coming Out, and Other Magical Acts." In *Negotiating Disability: Disclosure and Higher Education*, edited by Stephanie Kerschbaum, Laura Eisenmann, and James Jones, 15–24. Ann Arbor: University of Michigan Press, 2017.

Samuels, Ellen. "Six Ways of Looking at Crip Time." *Disability Studies Quarterly* 37:3 (2017). https://dsq-sds.org/article/view/5824/4684.

Sandahl, Carrie. "Queering the Crip or Cripping the Queer?: Intersections of Queer and Crip Identities in Solo Autobiographical Performance." *GLQ: A Journal of Lesbian and Gay Studies* 9 (April 1, 2003): 25–56. https://doi.org/10.1215/10642684-9-1-2-25.

Sandahl, Carrie. "Using Our Words: Exploring Representational Conundrums in Disability Drama and Performance." *Journal of Literary & Cultural Disability Studies* 12:2 (2018): 129–144. https://doi.org/10.3828/jlcds.2018.11.

Sanders, Lee. "Lois Curtis on Life after *Olmstead*." *Impact*. Accessed June 1, 2018. https://ici.umn.edu/products/impact/281/13.html.

Sapon-Shevin, Mara. "Inclusion: A Matter of Social Justice." *Educational Leadership* 61:2 (October 2003): 25–28.

Sauder, Kim. "Disabled People Don't Exist to Make You Look Good." *crippledscholar*, May 20, 2015. https://crippledscholar.com/tag/inspiration-porn/.

Sauder, Kim. "Inspiration Porn Is Not Progress, It's a New Kind of Oppression." *crippledscholar*, May 5, 2015. https://crippledscholar.com/tag/inspiration-porn/.

Sauder, Kim. "Media Roundup of Me before You Criticism." *crippledscholar*, May 28, 2016. https://crippledscholar.com/2016/05/28/media-roundup-of-me-before-you-criticism/.

Savarese, Emily Thorton and Ralph James Savarese. "The Superior Half of Speaking: An Introduction." *Disability Studies Quarterly* 30:1 (2010). https://dsq-sds.org/article/view/1062/1230.

Saxton, Marsha. "Born and Unborn: The Implications of Reproductive Technologies for People with Disabilities." In *Test-Tube Women: What Future For Motherhood?*, edited by Rita Arditti, Renate Duelli-Klein, and Shelley Minden, 298–312. London: Pandora Press, 1984.

Schalk, Sami. "Coming to Claim Crip: Disidentification with/in Disability Studies." *Disability Studies Quarterly* 33:2 (2013). http://dsq-sds.org/article/view/3705.

Schalk, Sami. "Reevaluating the Supercrip." *Journal of Literary & Cultural Disability Studies* 10:1 (January 2016): 71–86. https://doi.org/10.3828/jlcds.2016.5.

Scherman, Elizabeth. "The Speech That Didn't Fly: Polysemic Readings of Christopher Reeve's Speech to the 1996 Democratic National Convention." *Disability Studies Quarterly* 29:2 (2009). http://dsq-sds.org/article/view/918/1093.

Schulte, Brigid and Alieza Durana. "The Care Report." *New America*, September 2016. https://www.newamerica.org/in-depth/care-report/.

Schultz, Kirsten. "A Roundup of Posts Against Autism Speaks." *Medium*, March 29, 2017. https://medium.com/@KirstenSchultz/a-roundup-of-posts-against-autism-speaks-5dbf7f8cfcc6.

Schwarz, Alan. "The Selling of Attention Deficit Disorder." *The New York Times*, December 14, 2013. http://www.nytimes.com/2013/12/15/health/the-selling-of-attention-deficit-disorder.html?pagewanted=all.

Schweik, Susan. "Lomax's Matrix: Disability, Solidarity, and the Black Power of 504." *Disability Studies Quarterly* 31:1 (2011). http://dsq-sds.org/article/view/1371/1539.

Scott, Catherine. "Time Out of Joint: The Narcotic Effect of Prolepsis in Christopher Reeve's *Still Me*." *Biography* 29:2 (2006): 307–328.

Senator, Susan. *Making Peace with Autism: One Family's Story of Struggle, Discovery, and Unexpected Gifts*. Boston: Trumpeter Books, 2005.

Sequenzia, Amy. "Privacy and Parental Behavior." *Ollibean*. Accessed July 19, 2018. https://ollibean.com/privacy-and-parental-behavior/.

Sequenzia, Amy. "This is Autism." *Ollibean*. Accessed June 3, 2018. https://ollibean.com/autism/.

Shafer, Ellise. "Sia Adds Warning Label to 'Music' Movie, Apologizes to Autism Community on Heels of Golden Globes Nominations." *Variety*, February 3, 2021. https://variety.com/2021/film/news/sia-music-warning-label-apologizes-autism-community-12.

Shakespeare, Tom. "Christopher Reeve, 'You'll Believe a Man Can Walk.'" *Ouch!*, October 29, 2004. http://www.bbc.co.uk/ouch/features/christopher-reeve-you-ll-believe-a-man-can-walk.shtml.

Shakespeare, Tom. *Disability: The Basics*. New York: Routledge, 2018.

Shakespeare, Tom and Nicholas Watson. "Defending the Social Model." *Disability & Society* 12:2 (1997): 293–300. https://doi.org/10.1080/09687599727380.

Shang, Melissa. "Stories about Disability Don't Have to Be Sad." *The New York Times*, June 21, 2017. https://www.nytimes.com/2017/06/21/opinion/stories-about-disability-dont-have-to-be-sad.html.

Shapiro, Joseph. "Disability Pride: The High Expectations of a New Generation." *The New York Times*, July 17, 2020. https://www.nytimes.com/2020/07/17/style/americans-with-disabilities-act.html.

Shapiro, Joseph. *No Pity: People with Disabilities Forging a New Civil Rights Movement*. New York: Three Rivers Press, 1993.

Shildrick, Margrit. *Embodying the Monster: Encounters with the Vulnerable Self*. London: Sage Publications, 2002.

Shinn, Christopher. "Disability is Not Just a Metaphor." *The Atlantic*, July 23, 2014. https://www.theatlantic.com/entertainment/archive/2014/07/why-disabled-characters-are-never-played-by-disabled-actors/374822/.

"Sia Talks Directing Her First Feature Film *Music*." *YouTube*, October 29, 2020. https://www.youtube.com/watch?v=SIVppt0YPio&t=1607s.

Siebers, Tobin. *Disability Theory*. Ann Arbor: University of Michigan Press, 2008.

Silberman, Steve. "The Invisibility of Black Autism." *UNDARK*, May 17, 2016. https://undark.org/article/invisibility-black-autism/.

Silberman, Steve. *Neurotribes: The Legacy of Autism and the Future of Neurodiversity*. New York: Avery Books, 2015.

Simmons, James Q. and O. Ivar Lovaas. "Use of Pain and Punishment as Treatment Techniques with Childhood Schizophrenics." *American Journal of Psychotherapy* 23:1 (April 2018): 23–36. https://doi.org/10.1176/appi.psychotherapy.1969.23.1.23.

Singer, Judy. *Neurodiversity: The Birth of an Idea*. Judy Singer, 2017.

Smith, Anna Marie. *Welfare Reform and Sexual Regulation*. Cambridge: Cambridge University Press, 2007.

Smith, John. "Why the Americans with Disabilities Act Is Important to Me." *Impact*. Accessed August 13, 2018. https://ici.umn.edu/products/impact/281/4.html.

Smith, Stacy, Marc Choueiti, Katherine Peiper, Kevin Yao, Ariana Case, and Angel Choi. *Inequality in 1,200 Popular Films: Examining Portrayals of Gender, Race/Ethnicity, LGBTQ & Disability from 2007 to 2018*. Annenberg Foundation and

USC Annenberg, September 2019. http://assets.uscannenberg.org/docs/aii-inequ ality-report-2019-09-03.pdf.

Souderos, Trine. "Miracle Drug Called Junk Science." *Chicago Tribune*, May 21, 2009. http://www.chicagotribune.com/lifestyles/health/chi-autism-lupron-may21 -story.html.

Sousa, Amy. "From Refrigerator Mothers to Warrior-Heroes: The Cultural Identity Transformation of Mothers Raising Children with Intellectual Disabilities." *Symbolic Interaction* 34:2 (Spring 2011): 220–243. https://doi.org/10.1525/si.2011.34.2.220.

Sparrow, Maxfield. "ABA." *Unstrange Mind*, October 20, 2016. http://unstrangemind .com/aba/.

Spencer, Ashley. "The Golden Globes Celebrated Sia's 'Music.' Autistic Activists Wish They Hadn't." *The New York Times*, February 11, 2021. https://www.nyt imes.com/2021/02/11/movies/sia-music-autism-backlash.html.

Spencer, Robyn Ceanne. "Engendering the Black Freedom Struggle: Revolutionary Black Womanhood and the Black Panther Party in the Bay Area, California." *Journal of Women's History* 20:1 (Spring 2008): 90–113. https://doi.org/10.1353/ jowh.2008.0006.

Spivak, Gayatri Chakravoty. "Can the Subaltern Speak?" In *Colonial Discourse and Post- Colonial Theory: A Reader*, edited by Patrick Williams and Laura Chrismen, 66–111. New York: Columbia University Press, 1994.

Stern, Alexandra Minna. *Eugenic Nation: Faults and Frontiers of Better Breeding in Modern America*. Oakland: University of California Press, 2015.

Stevens, Sarah E. "Care Time." *Disability Studies Quarterly* 38:4 (2018). https://dsq -sds.org/article/view/6090/5136.

Stivers, Camilla. "Reflections on the Role of Personal Narrative in Social Science." *Signs: Journal of Women in Culture and Society* 18:2 (1993): 408–425. https://doi .org/10.1086/494800.

"The Story." *The Kids are All Right*. Accessed September 2, 2017. http://www.thek idsareallright.org/story.html.

Sullivan, Amanda and Aydin Bal. "Disproportionality in Special Education: Effects of Individual and School Variables on Disability Risk." *Exceptional Children* 79:4 (Summer 2013): 475–494.

Swaine, John, ed. "The Counted: About the Project." *The Guardian*. Accessed September 10, 2020. https://www.theguardian.com/us-news/ng-interac- tive/2015/ jun/01/about-the-counted.

Swaine, John, ed. "The Counted: People Killed by Police in the U.S., Recorded by the Guardian- With your Help." *The Guardian*. Accessed September 10, 2020. https:// www.theguardian.com/us-news/series/counted-us-police-killings.

Taylor, Luke E., Amy Swerdfeger, and Guy D. Eslick. "Vaccines Are Not Associated with Autism: An Evidence-Based Meta-Analysis of Case-Control and Cohort Studies." *Vaccine* 32:29 (June 17, 2014): 3623–3629. https://doi.org/10.1016/j .vaccine.2014.04.085.

Teleki, Stephanie. "Birthing a Movement to Reduce Unnecessary C-Sections: An Update From California." *Health Affairs,* October 31, 2017. https://www.healthaf fairs.org/do/10.1377/hblog20171031.709216/full/.

"Text of Robert Dole's Speech to the Republican National Convention, August 15, 1996." *CNN.* Accessed July 20, 2019. http://www.cnn.com/ALLPOLITICS/1996/conventions/san.diego/transcripts/0815/dole.fdch.shtml.

"This is What Disability Looks Like." *Facebook.* Accessed July 26, 2017. https://www.facebook.com/pg/ThisIsWhatDisabilityLooksLike/about/?ref=page_internal.

Thompson, Vilissa. "'Nothing about Us without Us'—Disability Representation in Media." *Center for Disability Rights.* Accessed October 25, 2019. http://cdrnys.org/blog/disability-dialogue/nothing-about-us-without-us-disability-representation-in-media/.

Thompson, Vilissa and Alice Wong. "#GetWokeADA26: Disabled People of Color Speak Out, Part Two. Ramp Your Voice!" *Disability Visibility Project*, July 26, 2016. http://wp.me/p4H7t1-MLn.

Tingley, Kim. "Do Brain Injuries Affect Women Differently?" *The New York Times Magazine*, June 26, 2019. https://www.nytimes.com/2019/06/26/magazine/do-brain-injuries-affect-women-differently-than-men.html.

Tonti, Stephen. "ADHD as a Difference in Cognition, Not a Disorder." Filmed April 11, 2013 at TEDxCMU, Carnegie Mellon University, Pittsburgh, PA. Video, 13:37. https://www.youtube.com/watch?v=uU6o2_UFSEY.

Travers, Jason C., Matt Tincani, and Michael P. Krezmien. "A Multiyear National Profile of Racial Disparity in Autism Identification." *Journal of Special Education* 47:1 (2013): 41–49. https://doi.org/10.1177/0022466911416247.

Tschantz, Jennifer and Joy Markowitz. "Gender and Special Education: Current State Data Collection." *Project Forum*, January 2003. http://www.nasdse.org/DesktopModules/DNNspot-Store/ProductFiles/143_49aabfa1-ef5c-4ece-9cbc-cedc6a405578.pdf.

Tuana, Nancy, ed. *Feminism and Science.* Bloomington: Indiana University Press, 1989.

The United States Commission on Civil Rights. "Minorities in Special Education." December 3, 2007. http://www.usccr.gov/pubs/MinoritiesinSpecialEducation.pdf.

United States Department of Education, Office of Special Education Programs. "IDEA Section 618 Data Products: Static Tables, Table 1–12: Children and Students Served under IDEA, Part B, in the U.S. and Outlying Areas, By Gender and Age Group." Accessed July 15, 2016. http://www.ideadata.org/tables30th/ar_1-12.htm.

United States Department of Health and Human Services. "Mental Health Myths and Facts." Accessed July 8, 2017. https://www.mentalhealth.gov/basics/myths-facts/.

United States Department of Health and Human Services, National Institutes of Health, and National Institute of Child Health and Human Development. "The NICHD Study of Early Child Care and Youth Development." 2006. http://www.nichd.nih.gov/sites/default/files/publications/pubs/documents/seccyd_06.pdf.

United States Department of Labor. "Health Benefits, Retirement Standards, and Workers' Compensation: Family and Medical Leave." Accessed May 31, 2019. https://webapps.dol.gov/elaws/elg/fmla.htm.

Ustaszewski, Anya. "I Don't Want to be 'Cured' of Autism, Thanks." *The Guardian*, January 14, 2009. https://www.theguardian.com/commentisfree/2009/jan/14/a utism-health.

Vagnerova, Kamila, Ines Koerner, and Patricia Hurn. "Gender and the Injured Brain." *Anesthesia & Analgesia* 107:1 (July 2008): 201–214. https://doi.org/10.1213/ane .0b013e31817326a5.

Valera, Eve and Aaron Kucyi. "Brain Injury in Women Experiencing Intimate Partner Violence: Neural Mechanistic Evidence of an 'Invisible' Trauma." *Brain Imaging Behaviour* 11:6 (December 2017): 1664–1677. https://doi.org/10.1007/s11682-016 -9643-1.

Valeras, Aimee Burke. "We Don't Have a Box": Understanding Hidden Disability Identity Utilizing Narrative Research Methodology." *Disability Studies Quarterly* 30:3/4 (2010). https://dsq-sds.org/article/view/1267/1297.

Verhovek, Sam Howe. "Parents Defend Decision to Keep Disabled Girl Small." *Los Angeles Times*, January 3, 2007. https://www.latimes.com/archives/la-xpm-2007- jan-03-na-stunt3-story.html.

Visser, Gerard H. A., Diogo Ayres-de-Campos, Eytan R. Barnea, Luc de Bernis, Gian Carlo Di Renzo, Maria Fernanda Escobar Vidarte, Isabel Lloyd, Anwar H. Nassar, Wanda Nicholson, P. K. Shah, et al. "FIGO Position Paper: How to Stop the Caesarean Section Epidemic." *The Lancet* 392:10155 (October 13, 2018): 1286–1287. https://doi.org/10.1016/S0140-6736(18)32113-5.

Visser, Irene. "Trauma Theory and Postcolonial Literary Studies." *Journal of Postcolonial Writing* 47:3 (2011): 270–282. https://doi.org/10.1080/17449855.20 11.569378.

Wade, Cheryl Marie. "I Am Not One of the." *Sinister Wisdom* 35 (Summer/Fall 1988): 24. http://www.sinisterwisdom.org/sites/default/files/Sinister%20Wisdom %2035.pdf.

Wagner, Aureen Pinto. *What to Do When Your Child Has Obsessive-Compulsive Disorder: Strategies and Solutions.* Mobile, AL: Lighthouse Press, 2002.

Walker, Nick. "Advice to Young Autistics: Stick Around and Be Awesome." *Neurocosmopolitanism*, August 21, 2014. http://neurocosmopolitanism.com/adv ice-to-young-autistics-stick-around-and-be-awesome/.

Walker, Nick. "What is Autism?" *Neurocosmopolitanism*, March 1, 2014. https://ne urocosmopolitanism.com/what-is-autism/.

Wall, Glenda. "Mothers' Experiences with Intensive Parenting and Brain Development Discourse." *Women's Studies International Forum* 33:3 (2010): 253–263. https:// doi.org/10.1016/j.wsif.2010.02.019.

Wall, Sarah. "An Autoethnography on Learning about Autoethnography." *International Journal of Qualitative Methods* 5:2 (2006): 146–160. https://doi.org /10.1177/160940690600500205.

Wallace, Kelly. "Mom Arrested for Leaving 9-Year-Old Alone at Park." *CNN*, July 21, 2014. https://www.cnn.com/2014/07/21/living/mom-arrested-left-girl-park -parents/index.html.

Walsh, Samantha. "'What Does It Matter?' A Meditation on the Social Positioning of Disability and Motherhood." In *Disability and Mothering: Liminal Spaces of*

Embodied Knowledge, edited by Cynthia Lewiecki-Wilson and Jen Cellio, 81–87. Syracuse: Syracuse University Press, 2011.

Wanshel, Elyse. "The MDA Telethon Is Back. Many Disabled People Aren't Happy About It." *Huffpost*, October 29, 2020. https://www.huffpost.com/entry/the-mda-t elethon-came-back-disabled-people-say-it-was-bad-and-always-has-been_n_5f95 cf48c5b6a2e1fb626c74.

Warner, Judith. *Perfect Madness: Motherhood in the Age of Anxiety*. New York: Riverhead Books, 2005.

Warner, Judith. *We've Got Issues: Children and Parents in the Age of Medication*. New York: Riverhead Books, 2010.

Washington, Harriet. *Medical Apartheid: The Dark History of Medical Experimentation on Black Americans from Colonial Times to the Present*. New York: Harlem Moon, 2006.

Watson, Nicholas, Linda McKie, Bill Hughes, Debra Hopkins, and Sue Gregory. "(Inter)Dependence, Needs and Care: The Potential for Disability and Feminist Theorists to Develop an Emancipatory Model." *Sociology* 38:2 (2004): 331–350. https://doi.org/10.1177/0038038504040867.

"We Have a Childcare Crisis in this Country. We Had the Solution 78 Years Ago?" *The Washington Post*, July 23, 2018. https://www.washingtonpost.com/news/post everything/wp/2018/07/23/we-have-a-childcare-crisis-in-this-country-we-had-the -solution-78-years-ago/?utm_term=.82618698c4a0.

Wendell, Susan. *The Rejected Body: Feminist Philosophical Reflections on Disability*. New York: Routledge, 1996.

Wendell, Susan. "Toward a Feminist Theory of Disability." *Hypatia* 4:2 (Summer 1989): 104–124. https://doi.org/10.1111/j.1527-2001.1989.tb00576.x.

Wendall, Susan. "Unhealthy Disabled: Treating Chronic Illnesses as Disabilities." *Hypatia* 16:4 (Autumn 2001): 17–33.

Weusten, Josje. "Narrative Constructions of Motherhood and Autism: Reading Embodied Language beyond Binary Oppositions." *Journal of Literary & Cultural Disability Studies* 5:1 (2011): 53–69. https://doi.org/10.3828/jlcds.2011.4.

"What Disability Means." *The New York Times*, August 25, 2016.

Whelton, Paul K., Robert M. Carey, Wilbert S. Aronow, Donald E. Casey, Jr., Karen J. Collins, Cheryl Dennison Himmelfarb, Sondra M. DePalma, Samuel Gidding, Kenneth A. Jamerson, Daniel W. Jones, et al. "Guideline for the Prevention, Detection, Evaluation, and Management of High Blood Pressure in Adults." A Report of the American College of Cardiology/American Heart Association Task Force on Clinical Practice Guidelines. *Hypertension* 71:6 (November 13, 2017): 13–115. https://doi.org/10.1161/HYP.0000000000000065.

Whimsy, Little Moon. "Autism Speaks Doesn't Speak for Autistics." *Saplings of Hope*, November 12, 2013. http://saplingstories.blogspot.com/2013/11/autism-speaks-doesn-speak-for-autistics.html?m=0.

White, Glen, Jamie Lloyd Simpson, Chiaki Gonda, Craig Ravesloot, and Zach Coble. "Moving from Independence to Interdependence: A Conceptual Model for Better Understanding Community Participation of Centers for Independent Living

Consumers." *Journal of Disability Policy Studies* 20:4 (2010): 233–240. https://do i.org/10.1177/1044207309350561.

"Why I Left ABA." *Socially Anxious Advocate*, May 22, 2015. https://sociallyanxi ousadvocate.wordpress.com.

Widegardner, Jean. "The Onus of Acceptance." *Autistic Women & Nonbinary Network*, October 7, 2013. https://autismwomensnetwork.org/the-onus-of-accept ance/.

Wiener, Jon. "The End of the Jerry Lewis Telethon—It's About Time." *The Nation*, September 2, 2011. https://www.thenation.com/article/end-jerry-lewis-telethon-its -about-time/.

Wiener, Lauren and Whitney C. Harris. "Could too Much Stress During Pregnancy Harm the Baby?" *Parents*. Accessed July 6, 2019. https://www.parents.com/pregna ncy/my-body/can-too-much-stress-during-pregnancy-be-bad-for-my-baby/.

Wigle, Stanley and Daryl Wilcox. "Inclusion." *Remedial and Special Education* 17:5 (September 1996): 323–329. https://doi.org/10.1177/074193259601700508.

Williams, John. *My Son is Not Rainman: One Man, One Autistic Boy, a Million Adventures*. London: Michael O'Mara Books, 2016.

Wilson, Jan Doolittle. "Reimagining Disability and Inclusive Education through Universal Design for Learning." *Disability Studies Quarterly* 37:2 (2017). https:// dsq-sds.org/article/view/5417/4650.

Wilson, Jan Doolittle. "'Who Has a Better Story Than Bran the Broken?' The Power of Disability Narratives." In *Behind the Throne: Essays on Power and Subversion in HBO's* Game of Thrones, edited by A. Keith Kelly. Jefferson, NC: McFarland, forthcoming.

Wolinksy, Emil. "Dear Kevin Hart, The MDA is Heartless." *Disability Visibility Project*, October 12, 2020. https://disabilityvisibilityproject.com/2020/10/12/dear -kevin-hart-the-mda-is-heartless/.

Wong, Alice. *Disability Visibility: First-Person Stories from the Twenty-First Century*. New York: Vintage, 2020.

Wood, Caitlin. "Introduction: Criptiques: A Daring Space." In *Criptiques*, edited by Caitlin Wood, 1–3. Portland, OR: May Day, 2014. https://criptiques.files.wordp ress.com/2014/05/crip-final-2.pdf.

Wood, Caitlin. "Tales from the Crip: Ready, Willing, and Disabled." *Bitch Media*, September 25, 2012. https://www.bitchmedia.org/post/tales-from-the-crip-ready -willing-and-disabled.

Woodburn, Danny and Kristina Kopic. *The Ruderman White Paper on Employment of Actors with Disabilities in Television*. Ruderman Family Foundation, July 2016. http://rudermanfoundation.org/wp-content/uploads/2016/07/TV-White-Paper_7-1 -003.pdf.

World Health Organization. "Ten Threats to Global Health in 2019." Accessed July 5, 2020. https://www.who.int/news-room/feature-stories/ten-threats-to-global-he alth-in-2019.

World Health Organization. "WHO Statement on Caesarean Section Rates." April 2015. https://www.who.int/reproductivehealth/publications/maternal_perinatal _health/cs-statement/en/.

World Health Organization. "World Report on Disability." Accessed September 21, 2019. https://www.who.int/disabilities/world_report/2011/report/en/.

Xu, Guifeng, Lane Strathearn, Buyun Liu, Binrang Yang, and Wei Bao. "Twenty-Year Trends in Diagnosed Attention-Deficit/Hyperactivity Disorder among U.S. Children and Adolescents, 1997–2016." *JAMA* Netw Open 1:4 (August 2018): 1–9. https://jamanetwork.com/journals/jamanetworkopen/fullarticle/2698633.

xxx. "Judge Rotenberg Center Survivor's Letter." *Autistic Hoya*, January 15, 2013. http://www.autistichoya.com/2013/01/judge-rotenberg-center-survivors-letter.html.

Yergeau, Melanie. *Authoring Autism: On Rhetoric and Neurological Queerness.* Durham: Duke University Press, 2018.

Yergeau, Melanie. "Circle Wars: Reshaping the Typical Autism Essay." *Disability Studies Quarterly* 30:1 (2010). http://dsq-sds.org/article/view/1063/1222.

Yergeau, Melanie. "Clinically Significant Disturbance: On Theorists Who Theorize Theory of Mind." *Disability Studies Quarterly* 33:4 (2013). https://dsq-sds.org/article/view/3876/3405.

Young, Stella. "I'm Not Your Inspiration, Thank You Very Much." Filmed April 2014 at TEDxSydney, Sydney, Australia. Video, 9:04. https://www.ted.com/talks/stella_young_i_m_not_your_inspiration_thank_you_very_much?language=en.

Index

ABA. *See* applied behavior analysis
ability-disability system, 3
able-bodiedness, 1, 18, 35, 64, 119, 227
ableism, 35, 57–58, 61, 120, 127–28, 160, 227, 246, 263
ableist, 8, 12n2, 35, 58, 63–64, 66, 80, 86, 96, 98, 120, 126–27, 133, 146, 148–49, 159, 164, 227, 232, 256, 263
ableist gaze, 80–81, 102
access intimacy, 11, 160–61, 164
ADA. *See* Americans with Disabilities Act
ADAPT. *See* American Disabled for Attendant Programs Today
ADHD. *See* attention-deficit/hyperactivity disorder
AfF. *See* Aspies for Freedom
Alliance Against Seclusion and Restraint, 96
American Association of People with Disabilities, 31, 42
American Horror Story, 85
American Psychiatric Association, 20
American Psycho, 85
American Disabled for Attendant Programs Today (ADAPT), 31, 37, 39, 94

Americans with Disabilities Act (ADA), 4, 11, 39–42, 44, 80, 99; Education and Reform Act, 42
anti-vaccine campaign, 76, 77
Anzaldúa, Gloria, 67, 147
APIDC. *See* Asians and Pacific Islanders with Disabilities of California
applied behavior analysis (ABA), 28–30
ASAN. *See* Autistic Self Advocacy Network
Ashley X case, 25–26
Asians and Pacific Islanders with Disabilities of California (APIDC), 61
Aspies for Freedom (AfF), 38
attention-deficit/hyperactivity disorder (ADHD), 176, 187–91, 197
autism, 2, 8–9, 58–59, 201–2; applied behavior analysis and, 29–30; high-functioning/low-functioning binary, 43–44, 174–76; identity-first language and, 17–18; media stereotypes of, 87–89, 91, 95–96; medicalization of, 20, 30, 76–77, 200, 230, 231; medical treatment of, 26–28; neurodiversity and, 17, 36, 43, 173–76, 190, 193, 197; racial and gender biases in diagnoses of, 21,

About the Author

Jan Doolittle Wilson is Wellspring Associate Professor of Gender Studies and History, co-director of the Women's and Gender Studies Program, and director of graduate studies in History at the University of Tulsa. She is the author of *The Women's Joint Congressional Committee and the Politics of Maternalism* (University of Illinois Press, 2007). Her work on gender and disability has appeared in the *Disability Studies Quarterly* and the *Journal of Women's History* and is forthcoming in anthologies such as the *Disability Studies Reader*, 6th ed., and *Behind the Throne: Essays on Power and Subversion in HBO's* Game of Thrones. Her TEDx talk on universal design for learning filmed at the University of Tulsa in April 2015 is used in several disability education and training programs across the nation, including those from the Office of Special Education Programs of the United States Department of Education and the Head Start and Early Learning Division of the Los Angeles County Office of Education.